The Story of My Life

HELEN KELLER AND ANNE SULLIVAN

THE STORY OF MY LIFE

By Helen Keller

With Her Letters (1887 — 1901) and
A Supplementary Account of Her Education
Including Passages from the Reports and Letters
of Her Teacher Anne Mansfield Sullivan
By John Albert Macy *Illustrated*.

WILDSIDE PRESS

To

ALEXANDER GRAHAM BELL

*WHO has taught the deaf to speak
and enabled the listening ear to hear
speech from the Atlantic to the Rockies,*

I Dedicate
this Story of My Life.

EDITOR'S PREFACE

THIS book is in three parts. The first two, Miss Keller's story and the extracts from her letters, form a complete account of her life as far as she can give it. Much of her education she cannot explain herself, and since a knowledge of that is necessary to an understanding of what she has written, it was thought best to supplement her autobiography with the reports and letters of her teacher, Miss Anne Mansfield Sullivan. The addition of a further account of Miss Keller's personality and achievements may be unnecessary; yet it will help to make clear some of the traits of her character and the nature of the work which she and her teacher have done.

For the third part of the book the Editor is responsible, though all that is valid in it he owes to authentic records and to the advice of Miss Sullivan.

The Editor desires to express his gratitude and the gratitude of Miss Keller and Miss Sullivan to *The Ladies' Home Journal* and to its editors, Mr. Edward Bok and Mr. William V. Alexander, who have been unfailingly kind and have given for use in this book all the photographs which were taken expressly for the *Journal;* and the Editor thanks Miss Keller's many friends who have lent him her letters to them and given him valuable information; especially Mrs. Laurence Hutton, who supplied him with her large collection of notes and anecdotes; Mr. John Hitz, Superintendent of the Volta Bureau for the Increase and Diffusion of Knowledge relating to the Deaf; and Mrs. Sophia C. Hopkins, to whom Miss Sullivan wrote those illuminating letters, the extracts from which give a better idea of her methods with her pupil than anything heretofore published.

Messrs. Houghton, Mifflin and Company have courteously permitted the reprinting of Miss Keller's letter to Dr. Holmes, which appeared in "Over the Teacups," and one of Whittier's letters to Miss Keller. Mr. S. T. Pickard, Whittier's literary executor, kindly sent the original of another letter from Miss Keller to Whittier.

JOHN ALBERT MACY.

Cambridge, Massachusetts, February 1, 1903.

TABLE OF CONTENTS

LIST OF ILLUSTRATIONS

I l e f t the w e l l - h ou s e

e a g er to l(ea)r n . Ever y th ing

h a d a n a m e , and e a ch

n a m e g a v e b i r th to a

n e w th ou gh t . A s w e

r e t u r n ed to the h ou s e ,

ever y o b j e c t I t ou ch ed

s e e m ed to q u i v er with l i f e .

Facsimile of the braille manuscript of the passage on page 24, with equivalents—slightly reduced. (Underlined combinations of letters have one sign in braille. Note the omission of the vowels before "r" in "learn," and the joining of the sign for "to" with the word that follows it.)

So. Boston,
May 1, 1891.

My dear Mr. Brooks;
Helen
sends you a loving greet
ing this bright May-day.
My teacher has just told
me that you have been
made a bishop, and that
your friends everywhere
are rejoicing because

one whom they love
has been greatly honor-
ed. I do not understand
very well what a
bishop's work is. but
I am sure it must be
good and helpful, and
I am glad that my
dear friend is brave,
and wise, and loving
enough to do it. It is
very beautiful to think
that you can tell so

PART I

THE STORY OF MY LIFE

THE STORY OF MY LIFE

CHAPTER I

IT is with a kind of fear that I begin to write the history of my life. I have, as it were, a superstitious hesitation in lifting the veil that clings about my childhood like a golden mist. The task of writing an autobiography is a difficult one. When I try to classify my earliest impressions, I find that fact and fancy look alike across the years that link the past with the present. The woman paints the child's experiences in her own fantasy. A few impressions stand out vividly from the first years of my life; but "the shadows of the prison-house are on the rest." Besides, many of the joys and sorrows of childhood have lost their poignancy; and many incidents of vital importance in my early education have been forgotten in the excitement of great discoveries. In order, therefore, not to be tedious I shall try to present in a series of sketches only the episodes that seem to me to be the most interesting and important.

I was born on June 27, 1880, in Tuscumbia, a little town of northern Alabama.

The family on my father's side is descended from Caspar Keller, a native of Switzerland, who settled in Maryland. One of my Swiss ancestors was the first teacher of the deaf in Zurich and wrote a book on the subject of their education—rather a singular

3

coincidence; though it is true that there is no king who has not had a slave among his ancestors, and no slave who has not had a king among his.

My grandfather, Caspar Keller's son, "entered" large tracts of land in Alabama and finally settled there. I have been told that once a year he went from Tuscumbia to Philadelphia on horseback to purchase supplies for the plantation, and my aunt has in her possession many of the letters to his family, which give charming and vivid accounts of these trips.

My Grandmother Keller was a daughter of one of Lafayette's aides, Alexander Moore, and granddaughter of Alexander Spotswood, an early Colonial Governor of Virginia. She was also second cousin to Robert E. Lee.

My father, Arthur H. Keller, was a captain in the Confederate Army, and my mother, Kate Adams, was his second wife and many years younger. Her grandfather, Benjamin Adams, married Susanna E. Goodhue, and lived in Newbury, Massachusetts, for many years. Their son, Charles Adams, was born in Newburyport, Massachusetts, and moved to Helena, Arkansas. When the Civil War broke out, he fought on the side of the South and became a brigadier-general. He married Lucy Helen Everett, who belonged to the same family of Everetts as Edward Everett and Dr. Edward Everett Hale. After the war was over the family moved to Memphis, Tennessee.

I lived, up to the time of the illness that deprived me of my sight and hearing, in a tiny house consisting of a large square room and a small one, in which the servant slept. It is a custom in the South to

"IVY GREEN," THE KELLER HOMESTEAD

build a small house near the homestead as an annex
to be used on occasion. Such a house my father
built after the Civil War, and when he married my
mother they went to live in it. It was completely
covered with vines, climbing roses and honeysuckles.
From the garden it looked like an arbour. The little
porch was hidden from view by a screen of yellow
roses and Southern smilax. It was the favourite
haunt of humming-birds and bees.

The Keller homestead, where the family lived,
was a few steps from our little rose-bower. It was
called "Ivy Green" because the house and the surrounding trees and fences were covered with
beautiful English ivy. Its old-fashioned garden
was the paradise of my childhood.

Even in the days before my teacher came, I used
to feel along the square stiff boxwood hedges, and,
guided by the sense of smell, would find the first
violets and lilies. There, too, after a fit of temper, I
went to find comfort and to hide my hot face in the
cool leaves and grass. What joy it was to lose
myself in that garden of flowers, to wander happily
from spot to spot, until, coming suddenly upon a
beautiful vine, I recognized it by its leaves and
blossoms, and knew it was the vine which covered
the tumble-down summer-house at the farther end
of the garden! Here, also, were trailing clematis,
drooping jessamine, and some rare sweet flowers
called butterfly lilies, because their fragile petals
resemble butterflies' wings. But the roses—they
were loveliest of all. Never have I found in the
greenhouses of the North such heart-satisfying roses
as the climbing roses of my southern home. They
used to hang in long festoons from our porch, filling

the whole air with their fragrance, untainted by any earthy smell; and in the early morning, washed in the dew, they felt so soft, so pure, I could not help wondering if they did not resemble the asphodels of God's garden.

The beginning of my life was simple and much like every other little life. I came, I saw, I conquered, as the first baby in the family always does. There was the usual amount of discussion as to a name for me. The first baby in the family was not to be lightly named, every one was emphatic about that. My father suggested the name of Mildred Campbell, an ancestor whom he highly esteemed, and he declined to take any further part in the discussion. My mother solved the problem by giving it as her wish that I should be called after her mother, whose maiden name was Helen Everett. But in the excitement of carrying me to church my father lost the name on the way, very naturally, since it was one in which he had declined to have a part. When the minister asked him for it, he just remembered that it had been decided to call me after my grandmother, and he gave her name as Helen Adams.

I am told that while I was still in long dresses I showed many signs of an eager, self-asserting disposition. Everything that I saw other people do I insisted upon imitating. At six months I could pipe out "How d'ye," and one day I attracted every one's attention by saying "Tea, tea, tea" quite plainly. Even after my illness I remembered one of the words I had learned in these early months. It was the word "water," and I continued to make some sound for that word after all other speech was lost. I ceased making the sound "wah-wah" only when I learned to spell the word.

They tell me I walked the day I was a year old. My mother had just taken me out of the bath-tub and was holding me in her lap, when I was suddenly attracted by the flickering shadows of leaves that danced in the sunlight on the smooth floor. I slipped from my mother's lap and almost ran toward them. The impulse gone, I fell down and cried for her to take me up in her arms.

These happy days did not last long. One brief spring, musical with the song of robin and mocking-bird, one summer rich in fruit and roses, one autumn of gold and crimson sped by and left their gifts at the feet of an eager, delighted child. Then, in the dreary month of February, came the illness which closed my eyes and ears and plunged me into the unconsciousness of a new-born baby. They called it acute congestion of the stomach and brain. The doctor thought I could not live. Early one morning, however, the fever left me as suddenly and mysteriously as it had come. There was great rejoicing in the family that morning, but no one, not even the doctor, knew that I should never see or hear again.

I fancy I still have confused recollections of that illness. I especially remember the tenderness with which my mother tried to soothe me in my waking hours of fret and pain, and the agony and bewilderment with which I awoke after a tossing half sleep, and turned my eyes, so dry and hot, to the wall, away from the once-loved light, which came to me dim and yet more dim each day. But, except for these fleeting memories, if, indeed, they be memories, it all seems very unreal, like a nightmare. Gradually

I got used to the silence and darkness that surrounded me and forgot that it had ever been different, until she came—my teacher—who was to set
my spirit free.   But during the first nineteen months
of my life I had caught glimpses of broad, green
fields, a luminous sky, trees and flowers which the
darkness that followed could not wholly blot out.
If we have once seen, "the day is ours, and what the
day has shown."

CHAPTER II

I CANNOT recall what happened during the first months after my illness. I only know that I sat in my mother's lap or clung to her dress as she went about her household duties. My hands felt every object and observed every motion, and in this way I learned to know many things. Soon I felt the need of some communication with others and began to make crude signs. A shake of the head meant "No" and a nod, "Yes," a pull meant "Come" and a push, "Go." Was it bread that I wanted? Then I would imitate the acts of cutting the slices and buttering them. If I wanted my mother to make ice-cream for dinner I made the sign for working the freezer and shivered, indicating cold. My mother, moreover, succeeded in making me understand a good deal. I always knew when she wished me to bring her something, and I would run upstairs or anywhere else she indicated. Indeed, I owe to her loving wisdom all that was bright and good in my long night.

I understood a good deal of what was going on about me. At five I learned to fold and put away the clean clothes when they were brought in from the laundry, and I distinguished my own from the rest. I knew by the way my mother and aunt dressed when they were going out, and I invariably begged to go with them. I was always sent for when there was company, and when the guests took

9

their leave, I waved my hand to them, I think with a vague remembrance of the meaning of the gesture. One day some gentlemen called on my mother, and I felt the shutting of the front door and other sounds that indicated their arrival. On a sudden thought I ran upstairs before any one could stop me, to put on my idea of a company dress. Standing before the mirror, as I had seen others do, I anointed mine head with oil and covered my face thickly with powder. Then I pinned a veil over my head so that it covered my face and fell in folds down to my shoulders, and tied an enormous bustle round my small waist, so that it dangled behind, almost meeting the hem of my skirt. Thus attired I went down to help entertain the company.

I do not remember when I first realized that I was different from other people; but I knew it before my teacher came to me. I had noticed that my mother and my friends did not use signs as I did when they wanted anything done, but talked with their mouths. Sometimes I stood between two persons who were conversing and touched their lips. I could not understand, and was vexed. I moved my lips and gesticulated frantically without result. This made me so angry at times that I kicked and screamed until I was exhausted.

I think I knew when I was naughty, for I knew that it hurt Ella, my nurse, to kick her, and when my fit of temper was over I had a feeling akin to regret. But I cannot remember any instance in which this feeling prevented me from repeating the naughtiness when I failed to get what I wanted.

In those days a little coloured girl, Martha Washington, the child of our cook, and Belle, an old setter

and a great hunter in her day, were my constant
companions. Martha Washington understood my
signs, and I seldom had any difficulty in making her
do just as I wished. It pleased me to domineer over
her, and she generally submitted to my tyranny
rather than risk a hand-to-hand encounter. I was
strong, active, indifferent to consequences. I knew
my own mind well enough and always had my own
way, even if I had to fight tooth and nail for it. We
spent a great deal of time in the kitchen, kneading
dough balls, helping make ice-cream, grinding coffee,
quarreling over the cake-bowl, and feeding the hens
and turkeys that swarmed about the kitchen steps.
Many of them were so tame that they would eat
from my hand and let me feel them. One big
gobbler snatched a tomato from me one day and
ran away with it. Inspired, perhaps, by Master
Gobbler's success, we carried off to the woodpile a
cake which the cook had just frosted, and ate every
bit of it. I was quite ill afterward, and I wonder
if retribution also overtook the turkey.

The guinea-fowl likes to hide her nest in out-of-
the-way places, and it was one of my greatest
delights to hunt for the eggs in the long grass. I
could not tell Martha Washington when I wanted
to go egg-hunting, but I would double my hands
and put them on the ground, which meant something round in the grass, and Martha always understood. When we were fortunate enough to find a
nest I never allowed her to carry the eggs home,
making her understand by emphatic signs that she
might fall and break them.

The sheds where the corn was stored, the stable
where the horses were kept, and the yard where the

cows were milked morning and evening were unfailing sources of interest to Martha and me. The milkers would let me keep my hands on the cows while they milked, and I often got well switched by the cow for my curiosity.

The making ready for Christmas was always a delight to me. Of course I did not know what it was all about, but I enjoyed the pleasant odours that filled the house and the tidbits that were given to Martha Washington and me to keep us quiet. We were sadly in the way, but that did not interfere with our pleasure in the least. They allowed us to grind the spices, pick over the raisins and lick the stirring spoons. I hung my stocking because the others did; I cannot remember, however, that the ceremony interested me especially, nor did my curiosity cause me to wake before daylight to look for my gifts.

Martha Washington had as great a love of mischief as I. Two little children were seated on the veranda steps one hot July afternoon. One was black as ebony, with little bunches of fuzzy hair tied with shoestrings sticking out all over her head like corkscrews. The other was white, with long golden curls. One child was six years old, the other two or three years older. The younger child was blind— that was I—and the other was Martha Washington. We were busy cutting out paper dolls; but we soon wearied of this amusement, and after cutting up our shoestrings and clipping all the leaves off the honeysuckle that were within reach, I turned my attention to Martha's corkscrews. She objected at first, but finally submitted. Thinking that turn and turn about is fair play, she seized the scissors and cut off one of my curls, and would have cut them all off but for my mother's timely interference.

Belle, our dog, my other companion, was old and lazy and liked to sleep by the open fire rather than to romp with me. I tried hard to teach her my sign language, but she was dull and inattentive. She sometimes started and quivered with excitement, then she became perfectly rigid, as dogs do when they point a bird. I did not then know why Belle acted in this way; but I knew she was not doing as I wished. This vexed me and the lesson always ended in a one-sided boxing match. Belle would get up, stretch herself lazily, give one or two contemptuous sniffs, go to the opposite side of the hearth and lie down again, and I, wearied and disappointed, went off in search of Martha.

Many incidents of those early years are fixed in my memory, isolated, but clear and distinct, making the sense of that silent, aimless, dayless life all the more intense.

One day I happened to spill water on my apron, and I spread it out to dry before the fire which was flickering on the sitting-room hearth. The apron did not dry quickly enough to suit me, so I drew nearer and threw it right over the hot ashes. The fire leaped into life; the flames encircled me so that in a moment my clothes were blazing. I made a terrified noise that brought Viny, my old nurse, to the rescue. Throwing a blanket over me, she almost suffocated me, but she put out the fire. Except for my hands and hair I was not badly burned.

About this time I found out the use of a key. One morning I locked my mother up in the pantry, where she was obliged to remain three hours, as the servants were in a detached part of the house. She kept pounding on the door, while I sat outside on the porch steps and laughed with glee as I felt the jar of the pounding. This most naughty prank of mine convinced my parents that I must be taught as soon as possible. After my teacher, Miss Sullivan, came to me, I sought an early opportunity to lock her in her room. I went upstairs with something which my mother made me understand I was to give to Miss Sullivan; but no sooner had I given it to her than I slammed the door to, locked it, and hid the key under the wardrobe in the hall. I could not be induced to tell where the key was. My father was obliged to get a ladder and take Miss Sullivan out through the window—much to my delight. Months after I produced the key.

When I was about five years old we moved from the little vine-covered house to a large new one. The family consisted of my father and mother, two older half-brothers, and, afterward, a little sister, Mildred. My earliest distinct recollection of my father is making my way through great drifts of newspapers to his side and finding him alone, holding a sheet of paper before his face. I was greatly puzzled to know what he was doing. I imitated this action, even wearing his spectacles, thinking they might help solve the mystery. But I did not find out the secret for several years. Then I learned what those papers were, and that my father edited one of them.

My father was most loving and indulgent, devoted to his home, seldom leaving us, except in the hunting season. He was a great hunter, I have been told,

and a celebrated shot. Next to his family he loved
his dogs and gun. His hospitality was great, almost
to a fault, and he seldom came home without bring-
·ng a guest. His special pride was the big garden
where, it was said, he raised the finest watermelons
and strawberries in the county; and to me he brought
the first ripe grapes and the choicest berries. I
remember his caressing touch as he led me from tree
to tree, from vine to vine, and his eager delight in
whatever pleased me.

He was a famous story-teller; after I had acquired
language he used to spell clumsily into my hand
his cleverest anecdotes, and nothing pleased him
more than to have me repeat them at an opportune
moment.

I was in the North, enjoying the last beautiful
days of the summer of 1896, when I heard the news
of my father's death. He had had a short illness,
there had been a brief time of acute suffering, then
all was over. This was my first great sorrow—my
first personal experience with death.

How shall I write of my mother? She is so near
to me that it almost seems indelicate to speak of her.

For a long time I regarded my little sister as an
intruder. I knew that I had ceased to be my
mother's only darling, and the thought filled me with
jealousy. She sat in my mother's lap constantly,
where I used to sit, and seemed to take up all her
care and time. One day something happened which
seemed to me to be adding insult to injury.

At that time I had a much-petted, much-abused
doll, which I afterward named Nancy. She was,
alas, the helpless victim of my outbursts of temper
and of affection, so that she became much the worse

for wear. I had dolls which talked, and cried, and opened and shut their eyes; yet I never loved one of them as I loved poor Nancy. She had a cradle, and I often spent an hour or more rocking her. I guarded both doll and cradle with the most jealous care; but once I discovered my little sister sleeping peacefully in the cradle. At this presumption on the part of one to whom as yet no tie of love bound me I grew angry. I rushed upon the cradle and overturned it, and the baby might have been killed had my mother not caught her as she fell. Thus it is that when we walk in the valley of twofold solitude we know little of the tender affections that grow out of endearing words and actions and companionship. But afterward, when I was restored to my human heritage, Mildred and I grew into each other's hearts, so that we were content to go hand-in-hand wherever caprice led us, although she could not understand my finger language, nor I her childish prattle.

CHAPTER III

MEANWHILE the desire to express myself grew. The few signs I used became less and less adequate, and my failures to make myself understood were invariably followed by outbursts of passion. I felt as if invisible hands were holding me, and I made frantic efforts to free myself. I struggled—not that struggling helped matters, but the spirit of resistance was strong within me; I generally broke down in tears and physical exhaustion. If my mother happened to be near I crept into her arms, too miserable even to remember the cause of the tempest. After awhile the need of some means of communication became so urgent that these outbursts occurred daily, sometimes hourly.

My parents were deeply grieved and perplexed. We lived a long way from any school for the blind or the deaf, and it seemed unlikely that any one would come to such an out-of-the-way place as Tuscumbia to teach a child who was both deaf and blind. Indeed, my friends and relatives sometimes doubted whether I could be taught. My mother's only ray of hope came from Dickens's "American Notes." She had read his account of Laura Bridgman, and remembered vaguely that she was deaf and blind, yet had been educated. But she also remembered with a hopeless pang that Dr. Howe, who had discovered the way to teach the deaf and blind, had been dead many years. His methods had probably died with him; and if they had not, how was a little girl in a far-off town in Alabama to receive the benefit of them?

When I was about six years old, my father heard of an eminent oculist in Baltimore, who had been successful in many cases that had seemed hopeless. My parents at once determined to take me to Baltimore to see if anything could be done for my eyes.

The journey, which I remember well, was very pleasant. I made friends with many people on the train. One lady gave me a box of shells. My father made holes in these so that I could string them, and for a long time they kept me happy and contented. The conductor, too, was kind. Often when he went his rounds I clung to his coat tails while he collected and punched the tickets. His punch, with which he let me play, was a delightful toy. Curled up in a corner of the seat I amused myself for hours making funny little holes in bits of cardboard.

My aunt made me a big doll out of towels. It was the most comical, shapeless thing, this improvised doll, with no nose, mouth, ears or eyes—nothing that even the imagination of a child could convert into a face. Curiously enough, the absence of eyes struck me more than all the other defects put together. I pointed this out to everybody with provoking persistency, but no one seemed equal to the task of providing the doll with eyes. A bright idea, however, shot into my mind, and the problem was solved. I tumbled off the seat and searched under it until I found my aunt's cape, which was trimmed with large beads. I pulled two beads off and indicated to her that I wanted her to sew them on my doll. She raised my hand to her eyes in a questioning way, and I nodded energetically. The beads were sewed in the right place and I could not contain myself for joy; but immediately I lost all interest in the doll. During the whole trip I did not have one fit of temper, there were so many things to keep my mind and fingers busy.

When we arrived in Baltimore, Dr. Chisholm received us kindly: but he could do nothing. He said, however, that I could be educated, and advised my father to consult Dr. Alexander Graham Bell, of Washington, who would be able to give him information about schools and teachers of deaf or blind children. Acting on the doctor's advice, we went immediately to Washington to see Dr. Bell, my father with a sad heart and many misgivings, I wholly unconscious of his anguish, finding pleasure in the excitement of moving from place to place. Child as I was, I at once felt the tenderness and sympathy which endeared Dr. Bell to so many hearts, as his wonderful achievements enlist their admiration. He held me on his knee while I examined his watch, and he made it strike for me. He understood my signs, and I knew it and loved him at once. But I did not dream that that interview would be the door through which I should pass from darkness into light, from isolation to friendship, companionship, knowledge, love.

Dr. Bell advised my father to write to Mr. Anagnos, director of the Perkins Institution in Boston, the scene of Dr. Howe's great labours for the blind, and ask him if he had a teacher competent to begin my education. This my father did at once, and in a few weeks there came a kind letter from Mr. Anagnos with the comforting assurance that a teacher had been found. This was in the summer of 1886. But Miss Sullivan did not arrive until the following March.

Thus I came up out of Egypt and stood before Sinai, and a power divine touched my spirit and gave it sight, so that I beheld many wonders. And from the sacred mountain I heard a voice which said, "Knowledge is love and light and vision."

CHAPTER IV

THE most important day I remember in all my life is the one on which my teacher, Anne Mansfield Sullivan, came to me. I am filled with wonder when I consider the immeasurable contrasts between the two lives which it connects. It was the third of March, 1887, three months before I was seven years old.

On the afternoon of that eventful day, I stood on the porch, dumb, expectant. I guessed vaguely from my mother's signs and from the hurrying to and fro in the house that something unusual was about to happen, so I went to the door and waited on the steps. The afternoon sun penetrated the mass of honeysuckle that covered the porch, and fell on my upturned face. My fingers lingered almost unconsciously on the familiar leaves and blossoms which had just come forth to greet the sweet southern spring. I did not know what the future held of marvel or surprise for me. Anger and bitterness had preyed upon me continually for weeks and a deep languor had succeeded this passionate struggle.

Have you ever been at sea in a dense fog, when it seemed as if a tangible white darkness shut you in, and the great ship, tense and anxious, groped her way toward the shore with plummet and sounding-line, and you waited with beating heart for something to happen? I was like that ship before my education began, only I was without compass or sounding-line, and had no way of knowing how near the harbour was. "Light! give me light!" was the wordless cry of my soul, and the light of love shone on me in that very hour.

I felt approaching footsteps. I stretched out my hand as I supposed to my mother. Some one took it, and I was caught up and held close in the arms of her who had come to reveal all things to me, and, more than all things else, to love me.

The morning after my teacher came she led me into her room and gave me a doll. The little blind children at the Perkins Institution had sent it and Laura Bridgman had dressed it; but I did not know this until afterward. When I had played with it a little while, Miss Sullivan slowly spelled into my hand the word "d-o-l-l." I was at once interested in this finger play and tried to imitate it. When I finally succeeded in making the letters correctly I was flushed with childish pleasure and pride. Running downstairs to my mother I held up my hand and made the letters for doll. I did not know that I was spelling a word or even that words existed; I was simply making my fingers go in monkey-like imitation. In the days that followed I learned to spell in this uncomprehending way a great many words, among them *pin, hat, cup* and a few verbs like *sit, stand* and *walk*. But my teacher had been with me several weeks before I understood that everything has a name.

One day, while I was playing with my new doll, Miss Sullivan put my big rag doll into my lap also, spelled "d-o-l-l" and tried to make me understand that "d-o-l-l" applied to both. Earlier in the day we had had a tussle over the words "m-u-g" and

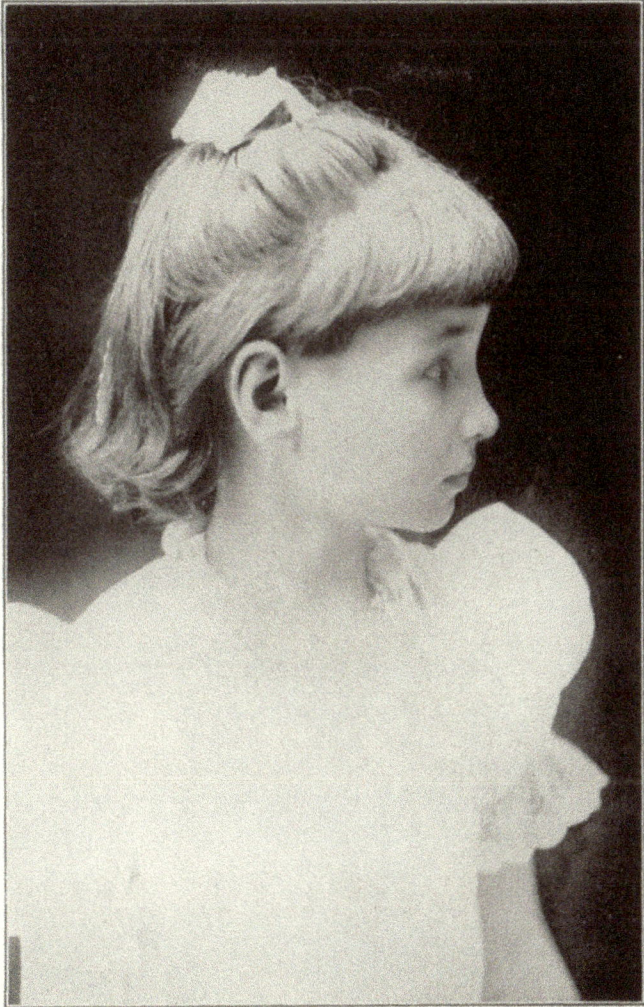

HELEN KELLER AT THE AGE OF SEVEN

"w-a-t-e-r." Miss Sullivan had tried to impress it upon me that "m-u-g" is *mug* and that "w-a-t-e-r" is *water*, but I persisted in confounding the two. In despair she had dropped the subject for the time, only to renew it at the first opportunity. I became impatient at her repeated attempts and, seizing the new doll, I dashed it upon the floor. I was keenly delighted when I felt the fragments of the broken doll at my feet. Neither sorrow nor regret followed my passionate outburst. I had not loved the doll. In the still, dark world in which I lived there was no strong sentiment or tenderness. I felt my teacher sweep the fragments to one side of the hearth, and I had a sense of satisfaction that the cause of my discomfort was removed. She brought me my hat, and I knew I was going out into the warm sunshine. This thought, if a wordless sensation may be called a thought, made me hop and skip with pleasure.

We walked down the path to the well-house, attracted by the fragrance of the honeysuckle with which it was covered. Some one was drawing water and my teacher placed my hand under the spout. As the cool stream gushed over one hand she spelled into the other the word *water*, first slowly, then rapidly. I stood still, my whole attention fixed upon the motions of her fingers. Suddenly I felt a misty consciousness as of something forgotten—a thrill of returning thought; and somehow the mystery of language was revealed to me. I knew then that "w-a-t-e-r" meant the wonderful cool something that was flowing over my hand. That living word awakened my soul, gave it light, hope, joy, set it free! There were barriers still, it is true, but barriers that could in time be swept away.*

I left the well-house eager to learn. Everything had a name, and each name gave birth to a new thought. As we returned to the house every object which I touched seemed to quiver with life. That was because I saw everything with the strange, new sight that had come to me. On entering the door I remembered the doll I had broken. I felt my way to the hearth and picked up the pieces. I tried vainly to put them together. Then my eyes filled with tears; for I realized what I had done, and for the first time I felt repentance and sorrow.

I learned a great many new words that day. I do not remember what they all were; but I do know that *mother, father, sister, teacher* were among them—words that were to make the world blossom for me, "like Aaron's rod, with flowers." It would have been difficult to find a happier child than I was as I lay in my crib at the close of that eventful day and lived over the joys it had brought me, and for the first time longed for a new day to come.

*See Miss Sullivan's letter, page 316.

CHAPTER V

I RECALL many incidents of the summer of 1887 that followed my soul's sudden awakening. I did nothing but explore with my hands and learn the name of every object that I touched; and the more I handled things and learned their names and uses, the more joyous and confident grew my sense of kinship with the rest of the world.

When the time of daisies and buttercups came Miss Sullivan took me by the hand across the fields, where men were preparing the earth for the seed, to the banks of the Tennessee River, and there, sitting on the warm grass, I had my first lessons in the beneficence of nature. I learned how the sun and the rain make to grow out of the ground every tree that is pleasant to the sight and good for food, how birds build their nests and live and thrive from land to land, how the squirrel, the deer, the lion and every other creature finds food and shelter. As my knowledge of things grew I felt more and more the delight of the world I was in. Long before I learned to do a sum in arithmetic or describe the shape of the earth, Miss Sullivan had taught me to find beauty in the fragrant woods, in every blade of grass, and in the curves and dimples of my baby sister's hand. She linked my earliest thoughts with nature, and made me feel that "birds and flowers and I were happy peers."

But about this time I had an experience which

taught me that nature is not always kind. One day my teacher and I were returning from a long ramble. The morning had been fine, but it was growing warm and sultry when at last we turned our faces homeward. Two or three times we stopped to rest under a tree by the wayside. Our last halt was under a wild cherry tree a short distance from the house. The shade was grateful, and the tree was so easy to climb that with my teacher's assistance I was able to scramble to a seat in the branches. It was so cool up in the tree that Miss Sullivan proposed that we have our luncheon there. I promised to keep still while she went to the house to fetch it.

Suddenly a change passed over the tree. All the sun's warmth left the air. I knew the sky was black, because all the heat, which meant light to me, had died out of the atmosphere. A strange odour came up from the earth. I knew it, it was the odour that always precedes a thunderstorm, and a nameless fear clutched at my heart. I felt absolutely alone, cut off from my friends and the firm earth. The immense, the unknown, enfolded me. I remained still and expectant; a chilling terror crept over me. I longed for my teacher's return; but above all things I wanted to get down from that tree.

There was a moment of sinister silence, then a multitudinous stirring of the leaves. A shiver ran through the tree, and the wind sent forth a blast that would have knocked me off had I not clung to the branch with might and main. The tree swayed and strained. The small twigs snapped and fell about me in showers. A wild impulse to jump seized me, but terror held me fast. I crouched down in the fork of the tree. The branches lashed about me. I felt the intermittent jarring that came now and then, as if something heavy had fallen and the shock had traveled up till it reached the limb I sat on. It worked my suspense up to the highest point, and just as I was thinking the tree and I should fall together, my teacher seized my hand and helped me down. I clung to her, trembling with joy to feel the earth under my feet once more. I had learned a new lesson—that nature "wages open war against her children, and under softest touch hides treacherous claws."

After this experience it was a long time before I climbed another tree. The mere thought filled me with terror. It was the sweet allurement of the mimosa tree in full bloom that finally overcame my fears. One beautiful spring morning when I was alone in the summer-house, reading, I became aware of a wonderful subtle fragrance in the air. I started up and instinctively stretched out my hands. It seemed as if the spirit of spring had passed through the summer-house. "What is it?" I asked, and the next minute I recognized the odour of the mimosa blossoms. I felt my way to the end of the garden, knowing that the mimosa tree was near the fence, at the turn of the path. Yes, there it was, all quivering in the warm sunshine, its blossom-laden branches almost touching the long grass. Was there ever anything so exquisitely beautiful in the world before! Its delicate blossoms shrank from the slightest earthly touch; it seemed as if a tree of paradise had been transplanted to earth. I made my way through a shower of petals to the great trunk and for one minute stood irresolute; then, putting my foot in the broad space between the forked branches, I pulled myself up into the tree. I had some difficulty in holding on, for the branches were very large and the bark hurt my hands. But I had a delicious sense that I was doing something unusual and wonderful, so I kept on climbing higher and higher, until I reached a little seat which somebody had built there so long ago that it had grown part of the tree itself. I sat there for a long, long time, feeling like a fairy on a rosy cloud. After that I spent many happy hours in my tree of paradise, thinking fair thoughts and dreaming bright dreams.

CHAPTER VI

I HAD now the key to all language, and I was eager to learn to use it. Children who hear acquire language without any particular effort; the words that fall from others' lips they catch on the wing, as it were, delightedly, while the little deaf child must trap them by a slow and often painful process. But whatever the process, the result is wonderful. Gradually from naming an object we advance step by step until we have traversed the vast distance between our first stammered syllable and the sweep of thought in a line of Shakespeare.

At first, when my teacher told me about a new thing I asked very few questions. My ideas were vague, and my vocabulary was inadequate; but as my knowledge of things grew, and I learned more and more words, my field of inquiry broadened, and I would return again and again to the same subject, eager for further information. Sometimes a new word revived an image that some earlier experience had engraved on my brain.

I remember the morning that I first asked the meaning of the word, "love." This was before I knew many words. I had found a few early violets in the garden and brought them to my teacher. She tried to kiss me; but at that time I did not like to have any one kiss me except my mother. Miss Sullivan put her arm gently round me and spelled into my hand, "I love Helen."

"What is love?" I asked.

She drew me closer to her and said, "It is here,"
pointing to my heart, whose beats I was conscious
of for the first time. Her words puzzled me very
much because I did not then understand anything
unless I touched it.

I smelt the violets in her hand and asked, half
in words, half in signs, a question which meant,
"Is love the sweetness of flowers?"

"No," said my teacher.

Again I thought. The warm sun was shining
on us.

"Is this not love?" I asked, pointing in the
direction from which the heat came, "Is this not
love?"

It seemed to me that there could be nothing more
beautiful than the sun, whose warmth makes all
things grow. But Miss Sullivan shook her head,
and I was greatly puzzled and disappointed. I
thought it strange that my teacher could not show
me love.

A day or two afterward I was stringing beads of
different sizes in symmetrical groups—two large
beads, three small ones, and so on. I had made
many mistakes, and Miss Sullivan had pointed
them out again and again with gentle patience.
Finally I noticed a very obvious error in the
sequence and for an instant I concentrated my attention on the lesson and tried to think how I should
have arranged the beads. Miss Sullivan touched
my forehead and spelled with decided emphasis,
"Think."

In a flash I knew that the word was the name of
the process that was going on in my head. This

was my first conscious perception of an abstract idea.

For a long time I was still—I was not thinking of the beads in my lap, but trying to find a meaning for "love" in the light of this new idea. The sun had been under a cloud all day, and there had been brief showers; but suddenly the sun broke forth in all its southern splendour.

Again I asked my teacher, "Is this not love?"

"Love is something like the clouds that were in the sky before the sun came out," she replied. Then in simpler words than these, which at that time I could not have understood, she explained: "You cannot touch the clouds, you know; but you feel the rain and know how glad the flowers and the thirsty earth are to have it after a hot day. You cannot touch love either; but you feel the sweetness that it pours into everything. Without love you would not be happy or want to play."

The beautiful truth burst upon my mind—I felt that there were invisible lines stretched between my spirit and the spirits of others.

From the beginning of my education Miss Sullivan made it a practice to speak to me as she would speak to any hearing child; the only difference was that she spelled the sentences into my hand instead of speaking them. If I did not know the words and idioms necessary to express my thoughts she supplied them, even suggesting conversation when I was unable to keep up my end of the dialogue.

This process was continued for several years; for the deaf child does not learn in a month, or even in two or three years, the numberless idioms and expressions used in the simplest daily intercourse.

The little hearing child learns these from constant repetition and imitation. The conversation he hears in his home stimulates his mind and suggests topics and calls forth the spontaneous expression of his own thoughts. This natural exchange of ideas is denied to the deaf child. My teacher, realizing this, determined to supply the kinds of stimulus I lacked. This she did by repeating to me as far as possible, verbatim, what she heard, and by showing me how I could take part in the conversation. But it was a long time before I ventured to take the initiative, and still longer before I could find something appropriate to say at the right time.

The deaf and the blind find it very difficult to acquire the amenities of conversation. How much more this difficulty must be augmented in the case of those who are both deaf and blind! They cannot distinguish the tone of the voice or, without assistance, go up and down the gamut of tones that give significance to words; nor can they watch the expression of the speaker's face, and a look is often the very soul of what one says.

CHAPTER VII

THE next important step in my education was learning to read.

As soon as I could spell a few words my teacher gave me slips of cardboard on which were printed words in raised letters. I quickly learned that each printed word stood for an object, an act, or a quality. I had a frame in which I could arrange the words in little sentences; but before I ever put sentences in the frame I used to make them in objects. I found the slips of paper which represented, for example, "doll," "is," "on," "bed" and placed each name on its object; then I put my doll on the bed with the words *is, on, bed* arranged beside the doll, thus making a sentence of the words, and at the same time carrying out the idea of the sentence with the things themselves.

One day, Miss Sullivan tells me, I pinned the word *girl* on my pinafore and stood in the wardrobe. On the shelf I arranged the words, *is, in, wardrobe*. Nothing delighted me so much as this game. My teacher and I played it for hours at a time. Often everything in the room was arranged in object sentences.

From the printed slip it was but a step to the printed book. I took my "Reader for Beginners" and hunted for the words I knew; when I found them my joy was like that of a game of hide-and-seek. Thus I began to read. Of the time

33

when I began to read connected stories I shall speak later.

For a long time I had no regular lessons. Even when I studied most earnestly it seemed more like play than work. Everything Miss Sullivan taught me she illustrated by a beautiful story or a poem. Whenever anything delighted or interested me she talked it over with me just as if she were a little girl herself. What many children think of with dread, as a painful plodding through grammar, hard sums and harder definitions, is to-day one of my most precious memories.

I cannot explain the peculiar sympathy Miss Sullivan had with my pleasures and desires. Perhaps it was the result of long association with the blind. Added to this she had a wonderful faculty for description. She went quickly over uninteresting details, and never nagged me with questions to see if I remembered the day-before-yesterday's lesson. She introduced dry technicalities of science little by little, making every subject so real that I could not help remembering what she taught.

We read and studied out of doors, preferring the sunlit woods to the house. All my early lessons have in them the breath of the woods—the fine, resinous odour of pine needles, blended with the perfume of wild grapes. Seated in the gracious shade of a wild tulip tree, I learned to think that everything has a lesson and a suggestion. "The loveliness of things taught me all their use." Indeed, everything that could hum, or buzz, or sing, or bloom, had a part in my education—noisy-throated frogs, katydids and crickets held in my hand until, forgetting their embarrassment, they trilled their reedy note, little downy chickens and wildflowers, the dogwood blossoms, meadow-violets and budding fruit trees. I felt the bursting cotton-bolls and fingered their soft fiber and fuzzy seeds; I felt the low soughing of the wind through the cornstalks, the silky rustling of the long leaves, and the indignant snort of my pony, as we caught him in the pasture and put the bit in his mouth—ah me! how well I remember the spicy, clovery smell of his breath!

Sometimes I rose at dawn and stole into the garden while the heavy dew lay on the grass and flowers. Few know what joy it is to feel the roses pressing softly into the hand, or the beautiful motion of the lilies as they sway in the morning breeze. Sometimes I caught an insect in the flower I was plucking, and I felt the faint noise of a pair of wings rubbed together in a sudden terror, as the little creature became aware of a pressure from without.

Another favourite haunt of mine was the orchard, where the fruit ripened early in July. The large, downy peaches would reach themselves into my hand, and as the joyous breezes flew about the trees the apples tumbled at my feet. Oh, the delight with which I gathered up the fruit in my pinafore, pressed my face against the smooth cheeks of the apples, still warm from the sun, and skipped back to the house!

Our favourite walk was to Keller's Landing, an old tumble-down lumber-wharf on the Tennessee River, used during the Civil War to land soldiers. There we spent many happy hours and played at learning geography. I built dams of pebbles, made islands and lakes, and dug river-beds, all for fun, and never dreamed that I was learning a lesson. I listened with increasing wonder to Miss Sullivan's descriptions of the great round world with its burning mountains, buried cities, moving rivers of ice, and many other things as strange. She made raised maps in clay, so that I could' feel the mountain ridges and valleys, and follow with my fingers the devious course of rivers. I liked this, too; but the division of the earth into zones and poles confused and teased my mind. The illustrative strings and the orange stick representing the poles seemed so real that even to this day the mere mention of temperate zone suggests a series of twine circles; and I believe that if any one should set about it he could convince me that white bears actually climb the North Pole.

Arithmetic seems to have been the only study I did not like. From the first I was not interested in the science of numbers. Miss Sullivan tried to teach me to count by stringing beads in groups, and by arranging kindergarten straws I learned to add and subtract. I never had patience to arrange more than five or six groups at a time. When I had accomplished this my conscience was at rest for the day, and I went out quickly to find my playmates.

In this same leisurely manner I studied zoölogy and botany.

Once a gentleman, whose name I have forgotten, sent me a collection of fossils—tiny mollusk shells beautifully marked, and bits of sandstone with the print of birds' claws, and a lovely fern in bas-relief. These were the keys which unlocked the treasures of the antediluvian world for me. With trembling fingers I listened to Miss Sullivan's descriptions of

the terrible beasts, with uncouth, unpronounceable
names, which once went tramping through the
primeval forests, tearing down the branches of
gigantic trees for food, and died in the dismal
swamps of an unknown age. For a long time these
strange creatures haunted my dreams, and this
gloomy period formed a somber background to
the joyous Now, filled with sunshine and roses
and echoing with the gentle beat of my pony's
hoof.

Another time a beautiful shell was given me, and
with a child's surprise and delight I learned how a
tiny mollusk had built the lustrous coil for his dwelling place, and how on still nights, when there is no
breeze stirring the waves, the Nautilus sails on the
blue waters of the Indian Ocean in his "ship of
pearl." After I had learned a great many interesting things about the life and habits of the children
of the sea—how in the midst of dashing waves the
little polyps build the beautiful coral isles of the
Pacific, and the foraminifera have made the chalk-
hills of many a land—my teacher read me "The
Chambered Nautilus," and showed me that the
shell-building process of the mollusks is symbolical
of the development of the mind. Just as the won-
der-working mantle of the Nautilus changes the
material it absorbs from the water and makes it a
part of itself, so the bits of knowledge one gathers
undergo a similar change and become pearls of
thought.

Again, it was the growth of a plant that furnished
the text for a lesson. We bought a lily and set it in
a sunny window. Very soon the green, pointed buds
showed signs of opening. The slender, fingerlike

leaves on the outside opened slowly, reluctant, I thought, to reveal the loveliness they hid; once having made a start, however, the opening process went on rapidly, but in order and systematically. There was always one bud larger and more beautiful than the rest, which pushed her outer covering back with more pomp, as if the beauty in soft, silky robes knew that she was the lily-queen by right divine, while her more timid sisters doffed their green hoods shyly, until the whole plant was one nodding bough of loveliness and fragrance.

Once there were eleven tadpoles in a glass globe set in a window full of plants. I remember the eagerness with which I made discoveries about them. It was great fun to plunge my hand into the bowl and feel the tadpoles frisk about, and to let them slip and slide between my fingers. One day a more ambitious fellow leaped beyond the edge of the bowl and fell on the floor, where I found him to all appearance more dead than alive. The only sign of life was a slight wriggling of his tail. But no sooner had he returned to his element than he darted to the bottom, swimming round and round in joyous activity. He had made his leap, he had seen the great world, and was content to stay in his pretty glass house under the big fuchsia tree until he attained the dignity of froghood. Then he went to live in the leafy pool at the end of the garden, where he made the summer nights musical with his quaint love-song.

Thus I learned from life itself. At the beginning I was only a little mass of possibilities. It was my teacher who unfolded and developed them. When she came, everything about me breathed of love and joy and was full of meaning. She has never since let pass an opportunity to point out the beauty that is in everything, nor has she ceased trying in thought and action and example to make my life sweet and useful.

It was my teacher's genius, her quick sympathy, her loving tact which made the first years of my education so beautiful. It was because she seized the right moment to impart knowledge that made it so pleasant and acceptable to me. She realized that a child's mind is like a shallow brook which ripples and dances merrily over the stony course of its education and reflects here a flower, there a bush, yonder a fleecy cloud; and she attempted to guide my mind on its way, knowing that like a brook it should be fed by mountain streams and hidden springs, until it broadened out into a deep river, capable of reflecting in its placid surface, billowy hills, the luminous shadows of trees and the blue heavens, as well as the sweet face of a little flower.

Any teacher can take a child to the classroom, but not every teacher can make him learn. He will not work joyously unless he feels that liberty is his, whether he is busy or at rest; he must feel the flush of victory and the heart-sinking of disappointment before he takes with a will the tasks distasteful to him and resolves to dance his way bravely through a dull routine of textbooks.

My teacher is so near to me that I scarcely think of myself apart from her. How much of my delight in all beautiful things is innate, and how much is due to her influence, I can never tell. I feel that her being is inseparable from my own, and that

the footsteps of my life are in hers.   All the best
of me belongs to her—there is not a talent, or an
aspiration or a joy in me that has not been awakened
by her loving touch.

CHAPTER VIII

THE first Christmas after Miss Sullivan came to Tuscumbia was a great event. Every one in the family prepared surprises for me, but what pleased me most, Miss Sullivan and I prepared surprises for everybody else. The mystery that surrounded the gifts was my greatest delight and amusement. My friends did all they could to excite my curiosity by hints and half-spelled sentences which they pretended to break off in the nick of time. Miss Sullivan and I kept up a game of guessing which taught me more about the use of language than any set lessons could have done. Every evening, seated round a glowing wood fire, we played our guessing game, which grew more and more exciting as Christmas approached.

On Christmas Eve the Tuscumbia schoolchildren had their tree, to which they invited me. In the centre of the schoolroom stood a beautiful tree ablaze and shimmering in the soft light, its branches loaded with strange, wonderful fruit. It was a moment of supreme happiness. I danced and capered round the tree in an ecstasy. When I learned that there was a gift for each child, I was delighted, and the kind people who had prepared the tree permitted me to hand the presents to the children. In the pleasure of doing this, I did not stop to look at my own gifts; but when I was ready for them, my impatience for the real Christmas to begin almost got beyond control. I knew the gifts

I already had were not those of which friends had thrown out such tantalizing hints, and my teacher said the presents I was to have would be even nicer than these. I was persuaded, however, to content myself with the gifts from the tree and leave the others until morning.

That night, after I had hung my stocking, I lay awake a long time, pretending to be asleep and keeping alert to see what Santa Claus would do when he came. At last I fell asleep with a new doll and a white bear in my arms. Next morning it was I who waked the whole family with my first "Merry Christmas!" I found surprises, not in the stocking only, but on the table, on all the chairs, at the door, on the very window-sill; indeed, I could hardly walk without stumbling on a bit of Christmas wrapped up in tissue paper. But when my teacher presented me with a canary, my cup of happiness overflowed.

Little Tim was so tame that he would hop on my finger and eat candied cherries out of my hand. Miss Sullivan taught me to take all the care of my new pet. Every morning after breakfast I prepared his bath, made his cage clean and sweet, filled his cups with fresh seed and water from the well-house, and hung a spray of chickweed in his swing.

One morning I left the cage on the window-seat while I went to fetch water for his bath. When I returned I felt a big cat brush past me as I opened the door. At first I did not realize what had happened; but when I put my hand in the cage and Tim's pretty wings did not meet my touch or his small pointed claws take hold of my finger, I knew that I should never see my sweet little singer again.

CHAPTER IX

THE next important event in my life was my visit to Boston, in May, 1888. As if it were yesterday I remember the preparations, the departure with my teacher and my mother, the journey, and finally the arrival in Boston. How different this journey was from the one I had made to Baltimore two years before! I was no longer a restless, excitable little creature, requiring the attention of everybody on the train to keep me amused. I sat quietly beside Miss Sullivan, taking in with eager interest all that she told me about what she saw out of the car window: the beautiful Tennessee River, the great cotton-fields, the hills and woods, and the crowds of laughing negroes at the stations, who waved to the people on the train and brought delicious candy and pop-corn balls through the car. On the seat opposite me sat my big rag doll, Nancy, in a new gingham dress and a beruffled sunbonnet, looking at me out of two bead eyes. Sometimes, when I was not absorbed in Miss Sullivan's descriptions, I remembered Nancy's existence and took her up in my arms, but I generally calmed my conscience by making myself believe that she was asleep.

As I shall not have occasion to refer to Nancy again, I wish to tell here a sad experience she had soon after our arrival in Boston. She was covered with dirt—the remains of mud pies I had compelled her to eat, although she had never shown any special liking for them. The laundress at the Perkins Institution secretly carried her off to give her a bath. This was too much for poor Nancy. When I next saw her she was a formless heap of cotton, which I should not have recognized at all except for the two bead eyes which looked out at me reproachfully.

When the train at last pulled into the station at Boston it was as if a beautiful fairy tale had come true. The "once upon a time" was now; the "far-away country" was here.

We had scarcely arrived at the Perkins Institution for the Blind when I began to make friends with the little blind children. It delighted me inexpressibly to find that they knew the manual alphabet. What joy to talk with other children in my own language! Until then I had been like a foreigner speaking through an interpreter. In the school where Laura Bridgman was taught I was in my own country. It took me some time to appreciate the fact that my new friends were blind. I knew I could not see; but it did not seem possible that all the eager, loving children who gathered round me and joined heartily in my frolics were also blind. I remember the surprise and the pain I felt as I noticed that they placed their hands over mine when I talked to them and that they read books with their fingers. Although I had been told this before, and although I understood my own deprivations, yet I had thought vaguely that since they could hear, they must have a sort of "second sight," and I was not prepared to find one child and another and yet another deprived of the same precious gift. But they were so happy and contented that I lost all sense of pain in the pleasure of their companionship.

One day spent with the blind children made me feel thoroughly at home in my new environment, and I looked eagerly from one pleasant experience to another as the days flew swiftly by. I could not quite convince myself that there was much world left, for I regarded Boston as the beginning and the end of creation.

While we were in Boston we visited Bunker Hill, and there I had my first lesson in history. The story of the brave men who had fought on the spot where we stood excited me greatly. I climbed the monument, counting the steps, and wondering as I went higher and yet higher if the soldiers had climbed this great stairway and shot at the enemy on the ground below.

The next day we went to Plymouth by water. This was my first trip on the ocean and my first voyage in a steamboat. How full of life and motion it was! But the rumble of the machinery made me think it was thundering, and I began to cry, because I feared if it rained we should not be able to have our picnic out of doors. I was more interested, I think, in the great rock on which the Pilgrims landed than in anything else in Plymouth. I could touch it, and perhaps that made the coming of the Pilgrims and their toils and great deeds seem more real to me. I have often held in my hand a little model of the Plymouth Rock which a kind gentleman gave me at Pilgrim Hall, and I have fingered its curves, the split in the centre and the embossed figures "1620," and turned over in my mind all that I knew about the wonderful story of the Pilgrims.

How my childish imagination glowed with the splendour of their enterprise! I idealized them as the bravest and most generous men that ever sought a home in a strange land. I thought they desired the freedom of their fellow men as well as their own. I was keenly surprised and disappointed years later to learn of their acts of persecution that make us tingle with shame, even while we glory in the courage and energy that gave us our "Country Beautiful."

Among the many friends I made in Boston were Mr. William Endicott and his daughter. Their kindness to me was the seed from which many pleasant memories have since grown. One day we visited their beautiful home at Beverly Farms. I remember with delight how I went through their rose-garden, how their dogs, big Leo and little curly-haired Fritz with long ears, came to meet me, and how Nimrod, the swiftest of the horses, poked his nose into my hands for a pat and a lump of sugar. I also remember the beach, where for the first time I played in the sand. It was hard, smooth sand, very different from the loose, sharp sand, mingled with kelp and shells, at Brewster. Mr. Endicott told me about the great ships that came sailing by from Boston, bound for Europe. I saw him many times after that, and he was always a good friend to me; indeed, I was thinking of him when I called Boston "the City of Kind Hearts."

CHAPTER X

JUST before the Perkins Institution closed for the summer, it was arranged that my teacher and I should spend our vacation at Brewster, on Cape Cod, with our dear friend, Mrs. Hopkins. I was delighted, for my mind was full of the prospective joys and of the wonderful stories I had heard about the sea.

My most vivid recollection of that summer is the ocean. I had always lived far inland and had never had so much as a whiff of salt air; but I had read in a big book called "Our World" a description of the ocean which filled me with wonder and an intense longing to touch the mighty sea and feel it roar. So my little heart leaped high with eager excitement when I knew that my wish was at last to be realized.

No sooner had I been helped into my bathing-suit than I sprang out upon the warm sand and without thought of fear plunged into the cool water. I felt the great billows rock and sink. The buoyant motion of the water filled me with an exquisite, quivering joy. Suddenly my ecstasy gave place to terror; for my foot struck against a rock and the next instant there was a rush of water over my head. I thrust out my hands to grasp some support, I clutched at the water and at the seaweed which the waves tossed in my face. But all my frantic efforts were in vain. The waves seemed to be playing a game with me, and tossed me from one to another in their wild frolic. It was fearful! The good, firm earth had slipped from my feet, and everything seemed shut out from this strange, all-enveloping element—life, air, warmth and love. At last, however, the sea, as if weary of its new toy, threw me back on the shore, and in another instant I was clasped in my teacher's arms. Oh, the comfort of the long, tender embrace! As soon as I had recovered from my panic sufficiently to say anything, I demanded: "Who put salt in the water?"

After I had recovered from my first experience in the water, I thought it great fun to sit on a big rock in my bathing-suit and feel wave after wave dash against the rock, sending up a shower of spray which quite covered me. I felt the pebbles rattling as the waves threw their ponderous weight against the shore; the whole beach seemed racked by their terrific onset, and the air throbbed with their pulsations. The breakers would swoop back to gather themselves for a mightier leap, and I clung to the rock, tense, fascinated, as I felt the dash and roar of the rushing sea!

I could never stay long enough on the shore. The tang of the untainted, fresh and free sea air was like a cool, quieting thought, and the shells and pebbles and the seaweed with tiny living creatures attached to it never lost their fascination for me. One day Miss Sullivan attracted my attention to a strange object which she had captured basking in the shallow water. It was a great horseshoe crab—the first one I had ever seen. I felt of him and thought it very strange that he should carry his house on his back. It suddenly occurred to me that he might make a delightful pet; so I seized him by the tail with both hands and carried him home. This feat pleased me highly, as his body was very heavy, and it took all my strength to drag him half a mile. I would not leave Miss Sullivan in peace until she had put the crab in a trough near the well where I was confident he would be secure. But next morning I went to the trough, and lo, he had disappeared! Nobody knew where he had gone, or how he had escaped. My disappointment was bitter at the time; but little by little I came to realize that it was not kind or wise to force this poor dumb creature out of his element, and after awhile I felt happy in the thought that perhaps he had returned to the sea.

CHAPTER XI

In the autumn I returned to my Southern home with a heart full of joyous memories. As I recall that visit North I am filled with wonder at the richness and variety of the experiences that cluster about it. It seems to have been the beginning of everything. The treasures of a new, beautiful world were laid at my feet, and I took in pleasure and information at every turn. I lived myself into all things. I was never still a moment; my life was as full of motion as those little insects that crowd a whole existence into one brief day. I met many people who talked with me by spelling into my hand, and thought in joyous sympathy leaped up to meet thought, and behold, a miracle had been wrought! The barren places between my mind and the minds of others blossomed like the rose.

I spent the autumn months with my family at our summer cottage, on a mountain about fourteen miles from Tuscumbia. It was called Fern Quarry, because near it there was a limestone quarry, long since abandoned. Three frolicsome little streams ran through it from springs in the rocks above, leaping here and tumbling there in laughing cascades wherever the rocks tried to bar their way. The opening was filled with ferns which completely covered the beds of limestone and in places hid the streams. The rest of the mountain was thickly wooded. Here were great oaks and splendid evergreens with trunks like mossy pillars, from the branches of which hung garlands of ivy and mistletoe, and persimmon trees, the odour of which pervaded every nook and corner of the wood—an illusive, fragrant something that made the heart glad. In places the wild muscadine and scuppernong vines stretched from tree to tree, making arbours which were always full of butterflies and buzzing insects. It was delightful to lose ourselves in the green hollows of that tangled wood in the late afternoon, and to smell the cool, delicious odours that came up from the earth at the close of day.

Our cottage was a sort of rough camp, beautifully situated on the top of the mountain among oaks and pines. The small rooms were arranged on each side of a long open hall. Round the house was a wide piazza, where the mountain winds blew, sweet with all wood-scents. We lived on the piazza most of the time—there we worked, ate and played. At the back door there was a great butternut tree, round which the steps had been built, and in front the trees stood so close that I could touch them and feel the wind shake their branches, or the leaves twirl downward in the autumn blast.

Many visitors came to Fern Quarry. In the evening, by the campfire, the men played cards and whiled away the hours in talk and sport. They told stories of their wonderful feats with fowl, fish and quadruped—how many wild ducks and turkeys they had shot, what "savage trout" they had caught, and how they had bagged the craftiest foxes, outwitted the most clever 'possums and overtaken the fleetest deer, until I thought that surely the lion, the tiger, the bear and the rest of the wild tribe would not be able to stand before these wily hunters. "To-morrow to the chase!" was their good-night shout as the circle of merry friends broke up for the night. The men slept in the hall outside our door, and I could feel the deep breathing of the dogs and the hunters as they lay on their improvised beds.

At dawn I was awakened by the smell of coffee, the rattling of guns, and the heavy footsteps of the men as they strode about, promising themselves the greatest luck of the season. I could also feel the stamping of the horses, which they had ridden out from town and hitched under the trees, where they stood all night, neighing loudly, impatient to be off. At last the men mounted, and, as they say in the old songs, away went the steeds with bridles ringing and whips cracking and hounds racing ahead, and away went the champion hunters "with hark and whoop and wild halloo!"

Later in the morning we made preparations for a barbecue. A fire was kindled at the bottom of a deep hole in the ground, big sticks were laid crosswise at the top, and meat was hung from them and turned on spits. Around the fire squatted negroes, driving away the flies with long branches. The savoury odour of the meat made me hungry long before the tables were set.

When the bustle and excitement of preparation was at its height, the hunting party made its appearance, struggling in by twos and threes, the men hot and weary, the horses covered with foam, and the jaded hounds panting and dejected—and not a single kill! Every man declared that he had seen at least one deer, and that the animal had come very close; but however hotly the dogs might pursue the game, however well the guns might be aimed, at the snap of the trigger there was not a deer in sight. They had been as fortunate as the little boy who said he came very near seeing a rabbit—he saw his tracks. The party soon forgot its disappointment, however, and we sat down, not to venison, but to a tamer feast of veal and roast pig.

One summer I had my pony at Fern Quarry. I called him Black Beauty, as I had just read the book, and he resembled his namesake in every way, from his glossy black coat to the white star on his forehead. I spent many of my happiest hours on his back. Occasionally, when it was quite safe, my teacher would let go the leading-rein, and the pony sauntered on or stopped at his sweet will to eat grass or nibble the leaves of the trees that grew beside the narrow trail.

On mornings when I did not care for the ride, my teacher and I would start after breakfast for a ramble in the woods, and allow ourselves to get lost amid the trees and vines, with no road to follow except the paths made by cows and horses. Frequently we came upon impassable thickets which forced us to take a roundabout way. We always returned to the cottage with armfuls of laurel, goldenrod, ferns and gorgeous swamp-flowers such as grow only in the South.

Sometimes I would go with Mildred and my little cousins to gather persimmons. I did not eat them; but I loved their fragrance and enjoyed hunting for them in the leaves and grass. We also went nutting, and I helped them open the chestnut burrs and break the shells of hickory-nuts and walnuts— the big, sweet walnuts!

At the foot of the mountain there was a railroad, and the children watched the trains whiz by. Sometimes a terrific whistle brought us to the steps, and Mildred told me in great excitement that a cow or a horse had strayed on the track. About a mile distant there was a trestle spanning a deep gorge. It was very difficult to walk over, the ties were wide apart and so narrow that one felt as if one were walking on knives. I had never crossed it until one day Mildred, Miss Sullivan and I were lost in the woods, and wandered for hours without finding a path.

Suddenly Mildred pointed with her little hand and exclaimed, "There's the trestle!" We would have taken any way rather than this; but it was late and growing dark, and the trestle was a short cut home. I had to feel for the rails with my toe; but I was not afraid, and got on very well, until all at once there came a faint "puff, puff" from the distance.

"I see the train!" cried Mildred, and in another minute it would have been upon us had we not climbed down on the crossbraces while it rushed over our heads. I felt the hot breath from the engine on my face, and the smoke and ashes almost choked us. As the train rumbled by, the trestle shook and swayed until I thought we should be dashed to the chasm below. With the utmost difficulty we regained the track. Long after dark we reached home and found the cottage empty; the family were all out hunting for us.

CHAPTER XII

AFTER my first visit to Boston, I spent almost every winter in the North. Once I went on a visit to a New England village with its frozen lakes and vast snow fields. It was then that I had opportunities such as had never been mine to enter into the treasures of the snow.

I recall my surprise on discovering that a mysterious hand had stripped the trees and bushes, leaving only here and there a wrinkled leaf. The birds had flown, and their empty nests in the bare trees were filled with snow. Winter was on hill and field. The earth seemed benumbed by his icy touch, and the very spirits of the trees had withdrawn to their roots, and there, curled up in the dark, lay fast asleep. All life seemed to have ebbed away, and even when the sun shone the day was

> Shrunk and cold,
> As if her veins were sapless and old,
> And she rose up decrepitly
> For a last dim look at earth and sea.

The withered grass and the bushes were transformed into a forest of icicles.

Then came a day when the chill air portended a snowstorm. We rushed out-of-doors to feel the first few tiny flakes descending. Hour by hour the flakes dropped silently, softly from their airy height to the earth, and the country became more and more level. A snowy night closed upon the world, and in the morning one could scarcely recognize a feature of the landscape. All the roads were hidden, not a single landmark was visible, only a waste of snow with trees rising out of it.

In the evening a wind from the northeast sprang up, and the flakes rushed hither and thither in furious mêlée. Around the great fire we sat and told merry tales, and frolicked, and quite forgot that we were in the midst of a desolate solitude, shut in from all communication with the outside world. But during the night the fury of the wind increased to such a degree that it thrilled us with a vague terror. The rafters creaked and strained, and the branches of the trees surrounding the house rattled and beat against the windows, as the winds rioted up and down the country.

On the third day after the beginning of the storm the snow ceased. The sun broke through the clouds and shone upon a vast, undulating white plain. High mounds, pyramids heaped in fantastic shapes, and impenetrable drifts lay scattered in every direction.

Narrow paths were shoveled through the drifts. I put on my cloak and hood and went out. The air stung my cheeks like fire. Half walking in the paths, half working our way through the lesser drifts, we succeeded in reaching a pine grove just outside a broad pasture. The trees stood motionless and white like figures in a marble frieze. There was no odour of pine-needles. The rays of the sun fell upon the trees, so that the twigs sparkled like diamonds and dropped in showers when we touched them. So dazzling was the light, it penetrated even the darkness that veils my eyes.

As the days wore on, the drifts gradually shrunk, but before they were wholly gone another storm came, so that I scarcely felt the earth under my feet once all winter. At intervals the trees lost their icy covering, and the bulrushes and underbrush were bare; but the lake lay frozen and hard beneath the sun.

Our favourite amusement during that winter was tobogganing. In places the shore of the lake rises abruptly from the water's edge. Down these steep slopes we used to coast. We would get on our toboggan, a boy would give us a shove, and off we went! Plunging through drifts, leaping hollows, swooping down upon the lake, we would shoot across its gleaming surface to the opposite bank. What joy! What exhilarating madness! For one wild, glad moment we snapped the chain that binds us to earth, and joining hands with the winds we felt ourselves divine!

CHAPTER XIII

It was in the spring of 1890 that I learned to speak.* The impulse to utter audible sounds had always been strong within me. I used to make noises, keeping one hand on my throat while the other hand felt the movements of my lips. I was pleased with anything that made a noise and liked to feel the cat purr and the dog bark. I also liked to keep my hand on a singer's throat, or on a piano when it was being played. Before I lost my sight and hearing, I was fast learning to talk, but after my illness it was found that I had ceased to speak because I could not hear. I used to sit in my mother's lap all day long and keep my hands on her face because it amused me to feel the motions of her lips; and I moved my lips, too, although I had forgotten what talking was. My friends say that I laughed and cried naturally, and for awhile I made many sounds and word-elements, not because they were a means of communication, but because the need of exercising my vocal organs was imperative. There was, however, one word the meaning of which I still remembered, *water*. I pronounced it "wa-wa." Even this became less and less intelligible until the time when Miss Sullivan began to teach me. I stopped using it only after I had learned to spell the word on my fingers.

I had known for a long time that the people about

*For Miss Sullivan's account see page 386.

me used a method of communication different from
mine; and even before I knew that a deaf child could
be taught to speak, I was conscious of dissatisfac-
tion with the means of communication I already
possessed.   One who is entirely dependent upon the
manual alphabet has always a sense of restraint, of
narrowness.   This feeling began to agitate me with
a vexing, forward-reaching sense of a lack that
should be filled.   My thoughts would often rise and
beat up like birds against the wind; and I persisted
in using my lips and voice.   Friends tried to discourage this tendency, fearing lest it would lead
to disappointment.   But I persisted, and an accident soon occurred which resulted in the breaking
down of this great barrier—I heard the story of
Ragnhild Kaata.

In 1890 Mrs. Lamson, who had been one of
Laura Bridgman's teachers, and who had just
returned from a visit to Norway and Sweden, came
to see me, and told me of Ragnhild Kaata, a deaf
and blind girl in Norway who had actually been
taught to speak.   Mrs. Lamson had scarcely finished telling me about this girl's success before I
was on fire with eagerness.   I resolved that I, too,
would learn to speak.   I would not rest satisfied
until my teacher took me, for advice and assistance,
to Miss Sarah Fuller, principal of the Horace Mann
School.   This lovely, sweet-natured lady offered to
teach me herself, and we began the twenty-sixth of
March, 1890.

Miss Fuller's method was this: she passed my
hand lightly over her face, and let me feel the position of her tongue and lips when she made a sound.
I was eager to imitate every motion and in an hour

had learned six elements of speech : M, P, A, S, T, I.
Miss Fuller gave me eleven lessons in all.   I shall
never forget the surprise and delight I felt when I
uttered my first connected sentence, "It is warm."
True, they were broken and stammering syllables;
but they were human speech.   My soul, conscious of
new strength, came out of bondage, and was
reaching through those broken symbols of speech to
all knowledge and all faith.

No deaf child who has earnestly tried to speak
the words which he has never heard—to come out
of the prison of silence, where no tone of love, no
song of bird, no strain of music ever pierces the
stillness—can forget the thrill of surprise, the joy of
discovery which came over him when he uttered
his first word.   Only such a one can appreciate the
eagerness with which I talked to my toys, to stones,
trees, birds and dumb animals, or the delight I felt
when at my call Mildred ran to me or my dogs
obeyed my commands.   It is an unspeakable boon
to me to be able to speak in winged words that need
no interpretation.   As I talked, happy thoughts
fluttered up out of my words that might perhaps
have struggled in vain to escape my fingers.

But it must not be supposed that I could really
talk in this short time.   I had learned only the
elements of speech.   Miss Fuller and Miss Sullivan
could understand me, but most people would not
have understood one word in a hundred.   Nor is it
true that, after I had learned these elements, I did
the rest of the work myself.   But for Miss Sullivan's
genius, untiring perseverance and devotion, I could
not have progressed as far as I have toward natural
speech.   In the first place, I laboured night and

day before I could be understood even by my most
intimate friends; in the second place, I needed Miss
Sullivan's assistance constantly in my efforts to
articulate each sound clearly and to combine all
sounds in a thousand ways.   Even now she calls
my attention every day to mispronounced words.

All teachers of the deaf know what this means,
and only they can at all appreciate the peculiar difficulties with which I had to contend.   In reading
my teacher's lips I was wholly dependent on my
fingers: I had to use the sense of touch in catching
the vibrations of the throat, the movements of the
mouth and the expression of the face; and often
this sense was at fault.   In such cases I was forced
to repeat the words or sentences, sometimes for
hours, until I felt the proper ring in my own
voice.   My work was practice, practice, practice.
Discouragement and weariness cast me down frequently; but the next moment the thought that I
should soon be at home and show my loved ones
what I had accomplished, spurred me on, and I
eagerly looked forward to their pleasure in my
achievement.

"My little sister will understand me now," was a
thought stronger than all obstacles.   I used to
repeat ecstatically, "I am not dumb now."   I could
not be despondent while I anticipated the delight of
talking to my mother and reading her responses from
her lips.   It astonished me to find how much easier
it is to talk than to spell with the fingers, and I discarded the manual alphabet as a medium of communication on my part; but Miss Sullivan and a few
friends still use it in speaking to me, for it is more
convenient and more rapid than lip-reading.

Just here, perhaps, I had better explain our use of the manual alphabet, which seems to puzzle people who do not know us. One who reads or talks to me spells with his hand, using the single-hand manual alphabet generally employed by the deaf. I place my hand on the hand of the speaker so lightly as not to impede its movements. The position of the hand is as easy to feel as it is to see. I do not feel each letter any more than you see each letter separately when you read. Constant practice makes the fingers very flexible, and some of my friends spell rapidly—about as fast as an expert writes on a typewriter. The mere spelling is, of course, no more a conscious act than it is in writing.

When I had made speech my own, I could not wait to go home. At last the happiest of happy moments arrived. I had made my homeward journey, talking constantly to Miss Sullivan, not for the sake of talking, but determined to improve to the last minute. Almost before I knew it, the train stopped at the Tuscumbia station, and there on the platform stood the whole family. My eyes fill with tears now as I think how my mother pressed me close to her, speechless and trembling with delight, taking in every syllable that I spoke, while little Mildred seized my free hand and kissed it and danced, and my father expressed his pride and affection in a big silence. It was as if Isaiah's prophecy had been fulfilled in me, "The mountains and the hills shall break forth before you into singing, and all the trees of the field shall clap their hands!"

CHAPTER XIV

THE winter of 1892 was darkened by the one cloud in my childhood's bright sky. Joy deserted my heart, and for a long, long time I lived in doubt, anxiety and fear. Books lost their charm for me, and even now the thought of those dreadful days chills my heart. A little story called "The Frost King," which I wrote and sent to Mr. Anagnos, of the Perkins Institution for the Blind, was at the root of the trouble. In order to make the matter clear, I must set forth the facts connected with this episode, which justice to my teacher and to myself compels me to relate.*

I wrote the story when I was at home, the autumn after I had learned to speak. We had stayed up at Fern Quarry later than usual. While we were there, Miss Sullivan had described to me the beauties of the late foliage, and it seems that her descriptions revived the memory of a story, which must have been read to me, and which I must have unconsciously retained. I thought then that I was "making up a story," as children say, and I eagerly sat down to write it before the ideas should slip from me. My thoughts flowed easily; I felt a sense of joy in the composition. Words and images came tripping to my finger ends, and as I thought out sentence after sentence, I wrote them on my braille slate. Now, if words and images come to me without effort, it is

*For the documents in this matter see page 396.

63

a pretty sure sign that they are not the offspring of my own mind, but stray waifs that I regretfully dismiss. At that time I eagerly absorbed everything I read without a thought of authorship, and even now I cannot be quite sure of the boundary line between my ideas and those I find in books. I suppose that is because so many of my impressions come to me through the medium of others' eyes and ears.

When the story was finished, I read it to my teacher, and I recall now vividly the pleasure I felt in the more beautiful passages, and my annoyance .t being interrupted to have the pronunciation of a word corrected. At dinner it was read to the assembled family, who were surprised that I could write so well. Some one asked me if I had read it in a book.

This question surprised me very much; for I had not the faintest recollection of having had it read to me. I spoke up and said, "Oh, no, it is my story, and I have written it for Mr. Anagnos."

Accordingly I copied the story and sent it to him for his birthday. It was suggested that I should change the title from "Autumn Leaves" to "The Frost King," which I did. I carried the little story to the post-office myself, feeling as if I were walking on air. I little dreamed how cruelly I should pay for that birthday gift.

Mr. Anagnos was delighted with "The Frost King," and published it in one of the Perkins Institution reports. This was the pinnacle of my happiness, from which I was in a little while dashed to earth. I had been in Boston only a short time when it was discovered that a story similar to "The Frost King," called "The Frost Fairies" by Miss

Margaret T. Canby, had appeared before I was born in a book called "Birdie and His Friends." The two stories were so much alike in thought and language that it was evident Miss Canby's story had been read to me, and that mine was—a plagiarism. It was difficult to make me understand this; but when I did understand I was astonished and grieved. No child ever drank deeper of the cup of bitterness than I did. I had disgraced myself; I had brought suspicion upon those I loved best. And yet how could it possibly have happened? I racked my brain until I was weary to recall anything about the frost that I had read before I wrote "The Frost King"; but I could remember nothing, except the common reference to Jack Frost, and a poem for children, "The Freaks of the Frost," and I knew I had not used that in my composition.

At first Mr. Anagnos, though deeply troubled, seemed to believe me. He was unusually tender and kind to me, and for a brief space the shadow lifted. To please him I tried not to be unhappy, and to make myself as pretty as possible for the celebration of Washington's birthday, which took place very soon after I received the sad news.

I was to be Ceres in a kind of masque given by the blind girls. How well I remember the graceful draperies that enfolded me, the bright autumn leaves that wreathed my head, and the fruit and grain at my feet and in my hands, and beneath all the gaiety of the masque the oppressive sense of coming ill that made my heart heavy.

The night before the celebration, one of the teachers of the Institution had asked me a question connected with "The Frost King," and I was telling her that Miss Sullivan had talked to me about Jack Frost and his wonderful works. Something I said made her think she detected in my words a confession that I did remember Miss Canby's story of "The Frost Fairies," and she laid her conclusions before Mr. Anagnos, although I had told her most emphatically that she was mistaken.

Mr. Anagnos, who loved me tenderly, thinking that he had been deceived, turned a deaf ear to the pleadings of love and innocence. He believed, or at least suspected, that Miss Sullivan and I had deliberately stolen the bright thoughts of another and imposed them on him to win his admiration. I was brought before a court of investigation composed of the teachers and officers of the Institution, and Miss Sullivan was asked to leave me. Then I was questioned and cross-questioned with what seemed to me a determination on the part of my judges to force me to acknowledge that I remembered having had "The Frost Fairies" read to me. I felt in every question the doubt and suspicion that was in their minds, and I felt, too, that a loved friend was looking at me reproachfully, although I could not have put all this into words. The blood pressed about my thumping heart, and I could scarcely speak, except in monosyllables. Even the consciousness that it was only a dreadful mistake did not lessen my suffering, and when at last I was allowed to leave the room, I was dazed and did not notice my teacher's caresses, or the tender words of my friends, who said I was a brave little girl and they were proud of me.

As I lay in my bed that night, I wept as I hope few children have wept. I felt so cold, I imagined I should die before morning, and the thought com-

forted me. I think if this sorrow had come to me
when I was older, it would have broken my spirit
beyond repairing. But the angel of forgetfulness
has gathered up and carried away much of
the misery and all the bitterness of those sad
days.

Miss Sullivan had never heard of "The Frost
Fairies" or of the book in which it was published.
With the assistance of Dr. Alexander Graham
Bell, she investigated the matter carefully, and at
last it came out that Mrs. Sophia C. Hopkins had a
copy of Miss Canby's "Birdie and His Friends" in
1888, the year that we spent the summer with her
at Brewster. Mrs. Hopkins was unable to find her
copy; but she has told me that at that time, while
Miss Sullivan was away on a vacation, she tried to
amuse me by reading from various books, and
although she could not remember reading "The
Frost Fairies" any more than I, yet she felt sure
that "Birdie and His Friends" was one of them.
She explained the disappearance of the book by the
fact that she had a short time before sold her house
and disposed of many juvenile books, such as old
school-books and fairy tales, and that "Birdie and
His Friends" was probably among them.

The stories had little or no meaning for me then;
but the mere spelling of the strange words was sufficient to amuse a little child who could do almost
nothing to amuse herself; and although I do not
recall a single circumstance connected with the reading of the stories, yet I cannot help thinking that I
made a great effort to remember the words, with the
intention of having my teacher explain them when
she returned. One thing is certain, the language

was ineffaceably stamped upon my brain, though for a long time no one knew it, least of all myself.

When Miss Sullivan came back, I did not speak to her about "The Frost Fairies," probably because she began at once to read "Little Lord Fauntleroy," which filled my mind to the exclusion of everything else. But the fact remains that Miss Canby's story was read to me once, and that long after I had forgotten it, it came back to me so naturally that I never suspected that it was the child of another mind.

In my trouble I received many messages of love and sympathy. All the friends I loved best, except one, have remained my own to the present time.

Miss Canby herself wrote kindly, "Some day you will write a great story out of your own head, that will be a comfort and help to many." But this kind prophecy has never been fulfilled. I have never played with words again for the mere pleasure of the game. Indeed, I have ever since been tortured by the fear that what I write is not my own. For a long time, when I wrote a letter, even to my mother, I was seized with a sudden feeling of terror, and I would spell the sentences over and over, to make sure that I had not read them in a book. Had it not been for the persistent encouragement of Miss Sullivan, I think I should have given up trying to write altogether.

I have read "The Frost Fairies" since, also the letters I wrote in which I used other ideas of Miss Canby's. I find in one of them, a letter to Mr. Anagnos, dated September 29, 1891, words and sentiments exactly like those of the book. At the time I was writing "The Frost King," and this letter, like many others, contains phrases which show that my mind was saturated with the story. I represent my teacher as saying to me of the golden autumn leaves, "Yes, they are beautiful enough to comfort us for the flight of summer"—an idea direct from Miss Canby's story.

This habit of assimilating what pleased me and giving it out again as my own appears in much of my early correspondence and my first attempts at writing. In a composition which I wrote about the old cities of Greece and Italy, I borrowed my glowing descriptions, with variations, from sources I have forgotten. I knew Mr. Anagnos's great love of antiquity and his enthusiastic appreciation of all beautiful sentiments about Italy and Greece. I therefore gathered from all the books I read every bit of poetry or of history that I thought would give him pleasure. Mr. Anagnos, in speaking of my composition on the cities, has said, "These ideas are poetic in their essence." But I do not understand how he ever thought a blind and deaf child of eleven could have invented them. Yet I cannot think that because I did not originate the ideas, my little composition is therefore quite devoid of interest. It shows me that I could express my appreciation of beautiful and poetic ideas in clear and animated language.

Those early compositions were mental gymnastics. I was learning, as all young and inexperienced persons learn, by assimilation and imitation, to put ideas into words. Everything I found in books that pleased me I retained in my memory, consciously or unconsciously, and adapted it. The young writer, as Stevenson has said, instinctively tries to copy whatever seems most admirable, and he shifts his admiration with astonishing versatility. It is only after years of this sort of practice that even great men have learned to marshal the legion of words which come thronging through every byway of the mind.

I am afraid I have not yet completed this process. It is certain that I cannot always distinguish my own thoughts from those I read, because what I read become the very substance and texture of my mind. Consequently, in nearly all that I write, I produce something which very much resembles the crazy patchwork I used to make when I first learned to sew. This patchwork was made of all sorts of odds and ends—pretty bits of silk and velvet; but the coarse pieces that were not pleasant to touch always predominated. Likewise my compositions are made up of crude notions of my own, inlaid with the brighter thoughts and riper opinions of the authors I have read. It seems to me that the great difficulty of writing is to make the language of the educated mind express our confused ideas, half feelings, half thoughts, when we are little more than bundles of instinctive tendencies. Trying to write is very much like trying to put a Chinese puzzle together. We have a pattern in mind which we wish to work out in words; but the words will not fit the spaces, or, if they do, they will not match the design. But we keep on trying because we know that others have succeeded, and we are not willing to acknowledge defeat.

"There is no way to become original, except to be born so," says Stevenson, and although I may not be original, I hope sometime to outgrow my artificial, periwigged compositions. Then, perhaps, my own thoughts and experiences will come to the surface. Meanwhile I trust and hope and persevere, and try not to let the bitter memory of "The Frost King" trammel my efforts.

So this sad experience may have done me good and set me thinking on some of the problems of composition. My only regret is that it resulted in the loss of one of my dearest friends, Mr. Anagnos.

Since the publication of "The Story of My Life" in the *Ladies' Home Journal*, Mr. Anagnos has made a statement, in a letter to Mr. Macy, that at the time of the "Frost King" matter, he believed I was innocent. He says, the court of investigation before which I was brought consisted of eight people: four blind, four seeing persons. Four of them, he says, thought I knew that Miss Canby's story had been read to me, and the others did not hold this view. Mr. Anagnos states that he cast his vote with those who were favourable to me.

But, however the case may have been, with whichever side he may have cast his vote, when I went into the room where Mr. Anagnos had so often held me on his knee and, forgetting his many cares, had shared in my frolics, and found there persons who seemed to doubt me, I felt that there was something hostile and menacing in the very atmosphere, and subsequent events have borne out this impression. For two years he seems to have held the belief that Miss Sullivan and I were innocent. Then he evidently retracted his favourable judgment, why I do not know. Nor did I know the details of the investigation. I never knew even the names of the members of the "court" who did not speak to me.

I was too excited to notice anything, too frightened to ask questions. Indeed, I could scarcely think what I was saying, or what was being said to me.

I have given this account of the "Frost King" affair because it was important in my life and education; and, in order that there might be no misunderstanding, I have set forth all the facts as they appear to me, without a thought of defending myself or of laying blame on any one.

CHAPTER XV

THE summer and winter following the "Frost King" incident I spent with my family in Alabama. I recall with delight that home-going. Everything had budded and blossomed. I was happy. "The Frost King" was forgotten.

When the ground was strewn with the crimson and golden leaves of autumn, and the musk-scented grapes that covered the arbour at the end of the garden were turning golden brown in the sunshine, I began to write a sketch of my life—a year after I had written "The Frost King."

I was still excessively scrupulous about everything I wrote. The thought that what I wrote might not be absolutely my own tormented me. No one knew of these fears except my teacher. A strange sensitiveness prevented me from referring to the "Frost King"; and often when an idea flashed out in the course of conversation I would spell softly to her, "I am not sure it is mine." At other times, in the midst of a paragraph I was writing, I said to myself, "Suppose it should be found that all this was written by some one long ago!" An impish fear clutched my hand, so that I could not write any more that day. And even now I sometimes feel the same uneasiness and disquietude. Miss Sullivan consoled and helped me in every way she could think of; but the terrible experience I had passed through left a lasting impression on my mind, the significance of which I am only just beginning to understand. It was with the hope of restoring my self-confidence that she persuaded me to write for the *Youth's Companion* a brief account of my life. I was then twelve years old. As I look back on my struggle to write that little story, it seems to me that I must have had a prophetic vision of the good that would come of the undertaking, or I should surely have failed.

I wrote timidly, fearfully, but resolutely, urged . on by my teacher, who knew that if I persevered, I should find my mental foothold again and get a grip on my faculties. Up to the time of the "Frost King" episode, I had lived the unconscious life of a little child; now my thoughts were turned inward, and I beheld things invisible. Gradually I emerged from the penumbra of that experience with a mind made clearer by trial and with a truer knowledge of life.

The chief events of the year 1893 were my trip to Washington during the inauguration of President Cleveland, and visits to Niagara and the World's Fair. Under such circumstances my studies were constantly interrupted and often put aside for many weeks, so that it is impossible for me to give a connected account of them.

We went to Niagara in March, 1893. It is difficult to describe my emotions when I stood on the point which overhangs the American Falls and felt the air vibrate and the earth tremble.

It seems strange to many people that I should be impressed by the wonders and beauties of Niagara. They are always asking: "What does this beauty or that music mean to you? You cannot see the

waves rolling up the beach or hear their roar.
What do they mean to you?" In the most evident
sense they mean everything. I cannot fathom or
define their meaning any more than I can fathom
or define love or religion or goodness.

During the summer of 1893, Miss Sullivan and
I visited the World's Fair with Dr. Alexander
Graham Bell. I recall with unmixed delight those
days when a thousand childish fancies became
beautiful realities. Every day in imagination I
made a trip round the world, and I saw many
wonders from the uttermost parts of the earth—
marvels of invention, treasuries of industry and skill
and all the activities of human life actually passed
under my finger tips.

I liked to visit the Midway Plaisance. It seemed
like the "Arabian Nights," it was crammed so full
of novelty and interest. Here was the India of my
books in the curious bazaar with its Shivas and
elephant-gods; there was the land of the Pyramids
concentrated in a model Cairo with its mosques
and its long processions of camels; yonder were the
lagoons of Venice, where we sailed every evening
when the city and the fountains were illuminated.
I also went on board a Viking ship which lay a short
distance from the little craft. I had been on a
man-of-war before, in Boston, and it interested me
to see, on this Viking ship, how the seaman was once
all in all—how he sailed and took storm and calm
alike with undaunted heart, and gave chase to
whosoever reëchoed his cry, "We are of the sea!"
and fought with brains and sinews, self-reliant,
self-sufficient, instead of being thrust into the background by unintelligent machinery, as Jack is

to-day. So it always is—"man only is interesting to man."

At a little distance from this ship there was a model of the *Santa Maria,* which I also examined. The captain showed me Columbus's cabin and the desk with an hour-glass on it. This small instrument impressed me most because it made me think how weary the heroic navigator must have felt as he saw the sand dropping grain by grain while desperate men were plotting against his life.

Mr. Higinbotham, President of the World's Fair, kindly gave me permission to touch the exhibits, and with an eagerness as insatiable as that with which Pizarro seized the treasures of Peru, I took in the glories of the Fair with my fingers. It was a sort of tangible kaleidoscope, this white city of the West. Everything fascinated me, especially the French bronzes. They were so lifelike, I thought they were angel visions which the artist had caught and bound in earthly forms.

At the Cape of Good Hope exhibit, I learned much about the processes of mining diamonds. Whenever it was possible, I touched the machinery while it was in motion, so as to get a clearer idea how the stones were weighed, cut, and polished. I searched in the washings for a diamond and found it myself—the only true diamond, they said, that was ever found in the United States.

Dr. Bell went everywhere with us and in his own delightful way described to me the objects of greatest interest. In the electrical building we examined the telephones, autophones, phonographs, and other inventions, and he made me understand how it is possible to send a message on wires that

MISS KELLER AND DR. ALEXANDER GRAHAM BELL

mock space and outrun time, and, like Prometheus, to draw fire from the sky. We also visited the anthropological department, and I was much interested in the relics of ancient Mexico, in the rude stone implements that are so often the only record of an age—the simple monuments of nature's unlettered children (so I thought as I fingered them) that seem bound to last while the memorials of kings and sages crumble in dust away—and in the Egyptian mummies, which I shrank from touching. From these relics I learned more about the progress of man than I have heard or read since.

All these experiences added a great many new terms to my vocabulary, and in the three weeks I spent at the Fair I took a long leap from the little child's interest in fairy tales and toys to the appreciation of the real and the earnest in the workaday world.

CHAPTER XVI

Before October, 1893, I had studied various subjects by myself in a more or less desultory manner. I read the histories of Greece, Rome and the United States. I had a French grammar in raised print, and as I already knew some French, I often amused myself by composing in my head short exercises, using the new words as I came across them, and ignoring rules and other technicalities as much as possible. I even tried, without aid, to master the French pronunciation, as I found all the letters and sounds described in the book. Of course this was tasking slender powers for great ends; but it gave me something to do on a rainy day, and I acquired a sufficient knowledge of French to read with pleasure La Fontaine's "Fables," "Le Medecin Malgrè Lui" and passages from "Athalie."

I also gave considerable time to the improvement of my speech, I read aloud to Miss Sullivan and recited passages from my favourite poets, which I had committed to memory; she corrected my pronunciation and helped me to phrase and inflect. It was not, however, until October, 1893, after I had recovered from the fatigue and excitement of my visit to the World's Fair, that I began to have lessons in special subjects at fixed hours.

Miss Sullivan and I were at that time in Hulton, Pennsylvania, visiting the family of Mr. William Wade. Mr. Irons, a neighbour of theirs, was a

good Latin scholar; it was arranged that I should
study under him.   I remember him as a man of rare,
sweet nature and of wide experience.   He taught
me Latin grammar principally; but he often helped
me in arithmetic, which I found as troublesome as
it was uninteresting.   Mr. Irons also read with me
Tennyson's "In Memoriam."   I had read many
books before, but never from a critical point of view.
I learned for the first time to know an author, to
recognize his style as I recognize the clasp of a
friend's hand.

At first I was rather unwilling to study Latin
grammar.   It seemed absurd to waste time analyz-
ing every word I came across—noun, genitive,
singular, feminine—when its meaning was quite
plain.   I thought I might just as well describe my
pet in order to know it—order, vertebrate; division,
quadruped; class, mammalia; genus, felinus; species,
cat; individual, Tabby.   But as I got deeper into
the subject, I became more interested, and the beauty
of the language delighted me.   I often amused myself by reading Latin passages, picking up words I
understood and trying to make sense.   I have never
ceased to enjoy this pastime.

There is nothing more beautiful, I think, than
the evanescent fleeting images and sentiments presented by a language one is just becoming familiar
with—ideas that flit across the mental sky, shaped
and tinted by capricious fancy.   Miss Sullivan
sat beside me at my lessons, spelling into my
hand whatever Mr. Irons said, and looking up
new words for me.   I was just beginning to read
Cæsar's "Gallic War" when I went to my home in
Alabama.

CHAPTER XVII

In the summer of 1894, I attended the meeting at Chautauqua of the American Association to Promote the Teaching of Speech to the Deaf. There it was arranged that I should go to the Wright-Humason School for the Deaf in New York City. I went there in October, 1894, accompanied by Miss Sullivan. This school was chosen especially for the purpose of obtaining the highest advantages in vocal culture and training in lip-reading. In addition to my work in these subjects, I studied, during the two years I was in the school, arithmetic, physical geography, French and German.

Miss Reamy, my German teacher, could use the manual alphabet, and after I had acquired a small vocabulary, we talked together in German whenever we had a chance, and in a few months I could understand almost everything she said. Before the end of the first year I read "Wilhelm Tell" with the greatest delight. Indeed, I think I made more progress in German than in any of my other studies. I found French much more difficult. I studied it with Madame Olivier, a French lady who did not know the manual alphabet, and who was obliged to give her instruction orally. I could not read her lips easily; so my progress was much slower than in German. I managed, however, to read "Le Medecin Malgrè Lui" again. It was very amusing but I did not like it nearly so well as "Wilhelm Tell."

My progress in lip-reading and speech was not what my teachers and I had hoped and expected it would be. It was my ambition to speak like other people, and my teachers believed that this could be accomplished; but, although we worked hard and faithfully, yet we did not quite reach our goal. I suppose we aimed too high, and disappointment was therefore inevitable. I still regarded arithmetic as a system of pitfalls. I hung about the dangerous frontier of "guess," avoiding with infinite trouble to myself and others the broad valley of reason. When I was not guessing, I was jumping at conclusions, and this fault, in addition to my dullness, aggravated my difficulties more than was right or necessary.

But although these disappointments caused me great depression at times, I pursued my other studies with unflagging interest, especially physical geography. It was a joy to learn the secrets of nature: how—in the picturesque language of the Old Testament—the winds are made to blow from the four corners of the heavens, how the vapours ascend from the ends of the earth, how rivers are cut out among the rocks, and mountains overturned by the roots, and in what ways man may overcome many forces mightier than himself. The two years in New York were happy ones, and I look back to them with genuine pleasure.

I remember especially the walks we all took together every day in Central Park, the only part of the city that was congenial to me. I never lost a jot of my delight in this great park. I loved to have it described every time I entered it; for it was beautiful in all its aspects, and these aspects were so many that it was beautiful in a different way each day of the nine months I spent in New York.

In the spring we made excursions to various places of interest. We sailed on the Hudson River and wandered about on its green banks, of which Bryant loved to sing. I liked the simple, wild grandeur of the palisades. Among the places I visited were West Point, Tarrytown, the home of Washington Irving, where I walked through "Sleepy Hollow."

The teachers at the Wright-Humason School were always planning how they might give the pupils every advantage that those who hear enjoy—how they might make much of few tendencies and passive memories in the cases of the little ones— and lead them out of the cramping circumstances in which their lives were set.

Before I left New York, these bright days were darkened by the greatest sorrow that I have ever borne, except the death of my father. Mr. John P. Spaulding, of Boston, died in February, 1896. Only those who knew and loved him best can understand what his friendship meant to me. He, who made every one happy in a beautiful, unobtrusive way, was most kind and tender to Miss Sullivan and me. So long as we felt his loving presence and knew that he took a watchful interest in our work, fraught with so many difficulties, we could not be discouraged. His going away left a vacancy in our lives that has never been filled.

CHAPTER XVIII

In October, 1896, I entered the Cambridge School for Young Ladies, to be prepared for Radcliffe.

When I was a little girl, I visited Wellesley and surprised, my friends by the announcement, "Some day I shall go to college—but I shall go to Harvard!" When asked why I would not go to Wellesley, I replied that there were only girls there. The thought of going to college took root in my heart and became an earnest desire, which impelled me to enter into competition for a degree with seeing and hearing girls, in the face of the strong opposition of many true and wise friends. When I left New York the idea had become a fixed purpose; and it was decided that I should go to Cambridge. This was the nearest approach I could get to Harvard and to the fulfillment of my childish declaration.

At the Cambridge School the plan was to have Miss Sullivan attend the classes with me and interpret to me the instruction given.

Of course my instructors had had no experience in teaching any but normal pupils, and my only means of conversing with them was reading their lips. My studies for the first year were English history, English literature, German, Latin, arithmetic, Latin composition and occasional themes. Until then I had never taken a course of study with the idea of preparing for college; but I had been well drilled in English by Miss Sullivan, and it soon became evident to my teachers that I needed no special instruction in this subject beyond a critical study of the books prescribed by the college. I had had, moreover, a good start in French, and received six months' instruction in Latin; but German was the subject with which I was most familiar.

In spite, however, of these advantages, there were serious drawbacks to my progress. Miss Sullivan could not spell out in my hand all that the books required, and it was very difficult to have text-books embossed in time to be of use to me, although my friends in London and Philadelphia were willing to hasten the work. For a while, indeed, I had to copy my Latin in braille, so that I could recite with the other girls. My instructors soon became sufficiently familiar with my imperfect speech to answer my questions readily and correct mistakes. I could not make notes in class or write exercises; but I wrote all my compositions and translations at home on my typewriter.

Each day Miss Sullivan went to the classes with me and spelled into my hand with infinite patience all that the teachers said. In study hours she had to look up new words for me and read and reread notes and books I did not have in raised print. The tedium of that work is hard to conceive. Frau Gröte, my German teacher, and Mr. Gilman, the principal, were the only teachers in the school who learned the finger alphabet to give me instruction. No one realized more fully than dear Frau Gröte how slow and inadequate her spelling was. Nevertheless, in the goodness of her heart she laboriously spelled out her instructions to me in special lessons twice a week, to give Miss Sullivan a little rest. But, though everybody was kind and ready to help us, there was only one hand that could turn drudgery into pleasure.

That year I finished arithmetic, reviewed my Latin grammar, and read three chapters of Cæsar's "Gallic War." In German I read, partly with my fingers and partly with Miss Sullivan's assistance, Schiller's "Lied von der Glocke" and "Taucher," Heine's "Harzreise," Freytag's "Aus dem Staat Friedrichs des Grossen," Riehl's "Fluch Der Schönheit," Lessing's "Minna von Barnhelm," and Goethe's "Aus meinem Leben." I took the greatest delight in these German books, especially Schiller's wonderful lyrics, the history of Frederick the Great's magnificent achievements and the account of Goethe's life. I was sorry to finish "Die Harzreise," so full of happy witticisms and charming descriptions of vine-clad hills, streams that sing and ripple in the sunshine, and wild regions, sacred to tradition and legend, the gray sisters of a long-vanished, imaginative age—descriptions such as can be given only by those to whom nature is "a feeling, a love and an appetite."

Mr. Gilman instructed me part of the year in English literature. We read together, "As You Like It," Burke's "Speech on Conciliation with America," and Macaulay's "Life of Samuel Johnson." Mr. Gilman's broad views of history and literature and his clever explanations made my work easier and pleasanter than it could have been had I only read notes mechanically with the necessarily brief explanations given in the classes. Burke's speech was more instructive than any other book on a political subject that I had ever read. My mind stirred with the stirring times, and the characters round which the life of two contending nations centred seemed to move right before me. I wondered more and more, while Burke's masterly speech rolled on in mighty surges of eloquence, how it was that King George and his ministers could have turned a deaf ear to his warning prophecy of our victory and their humiliation. Then I entered into the melancholy details of the relation in which the great statesman stood to his party and to the representatives of the people. I thought how strange it was that such precious seeds of truth and wisdom should have fallen among the tares of ignorance and corruption.

In a different way Macaulay's "Life of Samuel Johnson" was interesting. My heart went out to the lonely man who ate the bread of affliction in Grub Street, and yet, in the midst of toil and cruel suffering of body and soul, always had a kind word, and lent a helping hand to the poor and despised. I rejoiced over all his successes, I shut my eyes to his faults, and wondered, not that he had them, but that they had not crushed or dwarfed his soul. But in spite of Macaulay's brilliancy and his admirable faculty of making the commonplace seem fresh and picturesque, his positiveness wearied me at times, and his frequent sacrifices of truth to effect kept me in a questioning attitude very unlike the attitude of reverence in which I had listened to the Demosthenes of Great Britain.

At the Cambridge school, for the first time in my life, I enjoyed the companionship of seeing and hearing girls of my own age. I lived with several others

in one of the pleasant houses connected with the
school, the house where Mr. Howells used to live,
and we all had the advantage of home life.   I joined
them in many of their games, even blind man's
buff and frolics in the snow; I took long walks with
them; we discussed our studies and read aloud the
things that interested us.   Some of the girls learned
to speak to me, so that Miss Sullivan did not have
to repeat their conversation.

At Christmas, my mother and little sister spent
the holidays with me, and Mr. Gilman kindly offered
to let Mildred study in his school.   So Mildred
stayed with me in Cambridge, and for six happy
months we were hardly ever apart.   It makes me
most happy to remember the hours we spent helping
each other in study and sharing our recreation
together.

I took my preliminary examinations for Radcliffe
from the 29th of June to the 3rd of July in 1897.
The subjects I offered were Elementary and Advanced German, French, Latin, English, and Greek
and Roman history, making nine hours in all.   I
passed in everything, and received "honours" in
German and English.

Perhaps an explanation of the method that was
in use when I took my examinations will not be
amiss here.   The student was required to pass in
sixteen hours—twelve hours being called elementary
and four advanced.   He had to pass five hours at
a time to have them counted.   The examination
papers were given out at nine o'clock at Harvard
and brought to Radcliffe by a special messenger.
Each candidate was known, not by his name,
but by a number.   I was No. 233, but, as I

had to use a typewriter, my identity could not be concealed.

It was thought advisable for me to have my examinations in a room by myself, because the noise of the typewriter might disturb the other girls. Mr. Gilman read all the papers to me by means of the manual alphabet. A man was placed on guard at the door to prevent interruption.

The first day I had German. Mr. Gilman sat beside me and read the paper through first, then sentence by sentence, while I repeated the words aloud, to make sure that I understood him perfectly. The papers were difficult, and I felt very anxious as I wrote out my answers on the typewriter. Mr. Gilman spelled to me what I had written, and I made such changes as I thought necessary, and he inserted them. I wish to say here that I have not had this advantage since in any of my examinations. At Radcliffe no one reads the papers to me after they are written, and I have no opportunity to correct errors unless I finish before the time is up. In that case I correct only such mistakes as I can recall in the few minutes allowed, and make notes of these corrections at the end of my paper. If I passed with higher credit in the preliminaries than in the finals, there are two reasons. In the finals, no one read my work over to me, and in the preliminaries I offered subjects with some of which I was in a measure familiar before my work in the Cambridge school; for at the beginning of the year I had passed examinations in English, History, French and German, which Mr. Gilman gave me from previous Harvard papers.

Mr. Gilman sent my written work to the examiners with a certificate that I, candidate No. 233, had written the papers.

All the other preliminary examinations were conducted in the same manner.   None of them was so difficult as the first.   I remember that the day the Latin paper was brought to us, Professor Schilling came in and informed me I had passed satisfactorily in German.   This encouraged me greatly, and I sped on to the end of the ordeal with a light heart and a steady hand.

CHAPTER XIX

WHEN I began my second year at the Gilman school, I was full of hope and determination to succeed. But during the first few weeks I was confronted with unforeseen difficulties. Mr. Gilman had agreed that that year I should study mathematics principally. I had physics, algebra, geometry, astronomy, Greek and Latin. Unfortunately, many of the books I needed had not been embossed in time for me to begin with the classes, and I lacked important apparatus for some of my studies. The classes I was in were very large, and it was impossible for the teachers to give me special instruction. Miss Sullivan was obliged to read all the books to me, and interpret for the instructors, and for the first time in eleven years it seemed as if her dear hand would not be equal to the task.

It was necessary for me to write algebra and geometry in class and solve problems in physics, and this I could not do until we bought a braille writer, by means of which I could put down the steps and processes of my work. I could not follow with my eyes the geometrical figures drawn on the blackboard, and my only means of getting a clear idea of them was to make them on a cushion with straight and curved wires, which had bent and pointed ends. I had to carry in my mind, as Mr. Keith says in his report, the lettering of the figures, the hypothesis and conclusion, the construction and the process of the proof. In a word, every study had its obstacles. Sometimes I lost all courage and betrayed my feelings in a way I am ashamed to remember, especially as the signs of my trouble were afterward used against Miss Sullivan, the only person of all the kind friends I had there, who could make the crooked straight and the rough places smooth.

Little by little, however, my difficulties began to disappear. The embossed books and other apparatus arrived, and I threw myself into the work with renewed confidence. Algebra and geometry were the only studies that continued to defy my efforts to comprehend them. As I have said before, I had no aptitude for mathematics; the different points were not explained to me as fully as I wished. The geometrical diagrams were particularly vexing because I could not see the relation of the different parts to one another, even on the cushion. It was not until Mr. Keith taught me that I had a clear idea of mathematics.

I was beginning to overcome these difficulties when an event occurred which changed everything.

Just before the books came, Mr. Gilman had begun to remonstrate with Miss Sullivan on the ground that I was working too hard, and in spite of my earnest protestations, he reduced the number of my recitations. At the beginning we had agreed that I should, if necessary, take five years to prepare for college, but at the end of the first year the success of my examinations showed Miss Sullivan, Miss Harbaugh (Mr. Gilman's head teacher), and one other, that I could without too much effort complete my preparation in two years more. Mr. Gilman at first agreed to this; but when my tasks had become somewhat perplexing, he insisted that I was overworked, and that I should remain at his school three years longer. I did not like his plan, for I wished to enter college with my class.

On the seventeenth of November I was not very well, and did not go to school. Although Miss Sullivan knew that my indisposition was not serious, yet Mr. Gilman, on hearing of it, declared that I was breaking down and made changes in my studies which would have rendered it impossible for me to take my final examinations with my class. In the end the difference of opinion between Mr. Gilman and Miss Sullivan resulted in my mother's withdrawing my sister Mildred and me from the Cambridge School.

After some delay it was arranged that I should continue my studies under a tutor, Mr. Merton S. Keith, of Cambridge. Miss Sullivan and I spent the rest of the winter with our friends, the Chamberlins in Wrentham, twenty-five miles from Boston.

From February to July, 1898, Mr. Keith came out to Wrentham twice a week, and taught me algebra, geometry, Greek and Latin. Miss Sullivan interpreted his instruction.

In October, 1898, we returned to Boston. For eight months Mr. Keith gave me lessons five times a week, in periods of about an hour. He explained each time what I did not understand in the previous lesson, assigned new work, and took home with him the Greek exercises which I had written during the week on my typewriter, corrected them fully, and returned them to me.

In this way my preparation for college went on without interruption. I found it much easier and pleasanter to be taught by myself than to receive instruction in class. There was no hurry, no confusion. My tutor had plenty of time to explain what I did not understand, so I got on faster and did better work than I ever did in school. I still found more difficulty in mastering problems in mathematics than I did in any other of my studies. I wish algebra and geometry had been half as easy as the languages and literature. But even mathematics Mr. Keith made interesting; he succeeded in whittling problems small enough to get through my brain. He kept my mind alert and eager, and trained it to reason clearly, and to seek conclusions calmly and logically, instead of jumping wildly into space and arriving nowhere. He was always gentle and forbearing, no matter how dull I might be, and believe me, my stupidity would often have exhausted the patience of Job.

On the 29th and 30th of June, 1899, I took my final examinations for Radcliffe College. The first day I had Elementary Greek and Advanced Latin, and the second day Geometry, Algebra and Advanced Greek.

The college authorities did not allow Miss Sullivan to read the examination papers to me; so Mr. Eugene C. Vining, one of the instructors at the Perkins Institution for the Blind, was employed to copy the papers for me in American braille. Mr. Vining was a stranger to me, and could not communicate with me, except by writing braille. The proctor was also a stranger, and did not attempt to communicate with me in any way.

The braille worked well enough in the languages, but when it came to geometry and algebra, difficulties arose.* I was sorely perplexed, and felt discouraged wasting much precious time, especially in algebra. It is true that I was familiar with all literary braille in common use in this country—English, American, and New York Point; but the various signs and symbols in geometry and algebra in the three systems are very different, and I had used only the English braille in my algebra.

Two days before the examinations, Mr. Vining sent me a braille copy of one of the old Harvard papers in algebra. To my dismay I found that it was in the American notation. I sat down immediately and wrote to Mr. Vining, asking him to explain the signs. I received another paper and a table of signs by return mail, and I set to work to learn the notation. But on the night before the algebra examination, while I was struggling over some very complicated examples, I could not tell the combinations of bracket, brace and radical. Both Mr. Keith and I were distressed and full of forebodings for the morrow; but we went over to the college a little before the examination began, and had Mr. Vining explain more fully the American symbols.

In geometry my chief difficulty was that I had always been accustomed to read the propositions in line print, or to have them spelled into my hand; and somehow, although the propositions were right before me, I found the braille confusing, and could not fix clearly in my mind what I was reading. But when I took up algebra I had a harder time still. The signs, which I had so lately learned, and which I thought I knew, perplexed me. Besides, I could

*See Miss Keller's letter, page 259.

not see what I wrote on my typewriter. I had always done my work in braille or in my head. Mr. Keith had relied too much on my ability to solve problems mentally, and had not trained me to write examination papers. Consequently my work was painfully slow, and I had to read the examples over and over before I could form any idea of what I was required to do. Indeed, I am not sure now that I read all the signs correctly. I found it very hard to keep my wits about me.

But I do not blame any one. The administrative board of Radcliffe did not realize how difficult they were making my examinations, nor did they understand the peculiar difficulties I had to surmount. But if they unintentionally placed obstacles in my way, I have the consolation of knowing that I overcame them all.

CHAPTER XX

THE struggle for admission to college was ended, and I could now enter Radcliffe whenever I pleased. Before I entered college, however, it was thought best that I should study another year under Mr. Keith. It was not, therefore, until the fall of 1900 that my dream of going to college was realized.

I remember my first day at Radcliffe. It was a day full of interest for me. I had looked forward to it for years. A potent force within me, stronger than the persuasion of my friends, stronger even than the pleadings of my heart, had impelled me to try my strength by the standards of those who see and hear. I knew that there were obstacles in the way; but I was eager to overcome them. I had taken to heart the words of the wise Roman who said, "To be banished from Rome is but to live outside of Rome." Debarred from the great highways of knowledge, I was compelled to make the journey across country by unfrequented roads—that was all; and I knew that in college there were many bypaths where I could touch hands with girls who were thinking, loving and struggling like me.

I began my studies with eagerness. Before me I saw a new world opening in beauty and light, and I felt within me the capacity to know all things. In the wonderland of Mind I should be as free as another. Its people, scenery, manners, joys, tragedies should be living, tangible interpreters of

96

the real world. The lecture-halls seemed filled with the spirit of the great and the wise, and I thought the professors were the embodiment of wisdom. If I have since learned differently, I am not going to tell anybody.

But I soon discovered that college was not quite the romantic lyceum I had imagined. Many of the dreams that had delighted my young inexperience became beautifully less and "faded into the light of common day." Gradually I began to find that there were disadvantages in going to college.

The one I felt and still feel most is lack of time. I used to have time to think, to reflect, my mind and I. We would sit together of an evening and listen to the inner melodies of the spirit, which one hears only in leisure moments when the words of some loved poet touch a deep, sweet chord in the soul that until then had been silent. But in college there is no time to commune with one's thoughts. One goes to college to learn, it seems, not to think. When one enters the portals of learning, one leaves the dearest pleasures—solitude, books and imagination —outside with the whispering pines. I suppose I ought to find some comfort in the thought that I am laying up treasures for future enjoyment, but I am improvident enough to prefer present joy to hoarding riches against a rainy day.

My studies the first year were French, German, history, English composition and English literature. In the French course I read some of the works of Corneille, Molière, Racine, Alfred de Musset and Sainte-Beuve, and in the German those of Goethe and Schiller. I reviewed rapidly the whole period of history from the fall of the Roman Empire to the eighteenth century, and in English literature studied critically Milton's poems and "Areopagitica."

I am frequently asked how I overcome the peculiar conditions under which I work in college. In the classroom I am of course practically alone. The professor is as remote as if he were speaking through a telephone. The lectures are spelled into my hand as rapidly as possible, and much of the individuality of the lecturer is lost to me in the effort to keep in the race. The words rush through my hand like hounds in pursuit of a hare which they often miss. But in this respect I do not think I am much worse off than the girls who take notes. If the mind is occupied with the mechanical process of hearing and putting words on paper at pell-mell speed, I should not think one could pay much attention to the subject under consideration or the manner in which it is presented. I cannot make notes during the lectures, because my hands are busy listening. Usually I jot down what I can remember of them when I get home. I write the exercises, daily themes, criticisms and hour-tests, the mid-year and final examinations, on my typewriter, so that the professors have no difficulty in finding out how little I know. When I began the study of Latin prosody, I devised and explained to my professor a system of signs indicating the different meters and quantities.

I use the Hammond typewriter. I have tried many machines, and I find the Hammond is the best adapted to the peculiar needs of my work. With this machine movable type shuttles can be used, and one can have several shuttles, each with a different set of characters—Greek, French, or mathematical, according to the kind of writing one wishes to do on the typewriter. Without it, I doubt if I could go to college.

Very few of the books required in the various courses are printed for the blind, and I am obliged to have them spelled into my hand. Consequently I need more time to prepare my lessons than other girls. The manual part takes longer, and I have perplexities which they have not. There are days when the close attention I must give to details chafes my spirit, and the thought that I must spend hours reading a few chapters, while in the world without other girls are laughing and singing and dancing, makes me rebellious; but I soon recover my buoyancy and laugh the discontent out of my heart. For, after all, every one who wishes to gain true knowledge must climb the Hill Difficulty alone, and since there is no royal road to the summit, I must zigzag it in my own way. I slip back many times, I fall, I stand still, I run against the edge of hidden obstacles, I lose my temper and find it again and keep it better, I trudge on, I gain a little, I feel encouraged, I get more eager and climb higher and begin to see the widening horizon. Every struggle is a victory. One more effort and I reach the luminous cloud, the blue depths of the sky, the uplands of my desire. I am not always alone, however, in these struggles. Mr. William Wade and Mr. E. E. Allen, Principal of the Pennsylvania Institution for the Instruction of the Blind, get for me many of the books I need in raised print. Their thoughtfulness has been more of a help and encouragement to me than they can ever know.

Last year, my second year at Radcliffe, I studied English composition, the Bible as English literature, the governments of America and Europe, the Odes of Horace, and Latin comedy. The class in composition was the pleasantest. It was very lively. The lectures were always interesting, vivacious, witty; for the instructor, Mr. Charles Townsend Copeland, more than any one else I have had until this year, brings before you literature in all its original freshness and power. For one short hour you are permitted to drink in the eternal beauty of the old masters without needless interpretation or exposition. You revel in their fine thoughts. You enjoy with all your soul the sweet thunder of the Old Testament, forgetting the existence of Jahweh and Elohim; and you go home feeling that you have had "a glimpse of that perfection in which spirit and form dwell in immortal harmony; truth and beauty bearing a new growth on the ancient stem of time."

This year is the happiest because I am studying subjects that especially interest me, economics, Elizabethan literature, Shakespeare under Professor George L. Kittredge, and the History of Philosophy under Professor Josiah Royce. Through philosophy one enters with sympathy of comprehension into the traditions of remote ages and other modes of thought, which erewhile seemed alien and without reason.

But college is not the universal Athens I thought it was. There one does not meet the great and the wise face to face; one does not even feel their living touch. They are there, it is true; but they seem mummified. We must extract them from the crannied wall of learning and dissect and analyze them before we can be sure that we have a Milton or an Isaiah, and not merely a clever imitation. . Many scholars forget, it seems to me, that our enjoyment of the great works of literature depends more upon the depth of our sympathy than upon our understanding. The trouble is that very few of their laborious explanations stick in the memory. The mind drops them as a branch drops its overripe fruit. It is possible to know a flower, root and stem and all, and all the processes of growth, and yet to have no appreciation of the flower fresh bathed in heaven's dew. Again and again I ask impatiently, "Why concern myself with these explanations and hypotheses?" They fly hither and thither in my thought like blind birds beating the air with ineffectual wings. I do not mean to object to a thorough knowledge of the famous works we read. I object only to the interminable comments and bewildering criticisms that teach but one thing: there are as many opinions as there are men. But when a great scholar like Professor Kittredge interprets what the master said, it is "as if new sight were given the blind." He brings back Shakespeare, the poet.

There are, however, times when I long to sweep away half the things I am expected to learn; for the overtaxed mind cannot enjoy the treasure it has secured at the greatest cost. It is impossible, I think, to read in one day four or five different books in different languages and treating of widely different subjects, and not lose sight of the very ends for which one reads. When one reads hurriedly and nervously, having in mind written tests and examinations, one's brain becomes encumbered with a lot of choice bric-à-brac for which there seems to be little use. At the present time my mind is so full of heterogeneous matter that I almost despair of ever being able to put it in order. Whenever I enter the region that was the kingdom of my mind I feel like the proverbial bull in the china shop. A thousand odds and ends of knowledge come crashing about my head like hailstones, and when I try to escape them, theme-goblins and college nixies of all sorts pursue me, until I wish—oh, may I be forgiven the wicked wish!—that I might smash the idols I came to worship.

But the examinations are the chief bugbears of my college life. Although I have faced them many times and cast them down and made them bite the dust, yet they rise again and menace me with pale looks, until like Bob Acres I feel my courage oozing out at my finger ends. The days before these ordeals take place are spent in cramming your mind with mystic formulæ and indigestible dates—unpalatable diets, until you wish that books and science and you were buried in the depths of the sea.

At last the dreaded hour arrives, and you are a favoured being indeed if you feel prepared, and are able at the right time to call to your standard thoughts that will aid you in that supreme effort. It happens too often that your trumpet call is unheeded. It is most perplexing and exasperating that just at the moment when you need your memory and a nice sense of discrimination, these faculties take to themselves wings and fly away. The facts you have garnered with such infinite trouble invariably fail you at a pinch.

"Give a brief account of Huss and his work." Huss? Who was he and what did he do? The name looks strangely familiar. You ransack your

budget of historic facts much as you would hunt for
a bit of silk in a rag-bag.   You are sure it is somewhere in your mind near the top—you saw it there
the other day when you were looking up the begin-
nings of the Reformation.   But where is it now?
You fish out all manner of odds and ends of knowledge—revolutions, schisms, massacres, systems of
government; but Huss—where is he?   You are
amazed at all the things you know which are not on
the examination paper.   In desperation you seize
the budget and dump everything out, and there in a
corner is your man, serenely brooding on his own
private thought, unconscious of the catastrophe
which he has brought upon you.

Just then the proctor informs you that the time
is up.   With a feeling of intense disgust you kick
the mass of rubbish into a corner and go home, your
head full of revolutionary schemes to abolish the
divine right of professors to ask questions without
the consent of the questioned.

It comes over me that in the last two or three
pages of this chapter I have used figures which will
turn the laugh against me.   Ah, here they are—the
mixed metaphors mocking and strutting about before
me, pointing to the bull in the china shop assailed
by hailstones and the bugbears with pale looks,
an unanalyzed species!   Let them mock on.   The
words describe so exactly the atmosphere of jostling,
tumbling ideas I live in that I will wink at them for
once, and put on a deliberate air to say that my
ideas of college have changed.

While my days at Radcliffe were still in the future,
they were encircled with a halo of romance, which
they have lost; but in the transition from romantic

to actual I have learned many things I should never have known had I not tried the experiment. One of them is the precious science of patience, which teaches us that we should take our education as we would take a walk in the country, leisurely, our minds hospitably open to impressions of every sort. Such knowledge floods the soul unseen with a soundless tidal wave of deepening thought. "Knowledge is power." Rather, knowledge is happiness, because to have knowledge—broad, deep knowledge—is to know true ends from false, and lofty things from low. To know the thoughts and deeds that have marked man's progress is to feel the great heart-throbs of humanity through the centuries; and if one does not feel in these pulsations a heavenward striving, one must indeed be deaf to the harmonies of life.

CHAPTER XXI

I HAVE thus far sketched the events of my life, but I have not shown how much I have depended on books not only for pleasure and for the wisdom they bring to all who read, but also for that knowledge which comes to others through their eyes and their ears. Indeed, books have meant so much more in my education than in that of others, that I shall go back to the time when I began to read.

I read my first connected story in May, 1887, when I was seven years old, and from that day to this I have devoured everything in the shape of a printed page that has come within the reach of my hungry finger tips. As I have said, I did not study regularly during the early years of my education; nor did I read according to rule.

At first I had only a few books in raised print—"readers" for beginners, a collection of stories for children, and a book about the earth called "Our World." I think that was all; but I read them over and over, until the words were so worn and pressed I could scarcely make them out. Sometimes Miss Sullivan read to me, spelling into my hand little stories and poems that she knew I should understand; but I preferred reading myself to being read to, because I liked to read again and again the things that pleased me.

It was during my first visit to Boston that I really began to read in good earnest. I was permitted to spend a part of each day in the Institution library, and to wander from bookcase to bookcase, and take down whatever book my fingers lighted upon. And read I did, whether I understood one word in ten or two words on a page. The words themselves fascinated me; but I took no conscious account of what I read. My mind must, however, have been very impressionable at that period, for it retained many words and whole sentences, to the meaning of which I had not the faintest clue; and afterward, when I began to talk and write, these words and sentences would flash out quite naturally, so that my friends wondered at the richness of my vocabulary. I must have read parts of many books (in those early days I think I never read any one book through) and a great deal of poetry in this uncomprehending way, until I discovered "Little Lord Fauntleroy," which was the first book of any consequence I read understandingly.

One day my teacher found me in a corner of the library poring over the pages of "The Scarlet Letter." I was then about eight years old. I remember she asked me if I liked little Pearl, and explained some of the words that had puzzled me. Then she told me that she had a beautiful story about a little boy which she was sure I should like better than "The Scarlet Letter." The name of the story was "Little Lord Fauntleroy," and she promised to read it to me the following summer. But we did not begin the story until August; the first few weeks of my stay at the seashore were so full of discoveries and excitement that I forgot the very existence of books. Then my teacher went to visit some friends in Boston, leaving me for a short time.

When she returned almost the first thing we did
was to begin the story of "Little Lord Fauntleroy."
I recall distinctly the time and place when we read
the first chapters of the fascinating child's story.   It
was a warm afternoon in August.   We were sitting
together in a hammock which swung from two
solemn pines at a short distance from the house.
We had hurried through the dish-washing after
luncheon, in order that we might have as long an
afternoon as possible for the story.   As we hastened
through the long grass toward the hammock, the
grasshoppers swarmed about us and fastened themselves on our clothes, and I remember that my
teacher insisted upon picking them all off before we
sat down, which seemed to me an unnecessary waste
of time.   The hammock was covered with pine
needles, for it had not been used while my teacher
was away.   The warm sun shone on the pine trees
and drew out all their fragrance.   The air was
balmy, with a tang of the sea in it.   Before we began
the story Miss Sullivan explained to me the things
that she knew I should not understand, and as we
read on she explained the unfamiliar words.   At
first there were many words I did not know, and the
reading was constantly interrupted; but as soon as I
thoroughly comprehended the situation, I became
too eagerly absorbed in the story to notice mere
words, and I am afraid I listened impatiently to the
explanations that Miss Sullivan felt to be necessary.
When her fingers were too tired to spell another
word, I had for the first time a keen sense of my
deprivations.   I took the book in my hands and
tried to feel the letters with an intensity of longing
that I can never forget.

Afterward, at my eager request, Mr. Anagnos had this story embossed, and I read it again and again, until I almost knew it by heart; and all through my childhood "Little Lord Fauntleroy" was my sweet and gentle companion. I have given these details at the risk of being tedious, because they are in such vivid contrast with my vague, mutable and confused memories of earlier reading.

From "Little Lord Fauntleroy" I date the beginning of my true interest in books. During the next two years I read many books at my home and on my visits to Boston. I cannot remember what they all were, or in what order I read them; but I know that among them were "Greek Heroes," La Fontaine's "Fables," Hawthorne's "Wonder Book," "Bible Stories," Lamb's "Tales from Shakespeare," "A Child's History of England" by Dickens, "The Arabian Nights," "The Swiss Family Robinson," "The Pilgrim's Progress," "Robinson Crusoe," "Little Women," and "Heidi," a beautiful little story which I afterward read in German. I read them in the intervals between study and play with an ever-deepening sense of pleasure. I did not study nor analyze them—I did not know whether they were well written or not; I never thought about style or authorship. They laid their treasures at my feet, and I accepted them as we accept the sunshine and the love of our friends. I loved "Little Women" because it gave me a sense of kinship with girls and boys who could see and hear. Circumscribed as my life was in so many ways, I had to look between the covers of books for news of the world that lay outside my own.

I did not care especially for "The Pilgrim's

Progress," which I think I did not finish, or for the "Fables." I read La Fontaine's "Fables" first in an English translation, and enjoyed them only after a half-hearted fashion. Later I read the book again in French, and I found that, in spite of the vivid word-pictures, and the wonderful mastery of language, I liked it no better. I do not know why it is, but stories in which animals are made to talk and act like human beings have never appealed to me very strongly. The ludicrous caricatures of the animals occupy my mind to the exclusion of the moral.

Then, again, La Fontaine seldom, if ever, appeals to our higher moral sense. The highest chords he strikes are those of reason and self-love. Through all the fables runs the thought that man's morality springs wholly from self-love, and that if that self-love is directed and restrained by reason, happiness must follow. Now, so far as I can judge, self-love is the root of all evil; but, of course, I may be wrong, for La Fontaine had greater opportunities of observing men than I am likely ever to have. I do not object so much to the cynical and satirical fables as to those in which momentous truths are taught by monkeys and foxes.

But I love "The Jungle Book" and "Wild Animals I Have Known." I feel a genuine interest in the animals themselves, because they are real animals and not caricatures of men. One sympathizes with their loves and hatreds, laughs over their comedies, and weeps over their tragedies. And if they point a moral, it is so subtle that we are not conscious of it.

My mind opened naturally and joyously to a conception of antiquity. Greece, ancient Greece, exercised a mysterious fascination over me. In my fancy the pagan gods and goddesses still walked on earth and talked face to face with men, and in my heart I secretly built shrines to those I loved best. I knew and loved the whole tribe of nymphs and heroes and demigods—no, not quite all, for the cruelty and greed of Medea and Jason were too monstrous to be forgiven, and I used to wonder why the gods permitted them to do wrong and then punished them for their wickedness. And the mystery is still unsolved. I often wonder how

> God can dumbness keep
> While Sin creeps grinning through His house of Time.

It was the Iliad that made Greece my paradise. I was familiar with the story of Troy before I read it in the original, and consequently I had little difficulty in making the Greek words surrender their treasures after I had passed the borderland of grammar. Great poetry, whether written in Greek or in English, needs no other interpreter than a responsive heart. Would that the host of those who make the great works of the poets odious by their analysis, impositions and laborious comments might learn this simple truth! It is not necessary that one should be able to define every word and give it its principal parts and its grammatical position in the sentence in order to understand and appreciate a fine poem. I know my learned professors have found greater riches in the Iliad than I shall ever find; but I am not avaricious. I am content that others should be wiser than I. But with all their wide and comprehensive knowledge, they cannot measure their enjoyment of that splen-

did epic, nor can I. When I read the finest passages of the Iliad, I am conscious of a soul-sense
that lifts me above the narrow, cramping circumstances of my life. My physical limitations are
forgotten—my world lies upward, the length and
the breadth and the sweep of the heavens are
mine!

My admiration for the Æneid is not so great,
but it is none the less real. I read it as much as
possible without the help of notes or dictionary, and
I always like to translate the episodes that pleased
me especially. The word-painting of Virgil is wonderful sometimes; but his gods and men move
through the scenes of passion and strife and pity
and love like the graceful figures in an Elizabethan
mask, whereas in the Iliad they give three leaps
and go on singing. Virgil is serene and lovely
like a marble Apollo in the moonlight; Homer is a
beautiful, animated youth in the full sunlight with
the wind in his hair.

How easy it is to fly on paper wings! From
"Greek Heroes" to the Iliad was no day's journey,
nor was it altogether pleasant. One could have
traveled round the world many times while I trudged
my weary way through the labyrinthine mazes of
grammars and dictionaries, or fell into those dreadful pitfalls called examinations, set by schools and
colleges for the confusion of those who seek after
knowledge. I suppose this sort of Pilgrim's Progress was justified by the end; but it seemed interminable to me, in spite of the pleasant surprises
that met me now and then at a turn in the road.

I began to read the Bible long before I could
understand it. Now it seems strange to me that

there should have been a time when my spirit was deaf to its wondrous harmonies; but I remember well a rainy Sunday morning when, having nothing else to do, I begged my cousin to read me a story out of the Bible. Although she did not think I should understand, she began to spell into my hand the story of Joseph and his brothers. Somehow it failed to interest me. The unusual language and repetition made the story seem unreal and far away in the land of Canaan, and I fell asleep and wandered off to the land of Nod, before the brothers came with the coat of many colours unto the tent of Jacob and told their wicked lie! I cannot understand why the stories of the Greeks should have been so full of charm for me, and those of the Bible so devoid of interest, unless it was that I had made the acquaintance of several Greeks in Boston and been inspired by their enthusiasm for the stories of their country; whereas I had not met a single Hebrew or Egyptian, and therefore concluded that they were nothing more than barbarians, and the stories about them were probably all made up, which hypothesis explained the repetitions and the queer names. Curiously enough, it never occurred to me to call Greek patronymics "queer."

But how shall I speak of the glories I have since discovered in the Bible? For years I have read it with an ever-broadening sense of joy and inspiration; and I love it as I love no other book. Still there is much in the Bible against which every instinct of my being rebels, so much that I regret the necessity which has compelled me to read it through from beginning to end. I do not think that the knowledge which I have gained of its history and sources com-

pensates me for the unpleasant details it has forced
upon my attention.   For my part, I wish, with Mr.
Howells, that the literature of the past might be
purged of all that is ugly and barbarous in it,
although I should object as much as any one to
having these great works weakened or falsified.

There is something impressive, awful, in the simplicity and terrible directness of the book of Esther.
Could there be anything more dramatic than the
scene in which Esther stands before her wicked lord?
She knows her life is in his hands; there is no one to
protect her from his wrath.   Yet, conquering her
woman's fear, she approaches him, animated by the
noblest patriotism, having but one thought: "If I
perish, I perish; but if I live, my people shall live."

The story of Ruth, too—how Oriental it is!   Yet
how different is the life of these simple country folks
from that of the Persian capital!   Ruth is so loyal
and gentle-hearted, we cannot help loving her, as
she stands with the reapers amid the waving corn.
Her beautiful, unselfish spirit shines out like a bright
star in the night of a dark and cruel age.   Love like
Ruth's, love which can rise above conflicting creeds
and deep-seated racial prejudices, is hard to find in
all the world.

The Bible gives me a deep, comforting sense that
"things seen are temporal, and things unseen are
eternal."

I do not remember a time since I have been
capable of loving books that I have not loved
Shakespeare.   I cannot tell exactly when I began
Lamb's "Tales from Shakespeare"; but I know that
I read them at first with a child's understanding and
a child's wonder.   "Macbeth" seems to have im-

pressed me most. One reading was sufficient to stamp every detail of the story upon my memory forever. For a long time the ghosts and witches pursued me even into Dreamland. I could see, absolutely see, the dagger and Lady Macbeth's little white hand—the dreadful stain was as real to me as to the grief-stricken queen.

I read "King Lear" soon after "Macbeth," and I shall never forget the feeling of horror when I came to the scene in which Gloster's eyes are put out. Anger seized me, my fingers refused to move, I sat rigid for one long moment, the blood throbbing in my temples, and all the hatred that a child can feel concentrated in my heart.

I must have made the acquaintance of Shylock and Satan about the same time, for the two characters were long associated in my mind. I remember that I was sorry for them. I felt vaguely that they could not be good even if they wished to, because no one seemed willing to help them or to give them a fair chance. Even now I cannot find it in my heart to condemn them utterly. There are moments when I feel that the Shylocks, the Judases, and even the Devil, are broken spokes in the great wheel of good which shall in due time be made whole.

It seems strange that my first reading of Shakespeare should have left me so many unpleasant memories. The bright, gentle, fanciful plays—the ones I like best now—appear not to have impressed me at first, perhaps because they reflected the habitual sunshine and gaiety of a child's life. But "there is nothing more capricious than the memory of a child: what it will hold, and what it will lose."

I have since read Shakespeare's plays many times

and know parts of them by heart, but I cannot tell which of them I like best.   My delight in them is as varied as my moods.   The little songs and the sonnets have a meaning for me as fresh and wonderful as the dramas.   But, with all my love for Shakespeare, it is often weary work to read all the meanings into his lines which critics and commentators have given them.   I used to try to remember their interpretations, but they discouraged and vexed me; so I made a secret compact with myself not to try any more.   This compact I have only just broken in my study of Shakespeare under Professor Kittredge. I know there are many things in Shakespeare, and in the world, that I do not understand; and I am glad to see veil after veil lift gradually, revealing new realms of thought and beauty.

Next to poetry I love history.   I have read every historical work that I have been able to lay my hands on, from a catalogue of dry facts and dryer dates to Green's impartial, picturesque "History of the English People"; from Freeman's "History of Europe" to Emerton's "Middle Ages."   The first book that gave me any real sense of the value of history was Swinton's "World's History," which I received on my thirteenth birthday.   Though I believe it is no longer considered valid, yet I have kept it ever since as one of my treasures.   From it I learned how the races of men spread from land to land and built great cities, how a few great rulers, earthly Titans, put everything under their feet, and with a decisive word opened the gates of happiness for millions and closed them upon millions more: how different nations pioneered in art and knowledge and broke ground for the mightier growths of coming ages; how civilization underwent, as it were, the holocaust of a degenerate age, and rose again, like the Phœnix, among the nobler sons of the North; and how by liberty, tolerance and education the great and the wise have opened the way for the salvation of the whole world.

In my college reading I have become somewhat familiar with French and German literature. The German puts strength before beauty, and truth before convention, both in life and in literature. There is a vehement, sledge-hammer vigour about everything that he does. When he speaks, it is not to impress others, but because his heart would burst if he did not find an outlet for the thoughts that burn in his soul.

Then, too, there is in German literature a fine reserve which I like; but its chief glory is the recognition I find in it of the redeeming potency of woman's self-sacrificing love. This thought pervades all German literature and is mystically expressed in Goethe's "Faust":

> All things transitory
>   But as symbols are sent.
> Earth's insufficiency
>   Here grows to event.
> The indescribable
> Here it is done.
> The Woman Soul leads us upward and on!

Of all the French writers that I have read, I like Molière and Racine best. There are fine things in Balzac and passages in Mérimée which strike one like a keen blast of sea air. Alfred de Musset is impossible! I admire Victor Hugo—I appreciate his genius, his brilliancy, his romanticism; though he is not one of my literary passions. But Hugo and

Goethe and Schiller and all great poets of all great nations are interpreters of eternal things, and my spirit reverently follows them into the regions where Beauty and Truth and Goodness are one.

I am afraid I have written too much about my book-friends, and yet I have mentioned only the authors I love most; and from this fact one might easily suppose that my circle of friends was very limited and undemocratic, which would be a very wrong impression. I like many writers for many reasons—Carlyle for his ruggedness and scorn of shams; Wordsworth, who teaches the oneness of man and nature; I find an exquisite pleasure in the oddities and surprises of Hood, in Herrick's quaintness and the palpable scent of lily and rose in his verses; I like Whittier for his enthusiasms and moral rectitude. I knew him, and the gentle remembrance of our friendship doubles the pleasure I have in reading his poems. I love Mark Twain—who does not? The gods, too, loved him and put into his heart all manner of wisdom; then, fearing lest he should become a pessimist, they spanned his mind with a rainbow of love and faith. I like Scott for his freshness, dash and large honesty. I love all writers whose minds, like Lowell's, bubble up in the sunshine of optimism—fountains of joy and good will, with occasionally a splash of anger and here and there a healing spray of sympathy and pity.

In a word, literature is my Utopia. Here I am not disfranchised. No barrier of the senses shuts me out from the sweet, gracious discourse of my book-friends. They talk to me without embarrassment or awkwardness. The things I have learned and the things I have been taught seem of ridiculously little importance compared with their "large loves and heavenly charities."

CHAPTER XXII

I TRUST that my readers have not concluded from the preceding chapter on books that reading is my only pleasure; my pleasures and amusements are many and varied.

More than once in the course of my story I have referred to my love of the country and out-of-door sports. When I was quite a little girl, I learned to row and swim, and during the summer, when I am at Wrentham, Massachusetts, I almost live in my boat. Nothing gives me greater pleasure than to take my friends out rowing when they visit me. Of course, I cannot guide the boat very well. Some one usually sits in the stern and manages the rudder while I row. Sometimes, however, I go rowing without the rudder. It is fun to try to steer by the scent of watergrasses and lilies, and of bushes that grow on the shore. I use oars with leather bands, which keep them in position in the oarlocks, and I know by the resistance of the water when the oars are evenly poised. In the same manner I can also tell when I am pulling against the current. I like to contend with wind and wave. What is more exhilarating than to make your staunch little boat, obedient to your will and muscle, go skimming lightly over glistening, tilting waves, and to feel the steady, imperious surge of the water!

I also enjoy canoeing, and I suppose you will smile when I say that I especially like it on moonlight

119

nights. I cannot, it is true, see the moon climb up the sky behind the pines and steal softly across the heavens, making a shining path for us to follow; but I know she is there, and as I lie back among the pillows and put my hand in the water, I fancy that I feel the shimmer of her garments as she passes. Sometimes a daring little fish slips between my fingers, and often a pond-lily presses shyly against my hand. Frequently, as we emerge from the shelter of a cove or inlet, I am suddenly conscious of the spaciousness of the air about me. A luminous warmth seems to enfold me. Whether it comes from the trees which have been heated by the sun, or from the water, I can never discover. I have had the same strange sensation even in the heart of the city. I have felt it on cold, stormy days and at night. It is like the kiss of warm lips on my face.

My favourite amusement is sailing. In the summer of 1901 I visited Nova Scotia, and had opportunities such as I had not enjoyed before to make the acquaintance of the ocean. After spending a few days in Evangeline's country, about which Longfellow's beautiful poem has woven a spell of enchantment, Miss Sullivan and I went to Halifax, where we remained the greater part of the summer. The harbour was our joy, our paradise. What glorious sails we had to Bedford Basin, to McNabb's Island, to York Redoubt, and to the Northwest Arm! And at night what soothing, wondrous hours we spent in the shadow of the great, silent men-of-war. Oh, it was all so interesting, so beautiful! The memory of it is a joy forever.

One day we had a thrilling experience. There was a regatta in the Northwest Arm, in which the boats from the different warships were engaged. We went in a sail-boat along with many others to watch the races. Hundreds of little sail-boats swung to and fro close by, and the sea was calm. When the races were over, and we turned our faces homeward, one of the party noticed a black cloud drifting in from the sea, which grew and spread and thickened until it covered the whole sky. The wind rose, and the waves chopped angrily at unseen barriers. Our little boat confronted the gale fearlessly; with sails spread and ropes taut, she seemed to sit upon the wind. Now she swirled in the billows, now she sprang upward on a gigantic wave, only to be driven down with angry howl and hiss. Down came the mainsail. Tacking and jibbing, we wrestled with opposing winds that drove us from side to side with impetuous fury. Our hearts beat fast, and our hands trembled with excitement, not fear; for we had the hearts of vikings, and we knew that our skipper was master of the situation. He had steered through many a storm with firm hand and sea-wise eye. As they passed us, the large craft and the gunboats in the harbour saluted and the seamen shouted applause for the master of the only little sail-boat that ventured out into the storm. At last, cold, hungry and weary, we reached our pier.

Last summer I spent in one of the loveliest nooks of one of the most charming villages in New England. Wrentham, Massachusetts, is associated with nearly all of my joys and sorrows. For many years Red Farm, by King Philip's Pond, the home of Mr. J. E. Chamberlin and his family, was my home. I remember with deepest gratitude the kindness of these dear friends and the happy days I spent with them. The sweet companionship of their children meant much to me. I joined in all their sports and rambles through the woods and frolics in the water. The prattle of the little ones and their pleasure in the stories I told them of elf and gnome, of hero and wily bear, are pleasant things to remember. Mr. Chamberlin initiated me into the mysteries of tree and wild-flower, until with the little ear of love I heard the flow of sap in the oak, and saw the sun glint from leaf to leaf. Thus it is that

> Even as the roots, shut in the darksome earth,
> Share in the tree-top's joyance, and conceive
> Of sunshine and wide air and wingéd things,
> By sympathy of nature, so do I

gave evidence of things unseen.

It seems to me that there is in each of us a capacity to comprehend the impressions and emotions which have been experienced by mankind from the beginning. Each individual has a subconscious memory of the green earth and murmuring waters, and blindness and deafness cannot rob him of this gift from past generations. This inherited capacity is a sort of sixth sense—a soul-sense which sees, hears, feels, all in one.

I have many tree friends in Wrentham. One of them, a splendid oak, is the special pride of my heart. I take all my other friends to see this king-tree. It stands on a bluff overlooking King Philip's Pond, and those who are wise in tree lore say it must have stood there eight hundred or a thousand years. There is a tradition that under this tree King Philip, the heroic Indian chief, gazed his last on earth and sky.

I had another tree friend, gentle and more approachable than the great oak—a linden that grew in the dooryard at Red Farm.   One afternoon, during a terrible thunderstorm, I felt a tremendous crash against the side of the house and knew, even before they told me, that the linden had fallen. We went out to see the hero that had withstood so many tempests, and it wrung my heart to see him prostrate who had mightily striven and was now mightily fallen.

But I must not forget that I was going to write about last summer in particular. As soon as my examinations were over, Miss Sullivan and I hastened to this green nook, where we have a little cottage on one of the three lakes for which Wrentham is famous. Here the long, sunny days were mine, and all thoughts of work and college and the noisy city were thrust into the background.   In Wrentham we caught echoes of what was happening in the world —war, alliance, social conflict. We heard of the cruel, unnecessary fighting in the far-away Pacific, and learned of the struggles going on between capital and labour. We knew that beyond the border of our Eden men were making history by the sweat of their brows when they might better make a holiday. But we little heeded these things. These things would pass away; here were lakes and woods and broad daisy-starred fields and sweet-breathed meadows, and they shall endure forever.

People who think that all sensations reach us through the eye and the ear have expressed surprise that I should notice any difference, except possibly the absence of pavements, between walking in city streets and in country roads. They forget that my whole body is alive to the conditions about me. The rumble and roar of the city smite the nerves of my face, and I feel the ceaseless tramp of an unseen multitude, and the dissonant tumult frets my spirit. The grinding of heavy wagons on hard pavements and the monotonous clangour of machinery are all the more torturing to the nerves if one's attention is not diverted by the panorama that is always present in the noisy streets to people who can see.

In the country one sees only Nature's fair works, and one's soul is not saddened by the cruel struggle for mere existence that goes on in the crowded city. Several times I have visited the narrow, dirty streets where the poor live, and I grow hot and indignant to think that good people should be content to live in fine houses and become strong and beautiful, while others are condemned to live in hideous, sunless tenements and grow ugly, withered and cringing. The children who crowd these grimy alleys, half-clad and underfed, shrink away from your outstretched hand as if from a blow. Dear little creatures, they crouch in my heart and haunt me with a constant sense of pain. There are men and women, too, all gnarled and bent out of shape. I have felt their hard, rough hands and realized what an endless struggle their existence must be—no more than a series of scrimmages, thwarted attempts to do something. Their life seems an immense disparity between effort and opportunity. The sun and the air are God's free gifts to all, we say; but are they so? In yonder city's dingy alleys the sun shines not, and the air is foul. Oh, man, how dost thou forget and obstruct thy brother man, and say, "Give us this day our daily bread," when he has none! Oh, would that men would leave the city, its splendour and its tumult and its gold, and return to wood and field and simple, honest living! Then would their children grow stately as noble trees, and their thoughts sweet and pure as wayside flowers. It is impossible not to think of all this when I return to the country after a year of work in town.

What a joy it is to feel the soft, springy earth under my feet once more, to follow grassy roads that lead to ferny brooks where I can bathe my fingers in a cataract of rippling notes, or to clamber over a stone wall into green fields that tumble and roll and climb in riotous gladness!

Next to a leisurely walk I enjoy a "spin" on my tandem bicycle. It is splendid to feel the wind blowing in my face and the springy motion of my iron steed. The rapid rush through the air gives me a delicious sense of strength and buoyancy, and the exercise makes my pulses dance and my heart sing.

Whenever it is possible, my dog accompanies me on a walk or ride or sail. I have had many dog friends—huge mastiffs, soft-eyed spaniels, wood-wise setters and honest, homely bull terriers. At present the lord of my affections is one of these bull terriers. He has a long pedigree, a crooked tail and the drollest "phiz" in dogdom. My dog friends seem to understand my limitations, and always keep close beside me when I am alone. I love their affectionate ways and the eloquent wag of their tails.

When a rainy day keeps me indoors, I amuse myself after the manner of other girls. I like to knit and crochet; I read in the happy-go-lucky way

I love, here and there a line; or perhaps I play a game or two of checkers or chess with a friend. I have a special board on which I play these games. The squares are cut out, so that the men stand in them firmly. The black checkers are flat and the white ones curved on top. Each checker has a hole in the middle in which a brass knob can be placed to distinguish the king from the commons. The chessmen are of two sizes, the white larger than the black, so that I have no trouble in following my opponent's maneuvers by moving my hands lightly over the board after a play. The jar made by shifting the men from one hole to another tells me when it is my turn.

If I happen to be all alone and in an idle mood, I play a game of solitaire, of which I am very fond. I use playing cards marked in the upper right-hand corner with braille symbols which indicate the value of the card.

If there are children around, nothing pleases me so much as to frolic with them. I find even the smallest child excellent company, and I am glad to say that children usually like me. They lead me about and show me the things they are interested in. Of course the little ones cannot spell on their fingers; but I manage to read their lips. If I do not succeed they resort to dumb show. Sometimes I make a mistake and do the wrong thing. A burst of childish laughter greets my blunder, and the pantomime begins all over again. I often tell them stories or teach them a game, and the wingéd hours depart and leave us good and happy.

Museums and art stores are also sources of pleasure and inspiration. Doubtless it will seem strange to many that the hand unaided by sight can feel action, sentiment, beauty in the cold marble; and yet it is true that I derive genuine pleasure from touching great works of art.   As my finger tips trace line and curve, they discover the thought and emotion which the artist has portrayed.   I can feel in the faces of gods and heroes hate, courage and love, just as I can detect them in living faces I am permitted to touch.   I feel in Diana's posture the grace and freedom of the forest and the spirit that tames the mountain lion and subdues the fiercest passions. My soul delights in the repose and gracious curves of the Venus; and in Barré's bronzes the secrets of the jungle are revealed to me.

A medallion of Homer hangs on the wall of my study, conveniently low, so that I can easily reach it and touch the beautiful, sad face with loving reverence.   How well I know each line in that majestic brow—tracks of life and bitter evidences of struggle and sorrow; those sightless eyes seeking, even in the cold plaster, for the light and the blue skies of his beloved Hellas, but seeking in vain; that beautiful mouth, firm and true and tender.   It is the face of a poet, and of a man acquainted with sorrow.   Ah, how well I understand his deprivation—the perpetual night in which he dwelt—

> O dark, dark, amid the blaze of noon,
> Irrecoverably dark, total eclipse
> Without all hope of day!

In imagination I can hear Homer singing, as with unsteady, hesitating steps he gropes his way from camp to camp—singing of life, of love, of war, of the splendid achievements of a noble race.   It was a wonderful, glorious song, and it won the blind poet an immortal crown, the admiration of all ages.

I sometimes wonder if the hand is not more sensitive to the beauties of sculpture than the eye. I should think the wonderful rhythmical flow of lines and curves could be more subtly felt than seen. Be this as it may, I know that I can feel the heart-throbs of the ancient Greeks in their marble gods and goddesses.

Another pleasure, which comes more rarely than the others, is going to the theatre. I enjoy having a play described to me while it is being acted on the stage far more than reading it, because then it seems as if I were living in the midst of stirring events. It has been my privilege to meet a few great actors and actresses who have the power of so bewitching you that you forget time and place and live again in the romantic past. I have been permitted to touch the face and costume of Miss Ellen Terry as she impersonated our ideal of a queen; and there was about her that divinity that hedges sublimest woe. Beside her stood Sir Henry Irving, wearing the symbols of kingship; and there was majesty of intellect in his every gesture and attitude and the royalty that subdues and overcomes in every line of his sensitive face. In the king's face, which he wore as a mask, there was a remoteness and inaccessibility of grief which I shall never forget.

I also know Mr. Jefferson. I am proud to count him among my friends. I go to see him whenever I happen to be where he is acting. The first time I saw him act was while at school in New York. He played "Rip Van Winkle." I had often read the story, but I had never felt the charm of Rip's

slow, quaint, kind ways as I did in the play.   Mr.
Jefferson's beautiful, pathetic representation quite
carried me away with delight.   I have a picture of
old Rip in my fingers which they will never lose.
After the play Miss Sullivan took me to see him
behind the scenes, and I felt of his curious garb and
his flowing hair and beard.   Mr. Jefferson let me
touch his face so that I could imagine how he looked
on waking from that strange sleep of twenty years,
and he showed me how poor old Rip staggered to
his feet.

I have also seen him in "The Rivals."   Once
while I was calling on him in Boston he acted the
most striking parts of "The Rivals" for me.   The
reception-room where we sat served for a stage.   He
and his son seated themselves at the big table, and
Bob Acres wrote his challenge.   I followed all his
movements with my hands, and caught the drollery
of his blunders and gestures in a way that would have
been impossible had it all been spelled to me.   Then
they rose to fight the duel, and I followed the swift
thrusts and parries of the swords and the waverings
of poor Bob as his courage oozed out at his finger
ends.   Then the great actor gave his coat a hitch
and his mouth a twitch, and in an instant I was in the
village of Falling Water and felt Schneider's shaggy
head against my knee.   Mr. Jefferson recited the
best dialogues of "Rip Van Winkle," in which the
tear came close upon the smile.   He asked me to
indicate as far as I could the gestures and action
that should go with the lines.   Of course, I have no
sense whatever of dramatic action, and could make
only random guesses; but with masterful art he
suited the action to the word.   The sigh of Rip as

he murmurs, "Is a man so soon forgotten when he is gone?" the dismay with which he searches for dog and gun after his long sleep, and his comical irresolution over signing the contract with Derrick—all these seem to be right out of life itself; that is, the ideal life, where things happen as we think they should.

I remember well the first time I went to the theatre. It was twelve years ago. Elsie Leslie, the little actress, was in Boston, and Miss Sullivan took me to see her in "The Prince and the Pauper." I shall never forget the ripple of alternating joy and woe that ran through that beautiful little play, or the wonderful child who acted it. After the play I was permitted to go behind the scenes and meet her in her royal costume. It would have been hard to find a lovelier or more lovable child than Elsie, as she stood with a cloud of golden hair floating over her shoulders, smiling brightly, showing no signs of shyness or fatigue, though she had been playing to an immense audience. I was only just learning to speak, and had previously repeated her name until I could say it perfectly. Imagine my delight when she understood the few words I spoke to her and without hesitation stretched her hand to greet me.

Is it not true, then, that my life with all its limitations touches at many points the life of the World Beautiful? Everything has its wonders, even darkness and silence, and I learn, whatever state I may be in, therein to be content.

Sometimes, it is true, a sense of isolation enfolds me like a cold mist as I sit alone and wait at life's shut gate. Beyond there is light, and music, and sweet companionship; but I may not enter. Fate,

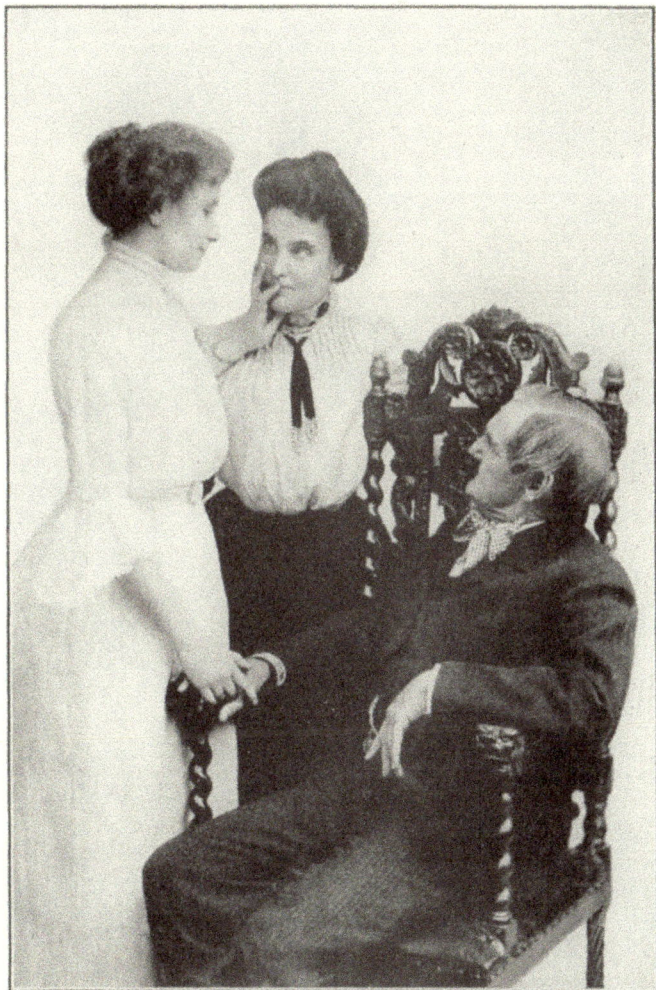

MISS KELLER, MISS SULLIVAN, AND
MR. JOSEPH JEFFERSON

silent, pitiless, bars the way. Fain would I question his imperious decree; for my heart is still undisciplined and passionate; but my tongue will not utter the bitter, futile words that rise to my lips, and they fall back into my heart like unshed tears. Silence sits immense upon my soul. Then comes hope with a smile and whispers, "There is joy in self-forgetfulness." So I try to make the light in others' eyes my sun, the music in others' ears my symphony, the smile on others' lips my happiness.

CHAPTER XXIII

WOULD that I could enrich this sketch with the names of all those who have ministered to my happiness! Some of them would be found written in our literature and dear to the hearts of many, while others would be wholly unknown to most of my readers. But their influence, though it escapes fame, shall live immortal in the lives that have been sweetened and ennobled by it. Those are red-letter days in our lives when we meet people who thrill us like a fine poem, people whose handshake is brimful of unspoken sympathy, and whose sweet, rich natures impart to our eager, impatient spirits a wonderful restfulness which, in its essence, is divine. The perplexities, irritations and worries that have absorbed us pass like unpleasant dreams, and we wake to see with new eyes and hear with new ears the beauty and harmony of God's real world. The solemn nothings that fill our everyday life blossom suddenly into bright possibilities. In a word, while such friends are near us we feel that all is well. Perhaps we never saw them before, and they may never cross our life's path again; but the influence of their calm, mellow natures is a libation poured upon our discontent, and we feel its healing touch, as the ocean feels the mountain stream freshening its brine.

I have often been asked, "Do not people bore you?" I do not understand quite what that means.

I suppose the calls of the stupid and curious, especially of newspaper reporters, are always inopportune. I also dislike people who try to talk down to my understanding. They are like people who when walking with you try to shorten their steps to suit yours; the hypocrisy in both cases is equally exasperating.

The hands of those I meet are dumbly eloquent to me. The touch of some hands is an impertinence. I have met people so empty of joy, that when I clasped their frosty finger-tips, it seemed as if I were shaking hands with a northeast storm. Others there are whose hands have sunbeams in them, so that their grasp warms my heart. It may be only the clinging touch of a child's hand; but there is as much potential sunshine in it for me as there is in a loving glance for others. A hearty handshake or a friendly letter gives me genuine pleasure.

I have many far-off friends whom I have never seen. Indeed they are so many that I have often been unable to reply to their letters; but I wish to say here that I am always grateful for their kind words, however insufficiently I acknowledge them.

I count it one of the sweetest privileges of my life to have known and conversed with many men of genius. Only those who knew Bishop Brooks can appreciate the joy his friendship was to those who possessed it. As a child I loved to sit on his knee and clasp his great hand with one of mine, while Miss Sullivan spelled into the other his beautiful words about God and the spiritual world. I heard him with a child's wonder and delight. My spirit could not reach up to his, but he gave me a real sense of joy in life, and I never left him without carrying away a fine thought that grew in beauty and depth of meaning as I grew.   Once, when I was puzzled to know why there were so many religions, he said: "There is one universal religion, Helen— the religion of love.   Love your Heavenly Father with your whole heart and soul, love every child of God as much as ever you can, and remember that the possibilities of good are greater than the possibilities of evil; and you have the key to Heaven." And his life was a happy illustration of this great truth.   In his noble soul love and widest knowledge were blended with faith that had become insight. He saw

> God in all that liberates and lifts,
> In all that humbles, sweetens and consoles.

Bishop Brooks taught me no special creed or dogma; but he impressed upon my mind two great ideas—the fatherhood of God and the brotherhood of man, and made me feel that these truths underlie all creeds and forms of worship.   God is love, God is our Father, we are His children; therefore the darkest clouds will break, and though right be worsted, wrong shall not triumph.

I am too happy in this world to think much about the future, except to remember that I have cherished friends awaiting me there in God's beautiful Somewhere.   In spite of the lapse of years, they seem so close to me that I should not think it strange if at any moment they should clasp my hand and speak words of endearment as they used to before they went away.

Since Bishop Brooks died I have read the Bible through; also some philosophical works on religion;

among them Swedenborg's "Heaven and Hell"
and Drummond's "Ascent of Man," and I have
found no creed or system more soul-satisfying than
Bishop Brooks's creed of love.   I knew Mr. Henry
Drummond, and the memory of his strong, warm
hand-clasp is like a benediction.   He was the most
sympathetic of companions.   He knew so much and
was so genial that it was impossible to feel dull in
his presence.

I remember well the first time I saw Dr. Oliver
Wendell Holmes.   He had invited Miss Sullivan
and me to call on him one Sunday afternoon.   It
was early in the spring, just after I had learned to
speak.   We were shown at once to his library where
we found him seated in a big armchair by an open
fire which glowed and crackled on the hearth, thinking, he said, of other days.

"And listening to the murmur of the River
Charles," I suggested.

"Yes," he replied, "the Charles has many dear
associations for me."   There was an odour of print
and leather in the room which told me that it was
full of books, and I stretched out my hand instinctively to find them.   My fingers lighted upon a
beautiful volume of Tennyson's poems, and when
Miss Sullivan told me what it was I began to recite:

> Break, break, break
> On thy cold gray stones, O sea!

But I stopped suddenly.   I felt tears on my hand.
I had made my beloved poet weep, and I was
greatly distressed.   He made me sit in his armchair, while he brought different interesting things
for me to examine, and at his request I recited

"The Chambered Nautilus," which was then my favorite poem.   After that I saw Dr. Holmes many times and learned to love the man as well as the poet.

One beautiful summer day, not long after my meeting with Dr. Holmes, Miss Sullivan and I visited Whittier in his quiet home on the Merrimac. His gentle courtesy and quaint speech won my heart. He had a book of his poems in raised print from which I read "In School Days."   He was delighted that I could pronounce the words so well, and said that he had no difficulty in understanding me. Then I asked many questions about the poem, and read his answers by placing my fingers on his lips. He said he was the little boy in the poem, and that the girl's name was Sally, and more which I have forgotten.   I also recited "Laus Deo," and as I spoke the concluding verses, he placed in my hands a statue of a slave from whose crouching figure the fetters were falling, even as they fell from Peter's limbs when the angel led him forth out of prison. Afterward we went into his study, and he wrote his* autograph for my teacher and expressed his admiration of her work, saying to me, "She is thy spiritual liberator."   Then he led me to the gate and kissed me tenderly on my forehead.   I promised to visit him again the following summer; but he died before the promise was fulfilled.

Dr. Edward Everett Hale is one of my very oldest friends.   I have known him since I was eight, and my love for him has increased with my years. His wise, tender sympathy has been the support of

* "With great admiration of thy noble work in releasing from bondage the mind of thy dear pupil, I am truly thy friend. JOHN G. WHITTIER."

MISS KELLER, MISS SULLIVAN, AND
DR. EDWARD EVERETT HALE

Miss Sullivan and me in times of trial and sorrow, and his strong hand has helped us over many rough places; and what he has done for us he has done for thousands of those who have difficult tasks to accomplish. He has filled the old skins of dogma with the new wine of love, and shown men what it is to believe, live and be free. What he has taught we have seen beautifully expressed in his own life—love of country, kindness to the least of his brethren, and a sincere desire to live upward and onward. He has been a prophet and an inspirer of men, and a mighty doer of the Word, the friend of all his race—God bless him!

I have already written of my first meeting with Dr. Alexander Graham Bell. Since then I have spent many happy days with him at Washington and at his beautiful home in the heart of Cape Breton Island, near Baddeck, the village made famous by Charles Dudley Warner's book. Here in Dr. Bell's laboratory, or in the fields on the shore of the great Bras d'Or, I have spent many delightful hours listening to what he had to tell me about his experiments, and helping him fly kites by means of which he expects to discover the laws that shall govern the future air-ship. Dr. Bell is proficient in many fields of science, and has the art of making every subject he touches interesting, even the most abstruse theories. He makes you feel that if you only had a little more time, you, too, might be an inventor. He has a humorous and poetic side, too. His dominating passion is his love for children. He is never quite so happy as when he has a little deaf child in his arms. His labours in behalf of the deaf will live on and bless generations of children yet to come; and we love him alike for what he himself has achieved and for what he has evoked from others.

During the two years I spent in New York I had many opportunities to talk with distinguished people whose names I had often heard, but whom I had never expected to meet. Most of them I met first in the house of my good friend, Mr. Laurence Hutton. It was a great privilege to visit him and dear Mrs. Hutton in their lovely home, and see their library and read the beautiful sentiments and bright thoughts gifted friends had written for them. It has been truly said that Mr. Hutton has the faculty of bringing out in every one the best thoughts and kindest sentiments. One does not need to read "A Boy I Knew" to understand him—the most generous, sweet-natured boy I ever knew, a good friend in all sorts of weather, who traces the footprints of love in the life of dogs as well as in that of his fellowmen.

Mrs. Hutton is a true and tried friend. Much that I hold sweetest, much that I hold most precious, I owe to her. She has oftenest advised and helped me in my progress through college. When I find my work particularly difficult and discouraging, she writes me letters that make me feel glad and brave; for she is one of those from whom we learn that one painful duty fulfilled makes the next plainer and easier.

Mr. Hutton introduced me to many of his literary friends, greatest of whom are Mr. William Dean Howells and Mark Twain. I also met Mr. Richard Watson Gilder and Mr. Edmund Clarence Stedman. I also knew Mr. Charles Dudley Warner, the most

MARK TWAIN
(Samuel Longhorne Clemens)

delightful of story-tellers and the most beloved
friend, whose sympathy was so broad that it may
be truly said of him, he loved all living things and
his neighbour as himself. Once Mr. Warner brought
to see me the dear poet of the woodlands—Mr. John
Burroughs. They were all gentle and sympathetic
and I felt the charm of their manner as much
as I had felt the brilliancy of their essays and poems.
I could not keep pace with all these literary folk as
they glanced from subject to subject and entered into
deep dispute, or made conversation sparkle with
epigrams and happy witticisms. I was like little
Ascanius, who followed with unequal steps the
heroic strides of Æneas on his march toward
mighty destinies. But they spoke many gracious
words to me. Mr. Gilder told me about his
moonlight journeys across the vast desert to the
Pyramids, and in a letter he wrote me he made
his mark under his signature deep in the paper so
that I could feel it. This reminds me that Dr. Hale
used to give a personal touch to his letters to me
by pricking his signature in braille. I read from
Mark Twain's lips one or two of his good stories.
He has his own way of thinking, saying and doing
everything. I feel the twinkle of his eye in his handshake. Even while he utters his cynical wisdom
in an indescribably droll voice, he makes you feel
that his heart is a tender Iliad of human sympathy.

There are a host of other interesting people I met
in New York: Mrs. Mary Mapes Dodge, the beloved editor of *St. Nicholas,* and Mrs. Riggs (Kate
Douglas Wiggin), the sweet author of "Patsy." I
received from them gifts that have the gentle con-
currence of the heart, books containing their own

thoughts, soul-illumined letters, and photographs that I love to have described again and again. But there is not space to mention all my friends, and indeed there are things about them hidden behind the wings of cherubim, things too sacred to set forth in cold print. It is with hesitancy that I have spoken even of Mrs. Laurence Hutton.

I shall mention only two other friends. One is Mrs. William Thaw, of Pittsburgh, whom I have often visited in her home, Lyndhurst. She is always doing something to make some one happy, and her generosity and wise counsel have never failed my teacher and me in all the years we have known her.

To the other friend I am also deeply indebted. He is well known for the powerful hand with which he guides vast enterprises, and his wonderful abilities have gained for him the respect of all. Kind to every one, he goes about doing good, silent and unseen. Again I touch upon the circle of honoured names I must not mention; but I would fain acknowledge his generosity and affectionate interest which make it possible for me to go to college.

Thus it is that my friends have made the story of my life. In a thousand ways they have turned my limitations into beautiful privileges, and enabled me to walk serene and happy in the shadow cast by my deprivation.

PART II

LETTERS (1887–1901)

INTRODUCTION

HELEN KELLER'S letters are important, not only as a supplementary story of her life, but as a demonstration of her growth in thought and expression—the growth which in itself has made her distinguished.

These letters, are, however, not merely remarkable as the productions of a deaf and blind girl, to be read with wonder and curiosity; they are good letters almost from the first. The best passages are those in which she talks about herself, and gives her world in terms of her experience of it. Her views on the precession of the equinoxes are not important, but most important are her accounts of what speech meant to her, of how she felt the statues, the dogs, the chickens at the poultry show, and how she stood in the aisle of St. Bartholomew's and felt the organ rumble. Those are passages of which one would ask for more. The reason they are comparatively few is that all her life she has been trying to be "like other people," and so she too often describes things not as they appear to her, but as they appear to one with eyes and ears.

One cause for the excellence of her letters is the great number of them. They are the exercises which have trained her to write. She has lived at different times in different parts of the country, and so has been separated from most of her friends and relatives. Of her friends, many have been distinguished people, to whom—not often, I think, at the sacrifice of spontaneity—she has felt it necessary to write well. To them and to a few friends with whom she is in closest sympathy she writes with intimate frankness whatever she is thinking about. Her naïve retelling of a child's tale she has heard, like the story of "Little Jakey," which she rehearses for Dr. Holmes and Bishop Brooks, is charming and her grave paraphrase of the day's lesson in geography or botany, her parrot-like repetition of what she has heard, and her conscious display of new words, are delightful and instructive; for they show not only what she was learning, but how, by putting it all into letters, she made the new knowledge and the new words her own.

So these selections from Miss Keller's correspondence are made with two purposes—to show her development and to preserve the most entertaining and significant passages from several hundred letters. Many of those written before 1892 were published in the reports of the Perkins Institution for the Blind. All letters up to that year are printed intact, for it is legitimate to be interested in the degree of skill the child showed in writing, even to details of punctuation; so it is well to preserve a literal integrity of reproduction. From the letters after the year 1892 I have culled in the spirit of one making an anthology, choosing the passages best in style and most important from the point of view of biography. Where I have been able to collate the original letters I have preserved everything as Miss Keller wrote it, punctuation, spelling, and all. I have done nothing but select and cut.

The letters are arranged in chronological order. One or two letters from Bishop Brooks, Dr. Holmes, and Whittier are put immediately after the letters to which they are replies. Except for two or three important letters of 1901, these selections cease with the year 1900. In that year Miss Keller entered college. Now that she is a grown woman, her mature letters should be judged like those of any other person, and it seems best that no more of her correspondence be published unless she should become distinguished beyond the fact that she is the only well-educated deaf and blind person in the world.

LETTERS (1887–1901)

Miss Sullivan began to teach Helen Keller on March 3rd, 1887. Three months and a half after the first word was spelled into her hand, she wrote in pencil this letter

TO HER COUSIN ANNA (MRS. GEORGE T. TURNER)

[TUSCUMBIA, ALABAMA, June 17, 1887.]
helen write anna george will give helen apple simpson will shoot bird jack will give helen stick of candy doctor will give mildred medicine mother will make mildred new dress
[No signature]

Twenty-five days later, while she was on a short visit away from home, she wrote to her mother. Two words are almost illegible, and the angular print slants in every direction.

TO MRS. KATE ADAMS KELLER

[HUNTSVILLE, ALABAMA, July 12, 1887.]
Helen will write mother letter papa did give helen medicine mildred will sit in swing mildred did

kiss helen teacher did give helen peach george is sick
in bed george arm is hurt anna did give helen lemon-
ade dog did stand up.

conductor did punch ticket papa did give helen
drink of water in car

carlotta did give helen flowers anna will buy helen
pretty new hat helen will hug and kiss mother helen
will come home grandmother does love helen

good-by

[No signature.]

By the following September Helen shows im·
provement in fulness of construction and more
extended relations of thought.

TO THE BLIND GIRLS AT THE PERKINS INSTITUTION
IN SOUTH BOSTON

[TUSCUMBIA, September, 1887.]

Helen will write little blind girls a letter
Helen and teacher will come to see little blind
girls Helen and teacher will go in steam car
to boston Helen and blind girls will have fun
blind girls can talk on fingers Helen will see Mr
anagnos Mr anagnos will love and kiss Helen Helen
will go to school with blind girls Helen can read
and count and spell and write like blind girls mildred will not go to boston Mildred does cry prince
and jumbo will go to boston papa does shoot ducks
with gun and ducks do fall in water and jumbo and
mamie do swim in water and bring ducks out in

mouth to papa Helen does play with dogs Helen
does ride on horseback with teacher Helen does give
handee grass in hand teacher does whip handee to
go fast Helen is blind Helen will put letter in envelope for blind girls good-by

HELEN KELLER

A few weeks later her style is more nearly correct and freer in movement. She improves in
idiom, although she still omits articles and uses the
"did" construction for the simple past. This is an
idiom common among children.

TO THE BLIND GIRLS AT THE PERKINS INSTITUTION

[TUSCUMBIA, October 24, 1887.]
dear little blind girls
I will write you a letter I thank you for pretty
desk I did write to mother in memphis on it
mother and mildred came home wednesday mother
brought me a pretty new dress and hat papa did go
to huntsville he brought me apples and candy I
and teacher will come to boston and see you nancy
is my doll she does cry I do rock nancy to sleep
mildred is sick doctor will give her medicine to
make her well. I and teacher did go to church
sunday mr. lane did read in book and talk Lady
did play organ. I did give man money in basket.
I will be good girl and teacher will curl my hair

lovely. I will hug and kiss little blind girls mr. anagnos will come to see me.

good-by
HELEN KELLER

TO MR. MICHAEL ANAGNOS, DIRECTOR OF THE
PERKINS INSTITUTION

[TUSCUMBIA, November, 1887.]

dear mr. anagnos I will write you a letter. I and teacher did have pictures. teacher will send it to you. photographer does make pictures. carpenter does build new houses. gardener does dig and hoe ground and plant vegetables. my doll nancy is sleeping. she is sick. mildred is well uncle frank has gone hunting deer. we will have venison for breakfast when he comes home. I did ride in wheel barrow and teacher did push it. simpson did give me popcorn and walnuts. cousin rosa has gone to see her mother. people do go to church sunday. I did read in my book about fox and box. fox can sit in the box. I do like to read in my book. you do love me. I do love you.

good-by
HELEN KELLER.

TO DR. ALEXANDER GRAHAM BELL

[TUSCUMBIA, November, 1887.]

DEAR MR. BELL.

I am glad to write you a letter. Father will

send you picture. I and Father and aunt did
go to see you in Washington. I did play with
your watch. I do love you. I saw doctor in
Washington. He looked at my eyes. I can read
stories in my book. I can write and spell and count.
good girl. My sister can walk and run. We do
have fun with Jumbo. Prince is not good dog. He
can not get birds. Rat did kill baby pigeons. I
am sorry. Rat does not know wrong. I and
mother and teacher will go to Boston in June. I
will see little blind girls. Nancy will go with me.
She is a good doll. Father will buy me lovely new
watch. Cousin Anna gave me a pretty doll. Her
name is Allie.

Good-by,

HELEN KELLER.

By the beginning of the next year her idioms are
firmer. More adjectives appear, including adjectives of colour. Although she can have no sensuous
knowledge of colour, she can use the words, as we
use most of our vocabulary, intellectually, with
truth, not to impression, but to fact. This letter
is to a school-mate at the Perkins Institution.

TO MISS SARAH TOMLINSON

TUSCUMBIA, Ala. Jan. 2nd 1888.

Dear Sarah

I am happy to write to you this morn-
ing. I hope Mr. Anagnos is coming to see me soon.

I will go to Boston in June and I will buy father gloves, and James nice collar, and Simpson cuffs. I saw Miss Betty and her scholars. They had a pretty Christmas-tree, and there were many pretty presents on it for little children. I had a mug, and little bird and candy. I had many lovely things for Christmas. Aunt gave me a trunk for Nancy and clothes. I went to party with teacher and mother. We did dance and play and eat nuts and candy and cakes and oranges and I did have fun with little boys and girls. Mrs. Hopkins did send me lovely ring, I do love her and little blind girls.

Men and boys do make carpets in mills. Wool grows on sheep. Men do cut sheep's wool off with large shears, and send it to the mill. Men and women do make wool cloth in mills.

Cotton grows on large stalks in fields. Men and boys and girls and women do pick cotton. We do make thread and cotton dresses of cotton. Cotton has pretty white and red flowers on it. Teacher did tear her dress. Mildred does cry. I will nurse Nancy. Mother will buy me lovely new aprons and dress to take to Boston. I went to Knoxville with father and aunt. Bessie is weak and little. Mrs. Thompson's chickens killed Leila's chickens. Eva does sleep in my bed. I do love good girls.

Good-by

HELEN KELLER.

The next two letters mention her visit in January to her relatives in Memphis, Tennessee. She was taken to the cotton exchange. When she felt the maps and blackboards she asked, "Do men go to school?" She wrote on the blackboard the names of all the gentlemen present. While at Memphis she went over one of the large Mississippi steamers.

TO DR. EDWARD EVERETT HALE

TUSCUMBIA, Alabama, February 15th [1888].
Dear Mr. Hale,

I am happy to write you a letter this morning. Teacher told me about kind gentleman I shall be glad to read pretty story I do read stories in my book about tigers and lions and sheep. I am coming to Boston in June to see little blind girls and I will come to see you. I went to Memphis to see grandmother and Aunt Nannie. Teacher bought me lovely new dress and cap and aprons. Little Natalie is a very weak and small baby. Father took us to see steamboat. It was on a large river. Boat is like house. Mildred is a good baby. I do love to play with little sister. Nancy was not a good child when I went to Memphis. She did cry loud. I will not write more to-day. I am tired.

Good-by

HELEN KELLER.

TO MR. MICHAEL ANAGNOS

TUSCUMBIA, Ala., Feb. 24th, 1888.
My dear Mr. Anagnos,—I am glad to write you a

letter in Braille.   This morning Lucien Thompson
sent me a beautiful bouquet of violets and crocuses
and jonquils.   Sunday Adeline Moses brought me
a lovely doll.   It came from New York.   Her name
is Adeline Keller.   She can shut her eyes and bend
her arms and sit down and stand up straight.   She
has on a pretty red dress.   She is Nancy's sister and
I am their mother.   Allie is their cousin.   Nancy
was a bad child when I went to Memphis she cried
loud, I whipped her with a stick.

Mildred does feed little chickens with crumbs.   I
love to play with little sister.

Teacher and I went to Memphis to see aunt
Nannie and grandmother.   Louise is aunt Nannie's
child.   Teacher bought me a lovely new dress and
gloves and stockings and collars and grandmother
made me warm flannels, and aunt Nannie made me
aprons.   Lady made me a pretty cap.   I went to
see Robert and Mr. Graves and Mrs. Graves and
little Natalie, and Mr. Farris and Mr. Mayo and
Mary and everyone.   I do love Robert and teacher.
She does not want me to write more today.   I feel
tired.

I found box of candy in Mr. Grave's pocket.
Father took us to see steam boat it is like house.
Boat was on very large river.   Yates plowed yard
today to plant grass.   Mule pulled plow.   Mother
will make garden of vegetables.   Father will plant
melons and peas and beans.

Cousin Bell will come to see us Saturday.   Mother
will make ice-cream for dinner, we will have ice-
cream and cake for dinner.   Lucien Thompson is
sick.   I am sorry for him.

Teacher and I went to walk in the yard, and I

learned about how flowers and trees grow. Sun rises in the east and sets in the west. Sheffield is north and Tuscumbia is south. We will go to Boston in June. I will have fun with little blind girls.

Good bye

HELEN KELLER.

"Uncle Morrie" of the next letter is Mr. Morrison Heady, of Normandy, Kentucky, who lost his sight and hearing when he was a boy. He is the author of some commendable verses.

TO MR. MORRISON HEADY

TUSCUMBIA, Ala., March 1st 1888.

My dear uncle Morrie,—I am happy to write you a letter, I do love you, and I will hug and kiss you when I see you.

Mr. Anagnos is coming to see me Monday. I do love to run and hop and skip with Robert in bright warm sun. I do know little girl in Lexington Ky. her name is Katherine Hobson.

I am going to Boston in June with mother and teacher, I will have fun with little blind girls, and Mr. Hale will send me pretty story. I do read stories in my book about lions and tigers and bears.

Mildred will not go to Boston, she does cry. I love to play with little sister, she is weak and small baby. Eva is better.

Yates killed ants, ants stung Yates. Yates is digging in garden. Mr. Anagnos did see oranges, they look like golden apples.

Robert will come to see me Sunday when sun shines and I will have fun with him.   My cousin Frank lives in Louisville.   I will come to Memphis again to see Mr. Farris and Mrs. Graves and Mr. Mayo and Mr. Graves.   Natalie is a good girl and does not cry, and she will be big and Mrs. Graves is making short dresses for her.   Natalie has a little carriage.   Mr. Mayo has been to Duck Hill and he brought sweet flowers home.

With much love and a kiss

HELEN A. KELLER.

In this account of the picnic we get an illuminating glimpse of Miss Sullivan's skill in teaching her pupil during play hours.   This was a day when the child's vocabulary grew.

TO MR. MICHAEL ANAGNOS

TUSCUMBIA, Ala. May 3rd 1888.

Dear Mr. Anagnos.—I am glad to write to you this morning, because I love you very much.   I was very happy to receive pretty book and nice candy and two letters from you.   I will come to see you soon and will ask you many questions about countries and you will love good child.

Mother is making me pretty new dresses to wear in Boston and I will look lovely to see little girls and boys and you.   Friday teacher and I went to a picnic with little children.   We played games and ate dinner under the trees, and we found ferns and wild. flowers. I walked in the woods and learned names of many trees. There are poplar and cedar and pine and oak and ash and hickory and maple trees. They make a pleasant shade and the little birds love to swing to and fro and sing sweetly up in the trees. Rabbits hop and squirrels run and ugly snakes do crawl in the woods. Geraniums and roses jasamines and japonicas are cultivated flowers. I help mother and teacher water them every night before supper.

Cousin Arthur made me a swing in the ash tree. Aunt Ev. has gone to Memphis. Uncle Frank is here. He is picking strawberries for dinner. Nancy is sick again, new teeth do make her ill. Adeline is well and she can go to Cincinnati Monday with me. Aunt Ev. will send me a boy doll, Harry will be Nancy's and Adeline's brother. Wee sister is a good girl. I am tired now and I do want to go down stairs. I send many kisses and hugs with letter.

Your darling child
HELEN KELLER.

Toward the end of May Mrs. Keller, Helen, and Miss Sullivan started for Boston. On the way they spent a few days in Washington, where they saw Dr. Alexander Graham Bell and called on President Cleveland. On May 26th they arrived in Boston and went to the Perkins Institution; here Helen met the little blind girls with whom she had corresponded the year before.

Early in July she went to Brewster, Massachusetts, and spent the rest of the summer. Here
occurred her first encounter with the sea, of which
she has since written.

TO MISS MARY C. MOORE

So. BOSTON, Mass. Sept. 1888

My dear Miss Moore

Are you very glad to receive a nice
letter from your darling little friend? I love you
very dearly because you are my friend. My
precious little sister is quite well now. She likes
to sit in my little rocking-chair and put her kitty to
sleep. Would you like to see darling little Mildred?
She is a very pretty baby. Her eyes are very big
and blue, and her cheeks are soft and round and rosy
and her hair is very bright and golden. She is very
good and sweet when she does not cry loud. Next
summer Mildred will go out in the garden with me
and pick the big sweet strawberries and then she will
be very happy. I hope she will not eat too many
of the delicious fruit for they will make her very ill.

Sometime will you please come to Alabama and
visit me? My uncle James is going to buy me a very
gentle pony and a pretty cart and I shall be very
happy to take you and Harry to ride. I hope Harry
will not be afraid of my pony. I think my father
will buy me a beautiful little brother some day. I
shall be very gentle and patient to my new little
brother. When I visit many strange countries my
brother and Mildred will stay with grandmother

because they will be too small to see a great many people and I think they would cry loud on the great rough ocean.

When Capt. Baker gets well he will take me in his big ship to Africa. Then I shall see lions and tigers and monkeys. I will get a baby lion and a white monkey and a mild bear to bring home. I had a very pleasant time at Brewster. I went in bathing almost every day and Carrie and Frank and little Helen and I had fun. We splashed and jumped and waded in the deep water. I am not afraid to float now. Can Harry float and swim? We came to Boston last Thursday, and Mr. Anagnos was delighted to see me, and he hugged and kissed me. The little girls are coming back to school next Wednesday.

Will you please tell Harry to write me a very long letter soon? When you come to Tuscumbia to see me I hope my father will have many sweet apples and juicy peaches and fine pears and delicious grapes and large water melons.

I hope you think about me and love me because I am a good little child.

With much love and two kisses

From your little friend
HELEN A. KELLER.

In this account of a visit to some friends, Helen's thought is much what one would expect from an ordinary child of eight, except perhaps her naïve satisfaction in the boldness of the young gentlemen.

TO MRS. KATE ADAMS KELLER

So. BOSTON, Mass, Sept. 24th [1888].
My dear Mother,
            I think you will be very glad to know
all about my visit to West Newton. Teacher and I
had a lovely time with many kind friends. West
Newton is not far from Boston and we went there
in the steam cars very quickly.

Mrs. Freeman and Carrie and Ethel and Frank
and Helen came to station to meet us in a huge
carriage. I was delighted to see my dear little
friends and I hugged and kissed them. Then we
rode for a long time to see all the beautiful things in
West Newton. Many very handsome houses and
large soft green lawns around them and trees and
bright flowers and fountains. The horse's name
was Prince and he was gentle and liked to trot very
fast. When we went home we saw eight rabbits
and two fat puppies, and a nice little white pony,
and two wee kittens and a pretty curly dog named
Don. Pony's name was Mollie and I had a nice ride
on her back; I was not afraid, I hope my uncle will
get me a dear little pony and a little cart very soon.

Clifton did not kiss me because he does not like
to kiss little girls. He is shy. I am very glad that
Frank and Clarence and Robbie and Eddie and
Charles and George were not very shy. I played
with many little girls and we had fun. I rode on
Carrie's tricicle and picked flowers and ate fruit
and hopped and skipped and danced and went to
ride. Many ladies and gentlemen came to see us.
Lucy and Dora and Charles were born in China. I
was born in America, and Mr. Anagnos was born in

Greece. Mr. Drew says little girls in China cannot talk on their fingers but I think when I go to China I will teach them. Chinese nurse came to see me, her name was Asu. She showed me a tiny atze that very rich ladies in China wear because their feet never grow large. Amah means a nurse. We came home in horse cars because it was Sunday and steam cars do not go often on Sunday. Conductors and engineers do get very tired and go home to rest. I saw little Willie Swan in the car and he gave me a juicy pear. He was six years old. What did I do when I was six years old? Will you please ask my father to come to train to meet teacher and me? I am very sorry that Eva and Bessie are sick. I hope I can have a nice party my birthday, and I do want Carrie and Ethel and Frank and Helen to come to Alabama to visit me. Will Mildred sleep with me when I come home.

With much love and thousand kisses.

From your dear little daughter.

HELEN A. KELLER.

Her visit to Plymouth was in July. This letter, written three months later, shows how well she remembered her first lesson in history.

TO MR. MORRISON HEADY

South Boston, Mass. October 1st, 1888.

My dear uncle Morrie,—I think you will be very glad to receive a letter from your dear little friend Helen. I am very happy to write to you because I

think of you and love you.   I read pretty stories in
the book you sent me, about Charles and his boat,
and Arthur and his dream, and Rosa and the sheep.

I have been in a large boat.   It was like a ship.
Mother and teacher and Mrs. Hopkins and Mr.
Anagnos and Mr. Rodocanachi and many other
friends went to Plymouth to see many old things.   I
will tell you a little story about Plymouth.

Many years ago there lived in England many good
people, but the king and his friends were not kind
and gentle and patient with good people, because
the king did not like to have the people disobey him.
People did not like to go to church with the king;
but they did like to build very nice little churches
for themselves.

The king was very angry with the people and they
were sorry and they said, we will go away to a
strange country to live and leave very dear home and
friends and naughty king.   So, they put all their
things into big boxes, and said, Good-bye.   I am
sorry for them because they cried much.   When they
went to Holland they did not know anyone; and they
could not know what the people were talking about
because they did not know Dutch.   But soon they
learned some Dutch words; but they loved their own
language and they did not want little boys and girls
to forget it and learn to talk funny Dutch.   So they
said, We must go to a new country far away and
build schools and houses and churches and make
new cities.   So they put all their things in boxes
and said, Good-bye to their new friends and sailed
away in a large boat to find a new country.   Poor
people were not happy for their hearts were full of
sad thoughts because they did not know much about

America. I think little children must have been afraid of a great ocean for it is very strong and it makes a large boat rock and then the little children would fall down and hurt their heads. After they had been many weeks on the deep ocean where they could not see trees or flowers or grass, but just water and the beautiful sky, for ships could not sail quickly then because men did not know about engines and steam. One day a dear little baby-boy was born. His name was Peregrine White. I am very sorry that poor little Peregrine is dead now. Every day the people went upon deck to look out for land. One day there was a great shout on the ship for the people saw the land and they were full of joy because they had reached a new country safely. Little girls and boys jumped and clapped their hands. They were all glad when they stepped upon a huge rock. I did see the rock in Plymouth and a little ship like the Mayflower and the cradle that dear little Peregrine slept in and many old things that came in the Mayflower. Would you like to visit Plymouth some time and see many old things.

Now I am very tired and I will rest.

With much love and many kisses, from your little friend.

HELEN A. KELLER.

The foreign words in these two letters, the first of which was written during a visit to the kindergarten for the blind, she had been told months before, and had stowed them away in her memory. She assimilated words and practised with them, sometimes using them intelligently, sometimes repeating them in a parrot-like fashion. Even when she did not fully understand words or ideas, she liked to set them down as though she did. It was in this way that she learned to use correctly words of sound and vision which express ideas outside of her experience. "Edith" is Edith Thomas.

TO MR. MICHAEL ANAGNOS

ROXBURY, MASS. Oct. 17th, 1888.

Mon cher Monsieur Anagnos,

I am sitting by the window and the beautiful sun is shining on me Teacher and I came to the kindergarten yesterday. There are twenty seven little children here and they are all blind. I am sorry because they cannot see much. Sometime will they have very well eyes? Poor Edith is blind and deaf and dumb. Are you very sad for Edith and me? Soon I shall go home to see my mother and my father and my dear good and sweet little sister. I hope you will come to Alabama to visit me and I will take you to ride in my little cart and I think you will like to see me on my dear little pony's back. I shall wear my lovely cap and my new riding dress. If the sun shines brightly I will take you to see Leila and Eva and Bessie. When I am thirteen years old I am going to travel in many strange and beautiful countries. I shall climb very high mountains in Norway and see much ice and snow. I hope I will not fall and hurt my head I shall visit little Lord Fauntleroy in England and he will be glad to show me his grand

and very ancient castle. And we will run with the deer and feed the rabbits and catch the squirrels. I shall not be afraid of Fauntleroy's great dog Dougal. I hope Fauntleroy take me to see a very kind queen. When I go to France I will take French. A little French boy will say, *Parlez-vous Francais?* and I will say, *Oui, Monsieur, vous avez un joli chapeau. Donnez moi un baiser.* I hope you will go with me to Athens to see the maid of Athens. She was very lovely lady and I will talk Greek to her. I will say, *se agapo* and, *pos echete* and I think she will say, *kalos,* and then I will say *chaere.* Will you please come to see me soon and take me to the theater? When you come I will say, *Kale emera,* and when you go home I will say, *Kale nykta.* Now I am too tired to write more. *Je vous time.* Au revoir

From your darling little friend
HÉLEN A. KELLER.

[So. BOSTON, Mass. October 29, 1888.]
TO MISS EVELINA H. KELLER

My dearest Aunt,—I am coming home very soon and I think you and every one will be very glad to see my teacher and me. I am very happy because I have learned much about many things. I am studying French and German and Latin and Greek. *Se agapo* is Greek, and it means I love thee. *J'ai une bonne petite sœur* is French, and it means I have a good little sister. *Nous avons un bon pere et une bonne mere* means, we have a good father and a

good mother. *Puer* is boy in Latin, and *Mutter* is
mother in German. I will teach Mildred many
languages when I come home.

HELEN A. KELLER.

TO MRS. SOPHIA C. HOPKINS

TUSCUMBIA, Ala. Dec. 11th, 1888.

My dear Mrs. Hopkins:—

 I have just fed my dear little
pigeon. My brother Simpson gave it to me
last Sunday. I named it Annie, for my teacher.
My puppy has had his supper and gone to bed.   My
rabbits are sleeping, too; and very soon I shall go
to bed.   Teacher is writing letters to her friends.
Mother and father and their friends have gone to
see a huge furnace.   The furnace is to make iron.
The iron ore is found in the ground; but it cannot be
used until it has been brought to the furnace and
melted, and all the dirt taken out, and just the pure
iron left.   Then it is all ready to be manufactured
into engines, stoves, kettles and many other things.
 Coal is found in the ground, too.   Many years
ago, before people came to live on the earth, great
trees and tall grasses and huge ferns and all the
beautiful flowers covered the earth.   When the
leaves and the trees fell, the water and the soil
covered them; and then more trees grew and fell
also, and were buried under water and soil.   After
they had all been pressed together for many thousands of years, the wood grew very hard, like rock,
and then it was all ready for people to burn.   Can
you see leaves and ferns and bark on the coal?

Men go down into the ground and dig out the coal,
and steam-cars take it to the large cities, and sell it
to people to burn, to make them warm and happy
when it is cold out of doors.

Are you very lonely and sad now? I hope you
will come to see me soon, and stay a long time.

With much love from your little friend

HELEN A. KELLER.

TO MISS DELLA BENNETT

TUSCUMBIA, ALA., Jan. 29, 1889.

My dear Miss Bennett:—I am delighted to write
to you this morning. We have just eaten our
breakfast. Mildred is running about downstairs.
I have been reading in my book about astronomers.
Astronomer comes from the Latin word *astra,* which
means stars; and astronomers are men who study
the stars, and tell us about them. When we are
sleeping quietly in our beds, they are watching the
beautiful sky through the telescope. A telescope
is like a very strong eye. The stars are so far away
that people cannot tell much about them, without
very excellent instruments. Do you like to look out
of your window, and see little stars? Teacher says
she can see Venus from our window, and it is a large
and beautiful star. The stars are called the earth's
brothers and sisters.

There are a great many instruments besides those
which the astronomers use. A knife is an instrument to cut with. I think the bell is an instrument,
too. I will tell you what I know about bells.

Some bells are musical and others are unmusical. Some are very tiny and some are very large. I saw a very large bell at Wellesley. It came from Japan. Bells are used for many purposes. They tell us when breakfast is ready, when to go to school, when it is time for church, and when there is a fire. They tell people when to go to work, and when to go home and rest. The engine-bell tells the passengers that they are coming to a station, and it tells the people to keep out of the way. Sometimes very terrible accidents happen, and many people are burned and drowned and injured. The other day I broke my doll's head off; but that was not a dreadful accident, because dolls do not live and feel, like people. My little pigeons are well, and so is my little bird. I would like to have some clay. Teacher says it is time for me to study now. Good-bye.

> With much love, and many kisses,
> HELEN A. KELLER.

TO DR. EDWARD EVERETT HALE

Tuscumbia, Alabama, February 21st, 1889.
My dear Mr. Hale,

I am very much afraid that you are thinking in your mind that little Helen has forgotten all about you and her dear cousins. But I think you will be delighted to receive this letter because then you will know that I of[ten] think about you and I love you dearly for you are my dear cousin. I have been at home a great many weeks now. It

made me feel very sad to leave Boston and I missed
all of my friends greatly, but of course I was glad
to get back to my lovely home once more. My
darling little sister is growing very fast. Sometimes
she tries to spell very short words on her small
[fingers] but she is too young to remember hard
words. When she is older I will teach her many
things if she is patient and obedient. My teacher
says, if children learn to be patient and gentle while
they are little, that when they grow to be young
ladies and gentlemen they will not forget to be kind
and loving and brave. I hope I shall be courageous
always. A little girl in a story was not courageous.
She thought she saw little elves with tall pointed
[hats] peeping from between the bushes and dancing
down the long alleys, and the poor little girl was
terrified. Did you have a pleasant Christmas? I
had many lovely presents given to me. The other
day I had a fine party. All of my dear little friends
came to see me. We played games, and ate ice-
cream and cake and fruit. Then we had great fun.
The sun is shining brightly to-day and I hope we
shall go to ride if the roads are dry. In a few days
the beautiful spring will be here. I am very glad
because I love the warm sunshine and the fragrant
flowers. I think Flowers grow to make people
happy and good. I have four dolls now. Cedric
is my little boy, he is named for Lord Fauntleroy.
He has big brown eyes and long golden hair and
pretty round cheeks. Ida is my baby. A lady
brought her to me from Paris. She can drink milk
like a real baby. Lucy is a fine young lady. She
has on a dainty lace dress and satin slippers. Poor
old Nancy is growing old and very feeble. She is

almost an invalid. I have two tame pigeons and
a tiny canary bird. Jumbo is very strong and
faithful. He will not let anything harm us at night.
I go to school every day I am studying reading,
writing, arithmetic, geography and language. My
Mother and teacher send you and Mrs. Hale their
kind greetings and Mildred sends you a kiss.
With much love and kisses, from your
Affectionate cousin
HELEN A. KELLER.

During the winter Miss Sullivan and her pupil
were working at Helen's home in Tuscumbia, and to
good purpose, for by spring Helen had learned to
write idiomatic English. After May, 1889, I find
almost no inaccuracies, except some evident slips of
the pencil. She uses words precisely and makes
easy, fluent sentences.

TO MR. MICHAEL ANAGNOS

TUSCUMBIA, ALA., May 18, 1889.
My Dear Mr. Anagnos:—You cannot imagine
how delighted I was to receive a letter from you
last evening. I am very sorry that you are going so
far away. We shall miss you very, very much. I
would love to visit many beautiful cities with you.
When I was in Huntsville I saw Dr. Bryson, and he
told me that he had been to Rome and Athens and
Paris and London. He had climbed the high mountains in Switzerland and visited beautiful churches in

Italy and France, and he saw a great many ancient castles. I hope you will please write to me from all the cities you visit. When you go to Holland please give my love to the lovely princess Wilhelmina. She is a dear little girl, and when she is old enough she will be the queen of Holland. If you go to Roumania please ask the good queen Elizabeth about her little invalid brother, and tell her that I am very sorry that her darling little girl died. I should like to send a kiss to Vittorio, the little prince of Naples, but teacher says she is afraid you will not remember so many messages. When I am thirteen years old I shall visit them all myself.

I thank you very much for the beautiful story about Lord Fauntleroy, and so does teacher.

I am so glad that Eva is coming to stay with me this summer. We will have fine times together. Give Howard my love, and tell him to answer my letter. Thursday we had a picnic. It was very pleasant out in the shady woods, and we all enjoyed the picnic very much.

Mildred is out in the yard playing, and mother is picking the delicious strawberries. Father and Uncle Frank are down town. Simpson is coming home soon. Mildred and I had our pictures taken while we were in Huntsville. I will send you one.

The roses have been beautiful. Mother has a great many fine roses. The La France and the Lamarque are the most fragrant; but the Marechal Neil, Solfaterre, Jacqueminot, Nipheots, Etoile de Lyon, Papa Gontier, Gabrielle Drevet and the Perle des Jardines are all lovely roses.

Please give the little boys and girls my love. I think of them every day and I love them dearly in

my heart.   When you come home from Europe I hope
you will be all well and very happy to get home again.
Do not forget to give my love to Miss Calliope
Kehayia and Mr. Francis Demetrios Kalopothakes.
Lovingly, your little friend,
HELEN ADAMS KELLER.

Like a good many of Helen Keller's early letters,
this to her French teacher is her re-phrasing of a
story.   It shows how much the gift of writing is, in
the early stages of its development, the gift of
mimicry.

TO MISS FANNIE S. MARRETT

TUSCUMBIA, ALA., May 17, 1889.
MY Dear Miss Marrett—I am thinking about
a dear little girl, who wept very hard.   She wept
because her brother teased her very much.   I will
tell you what he did, and I think you will feel very
sorry for the little child.   She had a most beautiful
doll given her.   Oh, it was a lovely and delicate
doll! but the little girl's brother, a tall lad, had taken
the doll, and set it up in a high tree in the garden,
and had run away.   The little girl could not reach
the doll, and could not help it down, and therefore
she cried.   The doll cried, too, and stretched out
its arms from among the green branches, and looked
distressed.   Soon the dismal night would come—
and was the doll to sit up in the tree all night, and

by herself? The little girl could not endure that thought. "I will stay with you," said she to the doll, although she was not at all courageous. Already she began to see quite plainly the little elves in their tall pointed hats, dancing down the dusky alleys, and peeping from between the bushes, and they seemed to come nearer and nearer; and she stretched her hands up towards the tree in which the doll sat and they laughed, and pointed their fingers at her. How terrified was the little girl; but if one has not done anything wrong, these strange little elves cannot harm one. "Have I done anything wrong? Ah, yes!" said the little girl. "I have laughed at the poor duck, with the red rag tied round its leg. It hobbled, and that made me laugh; but it is wrong to laugh at the poor animals!"

Is it not a pitiful story? I hope the father punished the naughty little boy. Shall you be very glad to see my teacher next Thursday? She is going home to rest, but she will come back to me next autumn.

Lovingly, your little friend,
HELEN ADAMS KELLER.

TO MISS MARY E. RILEY

TUSCUMBIA, ALA., May 27, 1889.
My Dear Miss Riley:—I wish you were here in the warm, sunny south today. Little sister and I would take you out into the garden, and pick the delicious raspberries and a few strawberries for you.

How would you like that? The strawberries are nearly all gone. In the evening, when it is cool and pleasant, we would walk in the yard, and catch the grasshoppers and butterflies. We would talk about the birds and flowers and grass and Jumbo and Pearl. If you liked, we would run and jump and hop and dance, and be very happy. I think you would enjoy hearing the mocking-birds sing. One sits on the twig of a tree, just beneath our window, and he fills the air with his glad songs. But I am afraid you cannot come to Tuscumbia; so I will write to you, and send you a sweet kiss and my love. How is Dick? Daisy is happy, but she would be happy ever if she had a little mate. My little children are all well except Nancy, and she is quite feeble. My grandmother and aunt Corinne are here. Grandmother is going to make me two new dresses. Give my love to all the little girls, and tell them that Helen loves them very, very much. Eva sends love to all.

With much love and many kisses, from your affectionate little friend,

HELEN ADAMS KELLER.

During the summer Miss Sullivan was away from Helen for three months and a half, the first separation of teacher and pupil. Only once afterward in fifteen years was their constant companionship broken for more than a few days at a time.

TO MISS ANNE MANSFIELD SULLIVAN

TUSCUMBIA, ALA., August 7, 1889.

Dearest Teacher—I am very glad to write to you this evening, for I have been thinking much about you all day. I am sitting on the piazza, and my little white pigeon is perched on the back of my chair, watching me write. Her little brown mate has flown away with the other birds; but Annie is not sad, for she likes to stay with me. Fauntleroy is asleep upstairs, and Nancy is putting Lucy to bed. Perhaps the mocking bird is singing them to sleep. All the beautiful flowers are in bloom now. The air is sweet with the perfume of jasmines, heliotropes and roses. It is getting warm here now, so father is going to take us to the Quarry on the 20th of August. I think we shall have a beautiful time out in the cool, pleasant woods. I will write and tell you all the pleasant things we do. I am so glad that Lester and Henry are good little infants. Give them many sweet kisses for me.

What was the name of the little boy who fell in love with the beautiful star? Eva has been telling me a story about a lovely little girl named Heidi. Will you please send it to me? I shall be delighted to have a typewriter.

Little Arthur is growing very fast. He has on short dresses now. Cousin Leila thinks he will walk in a little while. Then I will take his soft chubby hand in mine, and go out in the bright sunshine with him. He will pull the largest roses, and chase the gayest butterflies. I will take very good care of him, and not let him fall and hurt himself. Father and some other gentlemen went hunting yesterday.

Father killed thirty-eight birds. We had some of them for supper, and they were very nice. Last Monday Simpson shot a pretty crane. The crane is a large and strong bird. His wings are as long as my arm, and his bill is as long as my foot. He eats little fishes, and other small animals. Father says he can fly nearly all day without stopping.

Mildred is the dearest and sweetest little maiden in the world. She is very roguish, too. Sometimes, when mother does not know it, she goes out into the vineyard, and gets her apron full of delicious grapes. I think she would like to put her two soft arms around your neck and hug you.

Sunday I went to church. I love to go to church, because I like to see my friends.

A gentleman gave me a beautiful card. It was a picture of a mill, near a beautiful brook. There was a boat floating on the water, and the fragrant lilies were growing all around the boat. Not far from the mill there was an old house, with many trees growing close to it. There were eight pigeons on the roof of the house, and a great dog on the step. Pearl is a very proud mother-dog now. She has eight puppies, and she thinks there never were such fine puppies as hers.

I read in my books every day. I love them very, very, very much. I do want you to come back to me soon. I miss you so very, very much. I cannot know about many things, when my dear teacher is not here. I send you five thousand kisses, and more love than I can tell. I send Mrs. H. much love and a kiss.

From your affectionate little pupil,
HELEN A. KELLER.

In the fall Helen and Miss Sullivan returned to Perkins Institution at South Boston.

TO MISS MILDRED KELLER

SOUTH BOSTON, Oct. 24, 1889.

My Precious Little Sister:—Good morning. I am going to send you a birthday gift with this letter. I hope it will please you very much, because it makes me happy to send it. The dress is blue like your eyes, and candy is sweet just like your dear little self. I think mother will be glad to make the dress for you, and when you wear it you will look as pretty as a rose. The picture-book will tell you all about many strange and wild animals. You must not be afraid of them. They cannot come out of the picture to harm you.

I go to school every day, and I learn many new things. At eight I study arithmetic. I like that. At nine I go to the gymnasium with the little girls and we have great fun. I wish you could be here to play three little squirrels, and two gentle doves, and to make a pretty nest for a dear little robin. The mocking bird does not live in the cold north. At ten I study about the earth on which we all live. At eleven I talk with teacher and at twelve I study zoölogy. I do not know what I shall do in the afternoon yet.

Now, my darling little Mildred, good bye. Give father and mother a great deal of love and many hugs and kisses for me. Teacher sends her love too.

From your loving sister,

HELEN A. KELLER.

TO MR. WILLIAM WADE

South Boston, Mass., Nov. 20, 1889.
My Dear Mr. Wade:—I have just received a
letter from my mother, telling me that the beautiful
mastiff puppy you sent me had arrived in Tuscumbia
safely. Thank you very much for the nice gift. I
am very sorry that I was not at home to welcome
her; but my mother and my baby sister will be very
kind to her while her mistress is away. I hope she
is not lonely and unhappy. I think puppies can feel
very home-sick, as well as little girls. I should like
to call her Lioness, for your dog. May I? I hope
she will be very faithful,—and brave, too.

I am studying in Boston, with my dear teacher.
I learn a great many new and wonderful things. I
study about the earth, and the animals, and I like
arithmetic exceedingly. I learn many new words,
too. *Exceedingly* is one that I learned yesterday.
When I see Lioness I will tell her many things
which will surprise her greatly. I think she will
laugh when I tell her she is a vertebrate, a mammal,
a quadruped; and I shall be very sorry to tell her
that she belongs to the order Carnivora. I study
French, too. When I talk French to Lioness I will
call her *mon beau chien*. Please tell Lion that I
will take good care of Lioness. I shall be happy to
have a letter from you when you like to write to me.
From your loving little friend,
HELEN A. KELLER.
P. S. I am studying at the Institution for the
Blind. H. A. K.

This letter is indorsed in Whittier's hand, "Helen A. Keller—deaf dumb and blind—aged nine years." "Browns" is a lapse of the pencil for "brown eyes."

TO JOHN GREENLEAF WHITTIER

INST. FOR THE BLIND, SO. BOSTON, Mass.,
Nov. 27, 1889.

Dear Poet,

　　　I think you will be surprised to receive a letter from a little girl whom you do not know, but I thought you would be glad to hear that your beautiful poems make me very happy. Yesterday I read "In School Days" and "My Playmate," and I enjoyed them greatly. I was very sorry that the poor little girl with the browns and the "tangled golden curls" died. It is very pleasant to live here in our beautiful world. I cannot see the lovely things with my eyes, but my mind can see them all, and so I am joyful all the day long.

When I walk out in my garden I cannot see the beautiful flowers but I know that they are all around me; for is not the air sweet with their fragrance? I know too that the tiny lily-bells are whispering pretty secrets to their companions else they would not look so happy. I love you very dearly, because you have taught me so many lovely things about flowers, and birds, and people. Now I must say, good-bye. I hope [you] will enjoy the Thanksgiving very much.

From your loving little friend,

HELEN A. KELLER.

To Mr. John Greenleaf Whittier.

Whittier's reply, to which there is a reference in the following letter, has been lost.

TO MRS. KATE ADAMS KELLER

SOUTH BOSTON, Mass., Dec. 3, 1889.

My Dear Mother:—Your little daughter is very happy to write to you this beautiful morning. It is cold and rainy here to-day. Yesterday the Countess of Meath came again to see me. She gave me a beautiful bunch of violets. Her little girls are named Violet and May. The Earl said he should be delighted to visit Tuscumbia the next time he comes to America. Lady Meath said she would like to see your flowers, and hear the mocking-birds sing. When I visit England they want me to come to see them, and stay a few weeks. They will take me to see the Queen.

I had a lovely letter from the poet Whittier. He loves me. Mr. Wade wants teacher and me to come and see him next spring. May we go? He said you must feed Lioness from your hand, because she will be more gentle if she does not eat with other dogs.

Mr. Wilson came to call on us one Thursday. I was delighted to receive the flowers from home. They came while we were eating breakfast, and my friends enjoyed them with me. We had a very nice dinner on Thanksgiving day,—turkey and plum-pudding. Last week I visited a beautiful art store. I saw a great many statues, and the gentleman gave me an angel.

Sunday I went to church on board a great war-

ship.   After the services were over the soldier-
sailors showed us around.   There were four hundred and sixty sailors.   They were very kind to me.
One carried me in his arms so that my feet would
not touch the water.   They wore blue uniforms
and queer little caps.   There was a terrible fire
Thursday.   Many stores were burned, and four men
were killed.   I am very sorry for them.   Tell
father, please, to write to me.   How is dear little
sister?   Give her many kisses for me.   Now I must
close.   With much love, from your darling child,

HELEN A. KELLER.

TO MRS. KATE ADAMS KELLER

So. BOSTON, MASS., Dec. 24, 1889.
My dear Mother,
Yesterday I sent you a little Christmas box.   I am very sorry that I could not send
it before so that you would receive it to morrow,
but I could not finish the watch-case any sooner.
I made all of the gifts myself, excepting father's
handkerchief.   I wish I could have made father a
gift too, but I did not have sufficient time.   I hope
you will like your watch-case, for it made me very
happy to make it for you.   You must keep your
lovely new montre in it.   If it is too warm in
Tuscumbia for little sister to wear her pretty
mittens, she can keep them because her sister made
them for her.   I imagine she will have fun with the
little toy man.   Tell her to shake him, and then he
will blow his trumpet.   I thank my dear kind father

for sending me some money, to buy gifts for my friends. I love to make everybody happy. I should like to be at home on Christmas day. We would be very happy together. I think of my beautiful home every day. Please do not forget to send me some pretty presents to hang on my tree. I am going to have a Christmas tree, in the parlor and teacher will hang all of my gifts upon it. It will be a funny tree. All of the girls have gone home to spend Christmas. Teacher and I are the only babies left for Mrs. Hopkins to care for. Teacher has been sick in bed for many days. Her throat was very sore and the doctor thought she would have to go away to the hospital, but she is better now. I have not been sick at all. The little girls are well too. Friday I am going to spend the day with my little friends Carrie, Ethel, Frank and Helen Freeman. We will have great fun I am sure.

Mr. and Miss Endicott came to see me, and I went to ride in the carriage. They are going to give me a lovely present, but I cannot guess what it will be. Sammy has a dear new brother. He is very soft and delicate yet. Mr. Anagnos is in Athens now. He is delighted because I am here. Now I must say, good-bye. I hope I have written my letter nicely, but it is very difficult to write on this paper and teacher is not here to give me better. Give many kisses to little sister and much love to all. Lovingly   HELEN.

TO DR. EDWARD EVERETT HALE

SOUTH BOSTON, Jan. 8, 1890.
My dear Mr. Hale:
The beautiful shells came last night.
I thank you very much for them. I shall always
keep them, and it will make me very happy to
think that you found them, on that far away
island, from which Columbus sailed to discover
our dear country. When I am eleven years old it
will be four hundred years since he started with the
three small ships to cross the great strange ocean.
He was very brave. The little girls were delighted
to see the lovely shells. I told them all I knew
about them. Are you very glad that you could
make so many happy? I am. I should be very
happy to come and teach you the Braille sometime,
if you have time to learn, but I am afraid you are
too busy. A few days ago I received a little box
of English violets from Lady Meath. The flowers
were wilted, but the kind thought which came with
them was as sweet and as fresh as newly pulled
violets.

With loving greeting to the little cousins, and
Mrs. Hale and a sweet kiss for yourself,
From your little friend,
HELEN A. KELLER.

This, the first of Helen's letters to Dr. Holmes,
written soon after a visit to him, he published in
"Over the Teacups."

TO DR. OLIVER WENDELL HOLMES*

SOUTH BOSTON, MASS., March 1, 1890.

Dear, Kind Poet:—I have thought of you many times since that bright Sunday when I bade you good-bye; and I am going to write you a letter, because I love you. I am sorry that you have no little children to play with you sometimes; but I think you are very happy with your books, and your many, many friends. On Washington's birthday a great many people came here to see the blind children; and I read for them from your poems, and showed them some beautiful shells, which came from a little island near Palos.

I am reading a very sad story, called "Little Jakey." Jakey was the sweetest little fellow you can imagine, but he was poor and blind. I used to think—when I was small, and before I could read—that everybody was always happy, and at first it made me very sad to know about pain and great sorrow; but now I know that we could never learn to be brave and patient, if there were only joy in the world.

I am studying about insects in zoölogy, and I have learned many things about butterflies. They do not make honey for us, like the bees, but many of them are as beautiful as the flowers they light upon, and they always delight the hearts of little children. They live a gay life, flitting from flower to flower, sipping the drops of honeydew, without a thought for the morrow. They are just like little boys and girls when they forget books and studies, and run

*The *Atlantic Monthly*, May, 1890. By permission of Messrs. Houghton, Mifflin & Co.

away to the woods and the fields, to gather wild
flowers, or wade in the ponds for fragrant lilies,
happy in the bright sunshine.

If my little sister comes to Boston next June, will
you let me bring her to see you? She is a lovely
baby, and I am sure you will love her.

Now I must tell my gentle poet good-bye, for I
have a letter to write home before I go to bed.

From your loving little friend,
HELEN A. KELLER.

TO MISS SARAH FULLER*

SOUTH BOSTON, MASS., April 3, 1890.
My dear Miss Fuller,

My heart is full of joy this beautiful
morning, because I have learned to speak many
new words, and I can make a few sentences. Last
evening I went out in the yard and spoke to the
moon. I said, "O! moon come to me!" Do you
think the lovely moon was glad that I could speak to
her? How glad my mother will be. I can hardly
wait for June to come I am so eager to speak to her
and to my precious little sister. Mildred could not
understand me when I spelled with my fingers, but
now she will sit in my lap and I will tell her many
things to please her, and we shall be so happy
together. Are you very, very happy because you
can make so many people happy? I think you are
very kind and patient, and I love you very dearly.
My teacher told me Tuesday that you wanted to

*Miss Fuller gave Helen Keller her first lesson in articulation.
For an account of this see page 386.

know how I came to wish to talk with my mouth.   I will tell you all about it, for I remember my thoughts perfectly.   When I was a very little child I used to sit in my mother's lap all the time, because I was very timid, and did not like to be left by myself. And I would keep my little hand on her face all the while, because it amused me to feel her face and lips move when she talked with people.   I did not know then what she was doing, for I was quite ignorant of all things.   Then when I was older I learned to play with my nurse and the little negro children and I noticed that they kept moving their lips just like my mother, so I moved mine too, but sometimes it made me angry and I would hold my playmates' mouths very hard.   I did not know then that it was very naughty to do so.   After a long time my dear teacher came to me, and taught me to communicate with my fingers and I was satisfied and happy.   But when I came to school in Boston I met some deaf people who talked with their mouths like all other people, and one day a lady who had been to Norway came to see me, and told me of a blind and deaf girl* she had seen in that far away land who had been taught to speak and understand others when they spoke to her.   This good and happy news delighted me exceedingly, for then I was sure that I should learn also.   I tried to make sounds like my little playmates, but teacher told me that the voice was very delicate and sensitive and that it would injure it to make incorrect sounds, and promised to take me to see a kind and wise lady who would teach me rightly.   That lady was yourself.   Now I am as happy as the little birds, because I can speak and

*Ragnhild Kaata.

perhaps I shall sing too.   All of my friends will
be so surprised and glad.

Your loving little pupil,
HELEN A. KELLER.

When the Perkins Institution closed for the summer, Helen and Miss Sullivan went to Tuscumbia.
This was the first home-going after she had learned
to "talk with her mouth."

TO REV. PHILLIPS BROOKS

TUSCUMBIA, ALABAMA, July 14, 1890.

My dear Mr. Brooks, I am very glad to write
to you this beautiful day because you are my
kind friend and I love you, and because I wish to
know many things.   I have been at home three
weeks, and Oh, how happy I have been with dear
mother and father and precious little sister.   I was
very, very sad to part with all of my friends in
Boston, but I was so eager to see my baby sister I
could hardly wait for the train to take me home.
But I tried very hard to be patient for teacher's
sake.   Mildred has grown much taller and stronger
than she was when I went to Boston, and she is the
sweetest and dearest little child in the world.   My
parents were delighted to hear me speak, and I was
overjoyed to give them such a happy surprise.   I
think it is so pleasant to make everybody happy.
Why does the dear Father in heaven think it best
for us to have very great sorrow sometimes?   I am

always happy and so was Little Lord Fauntleroy, but dear Little Jakey's life was full of sadness. God did not put the light in Jakey's eyes and he was blind, and his father was not gentle and loving. Do you think poor Jakey loved his Father in heaven more because his other father was unkind to him? How did God tell people that his home was in heaven? When people do very wrong and hurt animals and treat children unkindly God is grieved, but what will he do to them to teach them to be pitiful and loving? I think he will tell them how dearly He loves them and that He wants them to be good and happy, and they will not wish to grieve their father who loves them so much, and they will want to please him in everything they do, so they will love each other and do good to everyone, and be kind to animals.

Please tell me something that you know about God. It makes me happy to know much about my loving Father, who is good and wise. I hope you will write to your little friend when you have time. I should like very much to see you to-day Is the sun very hot in Boston now? this afternoon if it is cool enough I shall take Mildred for a ride on my donkey. Mr. Wade sent Neddy to me, and he is the prettiest donkey you can imagine. My great dog Lioness goes with us when we ride to protect us. Simpson, that is my brother, brought me some beautiful pond lilies yesterday—he is a very brother to me.

Teacher sends you her kind remembrances, and father and mother also send their regards.

From your loving little friend,

HELEN A. KELLER.

DR. BROOKS'S REPLY

LONDON, August 3, 1890.

My Dear Helen—I was very glad indeed to get your letter. It has followed me across the ocean and found me in this magnificent great city which I should like to tell you all about if I could take time for it and make my letter long enough. Some time when you come and see me in my study in Boston I shall be glad to talk to you about it all if you care to hear.

But now I want to tell you how glad I am that you are so happy and enjoying your home so very much. I can almost think I see you with your father and mother and little sister, with all the brightness of the beautiful country about you, and it makes me very glad to know how glad you are.

I am glad also to know, from the questions which you ask me, what you are thinking about. I do not see how we can help thinking about God when He is so good to us all the time. Let me tell you how it seems to me that we come to know about our heavenly Father. It is from the power of love which is in our own hearts. Love is at the soul of everything. Whatever has not the power of loving must have a very dreary life indeed. We like to think that the sunshine and the winds and the trees are able to love in some way of their own, for it would make us know that they were happy if we knew that they could love. And so God who is the greatest and happiest of all beings is the most loving too. All the love that is in our hearts comes from him, as all the light which is in the

flowers comes from the sun.   And the more we love
the more near we are to God and His Love.

I told you that I was very happy because of your
happiness.   Indeed I am.   So are your Father and
your Mother and your Teacher and all your friends.
But do you not think that God is happy too because
you are happy?   I am sure He is.   And He is
happier than any of us because He is greater than
any of us, and also because He not merely *sees* your
happiness as we do, but He also *made* it.   He
gives it to you as the sun gives light and color
to the rose.   And we are always most glad of what
we not merely see our friends enjoy, but of what we
give them to enjoy.   Are we not?

But God does not only want us to be *happy;* He
wants us to be *good.*   He wants that most of all.
He knows that we can be really happy only when we
are good.   A great deal of the trouble that is in the
world is medicine which is very bad to take, but
which it is good to take because it makes us better.
We see how good people may be in great trouble
when we think of Jesus who was the greatest
sufferer that ever lived and yet was the best Being
and so, I am sure, the happiest Being that the world
has ever seen.

I love to tell you about God.   But He will tell you
Himself by the love which He will put into your
heart if you ask Him.   And Jesus, who is His Son,
but is nearer to Him than all of us His other
Children, came into the world on purpose to tell
us all about our Father's Love.   If you read His
words, you will see how full His heart is of the love
of God.   "We *know* that He loves us," He says.
And so He loved men Himself and though they

were very cruel to Him and at last killed Him, He was willing to die for them because He loved them so. And, Helen, He loves men still, and He loves us, and He tells us that we may love Him.

And so love is everything. And if anybody asks you, or if you ask yourself what God is, answer, "God is Love." That is the beautiful answer which the Bible gives.

All this is what you are to think of and to understand more and more as you grow older. Think of it now, and let it make every blessing brighter because your dear Father sends it to you.

You will come back to Boston I hope soon after I do. I shall be there by the middle of September. I shall want you to tell me all about everything, and not forget the Donkey.

I send my kind remembrance to your father and mother, and to your teacher. I wish I could see your little sister.

Good Bye, dear Helen. Do write to me soon again, directing your letter to Boston.

Your affectionate friend

PHILLIPS BROOKS.

DR. HOLMES'S REPLY

To a letter which has been lost.

BEVERLY FARMS, MASS., August 1, 1890.
My Dear Little Friend Helen:

I received your welcome letter several days ago, but I have so much writing to do that I am apt to make my letters wait a good while before they get answered.

It gratifies me very much to find that you remember me so kindly. Your letter is charming, and I am greatly pleased with it. I rejoice to know that you are well and happy. I am very much delighted to hear of your new acquisition—that you "talk with your mouth" as well as with your fingers. What a curious thing *speech* is! The tongue is so serviceable a member (taking all sorts of shapes, just as is wanted),—the teeth, the lips, the roof of the mouth, all ready to help, and so heap up the sound of the voice into the solid bits which we call consonants, and make room for the curiously shaped breathings which we call vowels! You have studied all this, I don't doubt, since you have practised vocal speaking.

I am surprised at the mastery of language which your letter shows. It almost makes me think the world would get along as well without seeing and hearing as with them. Perhaps people would be better in a great many ways, for they could not fight as they do now. Just think of an army of blind people, with guns and cannon! Think of the poor drummers! Of what use would they and their drumsticks be? You are spared the pain of many sights and sounds, which you are only too happy in escaping. Then think how much kindness you are sure of as long as you live. Everybody will feel an interest in dear little Helen; everybody will want to do something for her; and, if she becomes an ancient, gray-haired woman, she is still sure of being thoughtfully cared for.

Your parents and friends must take great satisfaction in your progress. It does great credit, not only to you, but to your instructors, who have so broken down the walls that seemed to shut you in that now your outlook seems more bright and cheerful than that of many seeing and hearing children.

Good-bye, dear little Helen! With every kind wish from your friend,

OLIVER WENDELL HOLMES.

This letter was written to some gentlemen in Gardiner, Maine, who named a lumber vessel after her.

TO MESSRS. BRADSTREET

TUSCUMBIA, ALA., July 14, 1890.

My Dear, Kind Friends:—I thank you very, very much for naming your beautiful new ship for me. It makes me very happy to know that I have kind and loving friends in the far-away State of Maine. I did not imagine, when I studied about the forests of Maine, that a strong and beautiful ship would go sailing all over the world, carrying wood from those rich forests, to build pleasant homes and schools and churches in distant countries. I hope the great ocean will love the new Helen, and let her sail over its blue waves peacefully. Please tell the brave sailors, who have charge of the HELEN KELLER, that little Helen who stays at home will often think of them with loving thoughts. I hope I shall see you and my beautiful namesake some time.

With much love, from your little friend,

HELEN A. KELLER.

To the Messrs. Bradstreet.

Helen and Miss Sullivan returned to the Perkins Institution early in November.

TO MRS. KATE ADAMS KELLER

SOUTH BOSTON, Nov. 10, 1890.

My Dearest Mother:—My heart has been full of thoughts of you and my beautiful home ever since we parted so sadly on Wednesday night. How I wish I could see you this lovely morning, and tell you all that has happened since I left home! And my darling little sister, how I wish I could give her a hundred kisses! And my dear father, how he would like to hear about our journey! But I cannot see you and talk to you, so I will write and tell you all that I can think of.

We did not reach Boston until Saturday morning. I am sorry to say that our train was delayed in several places, which made us late in reaching New York. When we got to Jersey City at six o'clock Friday evening we were obliged to cross the Harlem River in a ferry-boat. We found the boat and the transfer carriage with much less difficulty than teacher expected. When we arrived at the station they told us that the train did not leave for Boston until eleven o'clock, but that we could take the sleeper at nine, which we did. We went to bed and slept until morning. When we awoke we were in Boston. I was delighted to get there, though I was much disappointed because we did not arrive on Mr. Anagnos' birthday. We surprised our dear friends, however, for they did not expect us Saturday; but when the bell rung Miss Marrett guessed who was at the door, and Mrs. Hopkins jumped up from the breakfast table and ran to the door to meet us; she was indeed much astonished to see us. After we had had some breakfast we went up to see Mr. Anagnos. I was overjoyed to see my dearest and kindest friend once more. He gave me a beautiful watch. I have it pinned to my dress. I tell everybody the time when they ask me. I have only seen Mr. Anagnos twice. I have many questions to ask him about the countries he has been travelling in. But I suppose he is very busy now.

The hills in Virginia were very lovely. Jack Frost had dressed them in gold and crimson. The view was most charmingly picturesque. Pennsylvania is a very beautiful State. The grass was as green as though it was springtime, and the golden ears of corn gathered together in heaps in the great fields looked very pretty. In Harrisburg we saw a donkey like Neddy. How I wish I could see my own donkey and my dear Lioness! Do they miss their mistress very much? Tell Mildred she must be kind to them for my sake.

Our room is pleasant and comfortable.

My typewriter was much injured coming. The case was broken and the keys are nearly all out. Teacher is going to see if it can be fixed.

There are many new books in the library. What a nice time I shall have reading them! I have already read Sara Crewe. It is a very pretty story, and I will tell it to you some time. Now, sweet mother, your little girl must say good-bye.

With much love to father, Mildred, you and all the dear friends, lovingly your little daughter,

HELEN A. KELLER.

TO JOHN GREENLEAF WHITTIER

SOUTH BOSTON, Dec. 17, 1890.

Dear Kind Poet,

This is your birthday; that was the first thought which came into my mind when I awoke this morning; and it made me glad to think I could write you a letter and tell you how much your little friends love their sweet poet and his birthday. This evening they are going to entertain their friends with readings from your poems and music. I hope the swift winged messengers of love will be here to carry some of the sweet melody to you, in your little study by the Merrimac. At first I was very sorry when I found that the sun had hidden his shining face behind dull clouds, but afterwards I thought why he did it, and then I was happy. The sun knows that you like to see the world covered with beautiful white snow and so he kept back all his brightness, and let the little crystals form in the sky. When they are ready, they will softly fall and tenderly cover every object. Then the sun will appear in all his radiance and fill the world with light. If I were with you to-day I would give you eighty-three kisses, one for each year you have lived. Eighty-three years seems very long to me. Does it seem long to you? I wonder how many years there will be in eternity. I am afraid I cannot think about so much time. I received the letter which you wrote to me last summer, and I thank you for it. I am staying in Boston now at the Institution for the Blind, but I have not commenced my studies yet, because my dearest friend, Mr. Anagnos wants me to rest and play a great deal.

Teacher is well and sends her kind remembrance to you. The happy Christmas time is almost here! I can hardly wait for the fun to begin! I hope your Christmas Day will be a very happy one and that the New Year will be full of brightness and joy for you and every one.

　　　　　From your little friend

　　　　　　　　HELEN A. KELLER.

WHITTIER'S REPLY

My Dear Young Friend—I was very glad to have such a pleasant letter on my birthday. I had two or three hundred others and thine was one of the most welcome of all. I must tell thee about how the day passed at Oak Knoll. Of course the sun did not shine, but we had great open wood fires in the rooms, which were all very sweet with roses and other flowers, which were sent to me from distant friends; and fruits of all kinds from California and other places. Some relatives and dear old friends were with me through the day. I do not wonder thee thinks eighty three years a long time, but to me it seems but a very little while since I was a boy no older than thee, playing on the old farm at Haverhill. I thank thee for all thy good wishes, and wish thee as many. I am glad thee is at the Institution; it is an excellent place. Give my best regards to Miss Sullivan, and with a great deal of love I am

　　　　　Thy old friend,

　　　　　　　　JOHN G. WHITTIER.

Tommy Stringer, who appears in several of the following letters, became blind and deaf when he was four years old.   His mother was dead and his father was too poor to take care of him.   For a while he was kept in the general hospital at Allegheny.   From here he was to be sent to an almshouse, for at that time there was no other place for him in Pennsylvania.   Helen heard of him through Mr. J. G. Brown of Pittsburgh, who wrote her that he had failed to secure a tutor for Tommy.   She wanted him brought to Boston, and when she was told that money would be needed to get him a teacher, she answered, "We will raise it."   She began to solicit contributions from her friends, and saved her pennies.

Dr. Alexander Graham Bell advised Tommy's friends to send him to Boston, and the trustees of the Perkins Institution agreed to admit him to the kindergarten for the blind.

Meanwhile opportunity came to Helen to make a considerable contribution to Tommy's education. The winter before, her dog Lioness had been killed, and friends set to work to raise money to buy Helen another dog.   Helen asked that the contributions, which people were sending from all over America and England, be devoted to Tommy's education. Turned to this new use, the fund grew fast, and Tommy was provided for.   He was admitted to the kindergarten on the sixth of April.

Miss Keller wrote lately, "I shall never forget the pennies sent by many a poor child who could ill spare them, 'for little Tommy,' or the swift sympathy with which people from far and near, whom I had never seen, responded to the dumb cry of a little captive soul for aid."

TO MR. GEORGE R. KREHL

INSTITUTION FOR THE BLIND,
SOUTH BOSTON, MASS., March 20, 1891.

My Dear Friend, Mr. Krehl:—I have just heard,
through Mr. Wade, of your kind offer to buy me
a gentle dog, and I want to thank you for the
kind thought. It makes me very happy indeed to
know that I have such dear friends in other lands.
It makes me think that all people are good and loving. I have read that the English and Americans
are cousins; but I am sure it would be much truer to
say that we are brothers and sisters. My friends
have told me about your great and magnificent city,
and I have read a great deal that wise Englishmen
have written. I have begun to read "Enoch Arden,"
and I know several of the great poet's poems by
heart. I am eager to cross the ocean, for I want to
see my English friends and their good and wise
queen. Once the Earl of Meath came to see me,
and he told me that the queen was much beloved by
her people, because of her gentleness and wisdom.
Some day you will be surprised to see a little strange
girl coming into your office; but when you know it
is the little girl who loves dogs and all other animals,
you will laugh, and I hope you will give her a kiss,
just as Mr. Wade does. He has another dog for
me, and he thinks she will be as brave and faithful as
by beautiful Lioness. And now I want to tell you
what the dog lovers in America are going to do.
They are going to send me some money for a poor
little deaf and dumb and blind child. His name is
Tommy, and he is five years old. His parents are
too poor to pay to have the little fellow sent to
school; so, instead of giving me a dog, the gentle-

men are going to help make Tommy's life as bright and joyous as mine. Is it not a beautiful plan? Education will bring light and music into Tommy's soul, and then he cannot help being happy.

From your loving little friend,
HELEN A. KELLER

TO DR. OLIVER WENDELL HOLMES

[SOUTH BOSTON, MASS., April, 1891.]

Dear Dr. Holmes:—Your beautiful words about spring have been making music in my heart, these bright April days. I love every word of "Spring" and "Spring Has Come." I think you will be glad to hear that these poems have taught me to enjoy and love the beautiful springtime, even though I cannot see the fair, frail blossoms which proclaim its approach, or hear the joyous warbling of the home-coming birds. But when I read "Spring Has Come," lo! I am not blind any longer, for I see with your eyes and hear with your ears. Sweet Mother Nature can have no secrets from me when my poet is near. I have chosen this paper because I want the spray of violets in the corner to tell you of my grateful love. I want you to see baby Tom, the little blind and deaf and dumb child who has just come to our pretty garden. He is poor and helpless and lonely now, but before another April education will have brought light and gladness into Tommy's life. If you do come, you will want to ask the kind people of Boston to help brighten Tommy's whole life. Your loving friend,
HELEN KELLER.

TO SIR JOHN EVERETT MILLAIS

PERKINS INSTITUTION FOR THE BLIND,
SOUTH BOSTON, MASS., April 30, 1891.

My Dear Mr. Millais:—Your little American
sister is going to write you a letter, because she wants
you to know how pleased she was to hear you were
interested in our poor little Tommy, and had sent
some money to help educate him. It is very
beautiful to think that people far away in England
feel sorry for a little helpless child in America. I
used to think, when I read in my books about your
great city, that when I visited it the people would be
strangers to me, but now I feel differently. It seems
to me that all people who have loving, pitying hearts,
are not strangers to each other. I can hardly wait
patiently for the time to come when I shall see my
dear English friends, and their beautiful island
home. My favourite poet has written some lines
about England which I love very much. I think you
will like them too, so I will try to write them for you.

> "Hugged in the clinging billow's clasp,
>   From seaweed fringe to mountain heather,
> The British oak with rooted grasp
>   Her slender handful holds together,
> With cliffs of white and bowers of green,
>   And ocean narrowing to caress her,
> And hills and threaded streams between,
>   Our little mother isle, God bless her!"

You will be glad to hear that Tommy has a kind
lady to teach him, and that he is a pretty, active
little fellow. He loves to climb much better than to
spell, but that is because he does not know yet what
a wonderful thing language is. He cannot imagine
how very, very happy he will be when he can tell us

his thoughts, and we can tell him how we have loved him so long.

Tomorrow April will hide her tears and blushes beneath the flowers of lovely May. I wonder if the May-days in England are as beautiful as they are here.

Now I must say good-bye. Please think of me always as your loving little sister,

HELEN KELLER.

TO REV. PHILLIPS BROOKS

So. BOSTON, May 1, 1891.

My Dear Mr. Brooks:

Helen sends you a loving greeting this bright May-day. My teacher has just told me that you have been made a bishop, and that your friends everywhere are rejoicing because one whom they love has been greatly honored. I do not understand very well what a bishop's work is, but I am sure it must be good and helpful, and I am glad that my dear friend is brave, and wise, and loving enough to do it. It is very beautiful to think that you can tell so many people of the heavenly Father's tender love for all His children even when they are not gentle and noble as He wishes them to be. I hope the glad news which you will tell them will make their hearts beat fast with joy and love. I hope too, that Bishop Brooks' whole life will be as rich in happiness as the month of May is full of blossoms and singing birds.

From your loving little friend,

HELEN KELLER.

Before a teacher was found for Tommy and while he was still in the care of Helen and Miss Sullivan, a reception was held for him at the kindergarten. At Helen's request Bishop Brooks made an address. Helen wrote letters to the newspapers which brought many generous replies. All of these she answered herself, and she made public acknowledgment in letters to the newspapers. This letter is to the editor of the *Boston Herald,* enclosing a complete list of the subscribers. The contributions amounted to more than sixteen hundred dollars.

TO MR. JOHN H. HOLMES

SOUTH BOSTON, May 13, 1891.

Editor of the *Boston Herald:*

My Dear Mr. Holmes:—Will you kindly print in the *Herald,* the enclosed list? I think the readers of your paper will be glad to know that so much has been done for dear little Tommy, and that they will all wish to share in the pleasure of helping him. He is very happy indeed at the kindergarten, and is learning something every day. He has found out that doors have locks, and that little sticks and bits of paper can be got into the key-hole quite easily; but he does not seem very eager to get them out after they are in. He loves to climb the bed-posts and unscrew the steam valves much better than to spell, but that is because he does not understand that words would help him to make new and interesting discoveries. I hope that good people will continue to work for Tommy until his fund is completed, and education has brought light and music into his little life.   From your little friend,

HELEN KELLER.

TO DR. OLIVER WENDELL HOLMES

SOUTH BOSTON, May 27, 1891.

Dear, Gentle Poet:—I fear that you will think Helen a very troublesome little girl if she writes to you too often; but how is she to help sending you loving and grateful messages, when you do so much to make her glad? I cannot begin to tell you how delighted I was when Mr. Anagnos told me that you had sent him some money to help educate "Baby Tom." Then I knew that you had not forgotten the dear little child, for the gift brought with it the thought of tender sympathy. I am very sorry to say that Tommy has not learned any words yet. He is the same restless little creature he was when you saw him. But it is pleasant to think that he is happy and playful in his bright new home, and by and by that strange, wonderful thing teacher calls *mind,* will begin to spread its beautiful wings and fly away in search of knowledge-land. Words are the mind's wings, are they not?

I have been to Andover since I saw you, and I was greatly interested in all that my friends told me about Phillips Academy, because I knew you had been there, and I felt it was a place dear to you. I tried to imagine my gentle poet when he was a school-boy, and I wondered if it was in Andover he learned the songs of the birds and the secrets of the shy little woodland children. I am sure his heart was always full of music, and in God's beautiful world he must have heard love's sweet replying. When I came home teacher read to me "The School-boy," for it is not in our print.

Did you know that the blind children are going

to have their commencement exercises in Tremont
Temple, next Tuesday afternoon? I enclose a
ticket, hoping that you will come. We shall all be
proud and happy to welcome our poet friend. I
shall recite about the beautiful cities of sunny Italy.
I hope our kind friend Dr. Ellis will come too, and
take Tom in his arms.

　　With much love and a kiss, from your little friend,
　　　　　　　　　　HELEN A. KELLER.

TO REV. PHILLIPS BROOKS

　　　　　　　　SOUTH BOSTON, June 8, 1891.
My dear Mr. Brooks,
　I send you my picture as I promised, and I
hope when you look at it this summer your
thoughts will fly southward to your happy
little friend. I used to wish that I could see
pictures with my hands as I do statues, but now I
do not often think about it because my dear Father
has filled my mind with beautiful pictures, even of
things I cannot see. If the light were not in your
eyes, dear Mr. Brooks, you would understand better
how happy your little Helen was when her teacher
explained to her that the best and most beautiful
things in the world cannot be seen nor even touched,
but just felt in the heart. Every day I find out
something which makes me glad. Yesterday I
thought for the first time what a beautiful thing
motion was, and it seemed to me that everything
was trying to get near to God, does it seem that way
to you? It is Sunday morning, and while I sit here

in the library writing this letter you are teaching hundreds of people some of the grand and beautiful things about their heavenly Father.   Are you not very, very happy? and when you are a Bishop you will preach to more people and more and more will be made glad.   Teacher sends her kind remembrances, and I send you with my picture my dear love.

From your little friend

HELEN KELLER.

When the Perkins Institution closed in June, Helen and her teacher went south to Tuscumbia, where they remained until December.   There is a hiatus of several months in the letters, caused by the depressing effect on Helen and Miss Sullivan of the "Frost King" episode.   At the time this trouble seemed very grave and brought them much unhappiness.   An analysis of the case has been made elsewhere,* and Miss Keller has written her account of it.†

TO MR. ALBERT H. MUNSELL

BREWSTER, Mar. 10, 1892.

My dear Mr. Munsell,

Surely I need not tell you that your letter was very welcome.   I enjoyed every word of it and wished that it was longer.   I laughed when you spoke of old Neptune's wild moods.   He

* Page 396.   † Page 63.

has, in truth, behaved very strangely ever since we came to Brewster. It is evident that something has displeased his Majesty but I cannot imagine what it can be. His expression has been so turbulent that I have feared to give him your kind message. Who knows! Perhaps the Old Sea God as he lay asleep upon the shore, heard the soft music of growing things—the stir of life in the earth's bosom, and his stormy heart was angry, because he knew that his and Winter's reign was almost at an end. So together the unhappy monarch[s] fought most despairingly, thinking that gentle Spring would turn and fly at the very sight of the havoc caused by their forces. But lo! the lovely maiden only smiles more sweetly, and breathes upon the icy battlements of her enemies, and in a moment they vanish, and the glad Earth gives her a royal welcome. But I must put away these idle fancies until we meet again. Please give your dear mother my love. Teacher wishes me to say that she liked the photograph very much and she will see about having some when we return. Now, dear friend, Please accept these few words because of the love that is linked with them.

Lovingly yours

HELEN KELLER.

This letter was reproduced in facsimile in *St. Nicholas,* June, 1892. It is undated, but must have been written two or three months before it was published.

TO *St. Nicholas**

Dear St. Nicholas:

It gives me very great pleasure to send you my autograph because I want the boys and girls who read *St. Nicholas* to know how blind children write. I suppose some of them wonder how we keep the lines so straight so I will try to tell them how it is done. We have a grooved board which we put between the pages when we wish to write. The parallel grooves correspond to lines and when we have pressed the paper into them by means of the blunt end of the pencil it is very easy to keep the words even. The small letters are all made in the grooves, while the long ones extend above and below them. We guide the pencil with the right hand, and feel carefully with the forefinger of the left hand to see that we shape and space the letters correctly. It is very difficult at first to form them plainly, but if we keep on trying it gradually becomes easier, and after a great deal of practice we can write legible letters to our friends. Then we are very, very happy. Sometime they may visit a school for the blind. If they do, I am sure they will wish to see the pupils write.

Very sincerely your little friend
HELEN KELLER.

In May, 1892, Helen gave a tea in aid of the kindergarten for the blind. It was quite her own idea, and was given in the house of Mrs. Mahlon D. Spaulding, sister of Mr. John P. Spaulding, one of

* Reprinted by courteous permission of the Century Co.

Helen's kindest and most liberal friends. The tea brought more than two thousand dollars for the blind children.

TO MISS CAROLINE DERBY

South Boston, May 9, 1892.

My dear Miss Carrie:—I was much pleased to receive your kind letter. Need I tell you that I was more than delighted to hear that you are really interested in the "tea"? Of course we must not give it up. Very soon I am going far away, to my own dear home, in the sunny south, and it would always make me happy to think that the last thing which my dear friends in Boston did for my pleasure was to help make the lives of many little sightless children good and happy. I know that kind people cannot help feeling a tender sympathy for the little ones, who cannot see the beautiful light, or any of the wonderful things which give them pleasure; and it seems to me that all loving sympathy must express itself in acts of kindness; and when the friends of little helpless blind children understand that we are working for their happiness, they will come and make our "tea" a success, and I am sure I shall be the happiest little girl in all the world. Please let Bishop Brooks know our plans, so that he may arrange to be with us. I am glad Miss Eleanor is interested. Please give her my love. I will see you to-morrow and then we can make the rest of our plans. Please give your dear aunt teacher's and my love and tell her that we enjoyed our little visit very much indeed.

Lovingly yours,
Helen Keller. .

TO MR. JOHN P. SPAULDING

SOUTH BOSTON, May 11th, 1892.

My dear Mr. Spaulding:—I am afraid you will think your little friend, Helen, very troublesome when you read this letter; but I am sure you will not blame me when I tell you that I am very anxious about something. You remember teacher and I told you Sunday that I wanted to have a little tea in aid of the kindergarten. We thought everything was arranged: but we found Monday that Mrs. Elliott would not be willing to let us invite more than fifty people, because Mrs. Howe's house is quite small. I am sure that a great many people would like to come to the tea, and help me do something to brighten the lives of little blind children; but some of my friends say that I shall have to give up the idea of having a tea unless we can find another house. Teacher said yesterday, that perhaps Mrs. Spaulding would be willing to let us have her beautiful house, and [I] thought I would ask you about it. Do you think Mrs. Spaulding would help me, if I wrote to her? I shall be so disappointed if my little plans fail, because I have wanted for a long time to do something for the poor little ones who are waiting to enter the kindergarten. Please let me know what you think about the house, and try to forgive me for troubling you so much.

Lovingly your little friend,
HELEN KELLER.

TO MR. EDWARD H. CLEMENT

SOUTH BOSTON, May 18th, 1892.

My dear Mr. Clement:—I am going to write to you this beautiful morning because my heart is brimful of happiness and I want you and all my dear friends in the *Transcript* office to rejoice with me. The preparations for my tea are nearly completed, and I am looking forward joyfully to the event. I know I shall not fail. Kind people will not disappoint me, when they know that I plead for helpless little children who live in darkness and ignorance. They will come to my tea and buy light,—the beautiful light of knowledge and love for many little ones who are blind and friendless. I remember perfectly when my dear teacher came to me. Then I was like the little blind children who are waiting to enter the kindergarten. There was no light in my soul. This wonderful world with all its sunlight and beauty was hidden from me, and I had never dreamed of its loveliness. But teacher came to me and taught my little fingers to use the beautiful key that has unlocked the door of my dark prison and set my spirit free.

It is my earnest wish to share my happiness with others, and I ask the kind people of Boston to help me make the lives of little blind children brighter and happier.

Lovingly your little friend,
HELEN KELLER.

At the end of June Miss Sullivan and Helen went home to Tuscumbia.

TO MISS CAROLINE DERBY

TUSCUMBIA, ALABAMA, July 9th 1892.

My dear Carrie—You are to look upon it as a most positive proof of my love that I write to you to-day. For a whole week it has been "cold and dark and dreary" in Tuscumbia, and I must confess the continuous rain and dismalness of the weather fills me with gloomy thoughts and makes the writing of letters, or any pleasant employment, seem quite impossible. Nevertheless, I must tell you that we are alive,—that we reached home safely, and that we speak of you daily, and enjoy your interesting letters very much. I had a beautiful visit at Hulton. Everything was fresh and spring-like, and we stayed out of doors all day. We even ate our breakfast out on the piazza. Sometimes we sat in the hammock, and teacher read to me. I rode horseback nearly every evening and once I rode five miles at a fast gallop. O, it was great fun! Do you like to ride? I have a very pretty little cart now, and if it ever stops raining teacher and I are going to drive every evening. And I have another beautiful Mastiff—the largest one I ever saw—and he will go along to protect us. His name is Eumer. A queer name, is it not? I think it is Saxon. We expect to go to the mountains next week. My little brother, Phillips, is not well, and we think the clear mountain air will benefit him. Mildred is a sweet little sister and I am sure you would love her. I thank you very much for your photograph. I like to have my friends' pictures even though I cannot see them. I was greatly amused at the idea of your writing the square hand. I do not write on a Braille tablet, as you suppose, but on a grooved board like the piece which I enclose. You could not read Braille; for it is written in dots, not at all like ordinary letters. Please give my love to Miss Derby and tell her that I hope she gave my sweetest love to Baby Ruth. What was the book you sent me for my birthday? I received several, and I do not know which was from you. I had one gift which especially pleased me. It was a lovely cape crocheted, for me, by an old gentleman, seventy-five years of age. And every stitch, he writes, represents a kind wish for my health and happiness. Tell your little cousins I think they had better get upon the fence with me until after the election; for there are so many parties and candidates that I doubt if such youthful politicians would make a wise selection. Please give my love to Rosy when you write, and believe me,

Your loving friend
HELEN KELLER.

P. S. How do you like this type-written letter?

H. K.

TO MRS. GROVER CLEVELAND

My dear Mrs. Cleveland,

I am going to write you a little letter this beautiful morning because I love you and dear little Ruth very much indeed, and also because I wish to thank you for the loving message which you sent me through Miss Derby. I am glad, very glad that such a kind, beautiful lady loves me. I have loved you for a long time, but I did not think you had ever heard of me until your sweet message came. Please kiss your dear little baby for me, and tell her I have a little brother nearly sixteen months old. His name is Phillips Brooks. I named him myself after my dear friend Phillips Brooks. I send you with this letter a pretty book which my teacher thinks will interest you, and my picture. Please accept them with the love and good wishes of your friend,

HELEN KELLER.

TUSCUMBIA, ALABAMA.
November fourth. [1892.]

Hitherto the letters have been given in full; from this point on passages are omitted and the omissions are indicated.

TO MR. JOHN HITZ

TUSCUMBIA, ALABAMA, Dec. 19, 1892.
My Dear Mr. Hitz,

I hardly know how to begin a letter to you, it has been such a long time since your kind letter reached me, and there is so much that I would like to write if I could. You must have wondered why your letter has not had an answer, and perhaps you have thought Teacher and me very naughty indeed. If so, you will be very sorry when I tell you something. Teacher's eyes have been hurting her so that she could not write to any one, and I have been trying to fulfil a promise which I made last summer. Before I left Boston, I was asked to write a sketch of my life for the *Youth's Companion*. I had intended to write the sketch during my vacation: but I was not well, and I did not feel able to write even to my friends. But when the bright, pleasant autumn days came, and I felt strong again I began to think about the sketch. It was some time before I could plan it to suit me. You see, it is not very pleasant to write all about one's self. At last, however, I got something bit by bit that Teacher thought would do, and I set about putting the scraps together, which was not an easy task: for, although I worked some on it every day, I did not finish it until a week ago Saturday. I sent the sketch to the *Companion* as soon as it was finished; but I do not know that they will accept it. Since then, I have not been well, and I have been obliged to keep very quiet, and rest; but to-day I am better, and to-morrow I shall be well again, I hope.

The reports which you have read in the paper about me are not true at all. We received the *Silent Worker* which you sent, and I wrote right away to the editor to tell him that it was a mistake. Sometimes I am not well; but I am not a "wreck," and there is nothing "distressing" about my condition.

I enjoyed your dear letter so much! I am always delighted when anyone writes me a beautiful thought which I can treasure in my memory forever. It is because my books are full of the riches of which Mr. Ruskin speaks that I love them so dearly. I did not realize until I began to write the sketch for the *Companion*, what precious companions books have been to me, and how blessed even my life has been: and now I am happier than ever because I do realize the happiness that has come to me. I hope you will write to me as often as you can. Teacher and I are always delighted to hear from you. I want to write to Mr. Bell and send him my picture. I suppose he has been too busy to write to his little friend. I often think of the pleasant time we had all together in Boston last spring.

Now I am going to tell you a secret. I think we, Teacher, and my father and little sister, and myself, will visit Washington next March!!! Then I shall see you, and dear Mr. Bell, and Elsie and Daisy again! Would not it be lovely if Mrs. Pratt could meet us there? I think I will write to her and tell her the secret too. . . .

Lovingly your little friend,

HELEN KELLER.

P. S. Teacher says you want to know what kind of a pet I would like to have. I love all living things, —I suppose everyone does; but of course I cannot have a menagerie. I have a beautiful pony, and a large dog. And I would like a little dog to hold in my lap, or a big pussy (there are no fine cats in Tuscumbia) or a parrot. I would like to feel a parrot talk, it would be so much fun! but I would be pleased with, and love any little creature you send me.

H. K.

TO MISS CAROLINE DERBY

TUSCUMBIA, ALABAMA, February 18, 1893.
. . . You have often been in my thoughts during these sad days, while my heart has been grieving

over the loss of my beloved friend,* and I have
wished many times that I was in Boston with those
who knew and loved him as I did . . . he was
so much of a friend to me! so tender and loving
always! I do try not to mourn his death too sadly.
I do try to think that he is still near, very near; but
sometimes the thought that he is not here, that I
shall not see him when I go to Boston,—that he
is gone,—rushes over my soul like a great wave of
sorrow. But at other times, when I am happier, I
do feel his beautiful presence, and his loving hand
leading me in pleasant ways. Do you remember
the happy hour we spent with him last June when
he held my hand, as he always did, and talked to us
about his friend Tennyson, and our own dear poet
Dr. Holmes, and I tried to teach him the manual
alphabet, and he laughed so gaily over his mistakes,
and afterward I told him about my tea, and he
promised to come? I can hear him now, saying in
his cheerful, decided way, in reply to my wish that
my tea might be a success, "Of course it will, Helen.
Put your whole heart in the good work, my child,
and it cannot fail." I am glad the people are going
to raise a monument to his memory. . . .

In March Helen and Miss Sullivan went North,
and spent the next few months traveling and visiting friends.

In reading this letter about Niagara one should
remember that Miss Keller knows distance and
shape, and that the size of Niagara is within her

* Phillips Brooks, died January 23, 1893.

experience after she has explored it, crossed the bridge and gone down in the elevator. Especially important are such details as her feeling the rush of the water by putting her hand on the window. Dr. Bell gave her a down pillow, which she held against her to increase the vibrations.

TO MRS. KATE ADAMS KELLER

South Boston, April 13, 1893.

. . . Teacher, Mrs. Pratt and I very unexpectedly decided to take a journey with dear Dr. Bell   Mr. Westervelt, a gentleman whom father met in Washington, has a school for the deaf in Rochester. We went there first. . . .

Mr. Westervelt gave us a reception one afternoon. A great many people came. Some of them asked odd questions. A lady seemed surprised that I loved flowers when I could not see their beautiful colors, and when I assured her I did love them, she said, "no doubt you feel the colors with your fingers." But of course, it is not alone for their bright colors that we love the flowers. . . . A gentleman asked me what *beauty* meant to my mind. I must confess I was puzzled at first. But after a minute I answered that beauty was a form of goodness—and he went away.

When the reception was over we went back to the hotel and teacher slept quite unconscious of the surprise which was in store for her. Mr. Bell and I planned it together, and Mr. Bell made all the arrangements before we told teacher anything

about it. This was the surprise—I was to have
the pleasure of taking my dear teacher to see
Niagara Falls! . . .

The hotel was so near the river that I could feel
it rushing past by putting my hand on the window.
The next morning the sun rose bright and warm,
and we got up quickly for our hearts were full
of pleasant expectation. . . . You can never imagine how I felt when I stood in the presence of
Niagara until you have the same mysterious sensations yourself. I could hardly realize that it was
water that I felt rushing and plunging with impetuous fury at my feet. It seemed as if it were some
living thing rushing on to some terrible fate. I wish
I could describe the cataract as it is, its beauty and
awful grandeur, and the fearful and irresistible
plunge of its waters over the brow of the precipice.
One feels helpless and overwhelmed in the presence
of such a vast force. I had the same feeling once
before when I first stood by the great ocean and felt
its waves beating against the shore. I suppose you
feel so, too, when you gaze up to the stars in the
stillness of the night, do you not? . . . We went
down a hundred and twenty feet in an elevator that
we might see the violent eddies and whirlpools in
the deep gorge below the Falls. Within two miles
of the Falls is a wonderful suspension bridge. It is
thrown across the gorge at a height of two hundred
and fifty-eight feet above the water and is supported on each bank by towers of solid rock, which
are eight hundred feet apart. When we crossed
over to the Canadian side, I cried, "God save the
Queen!" Teacher said I was a little traitor. But
I do not think so. I was only doing as the

Canadians do, while I was in their country, and besides I honor England's good queen.

You will be pleased, dear Mother, to hear that a kind lady whose name is Miss Hooker is endeavoring to improve my speech.   Oh, I do so hope and pray that I shall speak well some day! . . .

Mr. Munsell spent last Sunday evening with us. How you would have enjoyed hearing him tell about Venice!   His beautiful word-pictures made us feel as if we were sitting in the shadow of San Marco, dreaming, or sailing upon the moonlit canal. . . . I hope when I visit Venice, as I surely shall some day, that Mr. Munsell will go with me.   That is my castle in the air.   You see, none of my friends describe things to me so vividly and so beautifully as he does. . . .

Her visit to the World's Fair she described in a letter to Mr. John P. Spaulding, which was published in *St. Nicholas,* and is much like the following letter.   In a prefatory note which Miss Sullivan wrote for *St. Nicholas,* she says that people frequently said to her, "Helen sees more with her fingers than we do with our eyes."   The President of the Exposition gave her this letter:

To the Chiefs of the Departments and Officers in charge of Buildings and Exhibits

GENTLEMEN—The bearer, Miss Helen Keller, accompanied by Miss Sullivan, is desirous of making a complete inspection of the Exposition in all

Departments. She is blind and deaf, but is able to converse, and is introduced to me as one having a wonderful ability to understand the objects she visits, and as being possessed of a high order of intelligence and of culture beyond her years. Please favour her with every facility to examine the exhibits in the several Departments, and extend to her such other courtesies as may be possible.

Thanking you in advance for the same, I am, with respect,

Very truly yours,
(signed) H. N. HIGINBOTHAM,
President.

TO MISS CAROLINE DERBY

HULTON, PENN., August 17, 1893.

. . . Every one at the Fair was very kind to me . . . Nearly all of the exhibitors seemed perfectly willing to let me touch the most delicate things, and they were very nice about explaining everything to me. A French gentleman, whose name I cannot remember, showed me the great French bronzes. I believe they gave me more pleasure than anything else at the Fair: they were so lifelike and wonderful to my touch. Dr. Bell went with us himself to the electrical building, and showed us some of the historical telephones. I saw the one through which Emperor Dom Pedro listened to the words, "To be, or not to be," at the Centennial. Dr. Gillett of Illinois took us to the Liberal Arts and Woman's buildings. In the former I visited Tiffany's exhibit, and held the beautiful Tiffany diamond, which is valued at one hundred thousand dollars, and touched many other rare and costly things. I sat in King Ludwig's armchair and felt like a queen when Dr. Gillett remarked that I had many loyal subjects. At the Woman's building we met the Princess Maria Schaovskoy of Russia, and a beautiful Syrian lady. I liked them both very much. I went to the Japanese department with Prof. Morse who is a well-known lecturer. I never realized what a wonderful people the Japanese are until I saw their most interesting exhibit. Japan must indeed be a paradise for children to judge from the great number of playthings which are manufactured there. The queer-looking Japanese musical instruments, and their beautiful works of art were interesting. The Japanese books are very odd. There are forty-seven letters in their alphabets. Prof. Morse knows a great deal about Japan, and is very kind and wise. He invited me to visit his museum in Salem the next time I go to Boston. But I think I enjoyed the sails on the tranquil lagoon, and the lovely scenes, as my friends described them to me, more than anything else at the Fair. Once, while we were out on the water, the sun went down over the rim of the earth, and threw a soft, rosy light over the White City, making it look more than ever like Dreamland. . . .

Of course, we visited the Midway Plaisance. It was a bewildering and fascinating place. I went into the streets of Cairo, and rode on the camel. That was fine fun. We also rode in the Ferris wheel, and on the ice-railway, and had a sail in the Whaleback. . . .

In the spring of 1893 a club was started in Tuscumbia, of which Mrs. Keller was president, to establish a public library.　Miss Keller says:

"I wrote to my friends about the work and enlisted their sympathy.　Several hundred books, including many fine ones, were sent to me in a short time, as well as money and encouragement.　This generous assistance encouraged the ladies, and they have gone on collecting and buying books ever since, until now they have a very respectable public library in the town."

TO MRS. CHARLES E. INCHES

HULTON, PENN., Oct. 21, 1893.
. . . We spent September at home in Tuscumbia . . . and were all very happy together. . . . Our quiet mountain home was especially attractive and restful after the excitement and fatigue of our visit to the World's Fair.　We enjoyed the beauty and solitude of the hills more than ever.

And now we are in Hulton, Penn. again where I am going to study this winter with a tutor assisted by my dear teacher.　I study Arithmetic, Latin and literature.　I enjoy my lessons very much.　It is so pleasant to learn about new things.　Every day I find how little I know, but I do not feel discouraged since God has given me an eternity in which to learn more.　In literature I am studying Longfellow's poetry.　I know a great deal of it by heart, for I loved it long before I knew a metaphor from a synecdoche.　I used to say I did not like arithmetic very well, but now I have changed my mind.

I see what a good and useful study it is, though I must confess my mind wanders from it sometimes! for, nice and useful as arithmetic is, it is not as interesting as a beautiful poem or a lovely story. But bless me, how time does fly. I have only a few moments left in which to answer your questions about the "Helen Keller" Public Library.

1. I think there are about 3,000 people in Tuscumbia, Ala., and perhaps half of them are colored people. 2. At present there is no library of any sort in the town. That is why I thought about starting one. My mother and several of my lady friends said they would help me, and they formed a club, the object of which is to work for the establishment of a free public library in Tuscumbia. They have now about 100 books and about $55 in money, and a kind gentleman has given us land on which to erect a library building. But in the meantime the club has rented a little room in a central part of the town, and the books which we already have are free to all. 3. Only a few of my kind friends in Boston know anything about the library. I did not like to trouble them while I was trying to get money for poor little Tommy; for of course it was more important that he should be educated than that my people should have books to read. 4. I do not know what books we have, but I think it is a miscellaneous (I think that is the word) collection. . . .

P. S.   My teacher thinks it would be more businesslike to say that a list of the contributors toward the building fund will be kept and published in my father's paper, the "North Alabamian."

H. K.

TO MISS CAROLINE DERBY

HULTON, PENN., December 28, 1893.
. . . Please thank dear Miss Derby for me for the pretty shield which she sent me. It is a very interesting souvenir of Columbus, and of the Fair White City; but I cannot imagine what discoveries I have made,—I mean new discoveries. We are all discoverers in one sense, being born quite ignorant of all things; but I hardly think that is what she meant. Tell her she must explain why I am a discoverer. . . .

TO DR. EDWARD EVERETT HALE

HULTON, PENNSYLVANIA, January 14, [1894].
My dear Cousin: I had thought to write to you long before this in answer to your kind letter which I was so glad to receive, and to thank you for the beautiful little book which you sent me; but I have been very busy since the beginning of the New Year. The publication of my little story in the *Youth's Companion* has brought me a large number of letters,—last week I received sixty-one!—and besides replying to some of these letters, I have many lessons to learn, among them Arithmetic and Latin; and, you know, Cæsar is Cæsar still, imperious and tyrannical, and if a little girl would understand so great a man, and the wars and conquests of which he tells in his beautiful Latin language, she must study much and think much, and study and thought require time.

I shall prize the little book always, not only for its own value; but because of its associations with you. It is a delight to think of you as the giver of one of your books into which, I am sure, you have wrought your own thoughts and feelings, and I thank you very much for remembering me in such a very beautiful way. . . .

In February Helen and Miss Sullivan returned to Tuscumbia. They spent the rest of the spring reading and studying. In the summer they attended the meeting at Chautauqua of the American Association for the Promotion of the Teaching of Speech to the Deaf, where Miss Sullivan read a paper on Helen Keller's education.

In the fall Helen and Miss Sullivan entered the Wright-Humason School in New York, which makes a specialty of lip-reading and voice-culture. The "singing lessons" were to strengthen her voice. She had taken a few piano lessons at the Perkins Institution. The experiment was interesting, but of course came to little.

TO MISS CAROLINE DERBY

THE WRIGHT-HUMASON SCHOOL.
42 West 76th St.
NEW YORK. Oct. 23, 1894.

. . . The school is very pleasant, and bless you! it is quite fashionable. . . . I study Arithmetic, English Literature and United States History as I did last winter. I also keep a diary.

I enjoy my singing lessons with Dr. Humason more
than I can say.　I expect to take piano lessons sometime. . . . .

Last Saturday our kind teachers planned a
delightful trip to Bedloe's Island to see Bartholdi's
great statue of Liberty enlightening the world.
. . . The ancient cannon, which look seaward,
wear a very menacing expression; but I doubt if
there is any unkindness in their rusty old hearts.

Liberty is a gigantic figure of a woman in Greek
draperies, holding in her right hand a torch. . . .
A spiral stairway leads from the base of this pedestal
to the torch.　We climbed up to the head which
will hold forty persons, and viewed the scene on
which Liberty gazes day and night, and O, how
wonderful it was! We did not wonder that the great
French artist thought the place worthy to be the
home of his grand ideal.　The glorious bay lay calm
and beautiful in the October sunshine, and the ships
came and went like idle dreams; those seaward going
slowly disappeared like clouds that change from
gold to gray; those homeward coming sped more
quickly like birds that seek their mother's nest. . . .

TO MISS CAROLINE DERBY

THE WRIGHT-HUMASON SCHOOL.
NEW YORK, March 15, 1895.
. . . I think I have improved a little in lip-
reading, though I still find it very difficult to read
rapid speech; but I am sure I shall succeed some day
if I only persevere.　Dr. Humason is still trying to

improve my speech. Oh, Carrie, how I should like to speak like other people! I should be willing to work night and day if it could only be accomplished. Think what a joy it would be to all of my friends to hear me speak naturally!! I wonder why it is so difficult and perplexing for a deaf child to learn to speak when it is so easy for other people; but I am sure I shall speak perfectly some time if I am only patient. . . .

Although I have been so busy, I have found time to read a good deal. . . . I have lately read "Wilhelm Tell" by Schiller, and "The Lost Vestal." . . . Now I am reading "Nathan the Wise" by Lessing and "King Arthur" by Miss Mulock.

. . . You know our kind teachers take us to see everything which they think will interest us, and we learn a great deal in that delightful way. On George Washington's birthday we all went to the Dog Show, and although there was a great crowd in the Madison Square Garden, and despite the bewilderment caused by the variety of sounds made by the dog-orchestra, which was very confusing to those who could hear them, we enjoyed the afternoon very much. Among the dogs which received the most attention were the bull-dogs. They permitted themselves startling liberties when any one caressed them, crowding themselves almost into one's arms and helping themselves without ceremony to kisses, apparently unconscious of the impropriety of their conduct. Dear me, what unbeautiful little beasts they are! But they are so good natured and friendly, one cannot help liking them.

Dr. Humason, Teacher, and I left the others at the Dog Show and went to a reception given by the

"Metropolitan Club." . . . It is sometimes called the "Millionaires' Club." The building is magnificent, being built of white marble; the rooms are large and splendidly furnished; but I must confess, so much splendor is rather oppressive to me; and I didn't envy the millionaires in the least all the happiness their gorgeous surroundings are supposed to bring them. . . .

TO MRS. KATE ADAMS KELLER

NEW YORK, March 31, 1895.

. . . Teacher and I spent the afternoon at Mr. Hutton's, and had a most delightful time! . . . We met Mr. Clemens and Mr. Howells there! I had known about them for a long time; but I had never thought that I should see them, and talk to them; and I can scarcely realize now that this great pleasure has been mine! But, much as I wonder that I, only a little girl of fourteen, should come in contact with so many distinguished people, I do realize that I am a very happy child, and very grateful for the many beautiful privileges I have enjoyed. The two distinguished authors were very gentle and kind, and I could not tell which of them I loved best. Mr. Clemens told us many entertaining stories, and made us laugh till we cried. I only wish you could have seen and heard him! He told us that he would go to Europe in a few days to bring his wife and his daughter, Jeanne, back to America, because Jeanne, who is studying in Paris, has learned so much in three years and a half that if he did not bring her home, she would soon know more than he did. I think Mark Twain is a very appropriate *nom de plume* for Mr. Clemens because it has a funny and quaint sound, and goes well with his amusing writings, and its nautical significance suggests the deep and beautiful things that he has written. I think he is very handsome indeed. . . . Teacher said she thought he looked something like Paradeuski. (If that is the way to spell the name.) Mr. Howells told me a little about Venice, which is one of his favorite cities, and spoke very tenderly of his dear little girl, Winnifred, who is now with God. He has another daughter, named Mildred, who knows Carrie. I might have seen Mrs. Wiggin, the sweet author of "Birds' Christmas Carol," but she had a dangerous cough and could not come. I was much disappointed not to see her; but I hope I shall have that pleasure some other time. Mr. Hutton gave me a lovely little glass, shaped like a thistle, which belonged to his dear mother, as a souvenir of my delightful visit. We also met Mr. Rogers . . . who kindly left his carriage to bring us home.

When the Wright-Humason School closed for the summer, Miss Sullivan and Helen went South.

TO MRS. LAURENCE HUTTON

Tuscumbia, Alabama, July 29, 1895.
. . . I am spending my vacation very quietly and pleasantly at my beautiful, sunny home, with

my loving parents, my darling little sister and my small brother, Phillips My precious teacher is with me too, and so of course I am happy I read a little, walk a little, write a little and play with the children a great deal, and the days slip by delightfully! . . .

My friends are so pleased with the improvement which I made in speech and lip-reading last year, that it has been decided best for me to continue my studies in New York another year I am delighted at the prospect of spending another year in your great city I used to think that I should never feel "at home" in New York; but since I have made the acquaintance of so many people, and can look back to such a bright and successful winter there, I find myself looking forward to next year, and anticipating still brighter and better times in the Metropolis

Please give my kindest love to Mr Hutton, and Mrs Riggs and Mr Warner too, although I have never had the pleasure of knowing him personally As I listen Venicewards, I hear Mr Hutton's pen dancing over the pages of his new book It is a pleasant sound because it is full of promise How much I shall enjoy reading it!

Please pardon me, my dear Mrs Hutton, for sending you a typewritten letter across the ocean I have tried several times to write with a pencil on my little writing machine since I came home; but I have found it very difficult to do so on account of the heat The moisture of my hand soils and blurs the paper so dreadfully, that I am compelled to use my typewriter altogether And it is not my "Remington" either, but a naughty little thing that gets

out of order on the slightest provocation, and cannot be induced to make a period . . .

TO MRS. WILLIAM THAW

NEW YORK, October 16, 1895.
Here we are once more in the great metropolis!
We left Hulton Friday night and arrived here
Saturday morning. Our friends were greatly surprised to see us, as they had not expected us before
the last of this month. I rested Saturday afternoon, for I was very tired, and Sunday I visited with
my schoolmates, and now that I feel quite rested, I
am going to write to you; for I know you will want
to hear that we reached New York safely. We
had to change cars at Philadelphia; but we did not
mind it much. After we had had our breakfast,
Teacher asked one of the train-men in the station if
the New York train was made up. He said no, it
would not be called for about fifteen minutes; so
we sat down to wait; but in a moment the man came
back and asked Teacher if we would like to go to
the train at once. She said we would, and he took
us way out on the track and put us on board our
train. Thus we avoided the rush and had a nice
quiet visit before the train started. Was that not
very kind? So it always is. Some one is ever
ready to scatter little acts of kindness along our
pathway, making it smooth and pleasant . . .
We had a quiet but very pleasant time in Hulton.
Mr. Wade is just as dear and good as ever! He has
lately had several books printed in England for me,

"Old Mortality," "The Castle of Otranto" and "King of No-land." . . .

TO MISS CAROLINE DERBY

NEW YORK, December 29, 1895.

. . . Teacher and I have been very gay of late. We have seen our kind friends, Mrs. Dodge, Mr. and Mrs. Hutton, Mrs. Riggs and her husband, and met many distinguished people, among whom were Miss Ellen Terry, Sir Henry Irving and Mr. Stockton! Weren't we very fortunate? Miss Terry was lovely. She kissed Teacher and said, "I do not know whether I am glad to see you or not; for I feel so ashamed of myself when I think of how much you have done for the little girl." We also met Mr. and Mrs. Terry, Miss Terry's brother and his wife. I thought her beauty angellic, and oh, what a clear, beautiful voice she had! We saw Miss Terry again with Sir Henry in "King Charles the First," a week ago last Friday, and after the play they kindly let me feel of them and get an idea of how they looked. How noble and kingly the King was, especially in his misfortunes! And how pretty and faithful the poor Queen was! The play seemed so real, we almost forgot where we were, and believed we were watching the genuine scenes as they were acted so long ago. The last act affected us most deeply, and we all wept, wondering how the executioner could have the heart to tear the King from his loving wife's arms.

I have just finished reading "Ivanhoe." It was very exciting; but I must say I did not enjoy it very much. Sweet Rebecca, with her strong, brave spirit and her pure, generous nature, was the only character which thoroughly won my admiration. Now I am reading "Stories from Scottish History," and they are very thrilling and absorbing! . . .

The next two letters were written just after the death of Mr. John P. Spaulding.

TO MRS. GEORGE H. BRADFORD

NEW YORK, February 4, 1896.

What can I say which will make you understand how much Teacher and I appreciate your thoughtful kindness in sending us those little souvenirs of the dear room where we first met the best and kindest of friends? Indeed, you can never know all the comfort you have given us. We have put the dear picture on the mantel-piece in our room where we can see it every day, and I often go and touch it, and somehow I cannot help feeling that our beloved friend is very near to me. . . . It was very hard to take up our school work again, as if nothing had happened; but I am sure it is well that we have duties which must be done, and which take our minds away for a time at least from our sorrow. . . .

TO MISS CAROLINE DERBY

NEW YORK, March 2nd, 1896.

. . . We miss dear King John sadly. It was so hard to lose him, he was the best and kindest of friends, and I do not know what we shall do without him. . . .

We went to a poultry-show . . . and the man there kindly permitted us to feel of the birds. They were so tame, they stood perfectly still when I handled them. I saw great big turkeys, geese, guineas, ducks and many others.

Almost two weeks ago we called at Mr. Hutton's and had a delightful time. We always do! We met Mr. Warner, the writer, Mr. Mabie, the editor of the *Outlook* and other pleasant people. I am sure you would like to know Mr. and Mrs. Hutton, they are so kind and interesting. I can never tell you how much pleasure they have given us.

Mr. Warner and Mr. Burroughs, the great lover of nature, came to see us a few days after, and we had a delightful talk with them. They were both very, very dear! Mr. Burroughs told me about his home near the Hudson, and what a happy place it must be! I hope we shall visit it some day. Teacher has read me his lively stories about his boyhood, and I enjoyed them greatly. Have you read the beautiful poem, "Waiting"? I know it, and it makes me feel so happy, it has such sweet thoughts. Mr. Warner showed me a scarf-pin with a beetle on it which was made in Egypt fifteen hundred years before Christ, and told me that the beetle meant immortality to the Egyptians because it wrapped itself up and went to sleep and came out again in a new form, thus renewing itself.

TO MISS CAROLINE DERBY

NEW YORK, April 25, 1896.

. . . My studies are the same as they were when I saw you, except that I have taken up French with a French teacher who comes three times a week. I read her lips almost exclusively, (she does not know the manual alphabet) and we get on quite well. I have read "Le Médecin Malgré Lui," a very good French comedy by Molière, with pleasure; and they say I speak French pretty well now, and German also. Anyway, French and German people understand what I am trying to say, and that is very encouraging. In voice-training I have still the same old difficulties to contend against; and the fulfilment of my wish to speak well seems O, so far away! Sometimes I feel sure that I catch a faint glimpse of the goal I am striving for; but in another minute a bend in the road hides it from my view, and I am again left wandering in the dark! But I try hard not to be discouraged. Surely we shall all find at last the ideals we are seeking. . . .

TO MR. JOHN HITZ

BREWSTER, MASS. July 15, 1896.

. . . As to the book, I am sure I shall enjoy it very much when I am admitted, by the magic of Teacher's dear fingers, into the companionship of the two sisters who went to the Immortal Fountain.

As I sit by the window writing to you, it is so lovely to have the soft, cool breezes fan my cheek, and to feel that the hard work of last year is over! Teacher seems to feel benefitted by the change too; for she is already beginning to look like her dear old self. We only need you, dear Mr. Hitz, to complete our happiness. Teacher and Mrs. Hopkins both say you *must* come as soon as you can! We will try to make you comfortable.

Teacher and I spent nine days at Philadelphia. Have you ever been at Dr. Crouter's Institution? Mr. Howes has probably given you a full account of our doings. We were busy all the time; we attended the meetings and talked with hundreds of people, among whom were dear Dr. Bell, Mr. Banerji of Calcutta, Monsieur Magnat of Paris with whom I conversed in French exclusively, and many other distinguished persons. We had looked forward to seeing you there, and so we were greatly disappointed that you did not come. We think of you so, so often! and our hearts go out to you in tenderest sympathy; and you know better than this poor letter can tell you how happy we always are to have you with us! I made a "speech" on July eighth, telling the members of the Association what an unspeakable blessing speech has been to me, and urging them to give every little deaf child an opportunity to learn to speak.* Every one said I spoke very well and intelligibly. After my little "speech," we attended a reception at which over six hundred people were present. I must confess I do not like such large receptions; the people crowd so, and we have to do so much talking; and yet it is at receptions like the one in Philadelphia that we often meet friends whom we learn to love afterwards. We left the city

*See page 392.

last Thursday night, and arrived in Brewster Friday afternoon.   We missed the Cape Cod train Friday morning, and so we came down to Province-town in the steamer *Longfellow*.   I am glad we did so; for it was lovely and cool on the water, and Boston Harbor is always interesting.

We spent about three weeks in Boston, after leaving New York, and I need not tell you we had a most delightful time.   We visited our good friends, Mr. and Mrs. Chamberlin, at Wrentham, out in the country, where they have a lovely home.   Their house stands near a charming lake where we went boating and canoeing, which was great fun.   We also went in bathing several times.   Mr. and Mrs. Chamberlin celebrated the 17th of June by giving a picnic to their literary friends.   There were about forty persons present, all of whom were writers and publishers.   Our friend, Mr. Alden, the editor of *Harper's* was there, and of course we enjoyed his society very much. . . .

TO CHARLES DUDLEY WARNER

BREWSTER, MASS., September 3, 1896.
. . . I have been meaning to write to you all summer; there were many things I wanted to tell you, and I thought perhaps you would like to hear about our vacation by the seaside, and our plans for next year; but the happy, idle days slipped away so quickly, and there were so many pleasant things to do every moment, that I never found time to clothe my thought in words, and send them to you.   I

wonder what becomes of lost opportunities. Perhaps our guardian angel gathers them up as we drop them, and will give them back to us in the beautiful sometime when we have grown wiser, and learned how to use them rightly. But, however this may be, I cannot now write the letter which has lain in my thought for you so long. My heart is too full of sadness to dwell upon the happiness the summer has brought me. My father is dead. He died last Saturday at my home in Tuscumbia, and I was not there. My own dear loving father! Oh, dear friend, how shall I ever bear it! . . .

On the first of October Miss Keller entered the Cambridge School for Young Ladies, of which Mr. Arthur Gilman is Principal. The "examinations" mentioned in this letter were merely tests given in the school, but as they were old Harvard papers, it is evident that in some subjects Miss Keller was already fairly well prepared for Radcliffe.

TO MRS. LAURENCE HUTTON

37 CONCORD AVENUE, CAMBRIDGE, MASS.
                              October 8, 1896.
. . . I got up early this morning, so that I could write you a few lines. I know you want to hear how I like my school. I do wish you could come and see for yourself what a beautiful school it is! There are about a hundred girls, and they are all so bright and happy; it is a joy to be with them.

You will be glad to hear that I passed my examinations successfully.   I have been examined in English, German, French, and Greek and Roman history. They were the entrance examinations for Harvard College; so I feel pleased to think I could pass them. This year is going to be a very busy one for Teacher and myself.   I am studying Arithmetic, English Literature, English History, German, Latin, and advanced geography; there is a great deal of preparatory reading required, and, as few of the books are in raised print, poor Teacher has to spell them all out to me; and that means hard work.

You must tell Mr. Howells when you see him, that we are living in his house. . . .

TO MRS. WILLIAM THAW

37 CONCORD AVENUE, CAMBRIDGE, MASS.,
December 2, 1896.

. . . It takes me a long time to prepare my lessons, because I have to have every word of them spelled out in my hand.   Not one of the text-books which I am obliged to use is in raised print; so of course my work is harder than it would be if I could read my lessons over by myself.   But it is harder for Teacher than it is for me because the strain on her poor eyes is so great, and I cannot help worrying about them.   Sometimes it really seems as if the task which we have set ourselves were more than we can accomplish; but at other times I enjoy my work more than I can say.

It is such a delight to be with the other girls, and

do everything that they do.　I study Latin, German, Arithmetic and English History, all of which I enjoy except Arithmetic.　I am afraid I have not a mathematical mind; for my figures always manage to get into the wrong places! . . .

TO MRS. LAURENCE HUTTON

CAMBRIDGE, MASS., May 3, 1897.
. . . You know I am trying very hard to get through with the reading for the examinations in June, and this, in addition to my regular school-work keeps me awfully busy.　But Johnson, and "The Plague" and everything else must wait a few minutes this afternoon, while I say, thank you, my dear Mrs. Hutton. . . .
. . . What a splendid time we had at the "Players' Club."　I always thought clubs were dull, smoky places, where men talked politics, and told endless stories, all about themselves and their wonderful exploits: but now I see, I must have been quite wrong. . . .

TO MR. JOHN HITZ

WRENTHAM, MASS. July 9, 1897.
. . . Teacher and I are going to spend the summer at Wrentham, Mass. with our friends, the Chamberlins.　I think you remember Mr. Chamberlin, the "Listener" in the *Boston Transcript*.　They are dear, kind people. . . .

But I know you want to hear about my examinations. I know that you will be glad to hear that I passed all of them successfully. The subjects I offered were elementary and advanced German, French, Latin, English, and Greek and Roman History. It seems almost too good to be true, does it not? All the time I was preparing for the great ordeal, I could not suppress an inward fear and trembling lest I should fail, and now it is an unspeakable relief to know that I have passed the examinations with credit. But what I consider my crown of success is the happiness and pleasure that my victory has brought dear Teacher. Indeed, I feel that the success is hers more than mine; for she is my constant inspiration. . . .

At the end of September Miss Sullivan and Miss Keller returned to the Cambridge School, where they remained until early in December. Then the interference of Mr. Gilman resulted in Mrs. Keller's withdrawing Miss Helen and her sister, Miss Mildred, from the school. Miss Sullivan and her pupil went to Wrentham, where they worked under Mr. Merton S. Keith, an enthusiastic and skilful teacher.

TO MRS. LAURENCE HUTTON

WRENTHAM, February 20, 1898.
. . . I resumed my studies soon after your departure, and in a very little while we were working as merrily as if the dreadful experience of a

month ago had been but a dream. I cannot tell you how much I enjoy the country. It is so fresh, and peaceful and free! I do think I could work all day long without feeling tired if they would let me. There are so many pleasant things to do—not always very easy things,—much of my work in Algebra and Geometry is hard: but I love it all, especially Greek. Just think, I shall soon finish my grammar! Then comes the "Iliad." What an inexpressible joy it will be to read about Achilles, and Ulysses, and Andromache and Athene, and the rest of my old friends in their own glorious language!! I think Greek is the loveliest language that I know anything about. If it is true that the violin is the most perfect of musical instruments, then Greek is the violin of human thought.

We have had some splendid toboganning this month. Every morning, before lesson-time, we all go out to the steep hill on the northern shore of the lake near the house, and coast for an hour or so. Some one balances the toboggan on the very crest of the hill, while we get on, and when we are ready, off we dash down the side of the hill in a headlong rush, and, leaping a projection, plunge into a snow-drift and go skimming far across the pond at a tremendous rate! . . .

TO MRS. LAURENCE HUTTON

[WRENTHAM] April 12, 1898.
. . . I am glad Mr. Keith is so well pleased with my progress. It is true that Algebra and

Geometry are growing easier all the time, especially algebra; and I have just received books in raised print which will greatly facilitate my work. . . .

I find I get on faster, and do better work with Mr. Keith than I did in the classes at the Cambridge School, and I think it was well that I gave up that kind of work. At any rate, I have not been idle since I left school; I have accomplished more, and been happier than I could have been there. . . .

TO MRS. LAURENCE HUTTON

[WRENTHAM] May 29, 1898.
 . . . My work goes on bravely. Each day is filled to the brim with hard study; for I am anxious to accomplish as much as possible before I put away my books for the summer vacation. You will be pleased to hear that I did three problems in Geometry yesterday without assistance. Mr. Keith and Teacher were quite enthusiastic over the achievement, and I must confess, I felt somewhat elated myself. Now I feel as if I should succeed in doing something in mathematics, although I cannot see why it is so very important to know that the lines drawn from the extremities of the base of an isosceles triangle to the middle points of the opposite sides are equal! The knowledge doesn't make life any sweeter or happier, does it? On the other hand, when we learn a new word, it is the key to untold treasures. . . .

TO CHARLES DUDLEY WARNER

WRENTHAM, MASS., June 7, 1898.

I am afraid you will conclude that I am not very anxious for a tandem after all, since I have let nearly a week pass without answering your letter in regard to the kind of wheel I should like. But really, I have been so constantly occupied with my studies since we returned from New York, that I have not had time even to think of the fun it would be to have a bicycle! You see, I am anxious to accomplish as much as possible before the long summer vacation begins. I am glad, though, that it is nearly time to put away my books; for the sunshine and flowers, and the lovely lake in front of our house are doing their best to tempt me away from my Greek and Mathematics, especially from the latter! I am sure the daisies and buttercups have as little use for the science of Geometry as I, in spite of the fact that they so beautifully illustrate its principles.

But bless me, I mustn't forget the tandem! The truth is, I know very little about bicycles. I have only ridden a "sociable," which is very different from the ordinary tandem. The "sociable" is safer, perhaps, than the tandem; but it is very heavy and awkward, and has a way of taking up the greater part of the road. Besides, I have been told that "sociables" cost more than other kinds of bicycles. My teacher and other friends think I could ride a Columbia tandem in the country with perfect safety. They also think your suggestion about a fixed handlebar a good one. I ride with a divided skirt, and so does my teacher; but it would be easier for her to mount a man's wheel than for me; so, if it could be arranged to have the ladies' seat behind, I think it would be better. . . .

TO MISS CAROLINE DERBY

WRENTHAM, September 11, 1898.

. . . I am out of doors all the time, rowing, swimming, riding and doing a multitude of other pleasant things. This morning I rode over twelve miles on my tandem! I rode on a rough road, and fell off three or four times, and am now awfully lame! But the weather and the scenery were so beautiful, and it was such fun to go scooting over the smoother part of the road, I didn't mind the mishaps in the least.

I have really learned to swim and dive—after a fashion! I can swim a little under water, and do almost anything I like, without fear of getting drowned! Isn't that fine? It is almost no effort for me to row around the lake, no matter how heavy the load may be. So you can well imagine how strong and brown I am. . . .

TO MRS. LAURENCE HUTTON

12 NEWBURY STREET, BOSTON,
October 23, 1898.

This is the first opportunity I have had to write to you since we came here last Monday. We have been in such a whirl ever since we decided to come to Boston; it seemed as if we should never get settled. Poor Teacher has had her hands full, attending to movers, and express-men, and all sorts of people. I wish it were not such a bother to move, especially as we have to do it so often! . . .

. . . Mr. Keith comes here at half past three every day except Saturday. He says he prefers to come here for the present. I am reading the "Iliad," and the "Æneid" and Cicero, besides doing a lot in Geometry and Algebra. The "Iliad" is beautiful with all the truth, and grace and simplicity of a wonderfully childlike people while the "Æneid" is more stately and reserved. It is like a beautiful maiden, who always lived in a palace, surrounded by a magnificent court; while the "Iliad" is like a splendid youth, who has had the earth for his playground.

The weather has been awfully dismal all the week; but to-day is beautiful, and our room floor is flooded with sunlight. By and by we shall take a little walk in the Public Gardens. I wish the Wrentham woods were round the corner! But alas! they are not, and I shall have to content myself with a stroll in the Gardens. Somehow, after the great fields and pastures and lofty pine-groves of the country, they seem shut-in and conventional. Even the trees seem citified and self-conscious. Indeed, I doubt if they are on speaking terms with their country cousins! Do you know, I cannot help feeling sorry for these trees with all their fashionable airs? They are like the people whom they see every day, who prefer the crowded, noisy city to the quiet and freedom of the country. They do not even suspect how circumscribed their lives are. They look down pityingly on the country-folk, who have never had an opportunity "to see the great world." Oh my! if they only realized their limitations, they would flee for their lives to the woods and fields. But what nonsense is this! You will think I'm pining away for my beloved Wrentham, which is true in one sense and not in another. I do miss Red Farm and the dear ones there dreadfully; but I am not unhappy. I have Teacher and my books, and I have the certainty that something sweet and good will come to me in this great city, where human beings struggle so bravely all their lives to wring happiness from cruel circumstances. Anyway, I am glad to have my share in life, whether it be bright or sad. . . .

TO MRS. WILLIAM THAW

BOSTON, December 6th, 1898.

My teacher and I had a good laugh over the girls' frolic. How funny they must have looked in their "rough-rider" costumes, mounted upon their fiery steeds! "Slim" would describe them, if they were anything like the saw-horses I have seen. What jolly times they must have at ———! I cannot help wishing sometimes that I could have some of the fun that other girls have. How quickly I should lock up all these mighty warriors, and hoary sages, and impossible heroes, who are now almost my only companions; and dance and sing and frolic like other girls! But I must not waste my time wishing idle wishes; and after all my ancient friends are very wise and interesting, and I usually enjoy their society

very much indeed. It is only once in a great while
that I feel discontented, and allow myself to wish for
things I cannot hope for in this life. But, as you
know, my heart is usually brimful of happiness.
The thought that my dear Heavenly Father is always near, giving me abundantly of all those things,
which truly enrich life and make it sweet and beautiful, makes every deprivation seem of little moment
compared with the countless blessings I enjoy.

TO MRS. WILLIAM THAW

12 Newbury Street, Boston,
December 19th, 1898.

. . . I realize now what a selfish, greedy girl
I was to ask that my cup of happiness should be
filled to overflowing, without stopping to think how
many other people's cups were quite empty. I feel
heartily ashamed of my thoughtlessness. One of
the childish illusions, which it has been hardest for
me to get rid of, is that we have only to make our
wishes known in order to have them granted. But I
am slowly learning that there is not happiness
enough in the world for everyone to have all that he
wants; and it grieves me to think that I should have
forgotten, even for a moment, that I already have
more than my share, and that like poor little Oliver
Twist I should have asked for "more." . . .

TO MRS. LAURENCE HUTTON

12 NEWBERRY STREET, BOSTON.
December 22, [1898]

. . . I suppose Mr. Keith writes you the work-a-day news. If so, you know that I have finished all the geometry, and nearly all the Algebra required for the Harvard examinations, and after Christmas I shall begin a very careful review of both subjects. You will be glad to hear that I enjoy Mathematics now. Why, I can do long, complicated quadratic equations in my head quite easily, and it is great fun! I think Mr. Keith is a wonderful teacher, and I feel very grateful to him for having made me see the beauty of Mathematics. Next to my own dear teacher, he has done more than any one else to enrich and broaden my mind.

TO MRS. LAURENCE HUTTON

12 NEWBURY STREET, BOSTON,
January 17, 1899.

. . . Have you seen Kipling's "Dreaming True," or "Kitchener's School?" It is a very strong poem and set me dreaming too. Of course you have read about the "Gordon Memorial College," which the English people are to erect at Khartoum. While I was thinking over the blessings that would come to the people of Egypt through this college, and eventually to England herself, there came into my heart the strong desire that my own dear country should in a similar way convert the terrible loss of her brave sons on the "Maine" into a like blessing to the people of Cuba. Would a college at Havana not be the noblest and most enduring monument that could be raised to the brave men of the "Maine," as well as a source of infinite good to all concerned? Imagine entering the Havana harbor, and having the pier, where the "Maine" was anchored on that dreadful night, when she was so mysteriously destroyed, pointed out to you, and being told that the great, beautiful building overlooking the spot was the "Maine Memorial College," erected by the American people, and having for its object the education both of Cubans and Spaniards! What a glorious triumph such a monument would be of the best and highest instincts of a Christian nation! In it there would be no suggestion of hatred or revenge, nor a trace of the old-time belief that might makes right. On the other hand, it would be a pledge to the world that we intend to stand by our declaration of war, and give Cuba to the Cubans, as soon as we have fitted them to assume the duties and responsibilities of a self-governing people. . . .

TO MR. JOHN HITZ

12 NEWBURY STREET, BOSTON,
February 3, 1899.
. . . I had an exceedingly interesting experience last Monday. A kind friend took me over in the morning to the Boston Art Museum. She had previously obtained permission from General Lor-

ing, Supt. of the Museum, for me to touch the statues, especially those which represented my old friends in the "Iliad" and "Aeneid." Was that not lovely? While I was there, General Loring himself came in, and showed me some of the most beautiful statues, among which were the Venus of Medici, the Minerva of the Parthenon, Diana, in her hunting costume, with her hand on the quiver and a doe by her side, and the unfortunate Laocoön and his two little sons, struggling in the fearful coils of two huge serpents, and stretching their arms to the skies with heart-rending cries. I also saw Apollo Belvidere. He had just slain the Python and was standing by a great pillar of rock, extending his graceful hand in triumph over the terrible snake. Oh, he was simply beautiful! Venus entranced me. She looked as if she had just risen from the foam of the sea, and her loveliness was like a strain of heavenly music. I also saw poor Niobe with her youngest child clinging close to her while she implored the cruel goddess not to kill her last darling. I almost cried, it was all so real and tragic. General Loring kindly showed me a copy of one of the wonderful bronze doors of the Baptistry of Florence, and I felt of the graceful pillars, resting on the backs of fierce lions. So you see, I had a foretaste of the pleasure which I hope some day to have of visiting Florence. My friend said, she would sometime show me the copies of the marbles brought away by Lord Elgin from the Parthenon. But somehow, I should prefer to see the originals in the place where Genius meant them to remain, not only as a hymn of praise to the gods, but also as a monument of the glory of Greece. It really seems wrong to snatch such sacred things away from the sanctuary of the Past where they belong. . . .

TO MR. WILLIAM WADE

Boston, February 19th, 1899.

Why, bless you, I thought I wrote to you the day after the "Eclogues" arrived, and told you how glad I was to have them! Perhaps you never got that letter. At any rate, I thank you, dear friend, for taking such a world of trouble for me. You will be glad to hear that the books from England are coming now. I already have the seventh and eighth books of the "Aeneid" and one book of the "Iliad," all of which is most fortunate, as I have come almost to the end of my embossed text-books.

It gives me great pleasure to hear how much is being done for the deaf-blind. The more I learn of them, the more kindness I find. Why, only a little while ago people thought it quite impossible to teach the deaf-blind anything; but no sooner was it proved possible than hundreds of kind, sympathetic hearts were fired with the desire to help them, and now we see how many of those poor, unfortunate persons are being taught to see the beauty and reality of life. Love always finds its way to an imprisoned soul, and leads it out into the world of freedom and intelligence!

As to the two-handed alphabet, I think it is much easier for those who have sight than the manual alphabet; for most of the letters look like the large capitals in books; but I think when it comes to teaching a deaf-blind person to spell, the manual alphabet is much more convenient, and less conspicuous. . . .

TO MRS. LAURENCE HUTTON

12 NEWBURY STREET, BOSTON,
March 5, 1899.

. . . I am now sure that I shall be ready for my examinations in June. There is but one cloud in my sky at present; but that is one which casts a dark shadow over my life, and makes me very anxious at times. My teacher's eyes are no better: indeed, I think they grow more troublesome, though she is very brave and patient, and will not give up. But it is most distressing to me to feel that she is sacrificing her sight for me. I feel as if I ought to give up the idea of going to college altogether: for not all the knowledge in the world could make me happy, if obtained at such a cost. I do wish, Mrs. Hutton, you would try to persuade Teacher to take a rest, and have her eyes treated. She will not listen to me.

I have just had some pictures taken, and if they are good, I would like to send one to Mr. Rogers, if you think he would like to have it. I would like so much to show him in some way how deeply I appreciate all that he is doing for me, and I cannot think of anything better to do.

Every one here is talking about the Sargent pictures. It is a wonderful exhibition of portraits, they say. How I wish I had eyes to see them! How I should delight in their beauty and color! However, I am glad that I am not debarred from all pleasure in the pictures. I have at least the satisfaction of seeing them through the eyes of my friends, which is a real pleasure. I am so thankful that I can rejoice in the beauties, which my friends gather and put into my hands!

We are all so glad and thankful that Mr. Kipling did not die! I have his "Jungle-Book" in raised print, and what a splendid, refreshing book it is! I cannot help feeling as if I knew its gifted author. What a real, manly, lovable nature his must be! . . .

TO DR. DAVID H. GREER

12 NEWBURY STREET, BOSTON,
May 8, 1899.

. . . Each day brings me all that I can possibly accomplish, and each night brings me rest, and the sweet thought that I am a little nearer to my goal than ever before. My Greek progresses finely. I have finished the ninth book of the "Iliad" and am just beginning the "Odyssey." I am also reading the "Aeneid" and the "Eclogues." Some of my friends tell me that I am very foolish to give so much time to Greek and Latin; but I am sure they would not think so, if they realized what a wonderful world of experience and thought Homer and Virgil have opened up to me. I think I shall enjoy the "Odyssey" most of all. The "Iliad" tells of almost nothing but war, and one sometimes wearies of the clash of spears and the din of battle; but the "Odyssey" tells of nobler courage—the courage of a soul sore tried, but steadfast to the end. I often wonder, as I read these splendid poems why, at the same time that Homer's songs of war fired the Greeks with valor, his songs of manly virtue did not have a stronger influence upon the spiritual life of the people.   Perhaps the reason is, that thoughts truly great are like seeds cast into the human mind, and either lie there unnoticed, or are tossed about and played with, like toys, until, grown wise through suffering and experience, a race discovers and cultivates them.   Then the world has advanced one step in its heavenward march.

I am working very hard just now.   I intend to take my examinations in June, and there is a great deal to be done, before I shall feel ready to meet the ordeal. . . .

You will be glad to hear that my mother, and little sister and brother are coming north to spend this summer with me.   We shall all live together in a small cottage on one of the lakes at Wrentham, while my dear teacher takes a much needed rest. She has not had a vacation for twelve years, think of it, and all that time she has been the sunshine of my life.   Now her eyes are troubling her a great deal, and we all think she ought to be relieved, for a while, of every care and responsibility.   But we shall not be quite separated; we shall see each other every day, I hope.   And, when July comes, you can think of me as rowing my dear ones around the lovely lake in the little boat you gave me, the happiest girl in the world! . . .

TO MRS. LAURENCE HUTTON

[BOSTON] May 28th [1899].
. . . We have had a hard day.   Mr. Keith was here for three hours this afternoon, pouring a

torrent of Latin and Greek into my poor bewildered brain. I really believe he knows more Latin and Greek Grammar than Cicero or Homer ever dreamed of! Cicero is splendid, but his orations are very difficult to translate. I feel ashamed sometimes, when I make that eloquent man say what sounds absurd or insipid; but how is a school-girl to interpret such genius? Why, I should have to be a Cicero to talk like a Cicero! . . .

Linnie Haguewood is a deaf-blind girl, one of the many whom Mr. William Wade has helped. She is being educated by Miss Dora Donald who, at the beginning of her work with her pupil, was supplied by Mr. Hitz, Superintendent of the Volta Bureau, with copies of all documents relating to Miss Sullivan's work with Miss Keller.

TO MR. WILLIAM WADE

WRENTHAM, MASS., June 5, 1899.

. . . Linnie Haguewood's letter, which you sent me some weeks ago, interested me very much. It seemed to show spontaneity and great sweetness of character. I was a good deal amused by what she said about history. I am sorry she does not enjoy it; but I too feel sometimes how dark, and mysterious and even fearful the history of old peoples, old religions and old forms of government really is.

Well, I must confess, I do not like the sign-language, and I do not think it would be of much use to the deaf-blind. I find it very difficult to follow the rapid motions made by the deaf-mutes, and besides, signs seem a great hindrance to them in acquiring the power of using language easily and freely. Why, I find it hard to understand them sometimes when they spell on their fingers. On the whole, if they cannot be taught articulation, the manual alphabet seems the best and most convenient means of communication. At any rate, I am sure the deaf-blind cannot learn to use signs with any degree of facility.

The other day, I met a deaf Norwegian gentle-nan, who knows Ragnhild Kaata and her teacher very well, and we had a very interesting conversation about her. He said she was very industrious and happy. She spins, and does a great deal of fancy work, and reads, and leads a pleasant, useful life. Just think, she cannot use the manual alphabet! She reads the lips well, and if she cannot understand a phrase, her friends write it in her hand; and in this way she converses with strangers. I cannot make out anything written in my hand, so you see, Ragnhild has got ahead of me in some things. I do hope I shall see her sometime. . . .

TO MRS. LAURENCE HUTTON

Wrentham, July 29, 1899.
. . . I passed in all the subjects I offered, and with credit in advanced Latin. . . . But I must confess, I had a hard time on the second day of my examinations. They would not allow Teacher

to read any of the papers to me; so the papers were copied for me in braille. This arrangement worked very well in the languages, but not nearly so well in the Mathematics. Consequently, I did not do so well as I should have done, if Teacher had been allowed to read the Algebra and Geometry to me. But you must not think I blame any one. Of course they did not realize how difficult and perplexing they were making the examinations for me. How could they— they can see and hear, and I suppose they could not understand matters from my point of view. . . .

Thus far my summer has been sweeter than anything I can remember. My mother, and sister and little brother have been here five weeks, and our happiness knows no bounds. Not only do we enjoy being together; but we also find our little home most delightful. I do wish you could see the view of the beautiful lake from our piazza, the islands looking like little emerald peaks in the golden sunlight, and the canoes flitting here and there, like autumn leaves in the gentle breeze, and breathe in the peculiarly delicious fragrance of the woods, which comes like a murmur from an unknown clime. I cannot help wondering if it is the same fragrance that greeted the Norsemen long ago, when, according to tradition, they visited our shores—an odorous echo of many centuries of silent growth and decay in flower and tree. . . .

TO MRS. SAMUEL RICHARD FULLER

WRENTHAM, October 20, 1899.
. . . I suppose it is time for me to tell you something about our plans for the winter. You

know it has long been my ambition to go to Radcliffe, and receive a degree, as many other girls have done; but Dean Irwin of Radcliffe, has persuaded me to take a special course for the present. She said I had already shown the world that I could do the college work, by passing all my examinations successfully, in spite of many obstacles. She showed me how very foolish it would be for me to pursue a four years' course of study at Radcliffe, simply to be like other girls, when I might better be cultivating whatever ability I had for writing. She said she did not consider a degree of any real value, but thought it was much more desirable to do something original than to waste one's energies only for a degree. Her arguments seemed so wise and practical, that I could not but yield. I found it hard, very hard, to give up the idea of going to college; it had been in my mind ever since I was a little girl; but there is no use doing a foolish thing, because one has wanted to do it a long time, is there?

But, while we were discussing plans for the winter, a suggestion which Dr. Hale had made long ago flashed across Teacher's mind—that I might take courses somewhat like those offered at Radcliffe, under the instruction of the professors in these courses. Miss Irwin seemed to have no objection to this proposal, and kindly offered to see the professors and find out if they would give me lessons. If they will be so good as to teach me and if we have money enough to do as we have planned, my studies this year will be English, English Literature of the Elizabethan period, Latin and German. . . .

TO MR. JOHN HITZ

138 BRATTLE ST., CAMBRIDGE,
Nov. 11, 1899.

. . . As to the braille question, I cannot tell how deeply it distresses me to hear that my statement with regard to the examinations has been doubted. Ignorance seems to be at the bottom of all these contradictions. Why, you yourself seem to think that I taught you American braille, when you do not know a single letter in the system! I could not help laughing when you said you had been writing to me in American braille—and there you were writing your letter in English braille!

The facts about the braille examinations are as follows:

How I passed my Entrance Examinations
for Radcliffe College.

On the 29th and 30th of June, 1899, I took my examinations for Radcliffe College. The first day I had elementary Greek and advanced Latin, and the second day Geometry, Algebra and advanced Greek.

The college authorities would not permit Miss Sullivan to read the examination papers to me; so Mr. Eugene C. Vining, one of the instructors at the Perkins Institution for the Blind, was employed to copy the papers for me in braille. Mr. Vining was a perfect stranger to me, and could not communicate with me except by writing in braille. The Proctor also was a stranger, and did not attempt to communicate with me in any way; and, as they were both unfamiliar with my speech, they could not readily understand what I said to them.

However, the braille worked well enough in **the**

languages; but when it came to Geometry and Algebra, it was different. I was sorely perplexed, and felt quite discouraged, and wasted much precious time, especially in Algebra. It is true that I am perfectly familiar with all literary braille— English, American, and New York Point; but the method of writing the various signs used in Geometry and Algebra in the three systems is very different, and two days before the examinations I knew only the English method. I had used it all through my school work, and never any other system.

In Geometry, my chief difficulty was, that I had always been accustomed to reading the propositions in Line Print, or having them spelled into my hand; and somehow, although the propositions were right before me, yet the braille confused me, and I could not fix in my mind clearly what I was reading. But, when I took up Algebra, I had a harder time still—I was terribly handicapped by my imperfect knowledge of the notation. The signs, which I had learned the day before, and which I thought I knew perfectly, confused me. Consequently my work was painfully slow, and I was obliged to read the examples over and over before I could form a clear idea what I was required to do. Indeed, I am not sure now that I read all the signs correctly, especially as I was much distressed, and found it very hard to keep my wits about me. . . .

Now there is one more fact, which I wish to state very plainly, in regard to what Mr. Gilman wrote to you. I never received any direct instruction in the Gilman School. Miss Sullivan always sat beside me, and told me what the teachers said. I did teach Miss Hall, my teacher in Physics, how

to write the American braille, but she never gave
me any instruction by means of it, unless a few
problems written for practice, which made me waste
much precious time deciphering them, can be called
instruction. Dear Frau Grote learned the manual
alphabet, and used to teach me herself; but this
was in private lessons, which were paid for by my
friends. In the German class Miss Sullivan interpreted to me as well as she could what the teacher
said.

Perhaps, if you would send a copy of this to the
head of the Cambridge School, it might enlighten
his mind on a few subjects, on which he seems to
be in total darkness just now. . . .

TO MISS MILDRED KELLER

138 BRATTLE STREET, CAMBRIDGE,
November 26, 1899.

. . . At last we are settled for the winter, and
our work is going smoothly. Mr. Keith comes
every afternoon at four o'clock, and gives me a
"friendly lift" over the rough stretches of road,
over which every student must go. I am studying
English history, English literature, French and
Latin, and by and by I shall take up German and
English composition—let us groan! You know,
I detest grammar as much as you do; but I suppose
I must go through it if I am to write, just as we had
to get ducked in the lake hundreds of times before
we could swim! In French Teacher is reading

"Columba" to me. It is a delightful novel, full of piquant expressions and thrilling adventures, (don't dare to blame me for using big words, since you do the same!) and, if you ever read it, I think you will enjoy it immensely. You are studying English history, aren't you. O but it's exceedingly interesting! I'm making quite a thorough study of the Elizabethan period—of the Reformation, and the Acts of Supremacy and Conformity, and the maritime discoveries, and all the big things, which the "deuce" seems to have invented to plague innocent youngsters like yourself! . . .

Now we have a swell winter outfit—coats, hats, gowns, flannels and all. We've just had four lovely dresses made by a French dressmaker. I have two, of which one has a black silk skirt, with a black lace net over it, and a waist of white poplin, with turquoise velvet and chiffon, and cream lace over a satin yoke. The other is woollen, and of a very pretty green. The waist is trimmed with pink and green brocaded velvet, and white lace, I think, and has double reefers on the front, tucked and trimmed with velvet, and also a row of tiny white buttons. Teacher too has a silk dress. The skirt is black, while the waist is mostly yellow, trimmed with delicate lavender chiffon, and black velvet bows and lace. Her other dress is purple, trimmed with purple velvet, and the waist has a collar of cream lace. So you may imagine that we look quite like peacocks, only we've no trains. . . .

A week ago yesterday there was [a] great football game between Harvard and Yale, and there was tremendous excitement here. We could hear the yells of the boys and the cheers of the lookers-on

MISS KELLER AND HER SISTER, MILDRED

as plainly in our room as if we had been on the field. Colonel Roosevelt was there, on Harvard's side; but bless you, he wore a white sweater, and no crimson that we know of! There were about twenty-five thousand people at the game, and, when we went out, the noise was so terrific, we nearly jumped out of our skins, thinking it was the din of war, and not of a football game that we heard. But, in spite of all their wild efforts, neither side was scored, and we all laughed and said, "Oh, well, now the pot can't call the kettle black!" . . .

TO MRS. LAURENCE HUTTON

559 MADISON AVENUE, NEW YORK,
January 2, 1900.

. . . We have been here a week now, and are going to stay with Miss Rhoades until Saturday. We are enjoying every moment of our visit, every one is so good to us. We have seen many of our old friends, and made some new ones. We dined with the Rogers last Friday, and oh, they were so kind to us! The thought of their gentle courtesy and genuine kindness brings a warm glow of joy and gratitude to my heart. I have seen Dr. Greer too. He has such a kind heart! I love him more than ever. We went to St. Bartholomew's Sunday, and I have not felt so much at home in a church since dear Bishop Brooks died. Dr. Greer read so slowly, that my teacher could tell me every word. His people must have wondered at his un-

usual deliberation. After the service he asked
Mr. Warren, the organist to play for me. I stood
in the middle of the church, where the vibrations
from the great organ were strongest, and I felt
the mighty waves of sound beat against me, as
the great billows beat against a little ship at sea.

TO MR. JOHN HITZ

138 BRATTLE STREET, CAMBRIDGE,
Feb. 3, 1900.
. . . My studies are more interesting than ever.
In Latin, I am reading Horace's odes. Although I
find them difficult to translate, yet I think they
are the loveliest pieces of Latin poetry I have read
or shall ever read. In French we have finished
"Colomba," and I am reading "Horace" by Corneille and La Fontaine's fables, both of which are
in braille. I have not gone far in either; but I know
I shall enjoy the fables, they are so delightfully
written, and give such good lessons in a simple and
yet attractive way. I do not think I have told you
that my dear teacher is reading "The Faery Queen"
to me. I am afraid I find fault with the poem as
much as I enjoy it. I do not care much for the
allegories, indeed I often find them tiresome, and
I cannot help thinking that Spenser's world of
knights, paynims, fairies, dragons and all sorts of
strange creatures is a somewhat grotesque and
amusing world; but the poem itself is lovely and as
musical as a running brook.

I am now the proud owner of about fifteen new books, which we ordered from Louisville. Among them are "Henry Esmond," "Bacon's Essays" and extracts from "English Literature." Perhaps next week I shall have some more books, "The Tempest," "A Midsummer Night's Dream" and possibly some selections from Green's history of England. Am I not very fortunate?

I am afraid this letter savors too much of books— but really they make up my whole life these days, and I scarcely see or hear of anything else! I do believe I sleep on books every night! You know a student's life is of necessity somewhat circumscribed and narrow and crowds out almost everything that is not in books. . . .

TO THE CHAIRMAN OF THE ACADEMIC BOARD
OF RADCLIFFE COLLEGE

138 BRATTLE STREET, CAMBRIDGE, MASS.,
May 5, 1900.

Dear Sir:

As an aid to me in determining my plans for study the coming year, I apply to you for information as to the possibility of my taking the regular courses in Radcliffe College.

Since receiving my certificate of admission to Radcliffe last July, I have been studying with a private tutor, Horace, Aeschylus, French, German, Rhetoric, English History, English Literature and Criticism, and English composition.

In college I should wish to continue most, if not all of these subjects. The conditions under which I work require the presence of Miss Sullivan, who has been my teacher and companion for thirteen years, as an interpreter of oral speech and as a reader of examination papers. In college she, or possibly in some subjects some one else, would of necessity be with me in the lecture-room and at recitations. I should do all my written work on a typewriter, and if a Professor could not understand my speech, I could write out my answers to his questions and hand them to him after the recitation.

Is it possible for the College to accommodate itself to these unprecedented conditions, so as to enable me to pursue my studies at Radcliffe? I realize that the obstacles in the way of my receiving a college education are very great—to others they may seem insurmountable; but, dear Sir, a true soldier does not acknowledge defeat before the battle.

TO MRS. LAURENCE HUTTON

138 BRATTLE STREET, CAMBRIDGE,
June 9, 1900.

. . . I have not yet heard from the Academic Board in reply to my letter; but I sincerely hope they will answer favorably. My friends think it very strange that they should hesitate so long, especially when I have not asked them to simplify my work in the least, but only to modify it so as to meet the existing circumstances. Cornell has offered to make arrangements suited to the conditions under which I work, if I should decide to go to that college, and the University of Chicago has made a similar offer; but I am afraid if I went to any other college, it would be thought that I did not pass my examinations for Radcliffe satisfactorily. . . .

In the fall Miss Keller entered Radcliffe College.

TO MR. JOHN HITZ

14 COOLIDGE AVE., CAMBRIDGE,
Nov. 26, 1900.

. . . —— has already communicated with you in regard to her and my plan of establishing an institution for deaf and blind children. At first I was most enthusiastic in its support, and I never dreamed that any grave objections could be raised except indeed by those who are hostile to Teacher; but now, after thinking most *seriously* and consulting my friends, I have decided that ——'s plan is by no means feasible. In my eagerness to make it possible for deaf and blind children to have the same advantages that I have had, I quite forgot that there might be many obstacles in the way of my accomplishing anything like what —— proposed.

My friends thought we might have one or two pupils in our own home, thereby securing to me the advantage of being helpful to others without any of the disadvantages of a large school. They were very kind; but I could not help feeling that they spoke more from a business than a humanitarian point of view.   I am sure they did not quite understand how passionately I desire that all who are afflicted like myself shall receive their rightful, inheritance of thought, knowledge and love.   Still I could not shut my eyes to the force and weight of their arguments, and I saw plainly that I must abandon ——'s scheme as impracticable.   They also said that I ought to appoint an advisory committee to control my affairs while I am at Radcliffe.   I considered this suggestion carefully, then I told Mr. Rhoades that I should be proud and glad to have wise friends to whom I could always turn for advice in all important matters.   For this committee I chose six, my mother, Teacher, because she is like a mother to me, Mrs. Hutton, Mr. Rhoades, Dr. Greer and Mr. Rogers, because it is they who have supported me all these years and made it possible for me to enter college.   Mrs. Hutton had already written to mother, asking her to telegraph if she was willing for me to have other advisers besides herself and Teacher.   This morning we received word that mother had given her consent to this arrangement.   Now it remains for me to write to Dr. Greer and Mr. Rogers. . . .

We had a long talk with Dr. Bell.   Finally he proposed a plan which delighted us all beyond words. He said that it was a gigantic blunder to attempt to found a school for deaf and blind children, because then they would lose the most precious opportunities of entering into the fuller, richer, freer life of seeing and hearing children.   I had had misgivings on this point; but I could not see how we were to help it.   However Mr. Bell suggested that ——

and all her friends who are interested in her scheme should organize an association for the promotion of the education of the deaf and blind, Teacher and myself being included of course. Under his plan they were to appoint Teacher to train others to instruct deaf and blind children in their own homes, just as she had taught me. Funds were to be raised for the teachers' lodgings and also for their salaries. At the same time Dr. Bell added that I could rest content and fight my way through Radcliffe in competition with seeing and hearing girls, while the great desire of my heart was being fulfilled. We clapped our hands and shouted; —— went away beaming with pleasure, and Teacher and I felt more light of heart than we had for sometime. Of course we can do nothing just now; but the painful anxiety about my college work and the future welfare of the deaf and blind has been lifted from our minds. Do tell me what you think about Dr. Bell's suggestion. It seems most practical and wise to me; but I must know all that there is to be known about it before I speak or act in the matter. . . .

TO MR. JOHN D. WRIGHT

CAMBRIDGE, December 9, 1900.

Do you think me a villain and—I can't think of a word bad enough to express your opinion of me, unless indeed horse-thief will answer the purpose. Tell me truly, do you think me as bad as that? I hope not; for I have thought many letters to you which never got on paper, and I am delighted to get your good letter, yes, I really was, and I intended to answer it immediately; but the days slip by unnoticed when one is busy, and I have been VERY busy this fall. You must believe that. Radcliffe girls are always up to their ears in work. If you doubt it, you'd better come and see for yourself.

Yes, I am taking the regular college course for a degree. When I am a B.A., I suppose you will not dare call me a villain! I am studying English— Sophomore English, if you please, (though I can't see that it is different from just plain English) German, French and History. I'm enjoying my work even more than I expected to, which is another way of saying that I'm glad I came. It is hard, very hard at times; but it hasn't swamped me yet. No, I am not studying Mathematics, or Greek or Latin either. The courses at Radcliffe are elective, only certain courses in English are prescribed. I passed off my English and advanced French before I entered college, and I choose the courses I like best. I don't however intend to give up Latin and Greek entirely. Perhaps I shall take up these studies later; but I've said goodbye to Mathematics forever, and I assure you, I was delighted to see the last of those horrid goblins! I hope to obtain my degree in four years; but I'm not very particular about that. There's no great hurry, and I want to get as much as possible out of my studies. Many of my friends would be well pleased if I would take two or even one course a year; but I rather object to spending the rest of my life in college. . . .

TO MR. WILLIAM WADE

14 COOLIDGE AVENUE, CAMBRIDGE,
December 9, 1900.

. . . Since you are so much interested in the
deaf and blind, I will begin by telling you of several
cases I have come across lately. Last October I
heard of an unusually bright little girl in Texas.
Her name is Ruby Rice, and she is thirteen years old,
I think. She has never been taught; but they
say she can sew and likes to help others in this sort
of work. Her sense of smell is wonderful. Why,
when she enters a store, she will go straight to the
showcases, and she can also distinguish her own
things. Her parents are very anxious indeed to
find a teacher for her. They have also written to
Mr. Hitz about her.

I also know a child at the Institution for the Deaf
in Mississippi. Her name is Maud Scott, and she
is six years old. Miss Watkins, the lady who has
charge of her wrote me a most interesting letter.
She said that Maud was born deaf and lost her sight
when she was only three months old, and that
when she went to the Institution a few weeks ago,
she was quite helpless. She could not even walk
and had very little use of her hands. When they
tried to teach her to string beads, her little hands fell
to her side. Evidently her sense of touch has not
been developed, and as yet she can walk only when
she holds some one's hand; but she seems to be an
exceedingly bright child. Miss Watkins adds that
she is very pretty. I have written to her that when
Maud learns to read, I shall have many stories to
send her. The dear, sweet little girl, it makes my

heart ache to think how utterly she is cut off from all that is good and desirable in life.   But Miss Watkins seems to be just the kind of teacher she needs.

I was in New York not long ago and I saw Miss Rhoades, who told me that she had seen Katie McGirr.   She said the poor young girl talked and acted exactly like a little child.   Katie played with Miss Rhoades's rings and took them away, saying with a merry laugh, "You shall not have them again!"   She could only understand Miss Rhoades when she talked about the simplest things.   The latter wished to send her some books; but she could not find anything simple enough for her!   She said Katie was very sweet indeed, but sadly in need of proper instruction.   I was much surprised to hear all this; for I judged from your letters that Katie was a very precocious girl. . . .

A few days ago I met Tommy Stringer in the railroad station at Wrentham.   He is a great, strong boy now, and he will soon need a man to take care of him; he is really too big for a lady to manage.   He goes to the public school, I hear, and his progress is astonishing, they say; but it doesn't show as yet in his conversation, which is limited to "Yes" and "No." . . .

TO MR. CHARLES T. COPELAND

DECEMBER 20, 1900.

My dear Mr. Copeland;

I venture to write to you because I am afraid that if I do not explain why I have stopped writing themes, you will think I have become discouraged, or perhaps that to escape criticism I have beat a cowardly retreat from your class. Please do not think either of these very unpleasant thoughts. I am not discouraged, nor am I afraid. I am confident that I could go on writing themes like those I have written, and I suppose I should get through the course with fairly good marks; but this sort of literary patch-work has lost all interest for me. I have never been satisfied with my work; but I never knew what my difficulty was until you pointed it out to me. When I came to your class last October, I was trying with all my might to be like everybody else, to forget as entirely as possible my limitations and peculiar environment. Now, however, I see the folly of attempting to hitch one's wagon to a star with harness that does not belong to it.

I have always accepted other people's experiences and observations as a matter of course. It never occurred to me that it might be worth while to make my own observations and describe the experiences peculiarly my own. Henceforth I am resolved to be myself, to live my own life and write my own thoughts when I have any. When I have written something that seems to be fresh and spontaneous and worthy of your criticisms, I will bring it to you, if I may, and if you think it good, I shall be happy; but if your verdict is unfavorable, I shall try again and yet again until I have succeeded in pleasing you . . .

14 COOLIDGE AVENUE, CAMBRIDGE,
December 27, 1900.

. . . So you read about our class luncheon in
the papers? How in the world do the papers find
out everything, I wonder. I am sure no reporter
was present. I had a splendid time; the toasts and
speeches were great fun. I only spoke a few words,
as I did not know I was expected to speak until a
few minutes before I was called upon. I think I
wrote you that I had been elected Vice-President of
the Freshman Class of Radcliffe.

Did I tell you in my last letter that I had a new
dress, a real party dress with low neck and short
sleeves and quite a train? It is pale blue, trimmed
with chiffon of the same color. I have worn it only
once, but then I felt that Solomon in all his glory
was not to be compared with me! Anyway, he
certainly never had a dress like mine! . . .

A gentleman in Philadelphia has just written to
my teacher about a deaf and blind child in Paris,
whose parents are Poles. The mother is a physician
and a brilliant woman, he says. This little boy
could speak two or three languages before he lost his
hearing through sickness, and he is now only about
five years old. Poor little fellow, I wish I could do
something for him; but he is so young, my teacher
thinks it would be too bad to separate him from his
mother. I have had a letter from Mrs. Thaw with
regard to the possibility of doing something for
these children. Dr. Bell thinks the present census

will show that there are more than a thousand*
in the United States alone; and Mrs. Thaw thinks
if all my friends were to unite their efforts, "it
would be an easy matter to establish at the beginning of this new century a new line upon which
mercy might travel," and the rescue of these unfortunate children could be accomplished. . . .

TO MR. WILLIAM WADE

CAMBRIDGE, February 2, 1901.

. . . By the way, have you any specimens of
English braille especially printed for those who have
lost their sight late in life or have fingers hardened
by long toil, so that their touch is less sensitive than
that of other blind people? I read an account of
such a system in one of my English magazines, and
I am anxious to know more about it. If it is as
efficient as they say, I see no reason why English
braille should not be adopted by the blind of all
countries. Why, it is the print that can be most
readily adapted to many different languages. Even
Greek can be embossed in it, as you know. Then,
too, it will be rendered still more efficient by the
"interpointing system," which will save an immense
amount of space and paper. There is nothing more
absurd, I think, than to have five or six different
prints for the blind. . . .

This letter was written in response to a tentative
offer from the editor of *The Great Round World* to

---

* The number of deaf-blind young enough to be benefited by
education is not so large as this; but the education of this class
of defectives has been neglected.

have the magazine published in raised type for the blind, if enough were willing to subscribe. It is evident that the blind should have a good magazine, not a special magazine for the blind, but one of our best monthlies, printed in embossed letters. The blind alone could not support it, but it would not take very much money to make up the additional expense.

TO *The Great Round World*

CAMBRIDGE, Feb. 16, 1901.

The Great Round World,
    New York City.
    Gentlemen: I have only to-day found time to reply to your interesting letter. A little bird had already sung the good news in my ear; but it was doubly pleasant to have it straight from you.
    It would be splendid to have *The Great Round World* printed in "language that can be felt." I doubt if any one who enjoys the wondrous privilege of seeing can have any conception of the boon such a publication as you contemplate would be to the sightless. To be able to read for one's self what is being willed, thought and done in the world—the world in whose joys and sorrows, failures and successes one feels the keenest interest—that would indeed be a happiness too deep for words. I trust that the effort of *The Great Round World* to bring light to those who sit in darkness will receive the encouragement and support it so richly deserves.
    I doubt, however, if the number of subscribers to an embossed edition of *The Great Round World* would ever be large; for I am told that the blind as

a class are poor. But why should not the friends of the blind assist *The Great Round World*, if necessary? Surely there are hearts and hands ever ready to make it possible for generous intentions to be wrought into noble deeds.

Wishing you godspeed in an undertaking that is very dear to my heart, I am, etc.

TO MISS NINA RHOADES

CAMBRIDGE, Sept. 25, 1901.

. . . We remained in Halifax until about the middle of August. . . . Day after day the Harbor, the warships, and the park kept us busy thinking and feeling and enjoying. . . . When the *Indiana* visited Halifax, we were invited to go on board, and she sent her own launch for us. I touched the immense cannon, read with my fingers several of the names of the Spanish ships that were captured at Santiago, and felt the places where she had been pierced with shells. The *Indiana* was the largest and finest ship in the Harbor, and we felt very proud of her.

After we left Halifax, we visited Dr. Bell at Cape Breton. He has a charming, romantic house on a mountain called Beinn Bhreagh, which overlooks the Bras d'Or Lake. . . .

Dr. Bell told me many interesting things about his work. He had just constructed a boat that could be propelled by a kite with the wind in its favor, and one day he tried experiments to see if

he could steer the kite against the wind. I was
there and really helped him fly the kites. On one
of them I noticed that the strings were of wire, and
having had some experience in bead work, I said I
thought they would break. Dr. Bell said "No!"
with great confidence, and the kite was sent up. It
began to pull and tug, and lo, the wires broke, and
off went the great red dragon, and poor Dr. Bell
stood looking forlornly after it. After that he
asked me if the strings were all right and changed
them at once when I answered in the negative.
Altogether we had great fun. . . .

TO DR. EDWARD EVERETT HALE*

CAMBRIDGE, Nov. 10, 1901.
My teacher and I expect to be present at the
meeting tomorrow in commemoration of the one
hundredth anniversary of Dr. Howe's birth; but
I very much doubt if we shall have an opportunity
to speak with you; so I am writing now to tell you
how delighted I am that you are to speak at the
meeting, because I feel that you, better than any one
I know will express the heartfelt gratitude of those
who owe their education, their opportunities, their
happiness to him who opened the eyes of the blind
and gave the dumb lip language.

Sitting here in my study, surrounded by my books,
enjoying the sweet and intimate companionship of

* Read by Dr. Hale at the celebration of the centenary of Dr.
Samuel Gridley Howe, at Tremont Temple, Boston, Nov. 11, 1901.

the great and the wise, I am trying to realize what my life might have been, if Dr. Howe had failed in the great task God gave him to perform. If he had not taken upon himself the responsibility of Laura Bridgman's education and led her out of the pit of Acheron back to her human inheritance, should I be a sophomore at Radcliffe College to-day—who can say? But it is idle to speculate about what might have been in connection with Dr. Howe's great achievement.

I think only those who have escaped that death-in-life existence, from which Laura Bridgman was rescued, can realize how isolated, how shrouded in darkness, how cramped by its own impotence is a soul without thought or faith or hope. Words are powerless to describe the desolation of that prison-house, or the joy of the soul that is delivered out of its captivity. When we compare the needs and helplessness of the blind before Dr. Howe began his work, with their present usefulness and independence, we realize that great things have been done in our midst. What if physical conditions have built up high walls about us? Thanks to our friend and helper, our world lies upward; the length and breadth and sweep of the heavens are ours!

It is pleasant to think that Dr. Howe's noble deeds will receive their due tribute of affection and gratitude, in the city, which was the scene of his great labors and splendid victories for humanity.

With kind greetings, in which my teacher joins me, I am

Affectionately your friend,
Helen Keller.

TO THE HON. GEORGE FRISBIE HOAR

CAMBRIDGE, MASS., November 25, 1901.

My Dear Senator Hoar:—

I am glad you liked my letter about Dr. Howe. It was written out of my heart, and perhaps that is why it met a sympathetic response in other hearts. I will ask Dr. Hale to lend me the letter, so that I can make a copy of it for you.

You see, I use a typewriter—it is my right hand man, so to speak. Without it I do not see how I could go to college. I write all my themes and examinations on it, even Greek. Indeed, it has only one drawback, and that probably is regarded as an advantage by the professors; it is that one's mistakes may be detected at a glance; for there is no chance to hide them in illegible writing.

I know you will be amused when I tell you that I am deeply interested in politics. I like to have the papers read to me, and I try to understand the great questions of the day; but I am afraid my knowledge is very unstable; for I change my opinions with every new book I read. I used to think that when I studied Civil Government and Economics, all my difficulties and perplexities would blossom into beautiful certainties; but alas, I find that there are more tares than wheat in these fertile fields of knowledge. . . .

PART III

A SUPPLEMENTARY ACCOUNT OF HELEN KELLER'S LIFE AND EDUCATION

The Writing of the Book.
Personality.
Education.
Speech.
Literary Style.

CHAPTER I

THE WRITING OF THE BOOK

IT is fitting that Miss Keller's "Story of My Life" should appear at this time. What is remarkable in her career is already accomplished, and whatever she may do in the future will be but a relatively slight addition to the success which distinguishes her now. That success has just been assured, for it is her work at Radcliffe during the last two years which has shown that she can carry her education as far as if she were studying under normal conditions. Whatever doubts Miss Keller herself may have had are now at rest.

Several passages of her autobiography, as it appeared in serial form, have been made the subject of a grave editorial in a Boston newspaper, in which the writer regretted Miss Keller's apparent disillusionment in regard to the value of her college life. He quoted the passages in which she explains that college is not the "universal Athens" she had hoped to find, and cited the cases of other remarkable persons whose college life had proved disappointing. But it is to be remembered that Miss Keller has written many things in her autobiography for the fun of writing them, and the disillusion, which the writer of the editorial took seriously, is in great part humorous. Miss Keller does not suppose her views to be of great importance, and when she utters her opinions on important matters she takes it for granted that her reader will receive them as the opinions of a junior in college, not of one who writes with the wisdom of maturity. For instance, it surprised her that some people were annoyed at what she said about the Bible, and she was amused that they did not see, what was plain enough, that she had been obliged to read the whole Bible in a course in English literature, not as a religious duty put upon her by her teacher or her parents.

I ought to apologize to the reader and to Miss Keller for presuming to say what her subject matter is worth, but one more

explanation is necessary. In her account of her early education Miss Keller is not giving a scientifically accurate record of her
life, nor even of the important events. She cannot know in
detail how she was taught, and her memory of her childhood
is in some cases an idealized memory of what she has learned
later from her teacher and others. She is less able to recall
events of fifteen years ago than most of us are to recollect our
childhood. That is why her teacher's records may be found
to differ in some particulars from Miss Keller's account.

The way in which Miss Keller wrote her story shows, as nothing else can show, the difficulties she had to overcome. When we
write, we can go back over our work, shuffle the pages, interline,
rearrange, see how the paragraphs look in proof, and so construct the whole work before the eye, as an architect constructs
his plans. When Miss Keller puts her work in typewritten form,
she cannot refer to it again unless some one reads it to her by
means of the manual alphabet.

This difficulty is in part obviated by the use of her braille
machine, which makes a manuscript that she can read; but as
her work must be put ultimately in typewritten form, and as
a braille machine is somewhat cumbersome, she has got into
the habit of writing directly on her typewriter. She depends so
little on her braille manuscript, that, when she began to write
her story more than a year ago and had put in braille a hundred
pages of material and notes, she made the mistake of destroying
these notes before she had finished her manuscript. Thus she
composed much of her story on the typewriter, and in constructing
it as a whole depended on her memory to guide her in putting
together the detached episodes, which Miss Sullivan read over
to her.

Last July, when she had finished under great pressure of work
her final chapter, she set to work to rewrite the whole story.
Her good friend, Mr. William Wade, had a complete braille
copy made for her from the magazine proofs. Then for the
first time she had her whole manuscript under her finger at
once. She saw imperfections in the arrangement of paragraphs
and the repetition of phrases. She saw, too, that her story properly
fell into short chapters and redivided it.

Partly from temperament, partly from the conditions of her
work, she has written rather a series of brilliant passages than a
unified narrative; in point of fact, several paragraphs of her

story are short themes written in her English courses, and the small unit sometimes shows its original limits.

In rewriting the story, Miss Keller made corrections on separate pages on her braille machine. Long corrections she wrote out on her typewriter, with catch-words to indicate where they belonged. Then she read from her braille copy the entire story, making corrections as she read, which were taken down on the manuscript that went to the printer. During this revision she discussed questions of subject matter and phrasing. She sat running her finger over the braille manuscript, stopping now and then to refer to the braille notes on which she had indicated her corrections, all the time reading aloud to verify the manuscript.

She listened to criticism just as any author listens to his friends or his editor. Miss Sullivan, who is an excellent critic, made suggestions at many points in the course of composition and revision. One newspaper suggested that Miss Keller had been led into writing the book and had been influenced to put certain things into it by zealous friends. As a matter of fact, most of the advice she has received and heeded has led to excisions rather than to additions. The book is Miss Keller's and is final proof of her independent power.

CHAPTER II

PERSONALITY

MARK TWAIN has said that the two most interesting characters of the nineteenth century are Napoleon and Helen Keller. The admiration with which the world has regarded her is more than justified by what she has done. No one can tell any great truth about her which has not already been written, and all that I can do is to give a few more facts about Miss Keller's work and add a little to what is known of her personality.

Miss Keller is tall and strongly built, and has always had good health. She seems to be more nervous than she really is, because she expresses more with her hands than do most English-speaking people. One reason for this habit of gesture is that her hands have been so long her instruments of communication that they have taken to themselves the quick shiftings of the eye, and express some of the things that we say in a glance. All deaf people naturally gesticulate. Indeed, at one time it was believed that the best way for them to communicate was through systematized gestures, the sign language invented by the Abbé de l'Epée.

When Miss Keller speaks, her face is animated and expresses all the modes of her thought—the expressions that make the features eloquent and give speech half its meaning. On the other hand she does not know another's expression. When she is talking with an intimate friend, however, her hand goes quickly to her friend's face to see, as she says, "the twist of the mouth." In this way she is able to get the meaning of those half sentences which we complete unconsciously from the tone of the voice or the twinkle of the eye.

Her memory of people is remarkable. She remembers the grasp of fingers she has held before, all the characteristic tightening of the muscles that makes one person's handshake different from that of another.

The trait most characteristic, perhaps, of Miss Keller (and also of Miss Sullivan) is humour. Skill in the use of words and her

286

habit of playing with them make her ready with *mots* and epigrams.

Some one asked her if she liked to study.

"Yes," she replied, "but I like to play also, and I feel sometimes as if I were a music box with all the play shut up inside me."

When she met Dr. Furness, the Shakespearean scholar, he warned her not to let the college professors tell her too many assumed facts about the life of Shakespeare; all we know, he said, is that Shakespeare was baptized, married, and died.

"Well," she replied, "he seems to have done all the essential things."

Once a friend who was learning the manual alphabet kept making "g," which is like the hand of a sign-post, for "h," which is made with two fingers extended. Finally Miss Keller told him to "fire both barrels."

Mr. Joseph Jefferson was once explaining to Miss Keller what the bumps on her head meant.

"That," he said, "is your prize-fighting bump."

"I never fight," she replied, "except against difficulties."

Miss Keller's humour is that deeper kind of humour which is courage.

Thirteen years ago she made up her mind to learn to speak, and she gave her teacher no rest until she was allowed to take lessons, although wise people, even Miss Sullivan, the wisest of them all, regarded it as an experiment unlikely to succeed and almost sure to make her unhappy. It was this same perseverance that made her go to college. After she had passed her examinations and received her certificate of admission, she was advised by the Dean of Radcliffe and others not to go on. She accordingly delayed a year. But she was not satisfied until she had carried out her purpose and entered college.

Her life has been a series of attempts to do whatever other people do, and to do it as well. Her success has been complete, for in trying to be like other people she has come most fully to be herself. Her unwillingness to be beaten has developed her courage. Where another can go, she can go. Her respect for physical bravery is like Stevenson's—the boy's contempt for the fellow who cries, with a touch of young bravado in it. She takes tramps in the woods, plunging through the underbrush, where she is scratched and bruised; yet you could not get her to admit that she is hurt, and you certainly could not persuade her to stay at home next time.

So when people try experiments with her, she displays a sportsmanlike determination to win in any test, however unreasonable, that one may wish to put her to.

If she does not know the answer to a question, she guesses with mischievous assurance. Ask her the colour of your coat (no blind person can tell colour), she will feel it and say "black." If it happens to be blue, and you tell her so triumphantly, she is likely to answer, "Thank you. I am glad you know. Why did you ask me?"

Her whimsical and adventuresome spirit puts her so much on her mettle that she makes rather a poor subject for the psychological experimenter. Moreover, Miss Sullivan does not see why Miss Keller should be subjected to the investigation of the scientist, and has not herself made many experiments. When a psychologist asked her if Miss Keller spelled on her fingers in her sleep, Miss Sullivan replied that she did not think it worth while to sit up and watch, such matters were of so little consequence.

Miss Keller likes to be part of the company. If any one whom she is touching laughs at a joke, she laughs, too, just as if she had heard it. If others are aglow with music, a responding glow, caught sympathetically, shines in her face. Indeed, she feels the movements of Miss Sullivan so minutely that she responds to her moods, and so she seems to know what is going on, even though the conversation has not been spelled to her for some time. In the same way her response to music is in part sympathetic, although she enjoys it for its own sake.

Music probably can mean little to her but beat and pulsation. She cannot sing and she cannot play the piano, although, as some early experiments show, she could learn mechanically to beat out a tune on the keys. Her enjoyment of music, however, is very genuine, for she has a tactile recognition of sound when the waves of air beat against her. Part of her experience of the rhythm of music comes, no doubt, from the vibration of solid objects which she is touching: the floor, or, what is more evident, the case of the piano, on which her hand rests. But she seems to feel the pulsation of the air itself. When the organ was played for her in St. Bartholomew's,* the whole building shook

*See page 263.

with the great pedal notes, but that does not altogether account for what she felt and enjoyed. The vibration of the air as the organ notes swelled made her sway in answer. Sometimes she puts her hand on a singer's throat to feel the muscular thrill and contraction, and from this she gets genuine pleasure. No one knows, however, just what her sensations are. It is amusing to read in one of the magazines of 1895 that Miss Keller "has a just and intelligent appreciation of different composers from having literally felt their music, Schumann being her favourite." If she knows the difference between Schumann and Beethoven, it is because she has read it, and if she has read it, she remembers it and can tell any one who asks her.

Miss Keller's effort to reach out and meet other people on their own intellectual ground has kept her informed of daily affairs. When her education became more systematic and she was busy with books, it would have been very easy for Miss Sullivan to let her draw into herself, if she had been so inclined. But every one who has met her has given his best ideas to her and she has taken them. If, in the course of a conversation, the friend next to her has ceased for some moments to spell into her hand, the question comes inevitably, "What are you talking about?" Thus she picks up the fragments of the daily intercourse of normal people, so that her detailed information is singularly full and accurate. She is a good talker on the little occasional affairs of life.

Much of her knowledge comes to her directly. When she is out walking she often stops suddenly, attracted by the odour of a bit of shrubbery. She reaches out and touches the leaves, and the world of growing things is hers, as truly as it is ours, to enjoy while she holds the leaves in her fingers and smells the blossoms, and to remember when the walk is done.

When she is in a new place, especially an interesting place like Niagara, whoever accompanies her—usually, of course, Miss Sullivan—is kept busy giving her an idea of visible details. Miss Sullivan, who knows her pupil's mind, selects from the passing landscape essential elements, which give a certain clearness to Miss Keller's imagined view of an outer world that to our eyes is confused and overloaded with particulars. If her companion does not give her enough details, Miss Keller asks questions until she has completed the view to her satisfaction.

She does not see with her eyes, but through the inner faculty to serve which eyes were given to us. When she returns from a walk and tells some one about it, her descriptions are accurate and vivid. A comparative experience drawn from written descriptions and from her teacher's words has kept her free from errors in her use of terms of sound and vision. True, her view of life is highly coloured and full of poetic exaggeration; the universe, as she sees it, is no doubt a little better than it really is. But her knowledge of it is not so incomplete as one might suppose. Occasionally she astonishes you by ignorance of some fact which no one happens to have told her; for instance, she did not know, until her first plunge into the sea, that it is salt. Many of the detached incidents and facts of our daily life pass around and over her unobserved; but she has enough detailed acquaintance with the world to keep her view of it from being essentially defective.

Most that she knows at first hand comes from her sense of touch. This sense is not, however, so finely developed as in some other blind people. Laura Bridgman could tell minute shades of difference in the size of thread, and made beautiful lace. Miss Keller used to knit and crochet, but she has had better things to do. With her varied powers and accomplishments, her sense of touch has not been used enough to develop it very far beyond normal acuteness. A friend tried Miss Keller one day with several coins. She was slower than he expected her to be in identifying them by their relative weight and size. But it should be said she almost never handles money—one of the many sordid and petty details of life, by the way, which she has been spared.

She recognizes the subject and general intention of a statuette six inches high. Anything shallower than a half-inch bas-relief is a blank to her, so far as it expresses an idea of beauty. Large statues, of which she can feel the sweep of line with her whole hand, she knows in their higher esthetic value. She suggests herself that she can know them better than we do, because she can get the true dimensions and appreciate more immediately the solid nature of a sculptured figure. When she was at the Museum of Fine Arts in Boston she stood on a step-ladder and let both hands play over the statues. When she felt a bas-relief of dancing girls she asked, "Where are the singers?" When she found them she said, "One is silent." The lips of the singer were closed.

It is, however, in her daily life that one can best measure the delicacy of her senses and her manual skill. She seems to have very little sense of direction. She gropes her way without much certainty in rooms where she is quite familiar. Most blind people are aided by the sense of sound, so that a fair comparison is hard to make, except with other deaf-blind persons. Her dexterity is not notable either in comparison with the normal person, whose movements are guided by the eye, or, I am told, with other blind people. She has practised no single constructive craft which would call for the use of her hands. When she was twelve, her friend Mr. Albert H. Munsell, the artist, let her experiment with a wax tablet and a stylus. He says that she did pretty well and managed to make, after models, some conventional designs of the outlines of leaves and rosettes. The only thing she does which requires skill with the hands is her work on the typewriter. Although she has used the typewriter since she was eleven years old, she is rather careful than rapid. She writes with fair speed and absolute sureness. Her manuscripts seldom contain typographical errors when she hands them to Miss Sullivan to read. Her typewriter has no special attachments. She keeps the relative position of the keys by an occasional touch of the little fingers on the outer edge of the board.

Miss Keller's reading of the manual alphabet by her sense of touch seems to cause some perplexity. Even people who know her fairly well have written in the magazines about Miss Sullivan's "mysterious telegraphic communications" with her pupil. The manual alphabet is that in use among all educated deaf people. Most dictionaries contain an engraving of the manual letters. The deaf person with sight looks at the fingers of his companion, but it is also possible to feel them. Miss Keller puts her fingers lightly over the hand of one who is talking to her and gets the words as rapidly as they can be spelled. As she explains, she is not conscious of the single letters or of separate words. Miss Sullivan and others who live constantly with the deaf can spell very rapidly—fast enough to get a slow lecture, not fast enough to get every word of a rapid speaker.

Anybody can learn the manual letters in a few minutes, use them slowly in a day, and in thirty days of constant use talk to Miss Keller or any other deaf person without realizing what his fingers are doing. If more people knew this, and the friends and relatives of deaf children learned the manual alphabet at once the deaf all over the world would be happier and better educated.

Miss Keller reads by means of embossed print or the various kinds of braille. The ordinary embossed book is made with roman letters, both small letters and capitals. These letters are of simple, square, angular design. The small letters are about three-sixteenths of an inch high, and are raised from the page the thickness of the thumbnail. The books are large, about the size of a volume of an encyclopedia. Green's "Short History of the English People" is in six large volumes. The books are not heavy, because the leaves with the raised type do not lie close. The time that one of Miss Keller's friends realizes most strongly that she is blind, is when he comes on her suddenly in the dark and hears the rustle of her fingers across the page.

The most convenient print for the blind is braille, which has several variations, too many, indeed—English, American, New York Point. Miss Keller reads them all. Most educated blind people know several, but it would save trouble if, as Miss Keller suggests, English braille were universally adapted. The facsimile on page xv gives an idea of how the raised dots look. Each character (either a letter or a special braille contraction) is a combination made by varying in place and number points in six possible positions. Miss Keller has a braille writer on which she keeps notes and writes letters to her blind friends. There are six keys, and by pressing different combinations at a stroke (as one plays a chord on the piano) the operator makes a character at a time in a sheet of thick paper, and can write about half as rapidly as on a typewriter. Braille is especially useful in making single manuscript copies of books.

Books for the blind are very limited in number. They cost a great deal to publish and they have not a large enough sale to make them profitable to the publisher; but there are several institutions with special funds to pay for embossed books. Miss Keller is more fortunate than most blind people in the kindness of her friends who have books made especially for her, and in the willingness of gentlemen, like Mr. E. E. Allen of the Pennsylvania Institute for the Instruction of the Blind, to print, as he has on several occasions, editions of books that she has needed.

Miss Keller does not as a rule read very fast, but she reads deliberately, not so much because she feels the words less quickly than we see them, as because it is one of her habits of mind to do things thoroughly and well. When a passage interests her, or she needs to remember it for some future use, she flutters it off swiftly on the fingers of her right hand. Sometimes this finger-play is unconscious. Miss Keller talks to herself absent-mindedly in the manual alphabet. When she is walking up or down the hall or along the veranda, her hands go flying along beside her like a confusion of birds' wings.

There is, I am told, tactile memory as well as visual and aural memory. Miss Sullivan says that both she and Miss Keller remember "in their fingers" what they have said. For Miss Keller to spell a sentence in the manual alphabet impresses it on her mind just as we learn a thing from having heard it many times and can call back the memory of its sound.

Like every deaf or blind person, Miss Keller depends on her sense of smell to an unusual degree. When she was a little girl she smelled everything and knew where she was, what neighbour's house she was passing, by the distinctive odours. As her intellect grew she became less dependent on this sense. To what extent she now identifies objects by their odour is hard to determine. The sense of smell has fallen into disrepute, and a deaf person is reluctant to speak of it. Miss Keller's acute sense of smell may account, however, in some part for that recognition of persons and things which it has been customary to attribute to a special sense, or to an unusual development of the power that we all seem to have of telling when some one is near.

The question of a special "sixth sense," such as people have ascribed to Miss Keller, is a delicate one. This much is certain, she cannot have any sense that other people may not have, and the existence of a special sense is not evident to her or to any one who knows her. Miss Keller is distinctly not a singular proof of occult and mysterious theories, and any attempt to explain her in that way fails to reckon with her normality. She is no more mysterious and complex than any other person. All that she is, all that she has done, can be explained directly, except such things in every human being as never can be explained. She does not, it would seem, prove the existence of spirit without matter, or of innate ideas, or of immortality, or anything else that any other human being does not prove. Philosophers have tried to find out what was her conception of abstract ideas before she learned language. If she had any conception, there is no way of discovering it now; for she cannot remember, and obviously there was no record at the time. She had no conception of God before she heard the word "God," as her comments very clearly show.*

Her sense of time is excellent, but whether it would have developed as a special faculty cannot be known, for she has had a watch since she was seven years old.

Miss Keller has two watches, which have been given her. They are, I think, the only ones of their kind in America. The watch has on the back cover a flat gold indicator which can be pushed freely around from left to right until, by means of a pin inside the case, it locks with the hour hand and takes a corresponding position. The point of this gold indicator bends over the edge of the case, round which are set eleven raised points—the stem forms the twelfth. Thus the watch, an ordinary watch with a white dial for the person who sees, becomes for a blind person by this special attachment in effect one with a single raised hour hand and raised figures. Though there is less than half an inch between the points—a space which represents sixty minutes— Miss Keller tells the time almost exactly. It should be said that any double-case watch with the crystal removed serves well enough for a blind person whose touch is sufficiently delicate to feel the position of the hands and not disturb or injure them.

The finer traits of Miss Keller's character are so well known that one needs not say much about them. Good sense, good humour, and imagination keep her scheme of things sane and beautiful. No attempt is made by those around her either to preserve or to break her illusions. When she was a little girl, a good many unwise and tactless things that were said for her benefit were not repeated to her, thanks to the wise watchfulness of Miss Sullivan. Now that she has grown up, nobody thinks of being less frank with her than with any other intelligent young woman. What her good friend, Charles Dudley Warner, wrote about her in *Harper's Magazine* in 1896 was true then, and it remains true now:

"I believe she is the purest-minded human being ever in existence. . . . The world to her is what her own mind is. She has not even learned that exhibition on which so many pride themselves, of 'righteous indignation.'

* See pages 369 and 371.

"Some time ago, when a policeman shot dead her dog, a dearly loved daily companion, she found in her forgiving heart no condemnation for the man; she only said, 'If he had only known what a good dog she was, he wouldn't have shot her.' It was said of old time, 'Lord forgive them, they know not what they do!'

"Of course the question will arise whether, if Helen Keller had not been guarded from the knowledge of evil, she would have been what she is to-day. . . . Her mind has neither been made effeminate by the weak and silly literature, nor has it been vitiated by that which is suggestive of baseness. In consequence her mind is not only vigorous, but it is pure. She is in love with noble things, with noble thoughts, and with the characters of noble men and women."

She still has a childlike aversion to tragedies. Her imagination is so vital that she falls completely under the illusion of a story, and lives in its world. Miss Sullivan writes in a letter of 1891:

"Yesterday I read to her the story of 'Macbeth,' as told by Charles and Mary Lamb. She was very greatly excited by it, and said: 'It is terrible! It makes me tremble!' After thinking a little while, she added, 'I think Shakespeare made it very terrible so that people would see how fearful it is to do wrong.'"

Of the real world she knows more of the good and less of the evil than most people seem to know. Her teacher does not harass her with the little unhappy things; but of the important difficulties they have been through, Miss Keller was fully informed, took her share of the suffering, and put her mind to the problems. She is logical and tolerant, most trustful of a world that has treated her kindly.

Once when some one asked her to define "love," she replied, "Why, bless you, that is easy; it is what everybody feels for everybody else."

"Toleration," she said once, when she was visiting her friend Mrs. Laurence Hutton, "is the greatest gift of the mind; it requires the same effort of the brain that it takes to balance oneself on a bicycle."

She has a large, generous sympathy and absolute fairness of temper. So far as she is noticeably different from other people she is less bound by convention. She has the courage of her metaphors and lets them take her skyward when we poor self-conscious folk would think them rather too bookish for ordinary conversation. She always says exactly what she thinks, without fear of the plain truth; yet no one is more tactful and adroit than she in turning an unpleasant truth so that it will do the least possible hurt to the feelings of others. Not all the attention that has been paid her since she was a child has made her take herself too seriously. Sometimes she gets started on a very solemn preachment. Then her teacher calls her an incorrigible little sermonizer, and she laughs at herself. Often, however, her sober ideas are not to be laughed at, for her earnestness carries her listeners with her. There is never the least false sententiousness in what she says. She means everything so thoroughly that her very quotations, her echoes from what she has read, are in truth original.

Her logic and her sympathy are in excellent balance. Her sympathy is of the swift and ministering sort which, fortunately, she has found so often in other people. And her sympathies go further and shape her opinions on political and national movements. She was intensely pro-Boer and wrote a strong argument in favour of Boer independence. When she was told of the surrender of the brave little people, her face clouded and she was silent a few minutes. Then she asked clear, penetrating questions about the terms of the surrender, and began to discuss them.

Both Mr. Gilman and Mr. Keith, the teachers who prepared her for college, were struck by her power of constructive reasoning; and she was excellent in pure mathematics, though she seems never to have enjoyed it much. Some of the best of her writing, apart from her fanciful and imaginative work, is her exposition in examinations and technical themes, and in some letters which she found it necessary to write to clear up misunderstandings, and which are models of close thinking enforced with sweet vehemence.

She is an optimist and an idealist.

"I hope," she writes in a letter, "that L—— isn't too practical, for if she is, I'm afraid she'll miss a great deal of pleasure."

In the diary that she kept at the Wright-Humason school in New York she wrote on October 18, 1894, "I find that I have four things to learn in my school life here, and indeed, in life—to think clearly without hurry or confusion, to love everybody sincerely, to act in everything with the highest motives, and to trust in dear God unhesitatingly."

CHAPTER III

EDUCATION

IT is now sixty-five years since Dr. Samuel Gridley Howe knew that he had made his way through Laura Bridgman's fingers to her intelligence. The names of Laura Bridgman and Helen Keller will always be linked together, and it is necessary to understand what Dr. Howe did for his pupil before one comes to an account of Miss Sullivan's work. For Dr. Howe is the great pioneer on whose work that of Miss Sullivan and other teachers of the deaf-blind immediately depends.

Dr. Samuel Gridley Howe was born in Boston, November 10, 1801, and died in Boston, January 9, 1876. He was a great philanthropist, interested especially in the education of all defectives, the feeble-minded, the blind, and the deaf. Far in advance of his time he advocated many public measures for the relief of the poor and the diseased, for which he was laughed at then, but which have since been put into practice. As head of the Perkins Institution for the Blind in Boston, he heard of Laura Bridgman and had her brought to the Institution on October 4, 1837.

Laura Bridgman was born at Hanover, New Hampshire, December 21, 1829; so she was almost eight years old when Dr. Howe began his experiments with her. At the age of twenty-six months scarlet fever left her without sight or hearing. She also lost her sense of smell and taste. Dr. Howe was an experimental scientist and had in him the spirit of New England transcendentalism with its large faith and large charities. Science and faith together led him to try to make his way into the soul which he believed was born in Laura Bridgman as in every other human being. His plan was to teach Laura by means of raised types. He pasted raised labels on objects and made her fit the labels to the objects and the objects to the labels. When she had learned in this way to associate raised words with things, in much the same manner, he says, as a dog learns tricks, he began to resolve the words into their letter elements and to teach her to put together "k-e-y," "c-a-p." His success convinced him that language can be conveyed through type to the mind of the blind-deaf child, who, before education, is in the state of the baby who has not learned to prattle; indeed, is in a much worse state, for the brain has grown in years without natural nourishment.

After Laura's education had progressed for two months with the use only of raised letters, Dr. Howe sent one of his teachers to learn the manual alphabet from a deaf-mute. She taught it to Laura, and from that time on the manual alphabet was the means of communicating with her.

After the first year or two Dr. Howe did not teach Laura Bridgman himself, but gave her over to other teachers, who under his direction carried on the work of teaching her language.*

Too much cannot be said in praise of Dr. Howe's work. As an investigator he kept always the scientist's attitude. He never forgot to keep his records of Laura Bridgman in the fashion of one who works in a laboratory. The result is, his records of her are systematic and careful. From a scientific standpoint, it is unfortunate that it was impossible to keep such a complete record of Helen Keller's development. This in itself is a great comment on the difference between Laura Bridgman and Helen Keller. Laura always remained an object of curious study. Helen Keller became so rapidly a distinctive personality that she kept her teacher in a breathless race to meet the needs of her pupil, with no time or strength to make a scientific study.

In some ways this is unfortunate. Miss Sullivan knew at the beginning that Helen Keller would be more interesting and successful than Laura Bridgman, and she expresses in one of her letters the need of keeping notes. But neither temperament nor training allowed her to make her pupil the object of any experiment or observation which did not help in the child's development. As soon as a thing was done, a definite goal passed, the teacher did not always look back and describe the way she had come. The explanation of the fact was unimportant compared to the fact itself and the need of hurrying on. There are two other reasons why Miss Sullivan's records are incomplete. It has always been a severe tax on her eyes to write, and she was early

*See "The Life and Education of Laura Dewey Bridgman," by Mrs. Mary Swift Lamson.

discouraged from publishing data by the inaccurate use made of what she at first supplied.

When she first wrote from Tuscumbia to Mr. Michael Anagnos, Dr. Howe's son-in-law and his successor as Director of the Perkins Institution, about her work with her pupil, the Boston papers began at once to publish exaggerated accounts of Helen Keller. Miss Sullivan protested. In a letter dated April 10, 1887, only five weeks after she went to Helen Keller, she wrote to a friend:

"—— sent me a *Boston Herald* containing a stupid article about Helen. How perfectly absurd to say that Helen is 'already talking fluently!' Why, one might just as well say that a two-year-old child converses fluently when he says 'apple give,' or 'baby walk go.' I suppose if you included his screaming, crowing, whimpering, grunting, squalling, with occasional kicks, in his conversation, it might be regarded as fluent—even eloquent. Then it is amusing to read of the elaborate preparation I underwent to fit me for the great task my friends entrusted to me. I am sorry that preparation didn't include spelling, it would have saved me such a lot of trouble."

On March 4, 1888, she writes in a letter:

"Indeed, I am heartily glad that I don't know all that is being said and written about Helen and myself. I assure you I know quite enough. Nearly every mail brings some absurd statement, printed or written. The truth is not wonderful enough to suit the newspapers; so they enlarge upon it and invent ridiculous embellishments. One paper has Helen demonstrating problems in geometry by means of her playing blocks. I expect to hear next that she has written a treatise on the origin and future of the planets!"

In December, 1887, appeared the first report of the Director of the Perkins Institution, which deals with Helen Keller. For this report Miss Sullivan prepared, in reluctant compliance with the request of Mr. Anagnos, an account of her work. This with the extracts from her letters, scattered through the report, is the first valid source of information about Helen Keller. Of this report Miss Sullivan wrote in a letter dated October 30, 1887:

"Have you seen the paper I wrote for the 'report'? Mr. Anagnos was delighted with it. He says Helen's progress has been 'a triumphal march from the beginning,' and he has many flattering things to say about her teacher. I think he is inclined to exaggerate; at all events, his language is too glowing, and simple facts are set forth in such a manner that they bewilder one. Doubtless the work of the past few months does seem like a triumphal march to him; but then people seldom see the halting and painful steps by which the most insignificant success is achieved."

As Mr. Anagnos was the head of a great institution, what he said had much more effect than the facts in Miss Sullivan's account on which he based his statements. The newspapers caught Mr. Anagnos's spirit and exaggerated a hundred-fold. In a year after she first went to Helen Keller, Miss Sullivan found herself and her pupil the centre of a stupendous fiction. Then the educators all over the world said their say and for the most part did not help matters. There grew up a mass of controversial matter which it is amusing to read now. Teachers of the deaf proved *a priori* that what Miss Sullivan had done could not be, and some discredit was reflected on her statements, because they were surrounded by the vague eloquence of Mr. Anagnos. Thus the story of Helen Keller, incredible when told with moderation, had the misfortune to be heralded by exaggerated announcements, and naturally met either an ignorant credulity or an incredulous hostility.

In November, 1888, another report of the Perkins Institution appeared with a second paper by Miss Sullivan, and then nothing official was published until November, 1891, when Mr. Anagnos issued the last Perkins Institution report containing anything about Helen Keller. For this report Miss Sullivan wrote the fullest and largest account she has ever written; and in this report appeared the "Frost King," which is discussed fully in a later chapter. Then the controversy waxed fiercer than ever.

Finding that other people seemed to know so much more about Helen Keller than she did, Miss Sullivan kept silent and has been silent for ten years, except for her paper in the first volta Bureau Souvenir of Helen Keller* and the paper which, at Dr. Bell's request, she prepared in 1894 for the meeting at Chautauqua of the American Association to Promote the Teaching of Speech to the Deaf. When Dr. Bell and others tell her, what is certainly true from an impersonal point of view, that she owes it to the cause of education to write what she knows, she answers

*See page 396.

very properly that she owes all her time and all her energies to her pupil.

Although Miss Sullivan is still rather amused than distressed when some one, even one of her friends, makes mistakes in published articles about her and Miss Keller, still she sees that Miss Keller's book should include all the information that the teacher could at present furnish. So she consented to the publication of extracts from letters which she wrote during the first year of her work with her pupil. These letters were written to Mrs. Sophia C. Hopkins, the only person to whom Miss Sullivan ever wrote freely. Mrs. Hopkins has been a matron at the Perkins Institution for twenty years, and during the time that Miss Sullivan was a pupil there she was like a mother to her. In these letters we have an almost weekly record of Miss Sullivan's work. Some of the details she had forgotten, as she grew more and more to generalize. Many people have thought that any attempt to find the principles in her method would be nothing but a later theory superimposed on Miss Sullivan's work. But it is evident that in these letters she was making a clear analysis of what she was doing. She was her own critic, and in spite of her later declaration, made with her modest carelessness, that she followed no particular method, she was very clearly learning from her task and phrasing at the time principles of education of unique value not only in the teaching of the deaf but in the teaching of all children. The extracts from her letters and reports form an important contribution to pedagogy, and more than justify the opinion of Dr. Daniel C. Gilman, who wrote in 1893, when he was President of Johns Hopkins University:

"I have just read . . . your most interesting account of the various steps you have taken in the education of your wonderful pupil, and I hope you will allow me to express my admiration for the wisdom that has guided your methods and the affection which has inspired your labours."

Miss Anne Mansfield Sullivan was born at Springfield, Massachusetts. Very early in her life she became almost totally blind, and she entered the Perkins Institution October 7, 1880, when she was fourteen years old. Later her sight was partially restored.

Mr. Anagnos says in his report of 1887: "She was obliged

to begin her education at the lowest and most elementary point; but she showed from the very start that she had in herself the force and capacity which insure success. . . . She has finally reached the goal for which she strove so bravely. The golden words that Dr. Howe uttered and the example that he left passed into her thoughts and heart and helped her on the road to usefulness; and now she stands by his side as his worthy successor in one of the most cherished branches of his work. . . . Miss Sullivan's talents are of the highest order."

In 1886 she graduated from the Perkins Institution. When Captain Keller applied to the director for a teacher, Mr. Anagnos recommended her. The only time she had to prepare herself for the work with her pupil was from August, 1886, when Captain Keller wrote, to February, 1887. During this time she read Dr. Howe's reports. She was further aided by the fact that during the six years of her school life she had lived in the house with Laura Bridgman. It was Dr. Howe who, by his work with Laura Bridgman, made Miss Sullivan's work possible: but it was Miss Sullivan who discovered the way to teach language to the deaf-blind.

It must be remembered that Miss Sullivan had to solve her problems unaided by previous experience or the assistance of any other teacher. During the first year of her work with Helen Keller, in which she taught her pupil language, they were in Tuscumbia; and when they came North and visited the Perkins Institution, Helen Keller was never a regular student there or subject to the discipline of the Institution. The impression that Miss Sullivan educated Helen Keller "under the direction of Mr. Anagnos" is erroneous. In the three years during which at various times Miss Keller and Miss Sullivan were guests of the Perkins Institution, the teachers there did not help Miss Sullivan, and Mr. Anagnos did not even use the manual alphabet with facility as a means of communication. Mr. Anagnos wrote in the report of the Perkins Institution, dated November 27, 1888: "At my urgent request, Helen, accompanied by her mother and her teacher, came to the North in the last week of May, and spent several months with us as our guests. . . . We gladly allowed her to use freely our library of embossed books, our collection of stuffed animals, sea-shells, models of flowers and plants, and the rest of our apparatus for instructing the blind through the sense of touch. I do not doubt that she derived from them much pleasure and not a little profit. But whether Helen stays at home or makes visits in other parts of the country, her education is always under the immediate direction and exclusive control of her teacher. No one interferes with Miss Sullivan's plans, or shares in her tasks. She has been allowed entire freedom in the choice of means and methods for carrying on her great work; and, as we can judge by the results, she has made a most judicious and discreet use of this privilege. What the little pupil has thus far accomplished is widely known, and her wonderful attainments command general admiration; but only those who are familiar with the particulars of the grand achievement know that the credit is largely due to the intelligence, wisdom, sagacity, unremitting perseverance and unbending will of the instructress, who rescued the child from the depths of everlasting night and stillness, and watched over the different phases of her mental and moral development with maternal solicitude and enthusiastic devotion."

Here follow in order Miss Sullivan's letters and the most important passages from the reports. I have omitted from each succeeding report what has already been explained and does not need to be repeated. For the ease of the reader I have, with Miss Sullivan's consent, made the extracts run together continuously and supplied words of connection and the resulting necessary changes in syntax, and Miss Sullivan has made slight changes in the phrasing of her reports and also of her letters, which were carelessly written. I have also italicized a few important passages. Some of her opinions Miss Sullivan would like to enlarge and revise. That remains for her to do at another time. At present we have here the fullest record that has been published. The first letter is dated March 6, 1887, three days after her arrival in Tuscumbia.

. . . It was 6.30 when I reached Tuscumbia. I found Mrs. Keller and Mr. James Keller waiting for me. They said somebody had met every train for two days. The drive from the station to the house, a distance of one mile, was very lovely and restful. I was surprised to find Mrs. Keller a very young-looking woman, not much older than myself, I should think. Captain Keller met us in the yard and gave me a cheery welcome and a hearty handshake. My first question was, "Where is Helen?" I tried with all my might to control the eagerness that made me tremble so that I could hardly walk. As we approached the house I saw a child standing in the doorway, and Captain Keller said, "There she is. She has known all day that some one was expected, and she has been wild ever since her mother went to the station for you." I had scarcely put my foot on the steps, when she rushed toward me with such force that she would have thrown me backward if Captain Keller had not been behind me. She felt my face and dress and my bag, which she took out of my hand and tried to open. It did not open easily, and she felt carefully to see if there was a key-hole. Finding that there was, she turned to me, making the sign of turning a key and pointing to the bag. Her mother interfered at this point and showed Helen by signs that she must not touch the bag. Her face flushed, and when her mother attempted to take the bag from her, she grew very angry. I attracted her attention by showing her my watch and letting her hold it in her hand. Instantly the tempest subsided, and we went upstairs together. Here I opened the bag, and she went through it eagerly, probably expecting to find something to eat. Friends had probably brought her candy in their bags, and she expected to find some in mine. I made her understand, by pointing to a trunk in the hall and to myself and nodding my head, that I had a trunk, and then made the sign that she had used for eating, and nodded again. She understood in a flash and ran downstairs to tell her mother, by means of emphatic signs, that there was some candy in a trunk for her. She returned in a few minutes and helped me put away my things. It was too comical to see her put on my bonnet and cock her head first on one side, then on the other, and look in the mirror, just as if she could see. Somehow I had expected to see a pale, delicate child—I suppose I got the idea from Dr. Howe's description of Laura Bridgman when she came to the Institution. But there's nothing pale or delicate about Helen. She is large, strong, and ruddy, and as unrestrained in her movements as a young colt. She has none of those nervous habits that are so noticeable and so distressing in blind children. Her body is well formed and vigorous, and Mrs. Keller says she has not been ill a day since the illness that deprived her of her sight and hearing. She has a fine head, and it is set on her shoulders just right. Her face is hard to describe. It is intelligent, but lacks mobility, or soul, or something. Her mouth is large and finely shaped. You see at a glance that she is blind. One eye is larger than the other, and protrudes noticeably. She rarely smiles; indeed, I have seen her smile only once or twice since I came. She is unresponsive and even impatient of caresses from any one except her mother. She is very quick-tempered and wilful, and nobody, except her brother James, has attempted to control her. The greatest problem I shall have to solve is how to discipline and control her without breaking her spirit. I shall go rather slowly at first and try to win her love. I shall not attempt to conquer her by force alone; but I shall insist on reasonable obedience from the start. One thing that impresses everybody is Helen's tireless activity. She is never still a moment. She is here, there, and everywhere. Her hands are in everything; but nothing holds her attention for long. Dear child, her restless spirit gropes in the dark. Her untaught, unsatisfied hands destroy whatever they touch because they do not know what else to do with things.

She helped me unpack my trunk when it came, and was delighted when she found the doll the little girls sent her. I thought it a good opportunity to teach her her first word. I spelled "d-o-l-l" slowly in her hand and pointed to the doll and nodded my head, which seems to be her sign for possession. Whenever anybody gives her anything, she points to it, then to herself, and nods her head. She looked puzzled and felt my hand, and I repeated the letters. She imitated them very well and pointed to the doll. Then I took the doll, meaning to give it back to her when she had made the letters; but she thought I meant to take it from her, and in an instant she was in a temper, and tried to seize the doll. I shook my head and tried to form the letters with her fingers; but she got more and more angry. I forced her into a chair and held her there until I was nearly exhausted. Then it occurred to me that it was useless to continue the struggle—I must do something to turn the current of her thoughts. I let her go, but refused to give up the doll. I went downstairs and got some cake (she is very fond of sweets). I showed Helen the cake and spelled "c-a-k-e" in her hand, holding the cake toward her. Of course she wanted it and tried to take it; but I spelled the word again and patted her hand. She made the letters rapidly, and I gave her the cake, which she ate in a great hurry, thinking, I suppose, that I might take it from her. Then I showed her the doll and spelled the word again, holding the doll toward her as I held the cake. She made the letters "d-o-l" and I made the other "l" and gave her the doll. She ran downstairs with it and could not be induced to return to my room all day.

Yesterday I gave her a sewing-card to do. I made the first row of vertical lines and let her feel it and notice that there were several rows of little holes. She began to work delightedly and finished the card in a few minutes, and did it very neatly indeed. I thought I would try another word; so I spelled "c-a-r-d." She made the "c-a," then stopped and thought, and making the sign for eating and pointing downward she pushed me toward the door, meaning that I must go downstairs for some cake. The two letters "c-a," you see, had reminded her of Friday's "lesson"—not that she had any idea that *cake* was the name of the thing, but it was simply a matter of association, I suppose. I finished the word "c-a-k-e" and obeyed her command. She was delighted. Then I spelled "d-o-l-l" and began to hunt for it. She follows with her hands every motion you make, and she knew that I was looking for the doll. She pointed down, meaning that the doll was downstairs. I made the signs that she had used when she wished me to go for the cake, and pushed her toward the door. She started forward, then hesitated a moment, evidently debating within herself whether she would go or not. She decided to send me instead. I shook my head and spelled "d-o-l-l" more emphatically, and opened the door for her; but she obstinately refused to obey. She had not finished the cake she was eating, and I took it away, indicating that if she brought the doll I would give her back the cake. She stood perfectly still for one long moment, her face crimson; then her desire for the cake triumphed, and she ran downstairs and brought the doll, and of course I gave her the cake, but could not persuade her to enter the room again.

She was very troublesome when I began to write this morning. She kept coming up behind me and putting her hand on the paper and into the ink-bottle. These blots are her handiwork. Finally I remembered the kindergarten beads, and set her to work stringing them. First I put on two wooden beads and one glass bead, then made her feel of the string and the two boxes of beads. She nodded and began at once to fill the string with wooden beads. I shook my head and took them all off and made her feel of the two wooden beads and the one glass bead. She examined them thoughtfully and began again. This time she put on the glass bead first and the two wooden ones next. I took them off and showed her that the two wooden ones must go on first, then the glass bead. She had no further trouble and filled the string quickly, too quickly, in fact. She tied the ends together when she had finished the string, and put the beads round her neck. I did not make the knot large enough in the next string, and the beads came off as fast as she put them on; but she solved the difficulty herself by putting the string through a bead and tying it. I thought this very clever. She amused herself with the beads until dinner-time, bringing the strings to me now and then for my approval.

My eyes are very much inflamed. I know this letter is very carelessly written. I had a lot to say, and couldn't stop to think how to express things neatly. Please do not show my letter to any one. If you want to, you may read it to my friends.

MONDAY P. M.

I had a battle royal with Helen this morning. Although I try very hard not to force issues, I find it very difficult to avoid them.

Helen's table manners are appalling. She puts her hands in our plates and helps herself, and when the dishes are passed, she grabs them and takes out whatever she wants. This morning I would not let her put her hand in my plate. She persisted, and a contest of wills followed. Naturally the family was much disturbed, and left the room. I locked the dining-room door, and proceeded to eat my breakfast, though the food almost choked me. Helen was lying on the floor, kicking and scream- ing and trying to pull my chair from under me. She kept this up for half an hour, then she got up to see what I was doing. I let her see that I was eating, but did not let her put her hand in the plate. She pinched me, and I slapped her every time she did it. Then she went all round the table to see who was there, and finding no one but me, she seemed bewildered. After a few minutes she came back to her place and began to eat her breakfast with her fingers. I gave her a spoon, which she threw on the floor. I forced her out of the chair and made her pick it up. Finally I succeeded in getting her back in her chair again, and held the spoon in her hand, compelling her to take up the food with it and put it in her mouth. In a few minutes she

yielded and finished her breakfast peaceably. Then we had
another tussle over folding her napkin. When she had finished,
she threw it on the floor and ran toward the door. Finding it
locked, she began to kick and scream all over again. It was
another hour before I succeeded in getting her napkin folded.
Then I let her out into the warm sunshine and went up to my
room and threw myself on the bed exhausted. I had a good
cry and felt better. I suppose I shall have many such battles
with the little woman before she learns the only two essential
things I can teach her, obedience and love.

Good-by, dear. Don't worry; I'll do my best and leave the
rest to whatever power manages that which we cannot. I like
Mrs. Keller very much.

TUSCUMBIA, ALABAMA, March 11, 1887.

Since I wrote you, Helen and I have gone to live all by ourselves in a little garden-house about a quarter of a mile from
her home, only a short distance from Ivy Green, the Keller
homestead. I very soon made up my mind that I could do
nothing with Helen in the midst of the family, who have always
allowed her to do exactly as she pleased. She has tyrannized
over everybody, her mother, her father, the servants, the little
darkies who play with her, and nobody had ever seriously
disputed her will, except occasionally her brother James, until I
came; and like all tyrants she holds tenaciously to her divine
right to do as she pleases. If she ever failed to get what she
wanted, it was because of her inability to make the vassals of
her household understand what it was. Every thwarted desire
was the signal for a passionate outburst, and as she grew older
and stronger, these tempests became more violent. As I began
to teach her, I was beset by many difficulties. She wouldn't
yield a point without contesting it to the bitter end. I couldn't
coax her or compromise with her. To get her to do the simplest
thing, such as combing her hair or washing her hands or button-
ing her boots, it was necessary to use force, and, of course, a distressing scene followed. The family naturally felt inclined to
interfere, especially her father, who cannot bear to see her cry.
So they were all willing to give in for the sake of peace. Besides,
her past experiences and associations were all against me. I
saw clearly that it was useless to try to teach her language

or anything else until she learned to obey me. I have thought about it a great deal, and the more I think, the more certain I am that obedience is the gateway through which knowledge, yes, and love, too, enter the mind of the child. As I wrote you, I meant to go slowly at first. I had an idea that I could win the love and confidence of my little pupil by the same means that I should use if she could see and hear. But I soon found that I was cut off from all the usual approaches to the child's heart. She accepted everything I did for her as a matter of course, and refused to be caressed, and there was no way of appealing to her affection or sympathy or childish love of appro-bation. She would or she wouldn't, and there was an end of it. Thus it is, we study, plan and prepare ourselves for a task, and when the hour for action arrives, we find that the system we have followed with such labour and pride does not fit the occasion; and then there's nothing for us to do but rely on something within us, some innate capacity for knowing and doing, which we did not know we possessed until the hour of our great need brought it to light.

I had a good, frank talk with Mrs. Keller, and explained to her how difficult it was going to be to do anything with Helen under the existing circumstances. I told her that in my opinion the child ought to be separated from the family for a few weeks at least—that she must learn to depend on and obey me before I could make any headway. After a long time Mrs. Keller said that she would think the matter over and see what Captain Keller thought of sending Helen away with me. Captain Keller fell in with the scheme most readily and suggested that the little garden-house at the "old place" be got ready for us. He said that Helen might recognize the place, as she had often been there; but she would have no idea of her surroundings, and they could come every day to see that all was going well, with the understanding, of course, that she was to know nothing of their visits. I hurried the preparations for our departure as much as possible, and here we are.

The little house is a genuine bit of paradise. It consists of one large square room with a great fireplace, a spacious bay-window, and a small room where our servant, a little negro boy, sleeps. There is a piazza in front, covered with vines that grow so luxuriantly that you have to part them to see the garden beyond. Our meals are brought from the house, and we usually eat on the piazza. The little negro boy takes care of the fire when we need one; so I can give my whole attention to Helen.

She was greatly excited at first, and kicked and screamed herself into a sort of stupor; but when supper was brought she ate heartily and seemed brighter, although she refused to let me touch her. She devoted herself to her dolls the first evening, and when it was bedtime she undressed very quietly; but when she felt me get into bed with her, she jumped out on the other side, and nothing that I could do would induce her to get in again. But I was afraid she would take cold, and I insisted that she must go to bed. We had a terrific tussle, I can tell you. The struggle lasted for nearly two hours. I never saw such strength and endurance in a child. But fortunately for us both, I am a little stronger, and quite as obstinate when I set out. I finally succeeded in getting her on the bed and covered her up, and she lay curled up as near the edge of the bed as possible.

The next morning she was very docile, but evidently homesick. She kept going to the door, as if she expected some one, and every now and then she would touch her cheek, which is her sign for her mother, and shake her head sadly. She played with her dolls more than usual, and would have nothing to do with me. It is amusing and pathetic to see Helen with her dolls. I don't think she has any special tenderness for them— I have never seen her caress them; but she dresses and undresses them many times during the day and handles them exactly as she has seen her mother and the nurse handle her baby sister.

This morning Nancy, her favourite doll, seemed to have some difficulty about swallowing the milk that was being administered to her in large spoonfuls; for Helen suddenly put down the cup and began to slap her on the back and turn her over on her knees, trotting her gently and patting her softly all the time. This lasted for several minutes; then this mood passed, and Nancy was thrown ruthlessly on the floor and pushed to one side, while a large, pink-cheeked, fuzzy-haired member of the family received the little mother's undivided attention.

Helen knows several words now, but has no idea how to use them, or that everything has a name. I think, however, she will learn quickly enough by and by. As I have said before, she is wonderfully bright and active and as quick as lightning in her movements.

March 13, 1887.

You will be glad to hear that my experiment is working out finely. I have not had any trouble at all with Helen, either yesterday or to-day. She has learned three new words, and when I give her the objects, the names of which she has learned, she spells them unhesitatingly; but she seems glad when the lesson is over.

We had a good frolic this morning out in the garden. Helen evidently knew where she was as soon as she touched the box-wood hedges, and made many signs which I did not understand. No doubt they were signs for the different members of the family at Ivy Green.

I have just heard something that surprised me very much. It seems that Mr. Anagnos had heard of Helen before he received Captain Keller's letter last summer. Mr. Wilson, a teacher at Florence, and a friend of the Kellers', studied at Harvard the summer before and went to the Perkins Institution to learn if anything could be done for his friend's child. He saw a gentleman whom he presumed to be the director, and told him about Helen. He says the gentleman was not particularly interested, but said he would see if anything could be done. Doesn't it seem strange that Mr. Anagnos never referred to this interview?

March 20, 1887.

My heart is singing for joy this morning. A miracle has happened! The light of understanding has shone upon my little pupil's mind, and behold, all things are changed!

The wild little creature of two weeks ago has been transformed into a gentle child. She is sitting by me as I write, her face serene and happy, crocheting a long red chain of Scotch wool. She learned the stitch this week, and is very proud of the achieve-ment. When she succeeded in making a chain that would reach across the room, she patted herself on the arm and put the first work of her hands lovingly against her cheek. She lets me kiss her now, and when she is in a particularly gentle mood, she will sit in my lap for a minute or two; but she does not return my caresses. The great step—the ·step that counts—has been taken. The little savage has learned her first lesson in obedience, and finds the yoke easy. It now remains my pleasant task to direct and mould the beautiful intelligence that is beginning to stir in the child-soul. Already people remark the change in Helen. Her father looks in at us morning and evening as he goes to and from his office, and sees her contentedly stringing her beads or making horizontal lines on her sewing-card, and exclaims, "How quiet she is!" When I came, her movements were so insistent that one always felt there was something unnatural and almost weird about her. I have noticed also that she eats much less, a fact which troubles her father so much that he is anxious to get her home. He says she is homesick. I don't agree with him; but I suppose we shall have to leave our little bower very soon.

Helen has learned several nouns this week. "M-u-g" and "m-i-l-k," have given her more trouble than other words. When she spells "milk," she points to the mug, and when she spells "mug," she makes the sign for pouring or drinking, which shows that she has confused the words. She has no idea yet that everything has a name.

Yesterday I had the little negro boy come in when Helen was having her lesson, and learn the letters, too. This pleased her very much and stimulated her ambition to excel Percy. She was delighted if he made a mistake, and made him form the letter over several times. When he succeeded in forming it to suit her, she patted him on his woolly head so vigorously that I thought some of his slips were intentional.

One day this week Captain Keller brought Belle, a setter of which he is very proud, to see us. He wondered if Helen would recognize her old playmate. Helen was giving Nancy a bath, and didn't notice the dog at first. She usually feels the softest step and throws out her arms to ascertain if any one is near her. Belle didn't seem very anxious to attract her attention. I imagine she has been rather roughly handled sometimes by her little mistress. The dog hadn't been in the room more than half a minute, however, before Helen began to sniff, and dumped the doll into the wash-bowl and felt about the room. She stumbled upon Belle, who was crouching near the window where Captain Keller was standing. It was *evident* that she recognized the dog; for she put her arms round her neck and squeezed her. Then Helen sat down by her and began to manipulate her claws. We couldn't think for a second what she was doing; but when we saw her make the letters "d-o-l-l" on her own fingers, we knew that she was trying to teach Belle to spell.

March 28, 1887.

Helen and I came home yesterday. I am sorry they wouldn't let us stay another week; but I think I have made the most I could of the opportunities that were mine the past two weeks, and I don't expect that I shall have any serious trouble with Helen in the future. The back of the greatest obstacle in the path of progress is broken. I think "no" and "yes," conveyed by a shake or a nod of my head, have become facts as apparent to her as hot and cold or as the difference between pain and pleasure. And I don't intend that the lesson she has learned at the cost of so much pain and trouble shall be unlearned. I shall stand between her and the over-indulgence of her parents. I have told Captain and Mrs. Keller that they must not interfere with me in any way. I have done my best to make them see the terrible injustice to Helen of allowing her to have her way in everything, and I have pointed out that the processes of teaching the child that everything cannot be as he wills it, are apt to be painful both to him and to his teacher. They have promised to let me have a free hand and help me as much as possible. The improvement they cannot help seeing in their child has given them more confidence in me. Of course, it is hard for them. I realize that it hurts to see their afflicted little child punished and made to do things against her will. Only a few hours after my talk with Captain and Mrs. Keller (and they had agreed to everything), Helen took a notion that she wouldn't use her napkin at table. I think she wanted to see what would happen. I attempted several times to put the napkin round her neck; but each time she tore it off and threw it on the floor and finally began to kick the table. I took her plate away and started to take her out of the room. Her father objected and said that no child of his should be deprived of his food on any account.

Helen didn't come up to my room after supper, and I didn't

see her again until breakfast-time. She was at her place when I came down. She had put the napkin under her chin, instead of pinning it at the back, as was her custom. She called my attention to the new arrangement, and when I did not object she seemed pleased and patted herself. When she left the dining-room, she took my hand and patted it. I wondered if she was trying to "make up." I thought I would try the effect of a little belated discipline. I went back to the dining-room and got a napkin. When Helen came upstairs for her lesson, I arranged the objects on the table as usual, except that the cake, which I always give her in bits as a reward when she spells a word quickly and correctly, was not there. She noticed this at once and made the sign for it. I showed her the napkin and pinned it round her neck, then tore it off and threw it on the floor and shook my head. I repeated this performance several times. I think she understood perfectly well; for she slapped her hand two or three times and shook her head. We began the lesson as usual. I gave her an object, and she spelled the name (she knows twelve now). After spelling half the words, she stopped suddenly, as if a thought had flashed into her mind, and felt for the napkin. She pinned it round her neck and made the sign for cake (it didn't occur to her to spell the word, you see). I took this for a promise that if I gave her some cake she would be a good girl. I gave her a larger piece than usual, and she chuckled and patted herself.

April 3, 1887.

We almost live in the garden, where everything is growing and blooming and glowing. After breakfast we go out and watch the men at work. Helen loves to dig and play in the dirt like any other child. This morning she planted her doll and showed me that she expected her to grow as tall as I. You must see that she is very bright, but you have no idea how cunning she is.

At ten we come in and string beads for a few minutes. She can make a great many combinations now, and often invents new ones herself. Then I let her decide whether she will sew or knit or crochet. She learned to knit very quickly, and is making a wash-cloth for her mother. Last week she made her doll an apron, and it was done as well as any child of her age could do it. But I am always glad when this work is over for the day. Sewing and crocheting are inventions of the devil, I 'think. I'd rather break stones on the king's highway than hem a handkerchief. At eleven we have gymnastics. She knows all the free-hand movements and the "Anvil Chorus" with the dumb-bells. Her father says he is going to fit up a gymnasium for her in the pump-house; but we both like a good romp better than set exercises. The hour from twelve to one is devoted to the learning of new words. *But you mustn't think this is the only time I spell to Helen; for I spell in her hand everything we do all day long, although she has no idea as yet what the spelling means.* After dinner I rest for an hour, and Helen plays with her dolls or frolics in the yard with the little darkies, who were her constant companions before I came. Later I join them, and we make the rounds of the outhouses. We visit the horses and mules in their stalls and hunt for eggs and feed the turkeys. Often, when the weather is fine, we drive from four to six, or go to see her aunt at Ivy Green or her cousins in the town. Helen's instincts are decidedly social; she likes to have people about her and to visit her friends, partly, I think, because they always have things she likes to eat. After supper we go to my room and do all sorts of things until eight, when I undress the little woman and put her to bed. She sleeps with me now. Mrs. Keller wanted to get a nurse for her; but I concluded I'd rather be her nurse than look after a stupid, lazy negress. Besides, I like to have Helen depend on me for everything, *and I find it much easier to teach her things at odd moments than at set times.*

On March 31st I found that Helen knew eighteen nouns and three verbs. Here is a list of the words. Those with a cross after them are words she asked for herself: *Doll, mug, pin, key, dog, hat, cup, box, water, milk, candy, eye (x), finger (x), toe (x), head (x), cake, baby, mother, sit, stand, walk.* On April 1st she learned the nouns *knife, fork, spoon, saucer, tea, papa, bed,* and the verb *run.*

April 5, 1887.

I must write you a line this morning because something very important has happened. Helen has taken the second great step in her education. She has learned that *everything has a name, and that the manual alphabet is the key to everything she wants to know.*

In a previous letter I think I wrote you that "mug" and "milk" had given Helen more trouble than all the rest. She confused the nouns with the verb "drink." She didn't know the word for "drink," but went through the pantomime of drinking whenever she spelled "mug" or "milk." This morning, while she was washing, she wanted to know the name for "water." When she wants to know the name of anything, she points to it and pats my hand. I spelled "w-a-t-e-r" and thought no more about it until after breakfast. Then it occurred to me that with the help of this new word I might succeed in straightening out the "mug-milk" difficulty. We went out to the pump-house, and I made Helen hold her mug under the spout while I pumped. As the cold water gushed forth, filling the mug, I spelled "w-a-t-e-r" in Helen's free hand. The word coming so close upon the sensation of cold water rushing over her hand seemed to startle her. She dropped the mug and stood as one transfixed. A new light came into her face. She spelled "water" several times. Then she dropped on the ground and asked for its name and pointed to the pump and the trellis, and suddenly turning round she asked for my name. I spelled "Teacher." Just then the nurse brought Helen's little sister into the pump-house, and Helen spelled "baby" and pointed to the nurse. All the way back to the house she was highly excited, and learned the name of every object she touched, so that in a few hours she had added thirty new words to her vocabulary. Here are some of them: *Door, open, shut, give, go, come,* and a great many more.

P. S.—I didn't finish my letter in time to get it posted last night; so I shall add a line. Helen got up this morning like a radiant fairy. She has flitted from object to object, asking the name of everything and kissing me for very gladness. Last night when I got in bed, she stole into my arms of her own accord and kissed me for the first time, and I thought my heart would burst, so full was it of joy.

April 10, 1887.

I see an improvement in Helen from day to day, almost from hour to hour. Everything must have a name now. Wherever we go, she asks eagerly for the names of things she has not learned at home. She is anxious for her friends to spell, and eager to teach the letters to every one she meets. She drops the

signs and pantomime she used before, as soon as she has words
to supply their place, and the acquirement of a new word affords
her the liveliest pleasure. And we notice that her face grows
more expressive each day.

*I have decided not to try to have regular lessons for the present.
I am going to treat Helen exactly like a two-year-old child. It
occurred to me the other day that it is absurd to require a child to
come to a certain place at a certain time and recite certain lessons,
when he has not yet acquired a working vocabulary.* I sent Helen
away and sat down to think. I asked myself, *"How does a normal child learn language?"* The answer was simple, "By imitation." The child comes into the world with the ability to learn,
and he learns of himself, provided he is supplied with sufficient
outward stimulus. He sees people do things, and he tries to do
them. He hears others speak, and he tries to speak. *But long
before he utters his first word, he understands what is said to
him.* I have been observing Helen's little cousin lately. She is
about fifteen months old, and already understands a great deal.
In response to questions she points out prettily her nose, mouth,
eye, chin, cheek, ear. If I say, "Where is baby's other ear?"
she points it out correctly. If I hand her a flower, and say,
"Give it to mamma," she takes it to her mother. If I say, "Where
is the little rogue?" she hides behind her mother's chair, or
covers her face with her hands and peeps out at me with an
expression of genuine roguishness. She obeys many commands
like these: "Come," "Kiss," "Go to papa," "Shut the door," "Give
me the biscuit." But I have not heard her try to say any of
these words, although they have been repeated hundreds of
times in her hearing, and it is perfectly evident that she understands them. These observations have given me a clue to the
method to be followed in teaching Helen language. *I shall talk
into her hand as we talk into the baby's ears.* I shall assume
that she has the normal child's capacity of assimilation and imitation. *I shall use complete sentences in talking to her,* and fill
out the meaning with gestures and her descriptive signs when
necessity requires it; but I shall not try to keep her mind fixed on
any one thing. I shall do all I can to interest and stimulate it,
and wait for results.

April 24, 1887.

The new scheme works splendidly. Helen knows the meaning of more than a hundred words now, and learns new ones daily without the slightest suspicion that she is performing a most difficult feat. She learns because she can't help it, just as the bird learns to fly. But don't imagine that she "talks fluently." Like her baby cousin, she expresses whole sentences by single words. "Milk," with a gesture means, "Give me more milk." "Mother," accompanied by an inquiring look, means, "Where is mother?" "Go" means, "I want to go out." But when I spell into her hand, "Give me some bread," she hands me the bread, or if I say, "Get your hat and we will go to walk," she obeys instantly. The two words, "hat" and "walk" would have the same effect; *but the whole sentence, repeated many times during the day, must in time impress itself upon the brain, and by and by she will use it herself.*

We play a little game which I find most useful in developing the intellect, and which incidentally answers the purpose of a language lesson. It is an adaptation of hide-the-thimble. I hide something, a ball or a spool, and we hunt for it. When we first played this game two or three days ago, she showed no ingenuity at all in finding the object. She looked in places where it would have been impossible to put the ball or the spool. For instance, when I hid the ball, she looked under her writing-board. Again, when I hid the spool, she looked for it in a little box not more than an inch long; and she very soon gave up the search. Now I can keep up her interest in the game for an hour or longer, and she shows much more intelligence, and often great ingenuity in the search. This morning I hid a cracker. She looked everywhere she could think of without success, and was evidently in despair when suddenly a thought struck her, and she came running to me and made me open my mouth very wide, while she gave it a thorough investigation. Finding no trace of the cracker there, she pointed to my stomach and spelled "eat," meaning, "Did you eat it?"

Friday we went down town and met a gentleman who gave Helen some candy, which she ate, except one small piece which she put in her apron pocket. When we reached home, she found her mother, and of her own accord said, "Give baby candy." Mrs. Keller spelled, "No—baby eat—no." Helen went to the cradle and felt of Mildred's mouth and pointed to her own teeth. Mrs.

Keller spelled "teeth." Helen shook her head and spelled "Baby teeth—no, baby eat—no," meaning of course, "Baby cannot eat because she has no teeth."

May 8, 1887.

No, I don't want any more kindergarten materials. I used my little stock of beads, cards and straws at first because I didn't know what else to do; but the need for them is past, for the present at any rate.

I am beginning to suspect all elaborate and special systems of education. They seem to me to be built up on the supposition that every child is a kind of idiot who must be taught to think. Whereas, if the child is left to himself, he will think more and better, if less showily. Let him go and come freely, let him touch real things and combine his impressions for himself, instead of sitting indoors at a little round table, while a sweet-voiced teacher suggests that he build a stone wall with his wooden blocks, or make a rainbow out of strips of coloured paper, or plant straw trees in bead flower-pots. Such teaching fills the mind with artificial associations that must be got rid of, before the child can develop independent ideas out of actual experiences.

Helen is learning adjectives and adverbs as easily as she learned nouns. The idea always precedes the word. She had signs for *small* and *large* long before I came to her. If she wanted a small object and was given a large one, she would shake her head and take up a tiny bit of the skin of one hand between the thumb and finger of the other. If she wanted to indicate something large, she spread the fingers of both hands as wide as she could, and brought them together, as if to clasp a big ball. The other day I substituted the words *small* and *large* for these signs, and she at once adopted the words and discarded the signs. I can now tell her to bring me a large book or a small plate, to go upstairs slowly, to run fast and to walk quickly. This morning she used the conjunction *and* for the first time. I told her to shut the door, and she added, "and lock."

She came tearing upstairs a few minutes ago in a state of great excitement. I couldn't make out at first what it was all about.

She kept spelling "dog—baby" and pointing to her five fingers one after another, and sucking them. My first thought was, one of the dogs has hurt Mildred; but Helen's beaming face set my fears at rest. Nothing would do but I must go somewhere with her to see something. She led the way to the pump-house, and there in the corner was one of the setters with five dear little pups! I taught her the word "puppy" and drew her hand over them all, while they sucked, and spelled "puppies." She was much interested in the feeding process, and spelled "mother-dog" and "baby" several times. Helen noticed that the puppies' eyes were closed, and she said, "Eyes—shut. Sleep—no," meaning, "The eyes are shut, but the puppies are not asleep." She screamed with glee when the little things squealed and squirmed in their efforts to get back to their mother, and spelled, "Baby—eat large." I suppose her idea was "Baby eats much." She pointed to each puppy, one after another, and to her five fingers, and I taught her the word *five*. Then she held up one finger and said "baby." I knew she was thinking of Mildred, and I spelled, "One baby and five puppies." After she had played with them a little while, the thought occurred to her that the puppies must have special names, like people, and she asked for the name of each pup. I told her to ask her father, and she said, "No—mother." She evidently thought mothers were more likely to know about babies of all sorts. She noticed that one of the puppies was much smaller than the others, and she spelled "small," making the sign at the same time, and I said "very small." She evidently understood that *very* was the name of the new thing that had come into her head; for all the way back to the house she used the word *very* correctly. One stone was "small," another was "very small." When she touched her little sister, she said: "Baby—small. Puppy—*very* small." Soon after, she began to vary her steps from large to small, and little mincing steps were "very small." She is going through the house now, applying the new words to all kinds of objects.

Since I have abandoned the idea of regular lessons, I find that Helen learns much faster. I am convinced that the time spent by the teacher in digging out of the child what she has put into him, for the sake of satisfying herself that it has taken root, is so much time thrown away. *It's much better, I think, to assume that the child is doing his part, and that the seed you have sown will bear fruit in due time.* It's only fair to the child, anyhow, and it saves you much unnecessary trouble.

May 16, 1887.

We have begun to take long walks every morning, immediately after breakfast. The weather is fine, and the air is full of the scent of strawberries. Our objective point is Keller's Landing, on the Tennessee, about two miles distant. We never know how we get there, or where we are at a given moment; but that only adds to our enjoyment, especially when everything is new and strange. Indeed, I feel as if I had never seen anything until now, Helen finds so much to ask about along the way. We chase butterflies, and sometimes catch one. Then we sit down under a tree, or in the shade of a bush, and talk about it. Afterwards, if it has survived the lesson, we let it go; but usually its life and beauty are sacrificed on the altar of learning, though in another sense it lives forever; for has it not been transformed into living thoughts? It is wonderful how words generate ideas! Every new word Helen learns seems to carry with it necessity for many more. Her mind grows through its ceaseless activity.

Keller's Landing was used during the war to land troops, but has long since gone to pieces, and is overgrown with moss and weeds. The solitude of the place sets one dreaming. Near the landing there is a beautiful little spring, which Helen calls "squirrel-cup," because I told her the squirrels came there to drink. She has felt dead squirrels and rabbits and other wild animals, and is anxious to see a "walk-squirrel," which interpreted, means, I think, a "live squirrel." We go home about dinner-time usually, and Helen is eager to tell her mother everything she has seen. *This desire to repeat what has been told her shows a marked advance in the development of her intellect, and is an invaluable stimulus to the acquisition of language. I ask all her friends to encourage her to tell them of her doings, and to manifest as much curiosity and pleasure in her little adventures as they possibly can.* This gratifies the child's love of approbation and keeps up her interest in things. This is the basis of real intercourse. She makes many mistakes, of course, twists words and phrases, puts the cart before the horse, and gets herself into hopeless tangles of nouns and verbs; but so does the hearing child. I am sure these difficulties will take care of themselves.

The impulse to tell is the important thing. I supply a word here and there, sometimes a sentence, and suggest something which she has omitted or forgotten. Thus her vocabulary grows apace, and the new words germinate and bring forth new ideas; and they are the stuff out of which heaven and earth are made.

May 22, 1887.

My work grows more absorbing and interesting every day. Helen is a wonderful child, so spontaneous and eager to learn. She knows about 300 words now and *a great many common idioms,* and it is not three months yet since she learned her first word. It is a rare privilege to watch the birth, growth, and first feeble struggles of a living mind; this privilege is mine; and moreover, it is given me to rouse and guide this bright intelligence.

If only I were better fitted for the great task! I feel every day more and more inadequate. My mind is full of ideas; but I cannot get them into working shape. You see, my mind is undisciplined, full of skips and jumps, and here and there a lot of things huddled together in dark corners. How I long to put it in order! Oh, if only there were some one to help me! I need a teacher quite as much as Helen. I know that the education of this child will be the distinguishing event of my life, if I have the brains and perseverance to accomplish it. I have made up my mind about one thing: Helen must learn to use books—indeed, we must both learn to use them, and that reminds me —will you please ask Mr. Anagnos to get me Perez's and Sully's Psychologies? I think I shall find them helpful.

We have reading lessons every day. Usually we take one of the little "Readers" up in a big tree near the house and spend an hour or two finding the words Helen already knows. *We make a sort of game of it* and try to see who can find the words most quickly, Helen with her fingers, or I with my eyes, and she learns as many new words as I can explain with the help of those she knows. When her fingers light upon words she knows, she fairly screams with pleasure and hugs and kisses me for joy, especially if she thinks she has me beaten. It would astonish you to see how many words she learns in an hour in this pleasant manner. Afterward I put the new words into little sentences in the frame, and sometimes it is possible to tell a little story about a bee or a cat or a little boy in this way. I can now tell her to go upstairs or down, out of doors or into the house, lock or unlock a door, take or bring objects, sit, stand, walk, run, lie, creep, roll, or climb. She is delighted with action-words; so it is no trouble at all to teach her verbs. She is always ready for a lesson, and the eagerness with which she absorbs ideas is very delightful. She is as triumphant over the conquest of a sentence as a general who has captured the enemy's stronghold.

One of Helen's old habits, that is strongest and hardest to correct, is a tendency to break things. If she finds anything in her way, she flings it on the floor, no matter what it is: a glass, a pitcher, or even a lamp. She has a great many dolls, and every one of them has been broken in a fit of temper or ennui. The other day a friend brought her a new doll from Memphis, and I thought I would see if I could make Helen understand that she must not break it. I made her go through the motion of knocking the doll's head on the table and spelled to her: "No, no, Helen is naughty. Teacher is sad," and let her feel the grieved expression on my face. Then I made her caress the doll and kiss the hurt spot and hold it gently in her arms, and I spelled to her, "Good Helen, teacher is happy," and let her feel the smile on my face. She went through these motions several times, mimicking every movement, then she stood very still for a moment with a troubled look on her face, which suddenly cleared, and she spelled, "Good Helen," and wreathed her face in a very large, artificial smile. Then she carried the doll upstairs and put it on the top shelf of the wardrobe, and she has not touched it since.

Please give my kind regards to Mr. Anagnos and let him see my letter, if you think best. I hear there is a deaf and blind child being educated at the Baltimore Institution.

June 2, 1887.

The weather is scorching. We need rain badly. We are all troubled about Helen. She is very nervous and excitable. She is restless at night and has no appetite. It is hard to know what to do with her. The doctor says her mind is too active; but how are we to keep her from thinking? She begins to spell the minute she wakes up in the morning, and continues all day long. If I refuse to talk to her, she spells into her own hand, and apparently carries on the liveliest conversation with herself.

I gave her my braille slate to play with, thinking that the mechanical pricking of holes in the paper would amuse her and rest her mind. But what was my astonishment when I found that the little witch was writing letters! I had no idea she knew what a letter was. She has often gone with me to the post-office to mail letters, and I suppose I have repeated to her things I wrote to you. She knew, too, that I sometimes write "letters to blind girls" on the slate; but I didn't suppose that she had any clear idea what a letter was. One day she brought me a sheet that she had punched full of holes, and wanted to put it in an envelope and take it to the post-office. She said, "Frank —letter." I asked her what she had written to Frank. She replied, "Much words. Puppy motherdog—five. Baby—cry. Hot. Helen walk—no. Sunfire—bad. Frank—come. Helen—kiss Frank Strawberries—very good."

Helen is almost as eager to read as she is to talk. I find she grasps the import of whole sentences, catching from the context the meaning of words she doesn't know; and her eager questions indicate the outward reaching of her mind and its unusual powers.

The other night when I went to bed, I found Helen sound asleep with a big book clasped tightly in her arms. She had evidently been reading, and fallen asleep. When I asked her about it in the morning, she said, "Book—cry," and completed her meaning by shaking and other signs of fear. I taught her the word *afraid,* and she said: "Helen is not afraid. Book is afraid. Book will sleep with girl." I told her that the book wasn't afraid, and must sleep in its case, and that "girl" mustn't read in bed. She looked very roguish, and apparently understood that I saw through her ruse.

I am glad Mr. Anagnos thinks so highly of me as a teacher. But "genius" and "originality" are words we should not use lightly. If, indeed, they apply to me even remotely, I do not see that I deserve any laudation on that account.

And right here I want to say something which is for your ears alone. Something within me tells me that I shall succeed beyond my dreams. Were it not for some circumstances that make such an idea highly improbable, even absurd, I should think Helen's education would surpass in interest and wonder Dr. Howe's achievement. I know that she has remarkable powers, and I believe that I shall be able to develop and mould them. I cannot tell how I know these things. I had no idea a short time ago how to go to work; I was feeling about in the dark; but somehow I know now, and I know that I know. I cannot explain it; but when difficulties arise, I am not perplexed or doubtful. I know how to meet them; I seem to divine Helen's peculiar needs. It is wonderful.

Already people are taking a deep interest in Helen. No one can see her without being impressed. She is no ordinary child, and people's interest in her education will be no ordinary interest. Therefore let us be exceedingly careful what we say and write about her. I shall write freely to you and tell you everything, on one condition: It is this: you must promise never to show my letters to any one. My beautiful Helen shall not be transformed into a prodigy if I can help it.

June 5, 1887.

The heat makes Helen languid and quiet. Indeed, the Tophetic weather has reduced us all to a semi-liquid state. Yesterday Helen took off her clothes and sat in her skin all the afternoon. When the sun got round to the window where she was sitting with her book, she got up impatiently and shut the window. But when the sun came in just the same, she came over to me with a grieved look and spelled emphatically: "Sun is bad boy. Sun must go to bed."

She is the dearest, cutest little thing now, and so loving! One day, when I wanted her to bring me some water, she said: "Legs very tired. Legs cry much."

She is much interested in some little chickens that are pecking their way into the world this morning. I let her hold a shell in her hand, and feel the chicken "chip, chip." Her astonishment, when she felt the tiny creature inside, cannot be put in a letter. The hen was very gentle, and made no objection to our investigations. Besides the chickens, we have several other additions to the family—two calves, a colt, and a penful of funny little pigs. You would be amused to see me hold a squealing pig in my arms, while Helen feels it all over, and asks countless questions—questions not easy to answer either. After seeing the chicken come out of the egg, she asked: "Did baby pig grow in egg? Where are many shells?"

Helen's head measures twenty and one-half inches, and mine measures twenty-one and one-half inches. You see, I'm only one inch ahead!

June 12, 1887.

The weather continues hot. Helen is about the same—pale and thin; but you mustn't think she is really ill. I am sure the heat, and not the natural, beautiful activity of her mind, is responsible for her condition. Of course, I shall not overtax her brain. We are bothered a good deal by people who assume the responsibility of the world when God is neglectful. They tell us that Helen is "overdoing," that her mind is too active (these very people thought she had no mind at all a few months ago!) and suggest many absurd and impossible remedies. But so far nobody seems to have thought of chloroforming her, which is, I think, the only effective way of stopping the natural exercise of her faculties. It's queer how ready people always are with advice in any real or imaginary emergency, and no matter how many times experience has shown them to be wrong, they continue to set forth their opinions, as if they had received them from the Almighty!

I am teaching Helen the square-hand letters as a sort of diversion. It gives her something to do, and keeps her quiet, which I think is desirable while this enervating weather lasts. She has a perfect mania for counting. She has counted everything in the house, and is now busy counting the words in her primer. I hope it will not occur to her to count the hairs of her head. If she could see and hear, I suppose she would get rid of her superfluous energy in ways which would not, perhaps, tax her brain so much, although I suspect that the ordinary child takes his play pretty seriously. The little fellow who whirls his "New York Flyer" round the nursery, making "horseshoe curves" undreamed of by less imaginative engineers, is concentrating his whole soul on his toy locomotive.

She just came to say, with a worried expression, "Girl—not count *very* large (many) words." I said, "No, go and play with Nancy." This suggestion didn't please her, however; for she replied, "No. Nancy is very sick." I asked what was the matter, and she said, "Much (many) teeth do make Nancy sick." (Mildred is teething.)

I happened to tell her the other day that the vine on the fence was a "creeper." She was greatly amused, and began at once to find analogies between her movements and those of the plants. They run, creep, hop, and skip, bend, fall, climb, and swing; but she tells me roguishly that she is "walk-plant."

Helen held some worsted for me last night while I wound it. Afterward she began to swing round and round, spelling to herself all the time, "Wind fast, wind slow," and apparently enjoying her conceit very much.

June 15, 1887.

We had a glorious thunder-tempest last night, and it's much cooler to-day. We all feel refreshed, as if we'd had a shower-bath. Helen's as lively as a cricket. She wanted to know if men were shooting in the sky when she felt the thunder, and if the trees and flowers drank all the rain.

June 19, 1887.*

My little pupil continues to manifest the same eagerness to learn as at first. Her every waking moment is spent in the endeavour to satisfy her innate desire for knowledge, and her mind works so incessantly that we have feared for her health. But her appetite, which left her a few weeks ago, has returned, and her sleep seems more quiet and natural. She will be seven years old the twenty-seventh of this month. Her height is four feet one inch, and her head measures twenty and one-half inches in circumference, the line being drawn round the head so as to pass over the prominences of the parietal and frontal bones. Above this line the head rises one and one-fourth inches.

During our walks she keeps up a continual spelling, and delights to accompany it with actions such as skipping, hopping, jumping, running, walking fast, walking slow, and the like. When she drops stitches she says, "Helen wrong, teacher will cry." If she wants water she says, "Give Helen drink water." She knows four hundred words besides numerous proper nouns.

*This extract was published in The Perkins Institution Report of 1887.

In one lesson I taught her these words: *bedstead, mattress, sheet, blanket, comforter, spread, pillow.* The next day I found that she remembered all but *spread.* The same day she had learned, at different times, the words: *house, weed, dust, swing, molasses, fast, slow, maple-sugar* and *counter,* and she had not forgotten one of these last. This will give you an idea of the retentive memory she possesses. She can count to thirty very quickly, and can write seven of the square-hand letters and the words which can be made with them. She seems to understand about writing letters, and is impatient to "write Frank letter." She enjoys punching holes in paper with the stiletto, and I supposed it was because she could examine the result of her work; but we watched her one day, and I was much surprised to find that she imagined she was writing a letter. She would spell "Eva" (a cousin of whom she is very fond) with one hand, then make believe to write it; then spell, "sick in bed," and write that. She kept this up for nearly an hour. She was (or imagined she was) putting on paper the things which had interested her. When she had finished the letter she carried it to her mother and spelled, "Frank letter," and gave it to her brother to take to the post-office. She had been with me to take letters to the post-office.

She recognizes instantly a person whom she has once met, and spells the name. Unlike Laura Bridgman, she is fond of gentlemen, and we notice that she makes friends with a gentleman sooner than with a lady.

She is always ready to share whatever she has with those about her, often keeping but very little for herself. She is very fond of dress and of all kinds of finery, and is very unhappy when she finds a hole in anything she is wearing. She will insist on having her hair put in curl papers when she is so sleepy she can scarcely stand. She discovered a hole in her boot the other morning, and, after breakfast, she went to her father and spelled, "Helen new boot Simpson (her brother) buggy store man." One can easily see her meaning.

July 3, 1887.

There was a great rumpus downstairs this morning. I heard Helen screaming, and ran down to see what was the matter. I found her in a terrible passion. I had hoped this would never happen again. She has been so gentle and obedient the past two months, I thought love had subdued the lion; but it seems he was only sleeping. At all events, there she was, tearing and scratching and biting Viney like some wild thing. It seems Viney had attempted to take a glass, which Helen was filling with stones, fearing that she would break it. Helen resisted, and Viney tried to force it out of her hand, and I suspect that she slapped the child, or did something which caused this unusual outburst of temper. When I took her hand she was trembling violently, and began to cry. I asked what was the matter, and she spelled: "Viney—bad," and began to slap and kick her with renewed violence. I held her hands firmly until she became more calm.

Later Helen came to my room, looking very sad, and wanted to kiss me. I said, "I cannot kiss naughty girl." She spelled, "Helen is good, Viney is bad." I said: "You struck Viney and kicked her and hurt her. You were very naughty, and I cannot kiss naughty girl." She stood very still for a moment, and it was evident from her face, which was flushed and troubled, that a struggle was going on in her mind. Then she said: "Helen did (does) not love teacher. Helen do love mother. Mother will whip Viney." I told her that she had better not talk about it any more, but think. She knew that I was much troubled, and would have liked to stay near me; but I thought it best for her to sit by herself. At the dinner-table she was greatly disturbed because I didn't eat, and suggested that "Cook make tea for teacher." But I told her that my heart was sad, and I didn't feel like eating. She began to cry and sob and clung to me.

She was very much excited when we went upstairs; so I tried to interest her in a curious insect called a stick-bug. It's the queerest thing I ever saw—a little bundle of fagots fastened together in the middle. I wouldn't believe it was alive until I saw it move. Even then it looked more like a mechanical toy than a living creature. But the poor little girl couldn't fix her attention. Her heart was full of trouble, and she wanted to talk about it. She said: "Can bug know about naughty girl? Is bug very happy?" Then, putting her arms round my neck, she said: "I am (will be) good to-morrow. Helen is (will be) good all days." I said, "Will you tell Viney you are very sorry you scratched and kicked her?" She smiled and answered, "Viney

(can) not spell words." "I will tell Viney you are very sorry,"
I said. "Will you go with me and find Viney?" She was very
willing to go, and let Viney kiss her, though she didn't return the
caress. She has been unusually affectionate since, and it seems
to me there is a sweetness—a soul-beauty in her face which I
have not seen before.

July 31, 1887.

Helen's pencil-writing is excellent, as you will see from the
enclosed letter, which she wrote for her own amusement. I am
teaching her the braille alphabet, and she is delighted to be able
to make words herself that she can feel.

She has now reached the question stage of her development.
It is "what?" "why?" "when?" especially "why?" all day long,
and as her intelligence grows her inquiries become more insistent.
I remember how unbearable I used to find the inquisitiveness of
my friends' children; but I know now that these questions indicate the child's growing interest in the cause of things. The
"why?" is the *door through which he enters the world of reason
and reflection*. "How does carpenter know to build house?"
"Who put chickens in eggs?" "Why is Viney black?" "Flies bite
—why?" "Can flies know not to bite?" "Why did father kill
sheep?" Of course she asks many questions that are not as intelligent as these. Her mind isn't more logical than the minds
of ordinary children. On the whole, her questions are analogous
to those that a bright three-year-old child asks; but her desire
for knowledge is so earnest, the questions are never tedious,
though they draw heavily upon my meager store of information,
and tax my ingenuity to the utmost.

I had a letter from Laura Bridgman last Sunday. Please give
her my love, and tell her Helen sends her a kiss. I read the
letter at the supper-table, and Mrs. Keller exclaimed: "Why,
Miss Annie, Helen writes almost as well as that now!" It is
true.

August 21, 1887.

We had a beautiful time in Huntsville. Everybody there was
delighted with Helen, and showered her with gifts and kisses.
The first evening she learned the names of all the people in the

hotel, about twenty, I think. The next morning we were astonished to find that she remembered all of them, and recognized
every one she had met the night before. She taught the young
people the alphabet, and several of them learned to talk with
her. One of the girls taught her to dance the polka, and a little
boy showed her his rabbits and spelled their names for her.
She was delighted, and showed her pleasure by hugging and
kissing the little fellow, which embarrassed him very much.

We had Helen's picture taken with a fuzzy, red-eyed little poodle,
who got himself into my lady's good graces by tricks and cunning devices known only to dogs with an instinct for getting what
they want.

She has talked incessantly since her return about what she
did in Huntsville, and we notice a very decided improvement
in her ability to use language. Curiously enough, a drive we
took to the top of Monte Sano, a beautiful mountain not far
from Huntsville, seems to have impressed her more than anything else, except the wonderful poodle. She remembers all
that I told her about it, and in telling her mother *repeated the
very words and phrases I had used in describing it to her.* In
conclusion she asked her mother if she should like to see "very
high mountain and beautiful cloud-caps." I hadn't used this
expression. I said, "The clouds touch the mountain softly, like
beautiful flowers." You see, I had to use words and images with
which she was familiar through the sense of touch. But it hardly
seems possible that any mere words should convey to one who
has never seen a mountain the faintest idea of its grandeur;
and I don't see how any one is ever to know what impression she did receive, or the cause of her pleasure in what
was told her about it. All that we do know certainly is that
she has a good memory and imagination and the faculty of association.

August 28, 1887.

I do wish things would stop being born! "New puppies,"
"new calves" and "new babies" keep Helen's interest in the why
and wherefore of things at white heat. The arrival of a new
baby at Ivy Green the other day was the occasion of a fresh
outburst of questions about the origin of babies and live things
in general. "Where did Leila get new baby? How did doc-

tor know where to find baby? Did Leila tell doctor to get
very small new baby? Where did doctor find Guy and
Prince?" (puppies) "Why is Elizabeth Evelyn's sister?" etc.,
etc. These questions were sometimes asked under circumstances which rendered them embarrassing, and I made up my
mind that something must be done. If it was natural for
Helen to ask such questions, it was my duty to answer them.
It's a great mistake, I think, to put children off with false-
hoods and nonsense, when their growing powers of observation
and discrimination excite in them a desire to know about things.
From the beginning, *I have made it a practice to answer all
Helen's questions to the best of my ability in a way intelligible to
her, and at the same time truthfully.* "Why should I treat these
questions differently?" I asked myself. I decided that there was
no reason, except my deplorable ignorance of the great facts
that underlie our physical existence. It was no doubt because
of this ignorance that I rushed in where more experienced angels
fear to tread. There isn't a living soul in this part of the
world to whom I can go for advice in this, or indeed, in any
other educational difficulty. The only thing for me to do in a
perplexity is to go ahead, and learn by making mistakes. But
in this case I don't think I made a mistake. I took Helen and
my Botany, "How Plants Grow," up in the tree, where we often
go to read and study, and I told her in simple words the
story of plant-life. I reminded her of the corn, beans and water-
melon-seed she had planted in the spring, and told her that
the tall corn in the garden, and the beans and watermelon
vines had grown from those seeds. I explained how the earth
keeps the seeds warm and moist, until the little leaves are
strong enough to push themselves out into the light and air
where they can breathe and grow and bloom and make more
seeds, from which other baby-plants shall grow. I drew an
analogy between plant and animal-life, and told her that seeds
are eggs as truly as hens' eggs and birds' eggs—that the mother
hen keeps her eggs warm and dry until the little chicks come
out. I made her understand that all life comes from an egg.
The mother bird lays her eggs in a nest and keeps them warm
until the birdlings are hatched. The mother fish lays her eggs
where she knows they will be moist and safe, until it is time
for the little fish to come out. I told her that she could call
the egg the cradle of life. Then I told her that other animals

like the dog and cow, and human beings, do not lay their eggs, but nourish their young in their own bodies. I had no difficulty in making it clear to her that if plants and animals didn't produce offspring after their kind, they would cease to exist, and everything in the world would soon die. But the function of sex I passed over as lightly as possible. I did, however, try to give her the idea that love is the great continuer of life. The subject was difficult, and my knowledge inadequate; but I am glad I didn't shirk my responsibility; for, stumbling, hesitating, and incomplete as my explanation was, it touched deep responsive chords in the soul of my little pupil, and the readiness with which she comprehended the great facts of physical life confirmed me in the opinion that the child has dormant within him, when he comes into the world, all the experiences of the race. These experiences are like photographic negatives, until language develops them and brings out the memory-images.

September 4, 1887.

Helen had a letter this morning from her uncle, Doctor Keller. He invited her to come to see him at Hot Springs. The name Hot Springs interested her, and she asked many questions about it. She knows about cold springs. There are several near Tuscumbia; one very large one from which the town got its name. "Tuscumbia" is the Indian for "Great Spring." But she was surprised that hot water should come out of the ground. She wanted to know who made fire under the ground, and if it was like the fire in stoves, and if it burned the roots of plants and trees.

She was much pleased with the letter, and after she had asked all the questions she could think of, she took it to her mother, who was sewing in the hall, and read it to her. It was amusing to see her hold it before her eyes and spell the sentences out on her fingers, just as I had done. Afterward she tried to read it to Belle (the dog) and Mildred. Mrs. Keller and I watched the nursery comedy from the door. Belle was sleepy, and Mildred inattentive. Helen looked very serious, and, once or twice, when Mildred tried to take the letter, she put her hand away impatiently. Finally Belle got up, shook herself, and was about to walk away, when Helen caught her by the neck and forced her to lie down again. In the meantime Mildred had got the letter and crept away with it. Helen felt on the floor for it, but not finding it there, she evidently suspected Mildred; for she made the little sound which is her "baby call." Then she got up and stood very still, as if listening with her feet for Mildred's "thump, thump." When she had located the sound, she went quickly toward the little culprit and found her chewing the precious letter! This was too much for Helen. She snatched the letter and slapped the little hands soundly. Mrs. Keller took the baby in her arms, and when we had succeeded in pacifying her, I asked Helen, "What did you do to baby?" She looked troubled, and hesitated a moment before answering. Then she said: "Wrong girl did eat letter. Helen did slap very wrong girl." I told her that Mildred was very small, and didn't know that it was wrong to put the letter in her mouth.

"I did tell baby, no, no, much (many) times," was Helen's reply.

I said, "Mildred doesn't understand your fingers, and we must be very gentle with her."

She shook her head.

"Baby—not think. Helen will give baby pretty letter," and with that she ran upstairs and brought down a neatly folded sheet of braille, on which she had written some words, and gave it to Mildred, saying, "Baby can eat all words."

September 18, 1887.

I do not wonder you were surprised to hear that I was going to write something for the report. I do not know myself how it happened, except that I got tired of saying "no," and Captain Keller urged me to do it. He agreed with Mr. Anagnos that it was my duty to give others the benefit of my experience. Besides, they said Helen's wonderful deliverance might be a boon to other afflicted children.

When I sit down to write, my thoughts freeze, and when I get them on paper they look like wooden soldiers all in a row, and if a live one happens along, I put him in a straitjacket. It's easy enough, however, to say Helen is wonderful, because she really is. I kept a record of everything she said last week, and I found that she knows six hundred words,

This does not mean, however, that she always uses them correctly. Sometimes her sentences are like Chinese puzzles; but they are the kind of puzzles children make when they try to express their half-formed ideas by means of arbitrary language. She has the true language-impulse, and shows great fertility of resource in making the words at her command convey her meaning.

Lately she has been much interested in colour. She found the word "brown" in her primer and wanted to know its meaning. I told her that her hair was brown, and she asked, "Is brown very pretty?" After we had been all over the house, and I had told her the colour of everything she touched, she suggested that we go to the hen-houses and barns; but I told her she must wait until another day because I was very tired. We sat in the hammock; but there was no rest for the weary there. Helen was eager to know "more colour." I wonder if she has any vague idea of colour—any reminiscent impression of light and sound. It seems as if a child who could see and hear until her nineteenth month must retain some of her first impressions, though ever so faintly. Helen talks a great deal about things that she cannot know of through the sense of touch. She asks many questions about the sky, day and night, the ocean and mountains. She likes to have me tell her what I see in pictures.

But I seem to have lost the thread of my discourse. "What colour is think?" was one of the restful questions she asked, as we swung to and fro in the hammock. I told her that when we are happy our thoughts are bright, and when we are naughty they are sad. Quick as a flash she said, "My think is white, Viney's think is black." You see, she had an idea that the colour of our thoughts matched that of our skin. I couldn't help laughing, for at that very moment Viney was shouting at the top of her voice:

> "I long to sit on dem jasper walls
> And see dem sinners stumble and fall!"

October 3, 1887.

My account for the report is finished and sent off. I have two copies, and will send you one; but you mustn't show it to anybody. It's Mr. Anagnos's property until it is published.

I suppose the little girls enjoyed Helen's letter.* She wrote it out of her own head, as the children say.

She talks a great deal about what she will do when she goes to Boston. She asked the other day, "Who made all things and Boston?" She says Mildred will not go there because "Baby does cry all days."

October 25, 1887.

Helen wrote another letter† to the little girls yesterday, and her father sent it to Mr. Anagnos. Ask him to let you see it. She has begun to use the pronouns of her own accord. This morning I happened to say, "Helen will go upstairs." She laughed and said, "Teacher is wrong. You will go upstairs." This is another great forward step. Thus it always is. Yesterday's perplexities are strangely simple to-day, and to-day's difficulties become to-morrow's pastime.

The rapid development of Helen's mind is beautiful to watch. I doubt if any teacher ever had a work of such absorbing interest. There must have been one lucky star in the heavens at my birth, and I am just beginning to feel its beneficent influence.

I had two letters from Mr. Anagnos last week. He is more grateful for my report than the English idiom will express. Now he wants a picture "of darling Helen and her illustrious teacher, to grace the pages of the forthcoming annual report."

October, 1887.‡

You have probably read, ere this, Helen's second letter to the little girls. I am aware that the progress which she has made between the writing of the two letters must seem incredible. Only those who are with her daily can realize the rapid advancement which she is making in the acquisition of language. You will see from her letter that she uses many pronouns correctly. She rarely misuses or omits one in conversation. Her passion for writing letters and putting her thoughts upon paper grows more intense. She now tells stories in which the imagination

*See page 146.   †See page 147.

‡This extract from a letter to Mr. Anagnos was published in the Perkins Institution Report of 1887.

plays an important part. She is also beginning to realize that she is not like other children. The other day she asked, "What do my eyes do?" I told her that I could see things with my eyes, and that she could see them with her fingers. After thinking a moment she said, "My eyes are bad!" then she changed it into "My eyes are sick!"

Miss Sullivan's first report, which was published in the official report of the Perkins Institution for the year 1887, is a short summary of what is fully recorded in the letters. Here follows the last part, beginning with the great day, April 5th, when Helen learned *water*.

In her reports Miss Sullivan speaks of "lessons" as if they came in regular order. This is the effect of putting it all in a summary. "Lesson" is too formal for the continuous daily work

One day I took her to the cistern. As the water gushed from the pump I spelled "w-a-t-er." Instantly she tapped my hand for a repetition, and then made the word herself with a radiant face. Just then the nurse came into the cistern-house bringing her little sister. I put Helen's hand on the baby and formed the letters "b-a-b-y," which she repeated without help and with the light of a new intelligence in her face.

On our way back to the house everything she touched had to be named for her, and repetition was seldom necessary. Neither the length of the word nor the combination of letters seems to make any difference to the child. Indeed, she remembers *heliotrope* and *chrysanthemum* more readily than she does shorter names. At the end of August she knew 625 words.

This lesson was followed by one on words indicative of place-relations. Her dress was put *in* a trunk, and then *on* it, and these prepositions were spelled for her. Very soon she learned the difference between *on* and *in*, though it was some time before she could use these words in sentences of her own. Whenever it was possible she was made the actor in the lesson, and was delighted to stand *on* the chair, and to be put *into* the wardrobe. In connection with this lesson she learned the names of the members of

the family and the word *is*. "Helen is in wardrobe," "Mildred is in crib," "Box is on table," "Papa is on bed," are specimens of sentences constructed by her during the latter part of
April.

Next came a lesson on words expressive of positive quality.
For the first lesson I had two balls, one made of worsted, large
and soft, the other a bullet. She perceived the difference in size
at once. Taking the bullet she made her habitual sign for *small*—
that is, by pinching a little bit of the skin of one hand. Then
she took the other ball and made her sign for *large* by spreading
both hands over it. I substituted the adjectives *large* and *small*
for those signs. Then her attention was called to the hardness
of the one ball and the softness of the other, and she learned
soft and *hard*. A few minutes afterward she felt of her little
sister's head and said to her mother, "Mildred's head is small
and hard." Next I tried to teach her the meaning of *fast* and
slow. She helped me wind some worsted one day, first rapidly
and afterward slowly. I then said to her with the finger alphabet, "wind fast," or "wind slow," holding her hands and showing
her how to do as I wished. The next day, while exercising, she
spelled to me, "Helen wind fast," and began to walk rapidly.
Then she said, "Helen wind slow," again suiting the action to the
words.

I now thought it time to teach her to read printed words. A
slip on which was printed, in raised letters, the word *box* was
placed on the object; and the same experiment was tried with
a great many articles, but she did not immediately comprehend
that the label-name represented the thing. Then I took an alphabet sheet and put her finger on the letter A, at the same time
making A with my fingers. She moved her finger from one printed
character to another as I formed each letter on my fingers. She
learned all the letters, both capital and small, in one day. Next
I turned to the first page of the primer and made her touch the
word *cat*, spelling it on my fingers at the same time. Instantly
she caught the idea, and asked me to find *dog* and many other
words. Indeed, she was much displeased because I could not
find her name in the book. Just then I had no sentences in
raised letters which she could understand; but she would sit for
hours feeling each word in her book. When she touched one
with which she was familiar, a peculiarly sweet expression lighted
her face. and we saw her countenance growing sweeter and more

earnest every day. About this time I sent a list of the words she knew to Mr. Anagnos, and he very kindly had them printed for her. Her mother and I cut up several sheets of printed words so that she could arrange them into sentences. This delighted her more than anything she had yet done; and the practice thus obtained prepared the way for the writing lessons. There was no difficulty in making her understand how to write the same sentences with pencil and paper which she made every day with the slips, and she very soon perceived that she need not confine herself to phrases already learned, but could communicate any thought that was passing through her mind. I put one of the writing boards used by the blind between the folds of the paper on the table, and allowed her to examine an alphabet of the square letters, such as she was to make. I then guided her hand to form the sentence, "Cat does drink milk." When she finished it she was overjoyed. She carried it to her mother, who spelled it to her.

Day after day she moved her pencil in the same tracks along the grooved paper, never for a moment expressing the least impatience or sense of fatigue.

As she had now learned to express her ideas on paper, I next taught her the braille system. She learned it gladly when she discovered that she could herself read what she had written; and this still affords her constant pleasure. For a whole evening she will sit at the table writing whatever comes into her busy brain; and I seldom find any difficulty in reading what she has written.

Her progress in arithmetic has been equally remarkable. She can add and subtract with great rapidity up to the sum of one hundred; and she knows the multiplication tables as far as the *fives*. She was working recently with the number forty, when I said to her, "Make twos." She replied immediately, "Twenty twos make forty." Later I said, "Make fifteen threes and count." I wished her to make the groups of threes and supposed she would then have to count them in order to know what number fifteen threes would make. But instantly she spelled the answer: "Fifteen threes make forty-five."

On being told that she was white and that one of the servants was black, she concluded that all who occupied a similar menial position were of the same hue; and whenever I asked her the colour of a servant she would say "black." When asked the colour of some one whose occupation she did not know she seemed bewildered, and finally said "blue."

She has never been told anything about death or the burial of the body, and yet on entering the cemetery for the first time in her life, with her mother and me, to look at some flowers, she laid her hand on our eyes and repeatedly spelled "cry—cry." Her eyes actually filled with tears. The flowers did not seem to give her pleasure, and she was very quiet while we stayed there.

On another occasion while walking with me she seemed conscious of the presence of her brother, although we were distant from him. She spelled his name repeatedly and started in the direction in which he was coming.

When walking or riding she often gives the names of the people we meet almost as soon as we recognize them.

The letters take up the account again.

November 13, 1887.

We took Helen to the circus, and had "the time of our lives"! The circus people were much interested in Helen, and did everything they could to make her first circus a memorable event. They let her feel the animals whenever it was safe. She fed the elephants, and was allowed to climb up on the back of the largest, and sit in the lap of the "Oriental Princess," while the elephant marched majestically around the ring. She felt some young lions. They were as gentle as kittens; but I told her they would get wild and fierce as they grew older. She said to the keeper, "I will take the baby lions home and teach them to be mild." The keeper of the bears made one big black fellow stand on his hind legs and hold out his great paw to us, which Helen shook politely. She was greatly delighted with the monkeys and kept her hand on the star performer while he went through his tricks, and laughed heartily when he took off his hat to the audience. One cute little fellow stole her hair-ribbon, and another tried to snatch the flowers out of her hat. I don't know who had the best time, the monkeys, Helen or the spectators.

One of the leopards licked her hands, and the man in charge of
the giraffes lifted her up in his arms so that she could feel their
ears and see how tall they were. She also felt a Greek chariot,
and the charioteer would have liked to take her round the ring;
but she was afraid of "many swift horses." The riders and
clowns and rope-walkers were all glad to let the little blind girl
feel their costumes and follow their motions whenever it was
possible, and she kissed them all, to show her gratitude. Some
of them cried, and the wild man of Borneo shrank from her
sweet little face in terror. She has talked about nothing but the
circus ever since. In order to answer her questions, I have been
obliged to read a great deal about animals. At present I feel
like a jungle on wheels!

December 12, 1887.

I find it hard to realize that Christmas is almost here, in spite
of the fact that Helen talks about nothing else. Do you remember
what a happy time we had last Christmas?

Helen has learned to tell the time at last, and her father is
going to give her a watch for Christmas.

Helen is as eager to have stories told her as any hearing child
I ever knew. She has made me repeat the story of little Red
Riding Hood so often that I believe I could say it backward.
She likes stories that make her cry—I think we all do, it's so
nice to feel sad when you've nothing particular to be sad about.
I am teaching her little rhymes and verses, too. They fix beautiful
thoughts in her memory. I think, too, that they quicken all the
child's faculties, because they stimulate the imagination. Of course
I don't try to explain everything. If I did, there would be no
opportunity for the play of fancy. *Too much explanation directs
the child's attention to words and sentences, so that he fails to
get the thought as a whole.* I do not think any one can read, or
talk for that matter, until he forgets words and sentences in the
technical sense.

January 1, 1888.

It is a great thing to feel that you are of some use in the world,
that you are necessary to somebody. Helen's dependence on me for
almost everything makes me strong and glad.

Christmas week was a very busy one here, too. Helen is invited to all the children's entertainments, and I take her to as many as I can. I want her to know children and to be with them as much as possible. Several little girls have learned to spell on their fingers and are very proud of the accomplishment. One little chap, about seven, was persuaded to learn the letters, and he spelled his name for Helen. She was delighted, and showed her joy, by hugging and kissing him, much to his embarrassment.

Saturday the school-children had their tree, and I took Helen. It was the first Christmas tree she had ever seen, and she was puzzled, and asked many questions. "Who made tree grow in house? Why? Who put many things on tree?" She objected to its miscellaneous fruits and began to remove them, evidently thinking they were all meant for her. It was not difficult, however, to make her understand that there was a present for each child, and to her great delight she was permitted to hand the gifts to the children. There were several presents for herself. She placed them in a chair, resisting all temptation to look at them until every child had received his gifts. One little girl had fewer presents than the rest, and Helen insisted on sharing her gifts with her. It was very sweet to see the children's eager interest in Helen, and their readiness to give her pleasure. The exercises began at nine, and it was one o'clock before we could leave. My fingers and head ached; but Helen was as fresh and full of spirit as when we left home.

After dinner it began to snow, and we had a good frolic and an interesting lesson about the snow. Sunday morning the ground was covered, and Helen and the cook's children and I played snowball. By noon the snow was all gone. It was the first snow I had seen here, and it made me a little homesick. The Christmas season has furnished many lessons, and added scores of new words to Helen's vocabulary.

For weeks we did nothing but talk and read and tell each other stories about Christmas. Of course I do not try to explain all the new words, nor does Helen fully understand the little stories I tell her; but constant repetition fixes the words and phrases in the mind, and little by little the meaning will come to her. *I see no sense in "faking" conversation for the sake of teaching language. It's stupid and deadening to pupil and teacher. Talk should be natural and have for its object an exchange of ideas.* If there is nothing in the child's mind to communicate, it hardly seems worth while to require him to write on the blackboard, or spell on his fingers, cut and dried sentences about "the cat," "the bird," "a dog." *I have tried from the beginning to talk naturally to Helen and to teach her to tell me only things that interest her and ask questions only for the sake of finding out what she wants to know.* When I see that she is eager to tell me something, but is hampered because she does not know the words, I supply them and the necessary idioms, and we get along finely. The child's eagerness and interest carry her over many obstacles that would be our undoing if we stopped to define and explain everything. What would happen, do you think, if some one should try to measure our intelligence by our ability to define the commonest words we use? I fear me, if I were put to such a test, I should be consigned to the primary class in a school for the feeble-minded.

It was touching and beautiful to see Helen enjoy her first Christmas. Of course, she hung her stocking—two of them lest Santa Claus should forget one, and she lay awake for a long time and got up two or three times to see if anything had happened. When I told her that Santa Claus would not come until she was asleep, she shut her eyes and said, "He will think girl is asleep." She was awake the first thing in the morning, and ran to the fireplace for her stocking; and when she found that Santa Claus had filled both stockings, she danced about for a minute, then grew very quiet, and came to ask me if I thought Santa Claus had made a mistake, and thought there were two little girls, and would come back for the gifts when he discovered his mistake. The ring you sent her was in the toe of the stocking, and when I told her you gave it to Santa Claus for her, she said, "I do love Mrs. Hopkins." She had a trunk and clothes for Nancy, and her comment was, "Now Nancy will go to party." When she saw the braille slate and paper, she said, "I will write many letters, and I will thank Santa Claus very much." It was evident that every one, especially Captain and Mrs. Keller, was deeply moved at the thought of the difference between this bright Christmas and the last, when their little girl had no conscious part in the Christmas festivities. As we came downstairs, Mrs. Keller said to me with tears in her eyes, "Miss Annie, I thank God every day of my life for sending you to us; but I never realized until this morning what a blessing you have been to us." Captain Keller took my hand, but could not speak. But his silence was more eloquent than words. My heart, too, was full of gratitude and solemn joy.

The other day Helen came across the word grandfather in a little story and asked her mother, "Where is grandfather?" meaning her grandfather. Mrs. Keller replied, "He is dead." "Did father shoot him?" Helen asked, and added, "I will eat grandfather for dinner." So far, her only knowledge of death is in connection with things to eat. She knows that her father shoots partridges and deer and other game.

This morning she asked me the meaning of "carpenter," and the question furnished the text for the day's lesson. After talking about the various things that carpenters make, she asked me, "Did carpenter make me?" and before I could answer, she spelled quickly, "No, no, photographer made me in Sheffield."

One of the greatest iron furnaces has been started in Sheffield, and we went over the other evening to see them make a "run." Helen felt the heat and asked, "Did the sun fall?"

January 9, 1888.

The report came last night. I appreciate the kind things Mr. Anagnos has said about Helen and me; but his extravagant way of saying them rubs me the wrong way. The simple facts would be so much more convincing! Why, for instance, does he take the trouble to ascribe motives to me that I never dreamed of? You know, and he knows, and I know, that my motive in coming here was not in any sense philanthropic. How ridiculous it is to say I had drunk so copiously of the noble spirit of Dr. Howe that I was fired with the desire to rescue from darkness and obscurity the little Alabamian! I came here simply because circumstances made it necessary for me to earn my living, and I seized upon the first opportunity that offered itself, although I did not suspect, nor did he, that I had any special fitness for the work.

January 26, 1888.

I suppose you got Helen's letter. The little rascal has taken it into her head not to write with a pencil. I wanted her to write to her Uncle Frank this morning, but she objected. She said: "Pencil is very tired in head. I will write Uncle Frank braille letter." I said, "But Uncle Frank cannot read braille." "I will teach him," she said. I explained that Uncle Frank was old, and couldn't learn braille easily. In a flash she answered, "I think Uncle Frank is much (too) old to read very small letters." Finally I persuaded her to write a few lines; but she broke her pencil six times before she finished it. I said to her, "You are a naughty girl." "No," she replied, "pencil is very weak." I think her objection to pencil-writing is readily accounted for by the fact that she has been asked to write so many specimens for friends and strangers. You know how the children at the Institution detest it. It is irksome because the process is so slow, and they cannot read what they have written or correct their mistakes.

Helen is more and more interested in colour. When I told her that Mildred's eyes were blue, she asked, "Are they like wee skies?" A little while after I had told her that a carnation that had been given her was red, she puckered up her mouth and said, "Lips are like one pink." I told her they were tulips; but of course she didn't understand the word-play. I can't believe that the colour-impressions she received during the year and a half she could see and hear are entirely lost. Everything we have seen and heard is in the mind somewhere. It may be too vague and confused to be recognizable, but it is there all the same, like the landscape we lose in the deepening twilight.

February 10, 1888.

We got home last night. We had a splendid time in Memphis, but I didn't rest much. It was nothing but excitement from first to last—drives, luncheons, receptions, and all that they involve when you have an eager, tireless child like Helen on your hands. She talked incessantly. I don't know what I should have done, had some of the young people not learned to talk with her. They relieved me as much as possible. But even then I can never have a quiet half hour to myself. It is always: "Oh, Miss Sullivan, please come and tell us what Helen means," or "Miss Sullivan, won't you please explain this to Helen? We can't make her understand." I believe half the white population of Memphis called on us. Helen was petted and caressed enough to spoil an angel; but I do not think it is possible to spoil her, she is too unconscious of herself, and too loving.

The stores in Memphis are very good, and I managed to spend all the money that I had with me. One day Helen said, "I must buy Nancy a very pretty hat." I said, "Very well, we will go shopping this afternoon." She had a silver dollar and a dime. When we reached the shop, I asked her how much she would pay for Nancy's hat. She answered promptly, "I will pay ten cents." "What will you do with the dollar?" I asked. "I will buy some good candy to take to Tuscumbia," was her reply.

We visited the Stock Exchange and a steamboat. Helen was greatly interested in the boat, and insisted on being shown every inch of it from the engine to the flag on the flagstaff. I was gratified to read what the *Nation* had to say about Helen last week.

Captain Keller has had two interesting letters since the publication of the "Report," one from Dr. Alexander Graham Bell, and the other from Dr. Edward Everett Hale. Dr. Hale claims kinship with Helen, and seems very proud of his little cousin. Dr. Bell writes that Helen's progress is without a parallel in the education of the deaf, or something like that and he says many nice things about her teacher.

March 5, 1888.

I did not have a chance to finish my letter yesterday. Miss Ev. came up to help me make a list of words Helen has learned. We have got as far as P, and there are 900 words to her credit. I had Helen begin a journal* March 1st. I don't know how long she will keep it up. It's rather stupid business, I think. Just now she finds it great fun. She seems to like to tell all she knows. This is what Helen wrote Sunday:

"I got up, washed my face and hands, combed my hair, picked three dew violets for Teacher and ate my breakfast. After breakfast I played with dolls short. Nancy was cross. Cross is cry and kick. I read in my book about large, fierce animals. Fierce is much cross and strong and very hungry. I do not

*Most of this journal was lost. Fortunately, however, Helen Keller wrote so many letters and exercises that there is no lack of records of that sort.

love fierce animals. I wrote letter to Uncle James. He lives
in Hotsprings. He is doctor. Doctor makes sick girl well. I
do not like sick. Then I ate my dinner. I like much icecream
very much. After dinner father went to Birmingham on train
far away. I had letter from Robert. He loves me. He said
Dear Helen, Robert was glad to get a letter from dear, sweet
little Helen. I will come to see you when the sun shines. Mrs.
Newsum is Robert's wife. Robert is her husband. Robert
and I will run and jump and hop and dance and swing and
talk about birds and flowers and trees and grass and Jumbo and
Pearl will go with us. Teacher will say, We are silly. She is
funny. Funny makes us laugh. Natalie is a good girl and does
not cry. Mildred does cry. She will be a nice girl in many days
and run and play with me. Mrs. Graves is making short dresses
for Natalie. Mr. Mayo went to Duckhill and brought home
many sweet flowers. Mr. Mayo and Mr. Farris and Mr. Graves
love me and Teacher. I am going to Memphis to see them soon,
and they will hug and kiss me. Thornton goes to school and
gets his face dirty. Boy must be very careful. After supper I
played romp with Teacher in bed. She buried me under the
pillows and then I grew very slow like tree out of ground. Now,
I will go to bed.   HELEN KELLER."

                                                April 16, 1888.

We are just back from church. Captain Keller said at breakfast this morning that he wished I would take Helen to church.
The Presbytery would be there in a body, and he wanted
the ministers to see Helen. The Sunday-school was in session
when we arrived, and I wish you could have seen the sensation
Helen's entrance caused. The children were so pleased to see
her at Sunday-school, they paid no attention to their teachers,
but rushed out of their seats and surrounded us. She kissed
them all, boys and girls, willing or unwilling. She seemed to
think at first that the children all belonged to the visiting
ministers; but soon she recognized some little friends among
them, and I told her the ministers didn't bring their children
with them. She looked disappointed and said, "I'll send them
many kisses." One of the ministers wished me to ask Helen,
"What do ministers do?" She said, "They read and talk loud
to people to be good." He put her answer down in his note

book. When it was time for the church service to begin, she
was in such a state of excitement that I thought it best to take
her away; but Captain Keller said, "No, she will be all right."
So there was nothing to do but stay. It was impossible to keep
Helen quiet. She hugged and kissed me, and the quiet-looking
divine who sat on the other side of her. He gave her his watch
to play with; but that didn't keep her still. She wanted to show
it to the little boy in the seat behind us. When the communion
service began, she smelt the wine, and sniffed so loud that every
one in the church could hear. When the wine was passed to our
neighbour, he was obliged to stand up to prevent her taking it
away from him. I never was so glad to get out of a place as I
was to leave that church! I tried to hurry Helen out-of-doors,
but she kept her arm extended, and every coat-tail she touched
must needs turn round and give an account of the children
he left at home, and receive kisses according to their number.
Everybody laughed at her antics, and you would have thought
they were leaving a place of amusement rather than a church.
Captain Keller invited some of the ministers to dinner. Helen
was irrepressible. She described in the most animated pantomime, supplemented by spelling, what she was going to do in
Brewster. Finally she got up from the table and went through
the motion of picking seaweed and shells, and splashing in the
water, holding up her skirts higher than was proper under the
circumstances. Then she threw herself on the floor and began
to swim so energetically that some of us thought we should be
kicked out of our chairs! Her motions are often more expressive
than any words, and she is as graceful as a nymph.

I wonder if the days seem as interminable to you as they do
to me. We talk and plan and dream about nothing but Boston,
Boston, Boston. I think Mrs. Keller has definitely decided to
go with us, but she will not stay all summer.

May 15, 1888.

Do you realize that this is the last letter I shall write to you
for a long, long time? The next word that you receive from
me will be in a yellow envelope, and it will tell you when we
shall reach Boston. I am too happy to write letters; but I must
tell you about our visit to Cincinnati.

We spent a delightful week with the "doctors." Dr. Keller

met us in Memphis. Almost every one on the train was a physician, and Dr. Keller seemed to know them all. When we reached Cincinnati, we found the place full of doctors. There were several prominent Boston physicians among them. We stayed at the Burnet House. Everybody was delighted with Helen. All the learned men marveled at her intelligence and gaiety. There is something about her that attracts people. I think it is her joyous interest in everything and everybody.

Wherever she went she was the centre of interest. She was delighted with the orchestra at the hotel, and whenever the music began she danced round the room, hugging and kissing every one she happened to touch. Her happiness impressed all; nobody seemed to pity her. One gentleman said to Dr. Keller, "I have lived long and seen many happy faces; but I have never seen such a radiant face as this child's before to-night." Another said, "Damn me! but I'd give everything I own in the world to have that little girl always near me." But I haven't time to write all the pleasant things people said— they would make a very large book, and the kind things they did for us would fill another volume. Dr. Keller distributed the extracts from the report that Mr. Anagnos sent me, and he could have disposed of a thousand if he had had them. Do you remember Dr. Garcelon, who was Governor of Maine several years ago? He took us to drive one afternoon, and wanted to give Helen a doll; but she said: "I do not like too many children. Nancy is sick, and Adeline is cross, and Ida is very bad." We laughed until we cried, she was so serious about it. "What would you like, then?" asked the Doctor. "Some beautiful gloves to talk with," she answered. The Doctor was puzzled. He had never heard of "talking-gloves"; but I explained that she had seen a glove on which the alphabet was printed, and evidently thought they could be bought. I told him he could buy some gloves if he wished, and that I would have the alphabet stamped on them.

We lunched with Mr. Thayer (your former pastor) and his wife. He asked me how I had taught Helen adjectives and the names of abstract ideas like goodness and happiness. These same questions had been asked me, a hundred times by the learned doctors. It seems strange that people should marvel at what is really so simple. Why, it is as easy to teach the name of an idea, if it is clearly formulated in the child's mind, as to teach the name of an object. It would indeed be a herculean task to teach the words if the ideas did not already exist in the child's mind. If his experiences and observations hadn't led him to the concepts, *small, large, good, bad, sweet, sour,* he would have nothing to attach the word-tags to.

I, little ignorant I, found myself explaining to the wise men of the East and the West such simple things as these: If you give a child something sweet, and he wags his tongue and smacks his lips and looks pleased, he has a very definite sensation; and if, every time he has this experience, he hears the word *sweet,* or has it spelled into his hand, he will quickly adopt this arbitrary sign for his sensation. Likewise, if you put a bit of lemon on his tongue, he puckers up his lips and tries to spit it out; and after he has had this experience a few times, if you offer him a lemon, he shuts his mouth and makes faces, clearly indicating that he remembers the unpleasant sensation. You label it *sour,* and he adopts your symbol. If you had called these sensations respectively *black* and *white,* he would have adopted them as readily; but he would mean by *black* and *white* the same things that he means by *sweet* and *sour.* In the same way the child learns from many experiences to differentiate his feelings, and we name them for him—*good, bad, gentle, rough, happy, sad.* It is not the word, but the capacity to experience the sensation that counts in his education.

This extract from one of Miss Sullivan's letters is added because it contains interesting casual opinions stimulated by observing the methods of others.

We visited a little school for the deaf. We were very kindly received, and Helen enjoyed meeting the children. Two of the teachers knew the manual alphabet, and talked to her without an interpreter. They were astonished at her command of language. Not a child in the school, they said, had anything like Helen's facility of expression, and some of them had been under instruction for two or three years. I was incredulous at first; but after I had watched the children at work for a couple of hours, I knew that what I had been told was true, and I wasn't surprised. In one room some little tots were standing before the blackboard, painfully constructing "simple sentences." A little girl had written: "I have a new dress. It is a pretty dress. My mamma made my pretty new dress. I love mamma." A curly-headed little boy was writing: "I have a large ball. I like to kick my large ball." When we entered the room, the children's attention was riveted on Helen. One of them pulled me by the sleeve and said, "Girl is blind." The teacher was writing on the blackboard: "The girl's name is Helen. She is deaf. She cannot see. We are very sorry." I said: "Why do you write those sentences on the board? Wouldn't the children understand if you talked to them about Helen?" The teacher said something about getting the correct construction, and continued to construct an exercise out of Helen. I asked her if the little girl who had written about the new dress was particularly pleased with her dress. "No," she replied, "I think not; but children learn better if they write about things that concern them personally." It seemed all so mechanical and difficult, my heart ached for the poor little children. Nobody thinks of making a hearing child say, "I have a pretty new dress," at the beginning. These children were older in years, it is true, than the baby who lisps, "Papa kiss baby—pretty," and fills out her meaning by pointing to her new dress; but their ability to understand and use language was no greater.

There was the same difficulty throughout the school. In every classroom I saw sentences on the blackboard, which evidently had been written to illustrate some grammatical rule, or for the purpose of using words that had previously been taught in the same, or in some other connection. This sort of thing may be necessary in some stages of education; but it isn't the way to acquire language. *Nothing, I think, crushes the child's impulse to talk naturally more effectually than these blackboard exercises.* The schoolroom is not the place to teach any young child language, least of all the deaf child. He must be kept as unconscious as the hearing child of the fact that he is learning words, *and he should be allowed to prattle on his fingers, or with his pencil, in monosyllables if he chooses, until such time as his growing intelligence demands the sentence.* Language should not be associated in his mind with endless hours in school, with puzzling questions in grammar, or with anything that is an enemy to joy. But I must not get into the habit of criticizing other people's methods too severely. I may be as far from the straight road as they.

Miss Sullivan's second report brings the account down to October 1st, 1888.

During the past year Helen has enjoyed excellent health. Her eyes and ears have been examined by specialists, and it is their opinion that she cannot have the slightest perception of either light or sound.

It is impossible to tell exactly to what extent the senses of smell and taste aid her in gaining information respecting physical qualities; but, according to eminent authority, these senses do exert a great influence on the mental and moral development. Dugald Stewart says, "Some of the most significant words relating to the human mind are borrowed from the sense of smell; and the conspicuous place which its sensations occupy in the poetical language of all nations shows how easily and naturally they ally themselves with the refined operations of the fancy and the moral emotions of the heart." Helen certainly derives great pleasure from the exercise of these senses. On entering a greenhouse her countenance becomes radiant, and she will tell the names of the flowers with which she is familiar, by the sense of smell alone. Her recollections of the sensations of smell are very vivid. She enjoys in anticipation the scent of a rose or a violet; and if she is promised a bouquet of these flowers, a peculiarly happy expression lights her face, indicating that in imagination she perceives their fragrance, and that it is pleasant to her. It frequently happens that the perfume of a flower or the flavour of a fruit recalls to her mind some happy event in home life, or a delightful birthday party.

Her sense of touch has sensibly increased during the year, and has gained in acuteness and delicacy. Indeed, her whole body is so finely organized that she seems to use it as a medium for bringing herself into closer relations with her fellow creatures.

She is able not only to distinguish with great accuracy the different undulations of the air and the vibrations of the floor made by various sounds and motions, and to recognize her friends and acquaintances the instant she touches their hands or clothing, but she also perceives the state of mind of those around her. It is impossible for any one with whom Helen is conversing to be particularly happy or sad, and withhold the knowledge of this fact from her.

She observes the slightest emphasis placed upon a word in conversation, and she discovers meaning in every change of position, and in the varied play of the muscles of the hand. She responds quickly to the gentle pressure of affection, the pat of approval, the jerk of impatience, the firm motion of command, and to the many other variations of the almost infinite language of the feelings; and she has become so expert in interpreting this unconscious language of the emotions that she is often able to divine our very thoughts.

In my account of Helen last year,* I mentioned several instances where she seemed to have called into use an inexplicable mental faculty; but it now seems to me, after carefully considering the matter, that this power may be explained by her perfect familiarity with the muscular variations of those with whom she comes into contact, caused by their emotions. She has been forced to depend largely upon this muscular sense as a means of ascertaining the mental condition of those about her. She has learned to connect certain movements of the body with anger, others with joy, and others still with sorrow. One day, while she was walking out with her mother and Mr. Anagnos, a boy threw a torpedo, which startled Mrs. Keller. Helen felt the change in her mother's movements instantly, and asked, "What are we afraid of?" On one occasion, while walking on the Common with her, I saw a police officer taking a man to the station-house. The agitation which I felt evidently produced a perceptible physical change; for Helen asked, excitedly, "What do you see?"

A striking illustration of this strange power was recently shown while her ears were being examined by the aurists in Cincinnati. Several experiments were tried, to determine positively whether or not she had any perception of sound.

*See Perkins Institution Report for 1887, page 105.

All present were astonished when she appeared not only to hear a whistle, but also an ordinary tone of voice. She would turn her head, smile, and act as though she had heard what was said. I was then standing beside her, holding her hand. Thinking that she was receiving impressions from me, I put her hands upon the table, and withdrew to the opposite side of the room. The aurists then tried their experiments with quite different results. Helen remained motionless through them all, not once showing the least sign that she realized what was going on. At my suggestion, one of the gentlemen took her hand, and the tests were repeated. This time her countenance changed whenever she was spoken to, but there was not such a decided lighting up of the features as when I had held her hand.

In the account of Helen last year it was stated that she knew nothing about death, or the burial of the body; yet on entering a cemetery for the first time in her life, she showed signs of emotion—her eyes actually filling with tears.

A circumstance equally remarkable occurred last summer; but, before relating it, I will mention what she now knows with regard to death. Even before I knew her, she had handled a dead chicken, or bird, or some other small animal. Some time after the visit to the cemetery before referred to, Helen became interested in a horse that had met with an accident by which one of his legs had been badly injured, and she went daily with me to visit him. The wounded leg soon became so much worse that the horse was suspended from a beam. The animal groaned with pain, and Helen, perceiving his groans, was filled with pity. At last it became necessary to kill him, and, when Helen next asked to go and see him, I told her that he was *dead*. This was the first time that she had heard the word. I then explained that he had been shot to relieve him from suffering, and that he was now *buried*—put into the ground. I am inclined to believe that the idea of his having been intentionally shot did not make much impression upon her; but I think she did realize the fact that life was extinct in the horse as in the dead birds she had touched, and also that he had been put into the ground. Since this occurrence, I have used the word *dead* whenever occasion required, but with no further explanation of its meaning.

While making a visit at Brewster, Massachusetts, she one day accompanied my friend and me through the graveyard. She examined one stone after another, and seemed pleased when she could decipher a name. She smelt of the flowers, but showed no desire to pluck them; and, when I gathered a few for her, she refused to have them pinned on her dress. When her attention was drawn to a marble slab inscribed with the name FLORENCE in relief, she dropped upon the ground as though looking for something, then turned to me with a face full of trouble, and asked, "Where is poor little Florence?" I evaded the question, but she persisted. Turning to my friend, she asked, "Did you cry loud for poor little Florence?" Then she added: "I think she is very dead. Who put her in big hole?" As she continued to ask these distressing questions, we left the cemetery. Florence was the daughter of my friend, and was a young lady at the time of her death; but Helen had been told nothing about her, nor did she even know that my friend had had a daughter. Helen had been given a bed and carriage for her dolls, which she had received and used like any other gift. On her return to the house after her visit to the cemetery, she ran to the closet where these toys were kept, and carried them to my friend, saying, "They are poor little Florence's." This was true, although we were at a loss to understand how she guessed it. A letter written to her mother in the course of the following week gave an account of her impression in her own words:

"I put my little babies to sleep in Florence's little bed, and I take them to ride in her carriage. Poor little Florence is dead. She was very sick and died. Mrs. H. did cry loud for her dear little child. She got in the ground, and she is very dirty, and she is cold. Florence was very lovely like Sadie, and Mrs. H. kissed her and hugged her much. Florence is very sad in big hole. Doctor gave her medicine to make her well, but poor Florence did not get well. When she was very sick she tossed and moaned in bed. Mrs. H. will go to see her soon."

Notwithstanding the activity of Helen's mind, she is a very natural child. She is fond of fun and frolic, and loves dearly to be with other children. She is never fretful or irritable, and I have never seen her impatient with her playmates because they failed to understand her. She will play for hours together with children who cannot understand a single word she spells, and it is pathetic to watch the eager gestures and excited pantomime through which her ideas and emotions find expression.

Occasionally some little boy or girl will try to learn the manual alphabet. Then it is beautiful to observe with what patience, sweetness, and perseverance Helen endeavours to bring the unruly fingers of her little friend into proper position.

One day, while Helen was wearing a little jacket of which she was very proud, her mother said: "There is a poor little girl who has no cloak to keep her warm. Will you give her yours?" Helen began to pull off the jacket, saying, "I must give it to a poor little strange girl."

She is very fond of children younger than herself, and a baby invariably calls forth all the motherly instincts of her nature. She will handle the baby as tenderly as the most careful nurse could desire. It is pleasant, too, to note her thoughtfulness for little children, and her readiness to yield to their whims.

She has a very sociable disposition, and delights in the companionship of those who can follow the rapid motions of her fingers; but if left alone she will amuse herself for hours at a time with her knitting or sewing.

She reads a great deal. She bends over her book with a look of intense interest, and as the forefinger of her left hand runs along the line, she spells out the words with the other hand; but often her motions are so rapid as to be unintelligible even to those accustomed to reading the swift and varied movements of her fingers.

Every shade of feeling finds expression through her mobile features. Her behaviour is easy and natural, and it is charming because of its frankness and evident sincerity. Her heart is too full of unselfishness and affection to allow a dream of fear or unkindness. She does not realize that one can be anything but kind-hearted and tender. She is not conscious of any reason why she should be awkward; consequently, her movements are free and graceful.

She is very fond of all the living things at home, and she will not have them unkindly treated. When she is riding in the carriage she will not allow the driver to use the whip, because, she says, "poor horses will cry." One morning she was greatly distressed by finding that one of the dogs had a block fastened to her collar. We explained that it was done to keep Pearl from running away. Helen expressed a great deal of sympathy, and at every opportunity during the day she would find Pearl and carry the burden from place to place.

Her father wrote to her last summer that the birds and bees were eating all his grapes. At first she was very indignant, and said the little creatures were "very wrong"; but she seemed pleased when I explained to her that the birds and bees were hungry, and did not know that it was selfish to eat all the fruit. In a letter written soon afterward she says:

"I am very sorry that bumblebees and hornets and birds and large flies and worms are eating all of my father's delicious grapes. They like juicy fruit to eat as well as people, and they are hungry. They are not very wrong to eat too many grapes because they do not know much."

She continues to make rapid progress in the acquisition of language as her experiences increase. While these were few and elementary, her vocabulary was necessarily limited; but, as she learns more of the world about her, her judgment grows more accurate, her reasoning powers grow stronger, more active and subtle, and the language by which she expresses this intellectual activity gains in fluency and logic.

When traveling she drinks in thought and language. Sitting beside her in the car, I describe what I see from the window— hills and valleys and the rivers; cotton-fields and gardens in which strawberries, peaches, pears, melons, and vegetables are growing; herds of cows and horses feeding in broad meadows, and flocks of sheep on the hillside; the cities with their churches and schools, hotels and warehouses, and the occupations of the busy people. While I am communicating these things, Helen manifests intense interest; and, in default of words, she indicates by gestures and pantomime her desire to learn more of her surroundings and of the great forces which are operating everywhere. In this way, she learns countless new expressions without any apparent effort.

From the day when Helen first grasped the idea that all objects have names, and that these can be communicated by certain movements of the fingers, I have talked to her exactly as I should have done had she been able to hear, with only this exception, that I have addressed the words to her fingers instead of to her ears. Naturally, there was at first a strong tendency on her part to use only the important words in a sentence. She would say: "Helen milk." I got the milk to show her that she had used the correct word; but I did not let her drink it until she had, with my assistance, made a complete sentence, as, "Give Helen some milk to drink." In these early lessons I encouraged her in the use of different forms of expression for conveying the same idea. If she was eating some candy, I said: "Will Helen please give teacher some candy?" or, "Teacher would like to eat some of Helen's candy," emphasizing the 's. She very soon perceived that the same idea could be expressed in a great many ways. In two or three months after I began to teach her she would say: "Helen wants to go to bed," or, "Helen is sleepy, and Helen will go to bed."

I am constantly asked the question, "How did you teach her the meaning of words expressive of intellectual and moral qualities?" I believe it was more through association and repetition than through any explanation of mine. This is especially true of her earlier lessons, when her knowledge of language was so slight as to make explanation impossible.

I have always made it a practice to use the words descriptive of emotions, of intellectual or moral qualities and actions, in connection with the circumstance which required these words. Soon after I became her teacher Helen broke her new doll, of which she was very fond. She began to cry. I said to her, "Teacher is *sorry.*" After a few repetitions she came to associate the word with the feeling.

The word *happy* she learned in the same way; also, *right, wrong, good, bad,* and other adjectives. The word *love* she learned as other children do—by its association with caresses.

One day I asked her a simple question in a combination of numbers, which I was sure she knew. She answered at random. I checked her, and she stood still, the expression of her face plainly showing that she was trying to think. I touched her forehead, and spelled "t-h-i-n-k." The word, thus connected with the act, seemed to impress itself on her mind much as if I had placed her hand upon an object and then spelled its name. Since that time she has always used the word *think.*

At a later period I began to use such words as *perhaps, suppose, expect, forget, remember.* If Helen asked, "Where is mother now?" I replied: "I do not know. *Perhaps* she is with Leila."

She is always anxious to learn the names of people we meet in the horse-cars or elsewhere, and to know where they are going, and what they will do. Conversations of this kind are frequent:

HELEN. What is little boy's name?

TEACHER. I do not know, for he is a little stranger; but *perhaps* his name is Jack.

HELEN. Where is he going?

TEACHER. He *may* be going to the Common to have fun with other boys.

HELEN. What will he play?

TEACHER. I *suppose* he will play ball.

HELEN. What are boys doing now?

TEACHER. *Perhaps* they are expecting Jack, and are waiting for him.

After the words have become familiar to her, she uses them in composition.

"September 26, [1888.]

"This morning teacher and I sat by the window and we saw a little boy walking on the sidewalk. It was raining very hard and he had a very large umbrella to keep off the rain-drops.

"I do not know how old he was but *think* he *may have been* six years old. *Perhaps* his name was Joe. I do not know where he was going because he was a little strange boy. But *perhaps* his mother sent him to a store to buy something for dinner. He had a bag in one hand. I *suppose* he was going to take it to his mother."

In teaching her the use of language, I have not confined myself to any particular theory or system. I have observed the spontaneous movements of my pupil's mind, and have tried to follow the suggestions thus given to me.

Owing to the nervousness of Helen's temperament, every precaution has been taken to avoid unduly exciting her already very active brain. The greater part of the year has been spent in travel and in visits to different places, and her lessons have been those suggested by the various scenes and experiences through which she has passed. She continues to manifest the same eagerness to learn as at first. It is never necessary to urge her to study. Indeed, I am often obliged to coax her to leave an example or a composition.

While not confining myself to any special system of instruction, I have tried to add to her general information and intelligence, to enlarge her acquaintance with things around her, and to bring her into easy and natural relations with people. I have encouraged her to keep a diary, from which the following selection has been made:

"March 22nd, 1888.

"Mr. Anagnos came to see me Thursday. I was glad to hug and kiss him. He takes care of sixty little blind girls and seventy little blind boys. I do love them. Little blind girls sent me a pretty workbasket. I found scissors and thread, and needlebook with many needles in it, and crochet hook and emery, and thimble, and box, and yard measure and buttons, and pincushion. I will write little blind girls a letter to thank them. I will make pretty clothes for Nancy and Adeline and Allie. I will go to Cincinnati in May and buy another child. Then I will have four children. New baby's name is Harry. Mr. Wilson and Mr. Mitchell came to see us Sunday. Mr. Anagnos went to Louisville Monday to see little blind children. Mother went to Huntsville. I slept with father, and Mildred slept with teacher. I did learn about calm. It does mean quiet and happy. Uncle Morrie sent me pretty stories. I read about birds. The quail lays fifteen or twenty eggs and they are white. She makes her nest on the ground. The blue-bird makes her nest in a hollow tree and her eggs are blue. The robin's eggs are green. I learned a song about spring. March, April, May are spring.

Now melts the snow.
The warm winds blow
The waters flow
And robin dear,
Is come to show
That Spring is here.

"James killed snipes for breakfast. Little chickens did get very cold and die. I am sorry. Teacher and I went to ride on Tennessee River, in a boat. I saw Mr. Wilson and James row with oars. Boat did glide swiftly and I put hand in water and felt it flowing.

"I caught fish with hook and line and pole. We climbed high hill and teacher fell and hurt her head. I ate very small fish for supper. I did read about cow and calf. The cow loves to eat grass as well as girl does bread and butter and milk. Little calf does run and leap in field. She likes to skip and play, for she is happy when the sun is bright and warm. Little boy did love his calf. And he did say, I will kiss you, little calf, and he put his arms around calf's neck and kissed her. The calf licked good boy's face with long rough tongue. Calf must not open mouth much to kiss. I am tired, and teacher does not want me to write more."

In the autumn she went to a circus. While we were standing before his cage the lion roared, and Helen felt the vibration of the air so distinctly that she was able to reproduce the noise quite accurately.

I tried to describe to her the appearance of a camel; but, as we were not allowed to touch the animal, I feared that she did not get a correct idea of its shape. A few days afterward, however, hearing a commotion in the schoolroom, I went in and found Helen on all fours with a pillow so strapped upon her back as to leave a hollow in the middle, thus making a hump on either side. Between these humps she had placed her doll, which she was giving a ride around the room. I watched her for some time as she moved about, trying to take long strides in order to carry out the idea I had given her of a camel's gait. When I asked her what she was doing, she replied, "I am a very funny camel."

During the next two years neither Mr. Anagnos, who was in Europe for a year, nor Miss Sullivan wrote anything about Helen Keller for publication. In 1892 appeared the Perkins Institution report for 1891, containing a full account of Helen Keller, including many of her letters, exercises, and compositions. As some of the letters and the story of the "Frost King" are published here, there is no need of printing any more samples of Helen Keller's writing during the third, fourth and fifth years of her education. It was the first two years that counted. From Miss Sullivan's part of this report I give her most important comments and such biographical matter as does not appear elsewhere in the present volume.

These extracts Mr. Anagnos took from Miss Sullivan's notes and memoranda.

One day, while her pony and her donkey were standing side by side, Helen went from one to the other, examining them closely. At last she paused with her hand upon Neddy's head, and addressed him thus: "Yes, dear Neddy, it is true that you are not as beautiful as Black Beauty. Your body is not so handsomely formed, and there is no proud look in your face, and your neck does not arch. Besides, your long ears make you look a little funny. Of course, you cannot help it, and I love you just as well as if you were the most beautiful creature in the world."

Helen has been greatly interested in the story of "Black Beauty." To show how quickly she perceives and associates ideas, I will give an instance which all who have read the book will be able to appreciate. I was reading the following paragraph to her:

"The horse was an old, worn-out chestnut, with an ill-kept coat, and bones that showed plainly through it; the knees knuckled over, and the forelegs were very unsteady. I had been eating some hay, and the wind rolled a little lock of it that way, and the poor creature put out her long, thin neck and picked it up, and then turned round and looked about for more. There was a hopeless look in the dull eye that I could not help noticing, and then, as I was thinking where I had seen that horse before, she looked full at me and said, 'Black Beauty, is that you?'"

At this point Helen pressed my hand to stop me. She was sobbing convulsively. "It was poor Ginger," was all she could say at first. Later, when she was able to talk about it, she said: "Poor Ginger! The words made a distinct picture in my mind. I could see the way Ginger looked; all her beauty gone, her beautiful arched neck drooping, all the spirit gone out of her flashing eyes, all the playfulness gone out of her manner. Oh, how terrible it was! I never knew before that there could be such a change in anything. There were very few spots of sunshine in poor Ginger's life, and the sadnesses were so many!" After a moment she added, mournfully, "I fear some people's lives are just like Ginger's."

This morning Helen was reading for the first time Bryant's poem, "Oh, mother of a mighty race!" I said to her, "Tell me, when you have read the poem through, who you think the mother is." When she came to the line, "There's freedom at thy gates, and rest," she exclaimed: "It means America! The gate, I suppose, is New York City, and Freedom is the great statue of Liberty." After she had read "The Battlefield," by the same author, I asked her which verse she thought was the most beautiful. She replied, "I like this verse best:

'Truth crushed to earth shall rise again;
The eternal years of God are hers;
But Error, wounded, writhes with pain,
And dies among his worshipers.' "

She is at once transported into the midst of the events of a story. She rejoices when justice wins, she is sad when virtue lies low, and her face glows with admiration and reverence when heroic deeds are described. She even enters into the spirit of battle; she says, "I think it is right for men to fight against wrongs and tyrants."

Here begins Miss Sullivan's connected account in the report of 1891:

During the past three years Helen has continued to make rapid progress in the acquisition of language. She has one advantage over ordinary children, that nothing from without distracts her attention from her studies.

But this advantage involves a corresponding disadvantage; the danger of unduly severe mental application. Her mind is so constituted that she is in a state of feverish unrest while conscious that there is something that she does not comprehend. I have never known her to be willing to leave a lesson when she felt that there was anything in it which she did not understand. If I suggest her leaving a problem in arithmetic until the next day, she answers, "I think it will make my mind stronger to do it now."

A few evenings ago we were discussing the tariff. Helen wanted me to tell her about it. I said: "No. You cannot understand it yet." She was quiet for a moment, and then asked, with spirit: "How do you know that I cannot understand?

I have a good mind! You must remember, dear teacher, that Greek parents were very particular with their children, and they used to let them listen to wise words, and I think they understood some of them." I have found it best not to tell her that she cannot understand, because she is almost certain to become excited.

Not long ago I tried to show her how to build a tower with her blocks. As the design was somewhat complicated, the slightest jar made the structure fall. After a time I became discouraged, and told her I was afraid she could not make it stand, but that I would build it for her; but she did not approve of this plan. She was determined to build the tower herself; and for nearly three hours she worked away, patiently gathering up the blocks whenever they fell, and beginning over again, until at last her perseverance was crowned with success. The tower stood complete in every part.

Until October, 1889, I had not deemed it best to confine Helen to any regular and systematic course of study. For the first two years of her intellectual life she was like a child in a strange country, where everything was new and perplexing; and, until she gained a knowledge of language, it was not possible to give her a definite course of instruction.

Moreover, Helen's inquisitiveness was so great during these years that it would have interfered with her progress in the acquisition of language, if a consideration of the questions which were constantly occurring to her had been deferred until the completion of a lesson. In all probability she would have forgotten the question, and a good opportunity to explain something of real interest to her would have been lost. Therefore it has always seemed best to me to teach anything whenever my pupil needed to know it, whether it had any bearing on the projected lesson or not; her inquiries have often led us far away from the subject under immediate consideration.

Since October, 1889, her work has been more regular and has included arithmetic, geography, zoölogy, botany and reading.

She has made considerable progress in the study of arithmetic. She readily explains the processes of multiplication, addition, subtraction, and division, and seems to understand the operations. She has nearly finished Colburn's mental arithmetic, her last work being in improper fractions. She has also done some good work in written arithmetic. Her mind works so rapidly, that it often happens, that when I give her an example she will give me the correct answer before I have time to write out the question. She pays little attention to the language used in stating a problem, and seldom stops to ask the meaning of unknown words or phrases until she is ready to explain her work. Once, when a question puzzled her very much, I suggested that we take a walk and then perhaps she would understand it. She shook her head decidedly, and said: "My enemies would think I was running away. I must stay and conquer them now," and she did.

The intellectual improvement which Helen has made in the past two years is shown more clearly in her greater command of language and in her ability to recognize nicer shades of meaning in the use of words, than in any other branch of her education.

Not a day passes that she does not learn many new words, nor are these merely the names of tangible and sensible objects. For instance, she one day wished to know the meaning of the following words: *Phenomenon, comprise, energy, reproduction, extraordinary, perpetual* and *mystery*. Some of these words have successive steps of meaning, beginning with what is simple and leading on to what is abstract. It would have been a hopeless task to make Helen comprehend the more abstruse meanings of the word *mystery,* but she understood readily that it signified something hidden or concealed, and when she makes greater progress she will grasp its more abstruse meaning as easily as she now does the simpler signification. In investigating any subject there must occur at the beginning words and phrases which cannot be adequately understood until the pupil has made considerable advancement; yet I have thought it best to go on giving my pupil simple definitions, thinking that, although these may be somewhat vague and provisional, they will come to one another's assistance, and that what is obscure to-day will be plain to-morrow.

I regard my pupil as a free and active being, whose own spontaneous impulses must be my surest guide. I have always talked to Helen exactly as I would talk to a seeing and hearing child, and I have insisted that other people should do the same. Whenever any one asks me if she will understand this or that word I always reply: "Never mind whether she understands each separate word of a sentence or not. She will guess the meanings of the new words from their connection with others which are already intelligible to her."

In selecting books for Helen to read, I have never chosen them with reference to her deafness and blindness. She always reads such books as seeing and hearing children of her age read and enjoy. Of course, in the beginning it was necessary that the things described should be familiar and interesting, and the English pure and simple. I remember distinctly when she first attempted to read a little story. She had learned the printed letters, and for some time had amused herself by making simple sentences, using slips on which the words were printed in raised letters; but these sentences had no special relation to one another. One morning we caught a mouse, and it occurred to me, with a live mouse and a live cat to stimulate her interest, that I might arrange some sentences in such a way as to form a little story, and thus give her a new conception of the use of language. So I put the following sentences in the frame, and gave it to Helen: "The cat is on the box. A mouse is in the box. The cat can see the mouse. The cat would like to eat the mouse. Do not let the cat get the mouse. The cat can have some milk, and the mouse can have some cake." The word *the* she did not know, and of course she wished it explained. At that stage of her advancement it would have been impossible to explain its use, and so I did not try, but moved her finger on to the next word, which she recognized with a bright smile. Then, as I put her hand upon puss sitting on the box, she made a little exclamation of surprise, and the rest of the sentence became perfectly clear to her. When she had read the words of the second sentence, I showed her that there really was a mouse in the box. She then moved her finger to the next line with an expression of eager interest. "The cat can see the mouse." Here I made the cat look at the mouse, and let Helen feel the cat. The expression of the little girl's countenance showed that she was perplexed. I called her attention to the following line, and, although she knew only the three words, *cat, eat* and *mouse*, she caught the idea. She pulled the cat away and put her on the floor, at the same time covering the box with the frame. When she read, "Do not let the cat get the mouse!" she recognized the negation in the sentence, and seemed to know that the cat must not get the mouse. *Get* and *let* were new words. She was familiar with the words of the last sentence, and was delighted when allowed to act them out. By signs she made me understand that she wished another story, and I gave her a book containing very short stories, written in the most elementary style. She ran her fingers along the lines, finding the words she knew and guessing at the meaning of others, in a way that would convince the most conservative of educators that a little deaf child, if given the opportunity, will learn to read as easily and naturally as ordinary children.

I am convinced that Helen's use of English is due largely to her familiarity with books. She often reads for two or three hours in succession, and then lays aside her book reluctantly. One day as we left the library I noticed that she appeared more serious than usual, and I asked the cause. "I am thinking how much wiser we always are when we leave here than we are when we come," was her reply.

When asked why she loved books so much, she once replied: "Because they tell me so much that is interesting about things I cannot see, and they are never tired or troubled like people. They tell me over and over what I want to know."

While reading from Dickens's "Child's History of England," we came to the sentence, "Still the spirit of the Britons was not broken." I asked what she thought that meant. She replied, "I think it means that the brave Britons were not discouraged because the Romans had won so many battles, and they wished all the more to drive them away." It would not have been possible for her to define the words in this sentence; and yet she had caught the author's meaning, and was able to give it in her own words. The next lines are still more idiomatic, "When Suetonius left the country, they fell upon his troops and retook the island of Anglesea." Here is her interpretation of the sentence: "It means that when the Roman general had gone away, the Britons began to fight again; and because the Roman soldiers had no general to tell them what to do, they were overcome by the Britons and lost the island they had captured."

She prefers intellectual to manual occupations, and is not so fond of fancy work as many of the blind children are; yet she is eager to join them in whatever they are doing. She has learned to use the Caligraph typewriter, and writes very correctly, but not rapidly as yet, having had less than a month's practice.

More than two years ago a cousin taught her the telegraph alphabet by making the dots and dashes on the back of her hand with his finger. Whenever she meets any one who is familiar with this system, she is delighted to use it in conversation. I have found it a convenient medium of communicating with Helen when she is at some distance from me, for it enables me to talk with her by tapping upon the floor with my foot. She feels the vibrations and understands what is said to her.

It was hoped that one so peculiarly endowed by nature as Helen, would, if left entirely to her own resources, throw some light upon such psychological questions as were not exhaustively investigated by Dr. Howe; but their hopes were not to be realized. In the case of Helen, as in that of Laura Bridgman, disappointment was inevitable. It is impossible to isolate a child in the midst of society, so that he shall not be influenced by the beliefs of those with whom he associates. In Helen's case such an end could not have been attained without depriving her of that intercourse with others, which is essential to her nature.

It must have been evident to those who watched the rapid unfolding of Helen's faculties that it would not be possible to keep her inquisitive spirit for any length of time from reaching out toward the unfathomable mysteries of life. But great care has been taken not to lead her thoughts prematurely to the consideration of subjects which perplex and confuse all minds. Children ask profound questions, but they often receive shallow answers, or, to speak more correctly, they are quieted by such answers.

"Where did I come from?" and "Where shall I go when I die?" were questions Helen asked when she was eight years old. But the explanations which she was able to understand at that time did not satisfy, although they forced her to remain silent, until her mind should begin to put forth its higher powers, and generalize from innumerable impressions and ideas which streamed in upon it from books and from her daily experiences. Her mind sought for the cause of things.

As her observation of phenomena became more extensive and her vocabulary richer and more subtle, enabling her to express her own conceptions and ideas clearly, and also to comprehend the thoughts and experiences of others, she became acquainted with the limit of human creative power, and perceived that some power, not human, must have created the earth, the sun, and the thousand natural objects with which she was perfectly familiar.

Finally she one day demanded a name for the power, the existence of which she had already conceived in her own mind.

Through Charles Kingsley's "Greek Heroes" she had become familiar with the beautiful stories of the Greek gods and goddesses, and she must have met with the words *God, heaven, soul,* and a great many similar expressions in books.

She never asked the meaning of such words, nor made any comment when they occurred; and until February, 1889, no one had ever spoken to her of God. At that time, a dear relative who was also an earnest Christian, tried to tell her about God but, as this lady did not use words suited to the comprehension of the child, they made little impression upon Helen's mind. When I subsequently talked with her she said: "I have something very funny to tell you. A. says God made me and every one out of sand; but it must be a joke. I am made of flesh and blood and bone, am I not?" Here she examined her arm with evident satisfaction, laughing heartily to herself. After a moment she went on: "A. says God is everywhere, and that He is all love; but I do not think a person can be made out of love. Love is only something in our hearts. Then A. said another very comical thing. She says He (meaning God) is my dear father. It made me laugh quite hard, for I know my father is Arthur Keller."

I explained to her that she was not yet able to understand what had been told her, and so easily led her to see that it would be better not to talk about such things until she was wiser.

She had met with the expression Mother Nature in the course of her reading, and for a long time she was in the habit of ascribing to Mother Nature whatever she felt to be beyond the power of man to accomplish. She would say, when speaking of the growth of a plant, "Mother Nature sends the sunshine and the rain to make the trees and the grass and the flowers grow." The following extract from my notes will show what were her ideas at this time:

Helen seemed a little serious after supper, and Mrs. H. asked her of what she was thinking. "I am thinking how very busy dear Mother Nature is in the springtime," she replied. When asked why, she answered: "Because she has so many children to take care of. She is the mother of everything; the flowers and trees and winds."

"How does Mother Nature take care of the flowers?" I asked. "She sends the sunshine and rain to make them grow," Helen replied; and after a moment she added, "I think the sunshine is Nature's warm smile, and the raindrops are her tears."

Later she said: "I do not know if Mother Nature made me. I think my mother got me from heaven, but I do not know where that place is. I know that daisies and pansies come from seeds which have been put in the ground; but children do not grow out of the ground, I am sure. I have never seen a plant-child! But I cannot imagine who made Mother Nature, can you? I love the beautiful spring, because the budding trees and the blossoming flowers and the tender green leaves fill my heart with joy. I must go now to see my garden. The daisies and the pansies will think I have forgotten them."

After May, 1890, it was evident to me that she had reached a point where it was impossible to keep from her the religious beliefs held by those with whom she was in daily contact. She almost overwhelmed me with inquiries which were the natural outgrowth of her quickened intelligence.

Early in May she wrote on her tablet the following list of questions:

"I wish to write about things I do not understand. Who made the earth and the seas, and everything? What makes the sun hot? Where was I before I came to mother? I know that plants grow from seeds which are in the ground, but I am sure people do not grow that way. I never saw a child-plant. Little birds and chickens come out of eggs. I have seen them. What was the egg before it was an egg? Why does not the earth fall, it is so very large and heavy? Tell me something that Father Nature does. May I read the book called the Bible? Please tell your little pupil many things when you have much time."

Can any one doubt after reading these questions that the child who was capable of asking them was also capable of understanding at least their elementary answers? She could not, of course, have grasped such abstractions as a complete answer to her questions would involve; but one's whole life is nothing more than a continual advance in the comprehension of the meaning and scope of such ideas.

Throughout Helen's education I have invariably assumed that

she can understand whatever it is desirable for her to know. Unless there had been in Helen's mind some such intellectual process as the questions indicate, any explanation of them would have been unintelligible to her. Without that degree of mental development and activity which perceives the necessity of super-human creative power, no explanation of natural phenomena is possible.

After she had succeeded in formulating the ideas which had been slowly growing in her mind, they seemed suddenly to absorb all her thoughts, and she became impatient to have everything explained. As we were passing a large globe a short time after she had written the questions, she stopped before it and asked, "Who made the *real* world?" I replied, "No one knows how the earth, the sun, and all the worlds which we call stars came to be; but I will tell you how wise men have tried to account for their origin, and to interpret the great and mysterious forces of nature."

She knew that the Greeks had many gods to whom they ascribed various powers, because they believed that the sun, the lightning, and a hundred other natural forces, were independent and superhuman powers. But after a great deal of thought and study, I told her, men came to believe that all forces were manifestations of one power, and to that power they gave the name *God*.

She was very still for a few minutes, evidently thinking earnestly. She then asked, "Who made God?" I was compelled to evade her question, for I could not explain to her the mystery of a self-existent being. Indeed, many of her eager questions would have puzzled a far wiser person than I am. Here are some of them: "What did God make the new worlds out of?" "Where did he get the soil, and the water, and the seeds, and the first animals?" "Where is God?" "Did you ever see God?" I told her that God was everywhere, and that she must not think of Him as a person, but as the life, the mind, the soul of everything. She interrupted me: "Everything does not have life. The rocks have not life, and they cannot think." It is often necessary to remind her that there are infinitely many things that the wisest people in the world cannot explain.

No creed or dogma has been taught to Helen, nor has any effort been made to force religious beliefs upon her attention. Being fully aware of my own incompetence to give her any adequate explanations of the mysteries which underlie the names of God, soul, and immortality, I have always felt obliged, by a sense of duty to my pupil, to say as little as possible about spiritual matters. The Rt. Rev. Phillips Brooks* has explained to her in a beautiful way the fatherhood of God.

She has not as yet been allowed to read the Bible, because I do not see how she can do so at present without getting a very erroneous conception of the attributes of God. I have already told her in simple language of the beautiful and helpful life of Jesus, and of his cruel death. The narrative affected her greatly when first she listened to it.

When she referred to our conversation again, it was to ask, "Why did not Jesus go away, so that his enemies could not find Him?" She thought the miracles of Jesus very strange. When told that Jesus walked on the sea to meet His disciples, she said, decidedly, "It does not mean *walked,* it means *swam.*" When told of the instance in which Jesus raised the dead, she was much perplexed, saying, "I did not know life could come back into the dead body!"

One day she said, sadly: "I am blind and deaf. That is why I cannot see God." I taught her the word *invisible,* and told her we could not see God with our eyes, because He was a spirit; but that when our hearts were full of goodness and gentleness, then we saw Him because then we were more like Him.

At another time she asked, "What is a soul?" "No one knows what the soul is like," I replied; "but we know that it is not the body, and it is that part of us which thinks and loves and hopes, and which Christian people believe will live on after the body is dead." I then asked her, "Can you think of your soul as separate from your body?" "Oh, yes!" she replied; "because last hour I was thinking very hard of Mr. Anagnos, and then my mind,"—then changing the word—"my soul was in Athens, but my body was here in the study." At this moment another thought seemed to flash through her mind, and she added, "But Mr. Anagnos did not speak to my soul." I explained to her that the soul, too, is invisible, or in other words, that it is without apparent form. "But if I write what my soul thinks," she said, "then it will be visible, and the words will be its body."

A long time ago Helen said to me, "I would like to live sixteen

*See page 187.

hundred years." When asked if she would not like to live *always* in a beautiful country called heaven, her first question was, "Where is heaven?" I was obliged to confess that I did not know, but suggested that it might be on one of the stars. A moment after she said, "Will you please go first and tell me all about it?" and then she added, "Tuscumbia is a very beautiful little town." It was more than a year before she alluded to the subject again, and when she did return to it, her questions were numerous and persistent. She asked: "Where is heaven, and what is it like? Why cannot we know as much about heaven as we do about foreign countries?" I told her in very simple language that there may be many places called heaven, but that essentially it was a condition—the fulfilment of the heart's desire, the satisfaction of its wants; and that heaven existed wherever *right* was acknowledged, believed in, and loved.

She shrinks from the thought of death with evident dismay. Recently, on being shown a deer which had been killed by her brother, she was greatly distressed, and asked sorrowfully, "Why must everything die, even the fleet-footed deer?" At another time she asked, "Do you not think we would be very much happier always, if we did not have to die?" I said, "No; because, if there were no death, our world would soon be so crowded with living creatures that it would be impossible for any of them to live comfortably." "But," said Helen, quickly, "I think God could make some more worlds as well as he made this one."

When friends have told her of the great happiness which awaits her in another life, she instantly asked: "How do you know, if you have not been dead?"

The literal sense in which she sometimes takes common words and idioms shows how necessary it is that we should make sure that she receives their correct meaning. When told recently that Hungarians were born musicians, she asked in surprise, "Do they sing when they are born?" When her friend added that some of the pupils he had seen in Budapest had more than one hundred tunes in their heads, she said, laughing, "I think their heads must be very noisy." She sees the ridiculous quickly, and, instead of being seriously troubled by metaphorical language, she is often amused at her own too literal conception of its meaning.

Having been told that the soul was without form, she was much perplexed at David's words, "He leadeth my soul." "Has it feet? Can it walk? Is it blind?" she asked; for in her mind the idea of being led was associated with blindness.

Of all the subjects which perplex and trouble Helen, none distresses her so much as the knowledge of the existence of evil, and of the suffering which results from it. For a long time it was possible to keep this knowledge from her; and it will always be comparatively easy to prevent her from coming in personal contact with vice and wickedness. The fact that sin exists, and that great misery results from it, dawned gradually upon her mind as she understood more and more clearly the lives and experiences of those around her. The necessity of laws and penalties had to be explained to her. She found it very hard to reconcile the presence of evil in the world with the idea of God which had been presented to her mind.

One day she asked, "Does God take care of us all the time?" She was answered in the affirmative. "Then why did he let little sister fall this morning, and hurt her head so badly?" Another time she was asking about the power and goodness of God. She had been told of a terrible storm at sea, in which several lives were lost, and she asked, "Why did not God save the people if he can do all things?"

Surrounded by loving friends and the gentlest influences, as Helen had always been, she has, from the earliest stage of her intellectual enlightenment, willingly done right. She knows with unerring instinct what is right, and does it joyously. She does not think of one wrong act as harmless, of another as of no consequence, and of another as not intended. To her pure soul all evil is equally unlovely.

These passages from the paper Miss Sullivan prepared for the meeting at Chautauqua, in July, 1894, of the American Association to Promote the Teaching of Speech to the Deaf, contain her latest written account of her methods.

You must not imagine that as soon as Helen grasped the idea that everything had a name she at once became mistress of the treasury of the English language, or that "her mental faculties emerged, full armed, from their then living tomb, as Pallas Athene from the head of Zeus," as one of her enthusiastic admirers would have us believe. At first, the words, phrases and sentences which she used in expressing her thoughts were all reproductions of what we had used in conversation with her, and which her memory had unconsciously retained. And indeed, this is true of the language of all children. Their language is the memory of the language they hear spoken in their homes. Countless repetition of the conversation of daily life has impressed certain words and phrases upon their memories, and when they come to talk themselves, memory supplies the words they lisp. Likewise, the language of educated people is the memory of the language of books.

Language grows out of life, out of its needs and experiences. At first my little pupil's mind was all but vacant. She had been living in a world she could not realize. *Language* and *knowledge* are indissolubly connected; they are interdependent. Good work in language presupposes and depends on a real knowledge of things. As soon as Helen grasped the idea that everything had a *name*, and that by means of the manual alphabet these names could be transmitted from one to another, I proceeded to awaken her further interest in the *objects* whose names she learned to spell with such evident joy. *I never taught language for the* PURPOSE *of teaching it;* but invariably used language as a medium for the communication of *thought;* thus the learning of language was *coincident* with the acquisition of knowledge. In order to use language intelligently, one must have something to talk *about,* and having something to talk about is the result of having had experiences; no amount of language training will enable our little children to use language with ease and fluency unless they have something clearly in their minds which they wish to communicate, or unless we succeed in awakening in them a desire to know what is in the minds of others.

At first I did not attempt to confine my pupil to any system. I always tried to find out what interested her most, and made that the starting-point for the new lesson, whether it had any bearing on the lesson I had planned to teach or not. During the first two years of her intellectual life, I required Helen to write very little. In order to write one must have something to write about, and having something to write about requires some mental preparation. The memory must be stored with ideas and the mind must be enriched with knowledge before writing becomes a natural and pleasurable effort. Too often, I think, children are required to write before they have anything to say. Teach them to think and read and talk without self-repression, and they will write because they cannot help it.

Helen acquired language by practice and habit rather than by study of rules and definitions. Grammar with its puzzling array of classifications, nomenclatures, and paradigms, was wholly discarded in her education. She learned language by being brought in contact with the *living* language itself; she was made to deal with it in everyday conversation, and in her books, and to turn it over in a variety of ways until she was able to use it correctly. No doubt I talked much more with my fingers, and more constantly than I should have done with my mouth; for had she possessed the use of sight and hearing, she would have been less dependent on me for entertainment and instruction.

I believe every child has hidden away somewhere in his being noble capacities which may be quickened and developed if we go about it in the right way; but we shall never properly develop the higher natures of our little ones while we continue to fill their minds with the so-called rudiments. Mathematics will never make them loving, nor will the accurate knowledge of the size and shape of the world help them to appreciate its beauties. Let us lead them during the first years to find their greatest pleasure in Nature. Let them run in the fields, learn about animals, and observe real things. Children will educate themselves under right conditions. They require guidance and sympathy far more than instruction.

I think much of the fluency with which Helen uses language is due to the fact that nearly every impression which she receives comes through the medium of language. But after due allowance has been made for Helen's natural aptitude for acquiring language, and for the advantage resulting from her peculiar environment, I think that we shall still find that the constant companionship of good books has been of supreme importance in her education. It may be true, as some maintain, that language cannot express to us much beyond what we have lived and experienced; but I have always observed that children manifest the greatest delight in the lofty, poetic language which we are too ready to think beyond their comprehension. "This is all you will understand," said a teacher to a class of little children, closing the book which she had been reading to them. "Oh, please read us the rest, even if we won't understand it," they pleaded, delighted with the rhythm, and the beauty which they felt, even though they could not have explained it. It is not necessary that a child should understand every word in a book before he can read with pleasure and profit. Indeed, only such explanations should be given as are really essential. Helen drank in language which she at first could not understand, and it remained in her mind until needed, when it fitted itself naturally and easily into her conversation and compositions. Indeed, it is maintained by some that she reads too much, that a great deal of originative force is dissipated in the enjoyment of books; that when she might see and say things for herself, she sees them only through the eyes of others, and says them in their language; but I am convinced that original composition without the preparation of much reading is an impossibility. Helen has had the best and purest models in language constantly presented to her, and her conversation and her writing are unconscious reproductions of what she has read. Reading, I think, should be kept independent of the regular school exercises. Children should be encouraged to read for the pure delight of it. The attitude of the child toward his books should be that of unconscious receptivity. The great works of the imagination ought to become a part of his life, as they were once of the very substance of the men who wrote them. It is true, the more sensitive and imaginative the mind is that receives the thought-pictures and images of literature, the more nicely the finest lines are reproduced. Helen has the vitality of feeling, the freshness and eagerness of interest, and the spiritual insight of the artistic temperament, and naturally she has a more active and intense joy in life, simply as life, and in nature, books, and people than less gifted mortals. Her mind is so filled with the beautiful thoughts and ideals of the great poets that nothing seems commonplace to her; for her imagination colours all life with its own rich hues.

There has been much discussion of such of Miss Sullivan's statements and explanations as have been published before. Too much has been written by people who do not know the problems of the deaf at first hand, and I do not care to add much to it. Miss Keller's education, however, is so fundamentally a question of language teaching that it rather includes the problems of the deaf than limits itself to the deaf alone. Teachers can draw their own conclusions. For the majority of readers, who will not approach Miss Keller's life from the educator's point of view, I will summarize a few principal things in Miss Sullivan's methods.

Miss Sullivan has begun where Dr. Howe left off. He invented the instrument, the physical means of working, but the teaching of language is quite another thing from the mechanical means by which language may be taught. By experiment, by studying other children, Miss Sullivan came upon the practical way of teaching language by the natural method. It was for this "natural method" that Dr. Howe was groping, but he never got to this idea, that a deaf child should not be taught each word separately by definition, but should be given language by endless repetition of language which it does not understand. And this is Miss Sullivan's great discovery. All day long in their play-time and work-time Miss Sullivan kept spelling into her pupil's hand, and by that Helen Keller absorbed words, just as the child in the cradle absorbs words by hearing thousands of them before he uses one and by associating the words with the occasion of their utterance. Thus he learns that words name things and actions and feelings. Now, that is the first principle in Miss Sullivan's method, one that had practical results, and one which, so far as I can discover, had never been put in practice in the education of a deaf child, not to say a deaf-blind child, until Miss Sullivan tried it with Helen Keller. And the principle had never been formulated clearly until Miss Sullivan wrote her letters.

The second principle in her method (the numerical order is, of course, arbitrary) is never to talk to the child about things distasteful or wearisome to him. In the first deaf school Miss Sullivan ever visited, the teacher was busy at the blackboard telling the children by written words something they did not want to know, while they were crowding round their visitor with wide-awake curiosity, showing there were a thousand things they did want to know. Why not, says Miss Sullivan, make a language lesson out of what they were interested in?*

Akin to this idea of talking to the child about what interests him, is the principle never to silence a child who asks questions, but to answer the questions as truly as possible; for, says Miss Sullivan, the question is the door to the child's mind. Miss Sullivan never needlessly belittled her ideas or expressions to suit the supposed state of the child's intelligence. She urged every one to speak to Helen naturally, to give her full sentences and intelligent ideas, never minding whether Helen understood or not. Thus Miss Sullivan knew what so many people do not understand, that after the first rudimentary definitions of *hat, cup, go, sit,* the unit of language, as the child learns it, is the sentence, which is also the unit of language in our adult experience. We do not take in a sentence word by word, but as a whole. It is the proposition, something predicated about something, that conveys an idea. True, single words do suggest and express ideas; the child may say simply "mamma" when he means "Where is mamma?" but he learns the expression of the ideas that relate to mamma—he learns language —by hearing complete sentences. And though Miss Sullivan did not force grammatical completeness upon the first finger-lispings of her pupil, yet when she herself repeated Helen's sentence, "mamma milk," she filled out the construction, completed the child's ellipsis and said, "Mamma will bring Helen some milk."

Thus Miss Sullivan was working out a natural method, which is so simple, so lacking in artificial system, that her method seems rather to be a destruction of method. It is doubtful if we should have heard of Helen Keller if Miss Sullivan had not been where there were other children. By watching them, she learned to treat her pupil as nearly as possible like an ordinary child.

The manual alphabet was not the only means of presenting words to Helen Keller's fingers. Books supplemented, perhaps equaled in importance, the manual alphabet, as a means of teaching language. Helen sat poring over them before she could read, not at first for the story, but to find words she knew; and the definition of new words which is implied in their con-

*Page 351.

text, in their position with reference to words known, added to Helen's vocabulary. Books are the storehouse of language, and any child, whether deaf or not, if he has his attention attracted in any way to printed pages, must learn. He learns not by reading what he understands, but by reading and remembering words he does not understand. And though perhaps few children will have as much precocious interest in books as did Helen Keller, yet the natural curiosity of every healthy child may be turned to printed pages, especially if the teacher is clever and plays a word game as Miss Sullivan did. Helen Keller is supposed to have a special aptitude for languages. It is true rather that she has a special aptitude for thinking, and her leaning toward language is due to the fact that language to her meant life. It was not a special subject, like geography or arithmetic, but her way to outward things.

When at the age of fourteen she had had but a few lessons in German, she read over the words of "Wilhelm Tell" and managed to get the story. Of grammar she knew nothing and she cared nothing for it. She got the language from the language itself, and this is, next to hearing the language spoken, the way for any one to get a foreign tongue, more vital and, in the end, easier than our schoolroom method of beginning with the grammar. In the same way she played with Latin, learning not only from the lessons her first Latin teacher gave her, but from going over and over the words of a text, a game she played by herself.

Mr. John D. Wright, one of her teachers at the Wright-Humason school, says in a letter to me:

"Often I found her, when she had a little leisure, sitting in her favourite corner, in a chair whose arms supported the big volume prepared for the blind, and passing her finger slowly over the lines of Moliere's 'Le Medecin Malgré Lui,' chuckling to herself at the comical situations and humorous lines. At that time her actual working vocabulary in French was very small, but by using her judgment, as we laughingly called the mental process, she could guess at the meanings of the words and put the sense together much as a child puzzles out a sliced object. The result was that in a few weeks she and I spent a most hilarious hour one evening while she poured out to me the whole story, dwelling with great gusto on its humour and sparkling wit. It was not a lesson, but only one of her recreations."

So Helen Keller's aptitude for language is her whole mental aptitude, turned to language because of its extraordinary value to her.

There have been many discussions of the question whether Helen Keller's achievements are due to her natural ability or to the method by which she was taught.

It is true that a teacher with ten times Miss Sullivan's genius could not have made a pupil so remarkable as Helen Keller out of a child born dull and mentally deficient. But it is also true that, with ten times her native genius, Helen Keller could not have grown to what she is, if she had not been excellently taught from the very start, and especially at the start. And the fact remains that she was taught by a method of teaching language to the deaf the essential principles of which are clearly expressed in Miss Sullivan's letters, written while she was discovering the method and putting it successfully into practice. And it can be applied by any teacher to any healthy deaf child, and in the broadest interpretation of the principles, can be applied to the teaching of language of all kinds to all children.

In the many discussions of this question writers seem to throw us from one horn to another of a dilemma—either a born genius in Helen Keller, or a perfect method in the teacher. Both things may be true at once, and there is another truth which makes the dilemma imperfect. Miss Sullivan is a person of extraordinary power. Her method might not succeed so completely in the hands of any one else. Miss Sullivan's vigorous, original mind has lent much of its vitality to her pupil. If Miss Keller is fond of language and not interested especially in mathematics, it is not surprising to find Miss Sullivan's interests very similar. And this does not mean that Miss Keller is unduly dependent on her teacher. It is told of her that, as a child of eight, when some one tried to interfere with her, she sat sober a few moments, and, when asked what was the trouble, answered, "I am preparing to assert my independence." Such an aggressive personality cannot grow up in mere dependence even under the guidance of a will like Miss Sullivan's. But Miss Sullivan by her "natural aptitude" has done for her pupil much that is not capable of analysis and reduction to principle; she has given the inspiration which is in all close friendship, and which rather develops than limits the powers of either person. Moreover, if Miss Keller is a "marvel of sweetness and goodness," if she has a love "of all things good and beautiful," this implies something about the teacher who has lived with her for sixteen years.

There is, then, a good deal that Miss Sullivan has done for Miss Keller which no other teacher can do in just the same way for any one else. To have another Helen Keller there must be another Miss Sullivan. To have another well-educated deaf and blind child, there need only be another teacher, living under favourable conditions, among plenty of external interests, unseparated from her pupil, allowed to have a free hand, and using as many as she needs of the principles which Miss Sullivan has saved her the trouble of finding out for herself, modifying and adding as she finds it necessary; and there must be a pupil in good health, of good native powers, young enough not to have grown beyond recovery in ignorance. Any deaf child or deaf and blind child in good health can be taught. And the one to do it is the parent or the special teacher, not the school. I know that this idea will be vigorously combated by those who conduct schools for the deaf. To be sure, the deaf school is the only thing possible for children educated by the State. But it is evident that precisely what the deaf child needs to be taught is what other children learn before they go to school at all. When Miss Sullivan went out in the barnyard and picked up a little chicken and talked to Helen about it, she was giving a kind of instruction impossible inside four walls, and impossible with more than one pupil at a time.

Surely Dr. Howe is wrong when he says, "A teacher cannot be a child." That is just what the teacher of the deaf child must be, a child ready to play and romp, and interested in all childish things.

The temptation to discuss, solely in the light of Helen Keller, the whole matter of educating the deaf is a dangerous one, and one which I have not taken particular care to avoid, because my opinions are of no authority and I have merely tried to suggest problems and reinforce some of the main ideas expressed by Miss Sullivan, who is an authority. It is a question whether Helen Keller's success has not led teachers to expect too much of other children, and I know of deaf-blind children who are dragged along by their teachers and friends, and become the subjects of glowing reports, which are pathetically untrue, because one sees behind the reports how the children are tugged at to bring them somewhere near the exaggerated things that are said about them.

Let me sum up a few of the elements that made Helen Keller what she is. In the first place she had nineteen months' experience of sight and sound. This meant some mental development. She had inherited vigour of body and mind. She expressed ideas in signs before she learned language. Mrs. Keller writes me that before her illness Helen made signs for everything, and her mother thought this habit the cause of her slowness in learning to speak. After the illness, when they were dependent on signs, Helen's tendency to gesture developed. How far she could receive communications is hard to determine, but she knew much that was going on around her. She recognized that others used their lips; she "saw" her father reading a paper and when he laid it down she sat in his chair and held the paper before her face. Her early rages were an unhappy expression of the natural force of character which instruction was to turn into trained and organized power.

It was, then, to a good subject that Miss Sullivan brought her devotion and intelligence, and fearless willingness to experiment. Miss Sullivan's methods were so good that even without the practical result, any one would recognize the truth of the teacher's ideas. Miss Sullivan has in addition a vigorous personality. And finally all the conditions were good for that first nature school, in which the teacher and pupil played together, exploring together and educating themselves, pupil and teacher inseparable.

Miss Keller's later education is easy to understand and needs no further explanation than she has given. Those interested may get on application to the Volta Bureau, Washington, D. C., the reports of the teachers who prepared her for college, Mr. Arthur Gilman of the Cambridge School for Young Ladies, and Mr. Merton S. Keith.

CHAPTER IV

SPEECH

THE two persons who have written authoritatively about Miss Keller's speech and the way she learned it are Miss Sarah Fuller,* of the Horace Mann School for the Deaf in Boston, Massachusetts, who gave her the first lessons, and Miss Sullivan, who, by her unremitting discipline, carried on the success of these first lessons.

Before I quote from Miss Sullivan's account, let me try to give some impression of what Miss Keller's speech and voice qualities are at present.

Her voice is low and pleasant to listen to. Her speech lacks variety and modulation; it runs in a sing-song when she is reading aloud; and when she speaks with fair degree of loudness, it hovers about two or three middle tones. Her voice has an aspirate quality; there seems always to be too much breath for the amount of tone. Some of her notes are musical and charming. When she is telling a child's story, or one with pathos in it, her voice runs into pretty slurs from one tone to another. This is like the effect of the slow dwelling on long words, not quite well managed, that one notices in a child who is telling a solemn story.

The principal thing that is lacking is sentence accent and variety in the inflection of phrases. Miss Keller pronounces each word as a foreigner does when he is still labouring with the elements of a sentence, or as children sometimes read in school when they have to pick out each word.

She speaks French and German. Her friend, Mr. John Hitz, whose native tongue is German, says that her pronunciation is excellent. Another friend, who is as familiar with French as with English, finds her French much more intelligible than her English. When she speaks English she distributes her

*Miss Fuller's account may be obtained on application to the Volta Bureau, Washington, D. C.

emphasis as in French and so does not put sufficient stress on accented syllables. She says for example, "pro -vo'-ca'-tion," "in'-di'-vi'-du'-al," with ever so little difference between the value of the syllables, and a good deal of inconsistency in the pronunciation of the same word one day and the next. It would, I think, be hard to make her feel just how to pronounce *dictionary* without her erring either toward *dictionayry* or *diction'ry*, and, of course the word is neither one nor the other. For no system of marks in a lexicon can tell one how to pronounce a word. The only way is to hear it, especially in a language like English which is so full of unspellable, suppressed vowels and quasi-vowels.

Miss Keller's vowels are not firm. Her *awful* is nearly *awfil*. The wavering is caused by the absence of accent on *ful*, for she pronounces *full* correctly.

She sometimes mispronounces as she reads aloud and comes on a word which she happens never to have uttered, though she may have written it many times. This difficulty and some others may be corrected when she and Miss Sullivan have more time. Since 1894, they have been so much in their books that they have neglected everything that was not necessary to the immediate task of passing the school years successfully. Miss Keller will never be able, I believe, to speak loud without destroying the pleasant quality and the distinctness of her words, but she can do much to make her speech clearer.

When she was at the Wright-Humason School in New York, Dr. Humason tried to improve her voice, not only her word pronunciation, but the voice itself, and gave her lessons in tone and vocal exercises.

It is hard to say whether or not Miss Keller's speech is easy to understand. Some understand her readily; others do not. Her friends grow accustomed to her speech and forget that it is different from that of any one else. Children seldom have any difficulty in understanding her; which suggests that her deliberate, measured speech is like theirs, before they come to the adult trick of running all the words of a phrase into one movement of the breath. I am told that Miss Keller speaks better than most other deaf people.

Miss Keller has told how she learned to speak.* Miss Sulli-

*Page 58.

van's account in her address at Chautauqua, in July, 1894, at the
meeting of The American Association to Promote the Teaching
of Speech to the Deaf, is substantially like Miss Keller's in points
of fact.

It was three years from the time when Helen began to communicate by means of the manual alphabet that she received
her first lesson in the more natural and universal medium of
human intercourse—oral language. She had become very proficient in the use of the manual alphabet, which was her only
means of communication with the outside world; through it
she had acquired a vocabulary which enabled her to converse
freely, read intelligently, and write with comparative ease
and correctness. Nevertheless, the impulse to utter audible sounds
was strong within her, and the constant efforts which I made to
repress this instinctive tendency, which I feared in time would
become unpleasant, were of no avail. I made no effort to teach
her to speak, because I regarded her inability to watch the
lips of others as an insurmountable obstacle. But she gradually
became conscious that her way of communicating was different
from that used by those around her, and one day her thoughts
found expression. "How do the blind girls know what to say
with their mouths? Why do you not teach me to talk like
them? Do deaf children ever learn to speak?" I explained
to her that some deaf children were taught to speak, but that
they could see their teachers' mouths, and that that was a very
great assistance to them. But she interrupted me to say she
was very sure she could feel my mouth very well. Soon after
this conversation, a lady came to see her and told her about the
deaf and blind Norwegian child, Ragnhild Kaata, who had been
taught to speak and understand what her teacher said to her
by touching his lips with her fingers. She at once resolved to
learn to speak, and from that day to this she has never wav-
ered in that resolution. She began immediately to make sounds
which she called speaking, and I saw the necessity of correct
instruction, since her heart was set upon learning to talk; and,
feeling my own incompetence to teach her, never having given the

subject of articulation serious study, I went with my pupil, for advice and assistance, to Miss Sarah Fuller. Miss Fuller was delighted with Helen's earnestness and enthusiasm, and at once began to teach her. In a few lessons she learned nearly all of the English sounds, and in less than a month she was able to articulate a great many words distinctly. From the first she was not content to be drilled in single sounds, but was impatient to pronounce words and sentences. The length of the word or the difficulty of the arrangement of the elements never seemed to discourage her. But, with all her eagerness and intelligence, learning to speak taxed her powers to the utmost. But there was satisfaction in seeing from day to day the evidence of growing mastery and the possibility of final success. And Helen's success has been more complete and inspiring than any of her friends expected, and the child's delight in being able to utter her thoughts in living and distinct speech is shared by all who witness her pleasure when strangers tell her that they understand her.

I have been asked a great many times whether I think Helen will ever speak naturally; that is, as other people speak. I am hardly prepared to decide that question, or even give an opinion regarding it. I believe that I have hardly begun yet to know what is possible. Teachers of the deaf often express surprise that Helen's speech is so good when she has not received any regular instruction in speech since the first few lessons given her by Miss Fuller. I can only say in reply, "This is due to habitual imitation and practice! practice! practice!" Nature has determined how the child shall learn to speak, and all we can do is to aid him in the simplest, easiest way possible, by encouraging him to observe and imitate the vibrations in the voice.

Some further details appear in an earlier, more detailed account, which Miss Sullivan wrote for the Perkins Institution Report of 1891.

I knew that Laura Bridgman had shown the same intuitive desire to produce sounds, and had even learned to pronounce a few simple words, which she took great delight in using, and I did not doubt that Helen could accomplish as much as this. I thought, however, that the advantage she would derive would not repay her for the time and labour that such an experiment would cost.

Moreover, the absence of hearing renders the voice monotonous and often very disagreeable; and such speech is generally unintelligible except to those familiar with the speaker.

The acquiring of speech by untaught deaf children is always slow and often painful. Too much stress, it seems to me, is often laid upon the importance of teaching a deaf child to articulate—a process which may be detrimental to the pupil's intellectual development. In the very nature of things, articulation is an unsatisfactory means of education; while the use of the manual alphabet quickens and invigorates mental activity, since through it the deaf child is brought into close contact with the English language, and the highest and most abstract ideas may be conveyed to the mind readily and accurately. Helen's case proved it to be also an invaluable aid in acquiring articulation. She was already perfectly familiar with words and the construction of sentences, and had only mechanical difficulties to overcome. Moreover, she knew what a pleasure speech would be to her, and this definite knowledge of what she was striving for gave her the delight of anticipation which made drudgery easy. The untaught deaf child who is made to articulate does not know what the goal is, and his lessons in speech are for a long time tedious and meaningless.

Before describing the process of teaching Helen to speak, it may be well to state briefly to what extent she had used the vocal organs before she began to receive regular instruction in articulation. When she was stricken down with the illness which resulted in her loss of sight and hearing, at the age of nineteen months, she was learning to talk. The unmeaning babblings of the infant were becoming day by day conscious and voluntary signs of what she felt and thought. But the disease checked her progress in the acquisition of oral language, and, when her physical strength returned, it was found that she had ceased to speak intelligibly because she could no longer hear a sound. She continued to exercise her vocal organs mechanically, as ordinary children do. Her cries and laughter and the tones of her voice as she pronounced many word elements were perfectly natural, but the child evidently attached no significance to them, and with one exception they were produced not with any intention of communicating with those around her, but from the sheer necessity of exercising her innate, organic, and hereditary faculty of expression. She always attached a meaning to the word *water*, which was one of the first sounds her baby lips learned to form, and it was the only word which she continued to articulate after she lost her hearing. Her pronunciation of this gradually became indistinct, and when I first knew her it was nothing more than a peculiar noise. Nevertheless, it was the only sign she ever made for water, and not until she had learned to spell the word with her fingers did she forget the spoken symbol. The word *water*, and the gesture which corresponds to the word *good-by*, seem to have been all that the child remembered of the natural and acquired signs with which she had been familiar before her illness.

As she became acquainted with her surroundings through the sense of feeling (I use the word in the broadest sense, as including all tactile impressions), she felt more and more the pressing necessity of communicating with those around her. Her little hands felt every object and observed every movement of the persons about her, and she was quick to imitate these movements. She was thus able to express her more imperative needs and many of her thoughts.

At the time when I became her teacher, she had made for herself upward of sixty signs, all of which were imitative and were readily understood by those who knew her. The only signs which I think she may have invented were her signs for *small* and *large*.* Whenever she wished for anything very much she would gesticulate in a very expressive manner. Failing to make herself understood, she would become violent. In the years of her mental imprisonment she depended entirely upon signs, and she did not work out for herself any sort of articulate language capable of expressing ideas. It seems, however, that, while she was still suffering from severe pain, she noticed the movements of her mother's lips.

When she was not occupied, she wandered restlessly about the house, making strange though rarely unpleasant sounds.

*See pages 319 and 338.

I have seen her rock her doll, making a continuous, monotonous sound, keeping one hand on her throat, while the fingers of the other hand noted the movements of her lips. This was in imitation of her mother's crooning to the baby. Occasionally she broke out into a merry laugh, and then she would reach out and touch the mouth of any one who happened to be near her, to see if he were laughing also. If she detected no smile, she gesticulated excitedly, trying to convey her thought; but if she failed to make her companion laugh, she sat still for a few moments, with a troubled and disappointed expression. She was pleased with anything which made a noise. She liked to feel the cat purr; and if by chance she felt a dog in the act of barking, she showed great pleasure. She always liked to stand by the piano when some one was playing and singing. She kept one hand on the singer's mouth, while the other rested on the piano, and she stood in this position as long as any one would sing to her; and afterward she would make a continuous sound which she called singing. The only words she had learned to pronounce with any degree of distinctness previous to March, 1890, were *papa, mamma, baby, sister*. These words she had caught without instruction from the lips of friends. It will be seen that they contain three vowel and six consonant elements, and these formed the foundation for her first real lesson in speaking.

At the end of the first lesson she was able to pronounce distinctly the following sounds: *a, ä, â, è, ĭ, ô, c* soft like *s* and hard like *k, g* hard, *b, l, n, m, t, p, s, u, k, f* and *d*. Hard consonants were, and indeed still are, very difficult for her to pronounce in connection with one another in the same word; she often suppresses the one and changes the other, and sometimes she replaces both by an analogous sound with soft aspiration. The confusion between *l* and *r* was very noticeable in her speech at first. She would repeatedly use one for the other. The great difficulty in the pronunciation of the *r* made it one of the last elements which she mastered. The *ch, sh* and soft *g* also gave her much trouble, and she does not yet enunciate them clearly.*

When she had been talking for less than a week, she met her friend, Mr. Rodocanachi, and immediately began to struggle

*The difficulties which Miss Sullivan found in 1891 are, in a measure, the difficulties which show in Miss Keller's speech to-day.

with the pronunciation of his name; nor would she give it up until she was able to articulate the word distinctly. Her interest never diminished for a moment; and, in her eagerness to overcome the difficulties which beset her on all sides, she taxed her powers to the utmost, and learned in eleven lessons all of the separate elements of speech.

Enough appears in the accounts by Miss Keller's teacher to show the process by which she reads the lips with her fingers, the process by which she was taught to speak, and by which, of course, she can listen to conversation now. In reading the lips she is not so quick or so accurate as some reports declare. It is a clumsy and unsatisfactory way of receiving communication, useless when Miss Sullivan or some one else who knows the manual alphabet is present to give Miss Keller the spoken words of others. Indeed, when some friend is trying to speak to Miss Keller, and the attempt is not proving successful, Miss Sullivan usually helps by spelling the lost words into Miss Keller's hand.

President Roosevelt had little difficulty last spring in making Miss Keller understand him, and especially requested Miss Sullivan not to spell into her hand. She got every word, for the President's speech is notably distinct. Other people say they have no success in making Miss Keller "hear" them.

A few friends to whom she is accustomed, like Mrs. A. C. Pratt, and Mr. J. E. Chamberlin, can pass a whole day with her and tell her everything without the manual alphabet. The ability to read the lips helps Miss Keller in getting corrections of her pronunciation from Miss Sullivan and others, just as it was the means of her learning to speak at all, but it is rather an accomplishment than a necessity.

It must be remembered that speech contributed in no way to her fundamental education, though without the ability to speak she could hardly have gone to higher schools and to college. But she knows better than any one else what value speech has had for her. The following is her address at the fifth meeting of the American Association to Promote the Teaching of Speech to the Deaf, at Mt. Airy, Philadelphia, Pennsylvania, July 8, 1896:

ADDRESS OF HELEN KELLER AT MT. AIRY

IF you knew all the joy I feel in being able to speak to you to-day, I think you would have some idea of the value of speech to the deaf, and you would understand why I want every little deaf child in all this great world to have an opportunity to learn to speak. I know that much has been said and written on this subject, and that there is a wide difference of opinion among teachers of the deaf in regard to oral instruction. It seems very strange to me that there should be this difference of opinion; I cannot understand how any one interested in our education can fail to appreciate the satisfaction we feel in being able to express our thoughts in living words. Why, I use speech constantly, and I cannot begin to tell you how much pleasure it gives me to do so. Of course I know that it is not always easy for strangers to understand me, but it will be by and by; and in the meantime I have the unspeakable happiness of knowing that my family and friends rejoice in my ability to speak. My little sister and baby brother love to have me tell them stories in the long summer evenings when I am at home; and my mother and teacher often ask me to read to them from my favourite books. I also discuss the political situation with my dear father, and we decide the most perplexing questions quite as satisfactorily to ourselves as if I could see and hear. So you see what a blessing speech is to me. It brings me into closer and tenderer relationship with those I love, and makes it possible for me to enjoy the sweet companionship of a great many persons from whom I should be entirely cut off if I could not talk.

I can remember the time before I learned to speak, and how I used to struggle to express my thoughts by means of the manual alphabet—how my thoughts used to beat against my finger tips like little birds striving to gain their freedom, until one day Miss Fuller opened wide the prison-door and let them escape. I wonder if she remembers how eagerly and gladly they spread their wings and flew away. Of course, it was not easy at first to fly. The speech-wings were weak and broken, and had lost all the grace and beauty that had once been theirs;

indeed, nothing was left save the impulse to fly, but that was something. One can never consent to creep when one feels an impulse to soar. But, nevertheless, it seemed to me sometimes that I could never use my speech-wings as God intended I should use them; there were so many difficulties in the way, so many discouragements; but I kept on trying, knowing that patience and perseverance would win in the end. And while I worked, I built the most beautiful air-castles, and dreamed dreams, the pleasantest of which was of the time when I should talk like other people; and the thought of the pleasure it would give my mother to hear my voice once more, sweetened every effort and made every failure an incentive to try harder next time. So I want to say to those who are trying to learn to speak and those who are teaching them: Be of good cheer. Do not think of to-day's failures, but of the success that may come to-morrow. You have set yourselves a difficult task, but you will succeed if you persevere; and you will find a joy in overcoming obstacles—a delight in climbing rugged paths, which you would perhaps never know if you did not sometime slip backward—if the road was always smooth and pleasant. Remember, no effort that we make to attain something beautiful is ever lost. Sometime, somewhere, somehow we shall find that which we seek. We shall speak, yes, and sing, too, as God intended we should speak and sing.

CHAPTER V

LITERARY STYLE

No one can have read Miss Keller's autobiography without feeling that she writes unusually fine English. Any teacher of composition knows that he can bring his pupils to the point of writing without errors in syntax or in the choice of words. It is just this accuracy which Miss Keller's early education fixes as the point to which any healthy child can be brought, and which the analysis of that education accounts for. Those who try to make her an exception, not to be explained by any such analysis of her early education, fortify their position by an appeal to the remarkable excellence of her use of language even when she was a child.

This appeal is to a certain degree valid; for, indeed, those additional harmonies of language and beauties of thought which make style are the gifts of the gods. No teacher could have made Helen Keller sensitive to the beauties of language and to the finer interplay of thought which demands expression in melodious word groupings.

At the same time the inborn gift of style can be starved or stimulated. No innate genius can invent fine language. The stuff of which good style is made must be given to the mind from without and given skilfully. A child of the muses cannot write fine English unless fine English has been its nourishment. In this, as in all other things, Miss Sullivan has been the wise teacher. If she had not had taste and an enthusiasm for good English, Helen Keller might have been brought up on the "Juvenile Literature," which belittles the language under pretense of being simply phrased for children; as if a child's book could not, like "Treasure Island" or "Robinson Crusoe" or the "Jungle Book," be in good style.

If Miss Sullivan wrote fine English, the beauty of Helen Keller's style would, in part, be explicable at once. But the extracts from Miss Sullivan's letters and from her reports, although they are clear and accurate, have not the beauty which distinguishes Miss Keller's English. Her service as a teacher of English is not to be measured by her own skill in composition. The reason why she read to her pupil so many good books is due, in some measure, to the fact that she had so recently recovered her eyesight. When she became Helen Keller's teacher she was just awakening to the good things that are in books, from which she had been shut out during her years of blindness.

In Captain Keller's library she found excellent books, Lamb's "Tales from Shakespeare," and better still, Montaigne. After the first year or so of elementary work she met her pupil on equal terms, and they read and enjoyed good books together.

Besides the selection of good books, there is one other cause for Miss Keller's excellence in writing, for which Miss Sullivan deserves unlimited credit. That is her tireless and unrelenting discipline, which is evident in all her work. She never allowed her pupil to send off letters which contained offenses against taste, but made her write them over until they were not only correct, but charming and well phrased.

Any one who has tried to write knows what Miss Keller owes to the endless practice which Miss Sullivan demanded of her. Let a teacher with a liking for good style insist on a child's writing a paragraph over and over again until it is more than correct, and he will be training, even beyond his own power of expression, the power of expression in the child.

How far Miss Sullivan carried this process of refinement and selection is evident from the humorous comment of Dr. Bell, that she made her pupil a little old woman, too widely different from ordinary children in her maturity of thought. When Dr. Bell said this he was arguing his own case. For it was Dr. Bell who first saw the principles that underlie Miss Sullivan's method, and explained the process by which Helen Keller absorbed language from books.

There is, moreover, a reason why Helen Keller writes good English, which lies in the very absence of sight and hearing. The disadvantages of being deaf and blind were overcome and the advantages remained. She excels other deaf people because she was taught as if she were normal. On the other hand, the peculiar value to her of language, which ordinary people take for granted as a necessary part of them like their right hand, made her think about language and love it.

Language was her liberator, and from the first she cherished it.

The proof of Miss Keller's early skill in the use of English, and the final comment on the excellence of this whole method of teaching, is contained in an incident, which, although at the time it seemed unfortunate, can no longer be regretted. I refer to the "Frost King" episode, which I shall explain in detail. Miss Keller has given her account of it, and the whole matter was discussed in the first Volta Bureau Souvenir from which I quote at length:

MISS SULLIVAN'S ACCOUNT OF THE "FROST KING"

HON. JOHN HITZ,

Superintendent of the Volta Bureau, Washington, D. C.

DEAR SIR: Since my paper was prepared for the second edition of the Souvenir "Helen Keller," some facts have been brought to my notice which are of interest in connection with the subject of the acquisition of language by my pupil, and if it is not already too late for publication in this issue of the Souvenir, I shall be glad if I may have opportunity to explain them in detail.

Perhaps it will be remembered that in my paper,* where allu-

---

*In this paper Miss Sullivan says: "During this winter (1891-92) I went with her into the yard while a light snow was falling, and let her feel the falling flakes. She appeared to enjoy it very much indeed. As we went in she repeated these words, 'Out of the cloud-folds of his garments Winter shakes the snow.' I inquired of her where she had read this; she did not remember having read it, did not seem to know that she had learned it. As I had never heard it, I inquired of several of my friends if they recalled the words; no one seemed to remember it. The teachers at the Institution expressed the opinion that the description did not appear in any book in raised print in that library; but one lady, Miss Marrett, took upon herself the task of examining books of poems in ordinary type, and was rewarded by finding the following lines in one of Longfellow's minor poems, entitled 'Snowflakes':

> 'Out of the bosom of the air,
> Out of the cloud-folds of her garments shaken,
> Over the woodlands brown and bare,
> Over the harvest-fields forsaken,
> Silent, and soft, and slow,
> Descends the snow.'

"It would seem that Helen had learned and treasured the memory of this expression of the poet, and this morning in the snow-storm had found its application."

sion is made to Helen's remarkable memory, it is noted that she appears to retain in her mind many forms of expression which, at the time they are received, she probably does not understand; but when further information is acquired, the language retained in her memory finds full or partial expression in her conversation or writing, according as it proves of greater or less value to her in the fitness of its application to the new experience. Doubtless this is true in the case of every intelligent child, and should not, perhaps, be considered worthy of especial mention in Helen's case, but for the fact that a child who is deprived of the senses of sight and hearing might not be expected to be as gifted mentally as this little girl proves to be; hence it is quite possible we may be inclined to class as marvelous many things we discover in the development of her mind which do not merit such an explanation.

In the hope that I may be pardoned if I appear to overestimate the remarkable mental capacity and power of comprehension and discrimination which my pupil possesses, I wish to add that, while I have always known that Helen made great use of such descriptions and comparisons as appeal to her imagination and fine poetic nature, yet recent developments in her writings convince me of the fact that I have not in the past been fully aware to what extent she absorbs the language of her favourite authors. In the early part of her education I had full knowledge of all the books she read and of nearly all the stories which were read to her, and could without difficulty trace the source of any adaptations noted in her writing or conversation; and I have always been much pleased to observe how appropriately she applies the expressions of a favourite author in her own compositions.

The following extracts from a few of her published letters give evidence of how valuable this power of retaining the memory of beautiful language has been to her. One warm, sunny day in early spring, when we were at the North, the balmy atmosphere appears to have brought to her mind the sentiment expressed by Longfellow in "Hiawatha," and she almost sings with the poet: "The ground was all aquiver with the stir of new life. My heart sang for very joy. I thought of my own dear home. I knew that in that sunny land spring had come in all its splendour. 'All its birds and all its blossoms, all its flowers and all its grasses.' "

About the same time, in a letter to a friend, in which she makes mention of her Southern home, she gives so close a reproduction from a poem by one of her favourite authors that I will give extracts from Helen's letter and from the poem itself:

EXTRACTS FROM HELEN'S LETTER

[*The entire letter is published on pp. 245 and 246 of the Report of the Perkins Institution for 1891*]

The blue-bird with his azure plumes, the thrush clad all in brown, the robin jerking his spasmodic throat, the oriole drifting like a flake of fire, the jolly bobolink and his happy mate, the mocking-bird imitating the notes of all, the red-bird with his one sweet trill, and the busy little wren, are all making the trees in our front yard ring with their glad songs.

FROM THE POEM ENTITLED "SPRING," BY OLIVER WENDELL HOLMES

The bluebird, breathing from his azure plumes
The fragrance borrowed from the myrtle blooms;
The thrush, poor wanderer, dropping meekly down,
Clad in his remnant of autumnal brown;
The oriole, drifting like a flake of fire
Rent by a whirlwind from a blazing spire;
The robin, jerking his spasmodic throat,
Repeats imperious, his staccato note;
The crack-brained bobolink courts his crazy mate,.
Poised on a bullrush tipsy with his weight:
Nay, in his cage the lone canary sings,
Feels the soft air, and spreads his idle wings.

On the last day of April she uses another expression from the same poem, which is more an adaptation than a reproduction: "To-morrow April will hide her tears and blushes beneath the flowers of lovely May."

In a letter to a friend* at the Perkins Institution, dated May 17, 1889, she gives a reproduction from one of Hans Christian

*Page 170.

Andersen's stories, which I had read to her not long before. This letter is published in the Perkins Institution Report (1891), p. 204. The original story was read to her from a copy of "Andersen's Stories," published by Leavitt & Allen Bros., and may be found on p. 97 of Part I. in that volume.

Her admiration for the impressive explanations which Bishop Brooks has given her of the Fatherhood of God is well known. In one of his letters, speaking of how God in every way tells us of his love, he says, "I think he writes it even upon the walls of the great house of nature which we live in, that he is our Father." The next year at Andover she said: "It seems to me the world is full of goodness, beauty, and love; and how grateful we must be to our heavenly Father, who has given us so much to enjoy! His love and care are written all over the walls of nature."

 In these later years, since Helen has come in contact with so many persons who are able to converse freely with her, she has made the acquaintance of some literature with which I am not familiar; she has also found in books printed in raised letters, in the reading of which I have been unable to follow her, much material for the cultivation of the taste she possesses for poetical imagery. The pages of the book she reads become to her like paintings, to which her imaginative powers give life and colour. She is at once transported into the midst of the events portrayed in the story she reads or is told, and the characters and descriptions become real to her; she rejoices when justice wins, and is sad when virtue goes unrewarded. The pictures the language paints on her memory appear to make an indelible impression; and many times, when an experience comes to her similar in character, the language starts forth with wonderful accuracy, like the reflection from a mirror.

Helen's mind is so gifted by nature that she seems able to understand with only the faintest touch of explanation every possible variety of external relations. One day in Alabama, as we were gathering wild flowers near the springs on the hillsides, she seemed to understand for the first time that the springs were surrounded by mountains, and she exclaimed: "The mountains are crowding around the springs to look at their own beautiful reflections!" I do not know where she obtained this language, yet it is evident that it must have come to her from without, as it would hardly be possible for a person derprived of the visual sense to originate such an idea. In mentioning a visit to Lexington, Mass., she writes: "As we rode along we could see the forest monarchs bend their proud forms to listen to the little children of the woodlands whispering their secrets. The anemone, the wild violet, the hepatica, and the funny little curled-up ferns all peeped out at us from beneath the brown leaves." She closes this letter with, "I must go to bed, for Morpheus has touched my eyelids with his golden wand." Here again, I am unable to state where she acquired these expressions.

She has always seemed to prefer stories which exercise the imagination, and catches and retains the poetic spirit in all such literature; but not until this winter have I been conscious that her memory absorbed the exact language to such an extent that she is herself unable to trace the source.

This is shown in a little story she wrote in October last at the home of her parents in Tuscumbia, which she called "Autumn Leaves." She was at work upon it about two weeks, writing a little each day, at her own pleasure. When it was finished, and we read it in the family, it occasioned much comment on account of the beautiful imagery, and we could not understand how Helen could describe such pictures without the aid of sight. As we had never seen or heard of any such story as this before, we inquired of her where she read it; she replied, "I did not read it; it is my story for Mr. Anagnos's birthday." While I was surprised that she could write like this, I was not more astonished than I had been many times before at the unexpected achievements of my little pupil, especially as we had exchanged many beautiful thoughts on the subject of the glory of the ripening foliage during the autumn of this year.

Before Helen made her final copy of the story, it was suggested to her to change its title to "The Frost King," as more appropriate to the subject of which the story treated; to this she willingly assented. The story was written by Helen in braille, as usual, and copied by her in the same manner; I then interlined the manuscript for the greater convenience of those who desired to read it. Helen wrote a little letter, and, enclosing the manuscript, forwarded both by mail to Mr. Anagnos for his birthday.

The story was printed in the January number of the *Mentor*

and, from a review of it in the *Goodson Gazette*, I was startled to find that a very similar story had been published in 1873, seven years before Helen was born. This story, "Frost Fairies," appeared in a book written by Miss Margaret T. Canby, entitled "Birdie and his Fairy Friends." The passages quoted from the two stories were so much alike in thought and expression as to convince me that Miss Canby's story must at some time have been read to Helen.

As I had never read this story, or even heard of the book, I inquired of Helen if she knew anything about the matter, and found she did not. She was utterly unable to recall either the name of the story or the book. Careful examination was made of the books in raised print in the library of the Perkins Institution to learn if any extracts from this volume could be found there; but nothing was discovered. I then concluded that the story must have been read to her a long time ago, as her memory usually retains with great distinctness facts and impressions which have been committed to its keeping.

After making careful inquiry, I succeeded in obtaining the information that our friend, Mrs. S. C. Hopkins, had a copy of this book in 1888 which was presented to her little daughter in 1873 or 1874. Helen and I spent the summer of 1888 with Mrs. Hopkins at her home in Brewster, Mass., where she kindly relieved me a part of the time, of the care of Helen. She amused and entertained Helen by reading to her from a collection of juvenile publications, among which was the copy of "Birdie and his Fairy Friends"; and, while Mrs. Hopkins does not remember this story of "Frost Fairies," she is confident that she read to Helen extracts, if not entire stories, from this volume. But as she was not able to find her copy, and applications for the volume at bookstores in Boston, New York, Philadelphia, Albany, and other places resulted only in failure, search was instituted for the author herself. This became a difficult task, as her publishers in Philadelphia had retired from business many years ago; however, it was eventually discovered that her residence is at Wilmington, Delaware, and copies of the second edition of the book, 1889, were obtained from her. She has since secured and forwarded to me a copy of the first edition.

The most generous and gratifying letters have been received from Miss Canby by Helen's friends, a few extracts from which are given:

Under date of February 24, 1892, after mentioning the order of the publication of the stories in the magazine, she writes:

"All the stories were revised before publishing them in book form; additions were made to the number as first published, I think, and some of the titles may have been changed."

In the same letter she writes:

"I hope that you will be able to make her understand that I am glad she enjoyed my story, and that I hope the new book will give her pleasure by renewing her friendship with the Fairies. I shall write to her in a short time. I am so much impressed with what I have learned of her that I have written a little poem entitled A Silent Singer, which I may send to her mother after a while. Can you tell me in what paper the article appeared accusing Helen of plagiarism, and giving passages from both stories? I should like much to see it, and to obtain a few copies if possible."

Under date of March 9, 1892, Miss Canby writes:

"I find traces, in the Report which you so kindly sent me, of little Helen having heard other stories than that of 'Frost Fairies.' On page 132, in a letter, there is a passage which must have been suggested by my story called 'The Rose Fairies' (see pp. 13–16 of 'Birdie') and on pages 93 and 94 of the Report the description of a thunderstorm is very much like Birdie's idea of the same in the 'Dew Fairies' on page 59 and 60 of my book. What a wonderfully active and retentive mind that gifted child must have! If she had remembered and written down accurately, a short story, and that soon after hearing it, it would have been a marvel; but to have heard the story once, three years ago, and in such a way that neither her parents nor teacher could ever allude to it or refresh her memory about it, and then to have been able to reproduce it so vividly, even adding some touches of her own in perfect keeping with the rest, which really improve the original, is something that very few girls of riper age, and with every advantage of sight, hearing, and even great talents for composition, could have done as well, if at all. Under the circumstances, I do not see how any one can be so unkind as to call it a plagiarism; it is a wonderful feat of memory, and stands *alone,* as doubtless much of her work will in future, if her mental powers grow and develop with her years as greatly as in the few years past. I have known many children well, have been surrounded by them all my life

anα love nothing better than to talk with them, amuse them,
and quietly notice their traits of mind and character; but I do
not recollect more than one girl of Helen's age who had the love
and thirst for knowledge, and the store of literary and general
information, and the skill in composition, which Helen possesses.
She is indeed a 'Wonder-Child.' Thank you very much for
the Report, *Gazette*, and Helen's Journal. The last made me
realize the great disappointment to the dear child more than
before. Please give her my warm love, and tell her not to feel
troubled about it any more. No one shall be allowed to think
it was anything wrong; and some day she will write a great,
beautiful story or poem that will make many people happy.
Tell her there are a few bitter drops in every one's cup, and the
only way is to take the bitter patiently, and the sweet thankfully.
I shall love to hear of her reception of the book and how she
likes the stories which are new to her."

I have now (March, 1892) read to Helen "The Frost Fairies,"
"The Rose Fairies," and a portion of "The Dew Fairies," but
she is unable to throw any light on the matter. She recognized
them at once as her own stories, with variations, and was much
puzzled to know how they could have been published before
she was born! She thinks it is wonderful that two people
should write stories so much alike; but she still considers her
own as original.

I give below a portion of Miss Canby's story, "The Rose
Fairies," and also Helen's letter to Mr. Anagnos containing her
"dream," so that the likenesses and differences may be studied
by those interested in the subject:

THE ROSE FAIRIES

[From "Birdie and his Fairy Friends," by Margaret T. Canby]

One pleasant morning little Birdie might have been seen sitting
quietly on the grass-plat at the side of his mother's house, looking
very earnestly at the rose-bushes.

It was quite early; great Mr. Sun, who is such an early riser
in summer time, had not been up very long; the birds were just
beginning to chirp their "good-mornings" to each other; and
as for the flowers, they were still asleep. But Birdie was so
busy all day, trotting about the house and garden, that he was
always ready for *his* nest at night, before the birds and flowers

had thought of seeking *theirs;* and so it came to pass that when Mr. Sun raised his head above the green woods and smiled lovingly upon the earth, Birdie was often the first to see him, and to smile back at him, all the while rubbing his eyes with his dimpled fists, until between smiling and rubbing, he was wide awake.

And what do you think he did next! Why, the little rogue rolled into his mamma's bed, and kissed her eyelids, her cheeks, and her mouth, until she began to dream that it was raining kisses; and at last she opened her eyes to see what it all meant, and found that it was Birdie, trying to "kiss her awake," as he said.

She loved her little boy very dearly, and liked to make him happy, and when he said, "Please dress me, dear mamma, and let me go out to play in the garden," she cheerfully consented; and, soon after, Birdie went downstairs in his morning-dress of cool linen, and with his round face bright and rosy from its bath, and ran out on the gravel path to play, until breakfast was ready.

He stood still a moment to look about him, and think what he should do first. The fresh morning air blew softly in his face, as if to welcome him and be his merry playmate; and the bright eye of Mr. Sun looked at him with a warm and glowing smile; but Birdie soon walked on to find something to play with. As he came in sight of the rose-bushes that grew near the side of the house, he suddenly clapped his hands, and with a little shout of joy stopped to look at them; they were all covered with lovely rosebuds. Some were red, some white, and others pale pink, and they were just peeping out of the green leaves, as rosy-faced children peep out from their warm beds in winter-time before they are quite willing to get up. A few days before, Birdie's papa had told him that the green balls on the rose-bushes had beautiful flowers shut up within them, but the little boy found it hard to believe, for he was so young that he did not remember how pretty the roses had been the summer before. Now he found out that his father's words were true, for a few days of warm weather had turned the green balls into rosebuds, and they were *so* beautiful that it was enough to make Birdie stand still before them, his blue eyes dancing with delight and his little hands clasped tightly together.

After awhile he went nearer, and looking closely at the

buds, found that they were folded up, leaf over leaf, as eyelids are folded over sleeping eyes, so that Birdie thought they must be asleep. "Lazy roses, wake up," said he, giving the branches a gentle shake; but only the dew fell off in bright drops, and the flowers were still shut up. At last Birdie remembered how he had awakened his mother with kisses, and thought he would try the same plan with the roses; so he drew up his red lips until *they* looked like a rosebud, too, and bending down a branch with a lovely pink bud upon it, he kissed it softly two or three times.

Here the similarity in the language of the story to that in the letter ceases.

(Written February 2 and 3, 1890.)
[*This letter was enclosed in another written in French, dated Le 1 fevrier* 1890.]

MY DEAR MR. ANAGNOS: You will laugh when you open your little friend's letter and see all the queer mistakes she has made in French, but I think you will be pleased to know that I can write even a short letter in French. It makes me very happy to please you and my dear teacher. I wish I could see your little niece Amelia. I am sure we should love each other. I hope you will bring some of Virginia Evanghelides' poems home with you, and translate them for me. Teacher and I have just returned from our walk. It is a beautiful day. We met a sweet little child. She was playing on the pier with a wee brother. She gave me a kiss and then ran away, because she was a shy little girl. I wonder if you would like to have me tell you a pretty dream which I had a long time ago when I was a very little child? Teacher says it was a day-dream, and she thinks you would be delighted to hear it. One pleasant morning in the beautiful springtime, I thought I was sitting on the soft grass under my dear mother's window, looking very earnestly at the rose-bushes which were growing all around me. It was quite early, the sun had not been up very long; the birds were just beginning to sing joyously. The flowers were still asleep. They would not awake until the sun had smiled lovingly upon them. I was a very happy little child with rosy cheeks, and large blue eyes, and the most beautiful golden ringlets you can imagine. The fresh morning air blew gently in my face, as if to welcome me, and be my merry playmate, and the sun looked at me with a warm and tender smile. I clapped my chubby hands for joy when I saw that the rose-bushes were covered with lovely buds. Some were red, some white, and others were delicate pink, and they were peeping out from between the green leaves like beautiful little fairies. I had never seen anything so lovely before, for I was very young and I could not remember how pretty the roses had been the summer before. My little heart was filled with a sweet joy, and I danced around the rose-bushes to show my delight. After a while I went very near to a beautiful white rose-bush which was completely covered with buds and sparkling with dew-drops; I bent down one of the branches with a lovely pure white bud upon it, and kissed it softly many times; just then I felt two loving arms steal gently around me, and loving lips kissing my eyelids, my cheeks, and my mouth, until I began to think it was raining kisses; and at last I opened my eyes to see what it all meant, and found it was my precious mother, who was bending over me, trying to kiss me awake. Do you like my day-dream? If you do, perhaps I will dream again for you some time.

Teacher and all of your friends send you their love. I shall be so glad when you come home, for I greatly miss you. Please give my love to your good Greek friends, and tell them that I shall come to Athens some day.

Lovingly your little friend and playmate,

HELEN A. KELLER.

"The Frost Fairies" and "The Frost King" are given in full, as the differences are as important as the resemblances:

THE FROST FAIRIES *[From "Birdie and his Fairy Friends"]* BY MARGARET T. CANBY	THE FROST KING BY HELEN A. KELLER
King Frost, or Jack Frost as he is sometimes called, lives in a cold country far to the North; but every year he takes a journey over the world in a	King Frost lives in a beautiful palace far to the North, in the land of perpetual snow. The palace, which is magni-

car of golden clouds drawn by a strong and rapid steed called "North Wind." Wherever he goes he does many wonderful things; he builds bridges over every stream, clear as glass in appearance but often strong as iron; he puts the flowers and plants to sleep by one touch of his hand, and they all bow down and sink into the warm earth, until spring returns; then, lest we should grieve for the flowers, he places at our windows lovely wreaths and sprays of his white northern flowers, or delicate little forests of fairy pine-trees, pure white and very beautiful. But his most wonderful work is the painting of the trees, which look, after his task is done, as if they were covered with the brightest layers of gold and rubies; and are beautiful enough to comfort us for the flight of summer.

I will tell you how King Frost first thought of this kind work, for it is a strange story. You must know that this King, like all other kings, has great treasures of gold and precious stones in his palace; but, being a good-hearted old fellow, he does not keep his riches locked up all the time, but tries to do good and make others happy with them. He has two neighbours, who live still farther north; one is ficent beyond description, was built centuries ago, in the reign of King Glacier. At a little distance from the palace we might easily mistake it for a mountain whose peaks were mounting heavenward to receive the last kiss of the departing day. But on nearer approach we should discover our error. What we had supposed to be peaks were in reality a thousand glittering spires. Nothing could be more beautiful than the architecture of this ice-palace. The walls are curiously constructed of massive blocks of ice which terminate in cliff-like towers. The entrance to the palace is at the end of an arched recess, and it is guarded night and day by twelve soldierly-looking white Bears.

But, children, you must make King Frost a visit the very first opportunity you have, and see for yourselves this wonderful palace. The old King will welcome you kindly, for he loves children, and it is his chief delight to give them pleasure.

King Winter, a cross and churlish old monarch, who is hard and cruel, and delights in making the poor suffer and weep; but the other neighbour is Santa Claus, a fine, good-natured, jolly old soul, who loves to do good, and who brings presents to the poor, and to nice little children at Christmas.

Well, one day King Forest was trying to think of some good that he could do with his treasure; and suddenly he concluded to send some of it to his kind neighbour, Santa Claus, to buy presents of food and clothing for the poor, that they might not suffer so much when King Winter went near their homes. So he called together his merry little fairies, and showing them a number of jars and vases filled with gold and precious stones, told them to carry those carefully to the palace of Santa Claus, and give them to him with the compliments of King Frost. "He will know how to make good use of the treasure," added Jack Frost; then he told the fairies not to loiter by the way, but to do his bidding quickly.

The fairies promised obedience and soon started on their journey, dragging the great glass jars and vases along, as well as they could, and now

You must know that King Frost, like all other kings, has great treasures of gold and precious stones; but as he is a generous old monarch, he endeavours to make a right use of his riches. So wherever he goes he does many wonderful works; he builds bridges over every stream, as transparent as glass, but often as strong as iron; he shakes the forest trees until the ripe nuts fall into the laps of laughing children; he puts the flowers to sleep with one touch of his hand; then, lest we should mourn for the bright faces of the flowers, he paints the leaves with gold and crimson and emerald, and when his task is done the trees are beautiful enough to comfort us for the flight of summer. I will tell you how King Frost happened to think of painting the leaves, for it is a strange story.

One day while King Frost was surveying his vast wealth and thinking what good he could do with it, he suddenly bethought him of his jolly old neighbour, Santa Claus.

and then grumbling a little at having such hard work to do, for they were idle fairies, and liked play better than work. At last they reached a great forest, and, being quite tired, they decided to rest awhile and look for nuts before going any further. But lest the treasure should be stolen from them, they hid the jars among the thick leaves of the forest trees, placing some high up near the top, and others in different parts of the various trees, until they thought no one could find them.

Then they began to wander about and hunt for nuts, and climb the trees to shake them down, and worked much harder for their own pleasure than they had done for their master's bidding, for it is a strange truth that fairies and children never complain of the toil and trouble they take in search of amusement, although they often grumble when asked to work for the good of others.

The frost fairies were so busy and so merry over their nutting frolic that they soon forgot their errand and their king's command to go quickly; but, as they played and loitered in the forest until noon, they found the reason why they were told to hasten; for although they had, as they

"I will send my treasures to Santa Claus," said the King to himself. "He is the very man to dispose of them satisfactorily, for he knows where the poor and the unhappy live, and his kind old heart is always full of benevolent plans for their relief." So he called together the merry little fairies of his household and, showing them the jars and vases containing his treasures, he bade them carry them to the palace of Santa Claus as quickly as they could. The fairies promised obedience, and were off in a twinkling, dragging the heavy jars and vases along after them as well as they could, now and then grumbling a little at having such a hard task, for they were idle fairies and loved to play better than to work. After awhile they came to a great forest and, being tired and hungry, they thought they would rest a little and look for nuts before continuing their journey. But thinking their treasure might be stolen from them, they hid the jars among the thick green leaves of the thought, hidden the treasure so carefully, they had not secured it from the power of Mr. Sun, who was an enemy of Jack Frost, and delighted to undo his work and weaken him whenever he could.

His bright eyes found out the jars of treasure among the trees, and as the idle fairies left them there until noon, at which time Mr. Sun is the strongest, the delicate glass began to melt and break, and before long every jar and vase was cracked or broken, and the precious treasures they contained were melting, too, and dripping slowly in streams of gold and crimson over the trees and bushes of the forest.

Still, for awhile, the frost fairies did not notice this strange occurrence, for they were down on the grass, so far below the tree-tops that the wonderful shower of treasure was a long time in reaching them; but at last one of them said, "Hark! I believe it is raining; I certainly hear the falling drops." The others laughed, and told him that it seldom rained when the sun was shining; but as they listened they plainly heard the tinkling of many drops falling through the forest, and sliding from leaf to leaf until they reached the bramble-bushes beside them, when, to their

various trees until they were sure that no one could find them. Then they began to wander merrily about search‑ing for nuts, climbing trees, peeping curiously into the empty birds' nests, and play‑ing hide and seek from behind the trees. Now, these naughty fairies were so busy and so merry over their frolic that they forgot all about their errand and their master's command to go quickly, but soon they found to their dis‑may why they had been bid‑den to hasten, for although they had, as they supposed, hidden the treasure carefully, yet the bright eyes of King Sun had spied out the jars among the leaves, and as he and King Frost could never agree as to what was the best way of benefiting the world, he was very glad of a good opportunity of playing a joke upon his rather sharp rival. King Sun laughed softly to himself when the delicate jars began to melt and break. At length every jar and vase was cracked or broken, and the precious stones they contained great dismay, they found that the *rain-drops* were *melted rubies,* which hardened on the leaves and turned them to bright crimson in a moment. Then looking more closely at the trees around, they saw that the treasure was all melting away, and that much of it was already spread over the leaves of the oak trees and maples, which were shining with their gorgeous dress of gold and bronze, crimson and emerald. It was very beautiful; but the idle fairies were too much frightened at the mischief their disobedience had caused, to admire the beauty of the forest, and at once tried to hide themselves among the bushes, lest King Frost should come and punish them.

Their fears were well founded, for their long absence had alarmed the king, and he had started out to look for his tardy servants, and just as they were all hidden, he came along slowly, looking on all sides for the fairies. Of course, he soon noticed the brightness of the leaves, and discovered the cause, too, when he caught sight of the broken jars and vases from which the melted treasure was still dropping. And when he came to the nut trees, and saw the shells left by the idle

were melting, too, and running in little streams over the trees and bushes of the forest.

Still the idle fairies did not notice what was happening, for they were down on the grass, and the wonderful shower of treasure was a long time in reaching them; but at last they plainly heard the tinkling of many drops falling like rain through the forest, and sliding from leaf to leaf until they reached the little bushes by their side, when to their astonishment they discovered that the rain-drops were melted rubies which hardened on the leaves, and turned them to crimson and gold in a moment. Then, looking around more closely, they saw that much of the treasure was already melted, for the oaks and maples were arrayed in gorgeous dresses of gold and crimson and emerald. It was very beautiful, but the disobedient fairies were too frightened to notice the beauty of the trees. They were afraid that King Frost would come and punish them. So they hid themselves among the bushes fairies and all the traces of their frolic, he knew exactly how they had acted, and that they had disobeyed him by playing and loitering on their way through the woods.

King Frost frowned and looked very angry at first, and his fairies trembled for fear and cowered still lower in their hiding-places; but just then two little children came dancing through the wood, and though they did not see King Frost or the fairies, they saw the beautiful colour of the leaves, and laughed with delight, and began picking great bunches to take to their mother. "The leaves are as pretty as flowers," said they; and they called the golden leaves "buttercups," and the red ones "roses," and were very happy as they went singing through the wood.

Their pleasure charmed away King Frost's anger, and he, too, began to admire the painted trees, and at last he said to himself, "My treasures are not wasted if they make little children happy. I will not be offended at my idle, thoughtless fairies, for they have taught me a new way of doing good." When the frost fairies heard these words they crept, one by one, from their corners, and, kneeling down before their master, confessed

and waited silently for something to happen. Their fears were well founded, for their long absence had alarmed the King, and he mounted North Wind and went out in search of his tardy couriers. Of course, he had not gone far when he noticed the brightness of the leaves, and he quickly guessed the cause when he saw the broken jars from which the treasure was still dropping. At first King Frost was very angry, and the fairies trembled and crouched lower in their hiding-places, and I do not know what might have happened to them if just then a party of boys and girls had not entered the wood. When the children saw the trees all aglow with brilliant colors they clapped their hands and shouted for joy, and immediately began to pick great bunches to take home. "The leaves are as lovely as the flowers!" cried they, in their delight. Their pleasure banished the anger from King Frost's heart and the frown from his brow, and he, too, began to admire the their fault, and asked his pardon. He frowned upon them for awhile, and scolded them, too, but he soon relented, and said he would forgive them this time, and would only punish them by making them carry more treasure to the forest, and hide it in the trees, until all the leaves, with Mr. Sun's help, were covered with gold and ruby coats.

Then the fairies thanked him for his forgiveness, and promised to work very hard to please him; and the good-natured king took them all up in his arms, and carried them safely home to his palace. From that time, I suppose, it has been part of Jack Frost's work to paint the trees with the glowing colours we see in the autumn; and if they are *not* covered with gold and precious stones, I do not know how he makes them so bright; *do you?*

painted trees. He said to himself, "My treasures are not wasted if they make little children happy. My idle fairies and my fiery enemy have taught me a new way of doing good."

When the fairies heard this, they were greatly relieved and came forth from their hiding-places, confessed their fault, and asked their master's forgiveness.

Ever since that time it has been King Frost's great delight to paint the leaves with the glowing colors we see in the autumn, and if they are not covered with gold and precious stones I cannot imagine what makes them so bright, can you?

If the story of "The Frost Fairies" was read to Helen in the summer of 1888, she could not have understood very much of it at that time, for she had only been under instruction since March, 1887.

Can it be that the language of the story had remained dormant in her mind until my description of the beauty of the autumn scenery in 1891 brought it vividly before her mental vision?

I have made careful investigation among Helen's friends in Alabama and in Boston and its vicinity, but thus far have been unable to ascertain any later date when it could have been read to her.

Another fact is of great significance in this connection. "The Rose Fairies" was published in the same volume with "The Frost Fairies," and, therefore, was probably read to Helen at or about the same time.

Now Helen, in her letter of February, 1890 (quoted above), alludes to this story of Miss Canby's as dream *"which I had a long time ago when I was a very little child."* Surely, a year and a half would appear "a long time ago" to a little girl like Helen; we therefore have reason to believe that the stories must have been read to her at least as early as the summer of 1888.

HELEN KELLER'S OWN STATEMENT

(*The following entry made by Helen in her diary speaks for itself.*)

1892. January 30. This morning I took a bath, and when teacher came upstairs to comb my hair she told me some very sad news which made me unhappy all day. Some one wrote to Mr. Anagnos that the story which I sent him as a birthday gift, and which I wrote myself, was not my story at all, but that a lady had written it a long time ago. The person said her story was called "Frost Fairies." I am sure I never heard it. It made us feel so bad to think that people thought we had been untrue and wicked. My heart was full of tears, for I love the beautiful truth with my whole heart and mind.

It troubles me greatly now. I do not know what I shall do. I never thought that people could make such mistakes. I am perfectly sure I wrote the story myself. Mr. Anagnos is much troubled. It grieves me to think that I have been the cause of his unhappiness, but of course I did not mean to do it.

I thought about my story in the autumn, because teacher told me about the autumn leaves while we walked in the woods at Fern Quarry. I thought fairies must have painted them because they are so wonderful, and I thought, too, that King Frost must have jars and vases containing precious treasures, because I knew that other kings long ago had, and because teacher told me that the leaves were painted ruby, emerald, gold, crimson, and brown; so that I thought the paint must be melted stones. I knew that they must make children happy because they are so lovely, and it made me very happy to think that the leaves were so beautiful and that the trees glowed so, although I could not see them.

I thought everybody had the same thought about the *leaves*, but I do not know now. I thought very much about the sad news when teacher went to the doctor's; she was not here at dinner and I missed her.

I do not feel that I can add anything more that will be of interest. My own heart is too "full of tears" when I remember how my dear little pupil suffered when she knew "that people thought we had been untrue and wicked," for I know that she does indeed "love the beautiful truth with her whole heart and mind."

Yours truly,

ANNIE M. SULLIVAN.

So much appears in the Volta Bureau Souvenir. The following letter from Mr. Anagnos is reprinted from the *American Annals of the Deaf*, April, 1892:

PERKINS INSTITUTION AND MASSACHUSETTS SCHOOL FOR
THE BLIND

So. BOSTON, March 11, 1892.

To THE EDITOR OF THE *Annals*.

SIR: In compliance with your wishes I make the following statement concerning Helen Keller's story of "King Frost." It was sent to me as a birthday gift on November 7th, from Tuscumbia, Alabama. Knowing as well as I do Helen's extraordinary abilities I did not hesitate to accept it as her own work; nor do I doubt to-day that she is fully capable of writing such a composition. Soon after its appearance in print I was pained to learn, through the *Goodson Gazette,* that a portion of the story (eight or nine passages) is either a reproduction or adaptation of Miss Margaret Canby's "Frost Fairies." I immediately instituted an inquiry to ascertain the facts in the case. None of our teachers or officers who are accustomed to converse with Helen ever knew or heard about Miss Canby's book, nor did the child's parents and relatives at home have any knowledge of it. Her father, Captain Keller, wrote to me as follows on the subject:

"I hasten to assure you that Helen could not have received any idea of the story from any of her relations or friends here, none of whom can communicate with her readily enough to impress her with the details of a story of that character."

At my request, one of the teachers in the girls' department examined Helen in regard to the construction of the story. Her testimony is as follows:

"I first tried to ascertain what had suggested to Helen's mind the particular fancies which made her story seem like a reproduction of one written by Miss Margaret Canby. Helen told me that for a long time she had thought of Jack Frost as a king, because of the many treasures which he possessed. Such rich treasures must be kept in a safe place, and so she had imagined them stored in jars and vases in one part of the royal palace. She said that one autumn day her teacher told her as they were walking together in the woods, about the many beautiful colours of the leaves, and she had thought that such beauty must make people very happy, and very grateful to King Frost. I asked Helen what stories she had read about Jack Frost. In answer to my question she recited a part of the poem called 'Freaks of the Frost,' and she referred to a little piece about winter, in one of the school readers. She could not remember that any one had ever read to her any stories about *King Frost,* but said she had talked with her teacher about *Jack Frost* and the wonderful things he did."

The only person that we supposed might possibly have read the story to Helen was her friend, Mrs. Hopkins, whom she was visiting at the time in Brewster. I asked Miss Sullivan to go at once to see Mrs. Hopkins and ascertain the facts in the matter. The result of her investigation is embodied in the printed note herewith enclosed.*

I have scarcely any doubt that Miss Canby's little book was read to Helen, by Mrs. Hopkins, in the summer of 1888. But the child has no recollection whatever of this fact. On Miss Sullivan's return to Brewster, she read to Helen the story of "Little Lord Fauntleroy," which she had purchased in Boston for the purpose. The child was at once fascinated and absorbed with the charming story, which evidently made a deeper impression upon her mind than any previously read to her, as was shown in the frequent reference to it, both in her conversation and letters, for many months afterward. Her intense interest

*This note is a statement of the bare facts and an apology, which Mr. Anagnos inserted in his report of the Perkins Institute.

in Fauntleroy must have buried all remembrance of "Frost Fairies," and when, more than three years later, she had acquired a fuller knowledge and use of language, and was told of Jack Frost and his work, the seed so long buried sprang up into new thoughts and fancies. This may explain the reason why Helen claims persistently that "The Frost King" is her own story. She seems to have some idea of the difference between original composition and reproduction. She did not know the meaning of the word "plagiarism" until quite recently, when it was explained to her. She is absolutely truthful. Veracity is the strongest element of her character. She was very much surprised and grieved when she was told that her composition was an adaptation of Miss Canby's story of "Frost Fairies." She could not keep back her tears, and the chief cause of her pain seemed to be the fear lest people should doubt her truthfulness. She said, with great intensity of feeling, "I love the beautiful truth." A most rigid examination of the child of about two hours' duration, at which eight persons were present and asked all sorts of questions with perfect freedom, failed to elicit in the least any testimony convicting either her teacher or any one else of the intention or attempt to practice deception.

In view of these facts I cannot but think that Helen, while writing "The Frost King," was entirely unconscious of ever having had the story of "Frost Fairies" read to her, and that her memory has been accompanied by such a loss of associations that she herself honestly believed her composition to be original. This theory is shared by many persons who are perfectly well acquainted with the child and who are able to rise above the clouds of a narrow prejudice.

Very sincerely yours,
M. ANAGNOS.
Director of the Perkins Institution and
Massachusetts School for the Blind.

The episode had a deadening effect on Helen Keller and on Miss Sullivan, who feared that she had allowed the habit of imitation, which has in truth made Miss Keller a writer, to go too far. Even to-day, when Miss Keller strikes off a fine phrase, Miss Sullivan says in humorous despair, "I wonder where she got that?" But she knows now, since she has studied with her pupil in college the problems of composition, under the wise advice of Mr. Charles T. Copeland, that the style of every writer and indeed, of every human being, illiterate or cultivated, is a composite reminiscence of all that he has read and heard. Of the sources of his vocabulary he is, for the most part, as unaware as he is of the moment when he ate the food which makes a bit of his thumbnail. With most of us the contributions from different sources are blended, crossed and confused. A child with but few sources may keep distinct what he draws from each. In this case Helen Keller held almost intact in her mind, unmixed with other ideas, the words of a story which at the time it was read to her she did not fully understand. The importance of this cannot be overestimated. It shows how the child-mind gathers into itself words it has heard, and how they lurk there ready to come out when the key that releases the spring is touched. The reason that we do not observe this process in ordinary children is, because we seldom observe them at all, and because they are fed from so many sources that the memories are confused and mutually destructive. The story of "The Frost King" did not, however, come from Helen Keller's mind intact, but had taken to itself the mould of the child's temperament and had drawn on a vocabulary that to some extent had been supplied in other ways. The style of her version is in some respects even better than the style of Miss Canby's story. It has the imaginative credulity of a primitive folk-tale; whereas Miss Canby's story is evidently told for children by an older person, who adopts the manner of a fairy tale and cannot conceal the mature mood which allows such didactic phrases as "Jack Frost as he is sometimes called," "Noon, at which time Mr. Sun is strongest." Most people will feel the superior imaginative quality of Helen Keller's opening paragraph. Surely the writer must become as a little child to see things like that. "Twelve soldierly looking white bears" is a stroke of genius, and there is beauty of rhythm throughout the child's narrative. It is original in the same way that a poet's version of an old story is original.

This little story calls into life all the questions of language and the philosophy of style. Some conclusions may be briefly suggested.

All use of language is imitative, and one's style is made up of all other styles that one has met.

The way to write good English is to read it and hear it. Thus it is that any child may be taught to use correct English by not being allowed to read or hear any other kind. In a child, the selection of the better from the worse is not conscious; he is the servant of his word experience.

The ordinary man will never be rid of the fallacy that words obey thought, that one thinks first and phrases afterward. There must first, it is true, be the intention, the desire to utter something, but the idea does not often become specific, does not take shape until it is phrased; certainly an idea is a different thing by virtue of being phrased. Words often make the thought, and the master of words will say things greater than are in him. A remarkable example is a paragraph from Miss Keller's sketch in the *Youth's Companion*. Writing of the moment when she learned that everything has a name, she says: "We met the nurse carrying my little cousin; and teacher spelled 'baby.' *And for the first time* I was impressed with the smallness and helplessness of a little baby, and mingled with the thought there was another one of myself, and I was glad I was myself, and not a baby." It was a word that created these thoughts in her mind. So the master of words is master of thoughts which the words create, and says things greater than he could otherwise know. Helen Keller writing "The Frost King" was building better than she knew and saying more than she meant.

Whoever makes a sentence of words utters not his wisdom, but the wisdom of the race whose life is in the words, though they have never been so grouped before. The man who can write stories thinks of stories to write. The medium calls forth the thing it conveys, and the greater the medium the deeper the thoughts.

The educated man is the man whose expression is educated. The substance of thought is language, and language is the one thing to teach the deaf child and every other child. Let him get language and he gets the very stuff that language is made of, the thought and the experience of his race. The language must be one used by a nation, not an artificial thing. Volapük is a paradox, unless one has French or English or German or some other language that has grown up in a nation. The deaf child who has only the sign language of De l'Épée is an intellectual Philip Nolan, an alien from all races, and his thoughts are not the thoughts of an Englishman, or a Frenchman, or a

Spaniard. The Lord's prayer in signs is not the Lord's prayer in English.

In his essay on style De Quincey says that the best English is to be found in the letters of the cultivated gentlewoman, because she has read only a few good books and has not been corrupted by the style of newspapers and the jargon of street, market-place, and assembly hall.

Precisely these outward circumstances account for Helen Keller's use of English. In the early years of her education she had only good things to read; some were, indeed, trivial and not excellent in style, but not one was positively bad in manner or substance. This happy condition has obtained throughout her life. She has been nurtured on imaginative literature, and she has gathered from it into her vigorous and tenacious memory the style of great writers. "A new word opens its heart to me," she writes in a letter; and when she uses the word its heart is still open. When she was twelve years old, she was asked what book she would take on a long railroad journey. "Paradise Lost," she answered, and she read it on the train.

Until the last year or two she has not been master of her style; rather has her style been master of her. It is only since she has made composition a more conscious study that she has ceased to be the victim of the phrase; the lucky victim, fortunately, of the good phrase.

When in 1892, she was encouraged to write a sketch of her life for the *Youth's Companion*, in the hope that it would reassure her and help her to recover from the effect of "The Frost King," she produced a piece of composition which is much more remarkable and in itself more entertaining at some points than the corresponding part of her story in this book. When she came to retell the story in a fuller form, the echo was still in her mind of the phrases she had written nine years before. Yet she had not seen her sketch in the *Youth's Companion* since she wrote it, except two passages which Miss Sullivan read to her to remind her of things she should say in this autobiography, and to show her, when her phrasing troubled her, how much better she did as a little girl.

From the early sketch I take a few passages which seem to me, without making very much allowance for difference in time, almost as good as anything she has written since:

I discovered the true way to walk when I was a year old, and
during the radiant summer days that followed I was never still
a minute. . . .

Then when my father came in the evening, I would run to
the gate to meet him, and he would take me up in his strong arms
and put back the tangled curls from my face and kiss me many
times, saying, "What has my Little Woman been doing
to-day?"

But the brightest summer has winter behind it. In the cold,
dreary month of February, when I was nineteen months old, I
had a serious illness. I still have confused memories of that illness. My mother sat beside my little bed and tried to soothe my
feverish moans while in her troubled heart she prayed, "Father
in Heaven, spare my baby's life!" But the fever grew and
flamed in my eyes, and for several days my kind physician thought
I would die.

But early one morning the fever left me as mysteriously and
unexpectedly as it had come, and I fell into a quiet sleep. Then
my parents knew I would live, and they were very happy. They
did not know for some time after my recovery that the cruel fever
had taken my sight and hearing; taken all the light and music
and gladness out of my little life.

But I was too young to realize what had happened. When I
awoke and found that all was dark and still, I suppose I thought
it was night, and I must have wondered why day was so long
coming. Gradually, however, I got used to the silence and darkness that surrounded me, and forgot that it had ever been
day.

I forgot everything that had been except my mother's tender
love. Soon even my childish voice was stilled, because I had
ceased to hear any sound.

But all was not lost! After all, sight and hearing are but
two of the beautiful blessings which God had given me. The
most precious, the most wonderful of His gifts was still mine.
My mind remained clear and active, "though fled fore'er the
light."

As soon as my strength returned, I began to take an interest
in what the people around me were doing. I would cling to
my mother's dress as she went about her household duties, and
my little hands felt every object and observed every motion, and
in this way I learned a great many things.

When I was a little older I felt the need of some means of communication with those around me, and I began to make simple signs which my parents and friends readily understood; but it often happened that I was unable to express my thoughts intelligibly, and at such times I would give way to my angry feelings utterly. . . .

Teacher had been with me nearly two weeks, and I had learned eighteen or twenty words, before that thought flashed into my mind, as the sun breaks upon the sleeping world; and in that moment of illumination the secret of language was revealed to me, and I caught a glimpse of the beautiful country I was about to explore.

Teacher had been trying all the morning to make me understand that the mug and the milk in the mug had different names; but I was very dull, and kept spelling *milk* for mug, and *mug* for milk until teacher must have lost all hope of making me see my mistake. At last she got up, gave me the mug, and led me out of the door to the pump-house. Some one was pumping water, and as the cool fresh stream burst forth, teacher made me put my mug under the spout and spelled "w-a-t-e-r," Water!

That word startled my soul, and it awoke, full of the spirit of the morning, full of joyous, exultant song. Until that day my mind had been like a darkened chamber, waiting for words to enter and light the lamp, which is thought. . . .

I learned a great many words that day. I do not remember what they all were; but I do know that *mother, father, sister* and *teacher* were among them. It would have been difficult to find a happier little child than I was that night as I lay in my crib and thought over the joy the day had brought me, and for the first time longed for a new day to come.

The next morning I awoke with joy in my heart. Everything I touched seemed to quiver with life. It was because I saw everything with the new, strange, beautiful sight which had been given me. I was never angry after that because I understood what my friends said to me, and I was very busy learning many wonderful things. I was never still during the first glad days of my freedom. I was continually spelling and acting out the words as I spelled them. I would run, skip, jump and swing, no matter where I happened to be. Everything was budding and blossoming. The honeysuckle hung in long garlands, deliciously fragrant, and the roses had never been so beautiful before. Teacher and I lived out-of-doors from morning until night, and I rejoiced greatly in the forgotten light and sunshine found again. . . .

The morning after our arrival I awoke bright and early. A beautiful summer day had dawned, the day on which I was to make the acquaintance of a somber and mysterious friend. I got up, and dressed quickly and ran downstairs. I met Teacher in the hall, and begged to be taken to the sea at once. "Not yet," she responded, laughing. "We must have breakfast first." As soon as breakfast was over we hurried off to the shore. Our pathway led through low, sandy hills, and as we hastened on, I often caught my feet in the long, coarse grass, and tumbled, laughing, in the warm, shining sand. The beautiful, warm air was peculiarly fragrant, and I noticed it got cooler and fresher as we went on.

Suddenly we stopped, and I knew, without being told, the Sea was at my feet. I knew, too, it was immense! awful! and for a moment some of the sunshine seemed to have gone out of the day. But I do not think I was afraid; for later, when I had put on my bathing-suit, and the little waves ran up on the beach and kissed my feet, I shouted for joy, and plunged fearlessly into the surf. But, unfortunately, I struck my foot on a rock and fell forward into the cold water.

Then a strange, fearful sense of danger terrified me. The salt water filled my eyes, and took away my breath, and a great wave threw me up on the beach as easily as if I had been a little pebble. For several days after that I was very timid, and could hardly be persuaded to go in the water at all; but by degrees my courage returned, and almost before the summer was over, I thought it the greatest fun to be tossed about by the sea-waves. . . .

I do not know whether the difference or the similarity in phrasing between the child's version and the woman's is the more remarkable. The early story is simpler and shows less deliberate artifice, though even then Miss Keller was prematurely conscious of style; but the art of the later narrative, as in the passage about the sea, or the passage on the medallion of Homer, is surely a fulfilment of the promise of the early story. It was in these early days that Dr. Holmes wrote to her: "I am delighted with the style of your letters. There is no affectation about them, and as they come straight from your heart, so they go straight to mine."

In the years when she was growing out of childhood, her style lost its early simplicity and became stiff and, as she says, "periwigged." In these years the fear came many times to Miss Sullivan lest the success of the child was to cease with childhood. At times Miss Keller seemed to lack flexibility; her thoughts ran in set phrases which she seemed to have no power to revise or turn over in new ways.

Then came the work in college—original theme writing with new ideals of composition or at least new methods of suggesting those ideals. Miss Keller began to get the better of her old friendly taskmaster, the phrase. This book, her first mature experiment in writing, settles the question of her ability to write.

The style of the Bible is everywhere in Miss Keller's work, just as it is in the style of most great English writers. Stevenson, whom Miss Sullivan likes and used to read to her pupil, is another marked influence. In her autobiography are many quotations, chiefly from the Bible and Stevenson, distinct from the context or interwoven with it, the whole a fabric quite of her own design. Her vocabulary has all the phrases that other people use, and the explanation of it, and the reasonableness of it ought to be evident by this time. There is no reason why she should strike from her vocabulary all words of sound and vision. Writing for other people, she should in many cases be true to outer fact rather than to her own experience. So long as she uses words correctly, she should be granted the privilege of using them freely, and not be expected to confine herself to a vocabulary true to her lack of sight and hearing. In her style, as in what she writes about, we must concede to the artist what we deny to the autobiographer. It should be explained, too, that *look* and *see* are used by the blind, and *hear* by the deaf, for *perceive;* they are simple and more convenient words. Only a literal person could think of holding the blind to *perception* or *apperception,* when *seeing* and *looking* are so much easier, and have, moreover, in the speech of all men the meaning of intellectual recognition as well as recognition through the sense of sight. When Miss

Keller examines a statue, she says in her natural idiom, as her fingers run over the marble, "It looks like a head of Flora."

It is true, on the other hand, that in her descriptions, she is best from the point of view of art when she is faithful to her own sensations; and this is precisely true of all artists.

Her recent training has taught her to drop a good deal of her conventionality and to write about experiences in her life which are peculiar to her and which, like the storm in the wild cherry tree, mean most and call for the truest phrasing. She has learned more and more to give up the style she borrowed from books and tried to use, because she wanted to write like other people; she has learned that she is at her best when she "feels" the lilies sway; lets the roses press into her hands and speaks of the heat which to her means light.

Miss Keller's autobiography contains almost everything that she ever intended to publish. It seems worth while, however, to quote from some of her chance bits of writing, which are neither so informal as her letters nor so carefully composed as her story of her life. These extracts are from her exercises in her course in composition, where she showed herself at the beginning of her college life quite without rival among her classmates. Mr. Charles T. Copeland, who has been for many years instructor in English and Lecturer on English Literature at Harvard and Radcliffe, said to me: "In some of her work she has shown that she can write better than any pupil I ever had, man or woman. She has an excellent 'ear' for the flow of sentences." The extracts follow:

A few verses of Omar Khayyám's poetry have just been read to me, and I feel as if I had spent the last half-hour in a magnificent sepulcher. Yes, it is a tomb in which hope, joy and the power of acting nobly lie buried. Every beautiful description, every deep thought glides insensibly into the same mournful chant of the brevity of life, of the slow decay and dissolution of all earthly things. The poet's bright, fond memories of love, youth and beauty are but the funeral torches shedding their light on this tomb, or to modify the image a little, they are the flowers that bloom on it, watered with tears and fed by a bleeding heart. Beside the tomb sits a weary soul, rejoicing neither in the joys of the past nor in the possibilities of the future, but seeking consolation in forgetfulness. In vain the inspiring sea shouts to this languid soul, in vain the heavens strive with its weakness; it still persists in regretting and seeks a refuge in oblivion from the pangs of present woe. At times it catches some faint echo from the living, joyous, real world, a gleam of the perfection that is to be; and, thrilled out of its despondency, feels capable of working out a grand ideal even "in the poor, miserable, hampered actual," wherein it is placed; but in a moment the inspiration, the vision is gone, and this great, much-suffering soul is again enveloped in the darkness of uncertainty and despair.

It is wonderful how much time good people spend fighting the devil. If they would only expend the same amount of energy loving their fellow men, the devil would die in his own tracks of ennui.

I often think that beautiful ideas embarrass most people as much as the company of great men. They are regarded generally as far more appropriate in books and in public discourses than in the parlor or at the table. Of course I do not refer to beautiful sentiments, but to the higher truths relating to everyday life. Few people that I know seem ever to pause in their daily intercourse to wonder at the beautiful bits of truth they have gathered during their years of study. Often when I speak enthusiastically of something in history or in poetry, I receive no response, and I feel that I must change the subject and return to the commonest topics, such as the weather, dressmaking, sports, sickness, "blues" and "worries." To be sure, I take the keenest interest in everything that concerns those who surround me; it is this very interest which makes it so difficult for me to carry on a conversation with some people who will not talk or say what they think; but I should not be sorry to find more friends ready to talk with me now and then about the wonderful things I read. We need not be like "Les Femmes Savantes" but we ought to have something to say about what we learn as well as about what we *must* do, and what our professors say or how they mark our themes.

To-day I took luncheon with the Freshman Class of Radcliffe.

This was my first real experience in college life, and a delightful experience it was! For the first time since my entrance into Radcliffe I had the opportunity to make friends with all my classmates, and the pleasure of knowing that they regarded me as one of themselves, instead of thinking of me as living apart and taking no interest in the everyday nothings of their life, as I had sometimes feared they did. I have often been surprised to hear this opinion expressed or rather implied by girls of my own age and even by people advanced in years. Once some one wrote to me that in his mind I was always "sweet and earnest," thinking only of what is wise, good and interesting—as if he thought I was one of those wearisome saints of whom there are only too many in the world! I always laugh at these foolish notions, and assure my friends that it is much better to have a few faults and be cheerful and responsive in spite of all deprivations than to retire into one's shell, pet one's affliction, clothe it with sanctity, and then set one's self up as a monument of patience, virtue, goodness and all in all; but even while I laugh I feel a twinge of pain in my heart, because it seems rather hard to me that any one should imagine that I do not feel the tender bonds which draw me to my young sisters—the sympathies springing from what we have in common—youth, hope, a half-eager, half-timid attitude towards the life before us and above all the royalty of maidenhood.

Sainte-Beuve says, *"Il vient un age peut-être quand on n'ecrit plus."* This is the only allusion I have read to the possibility that the sources of literature, varied and infinite as they seem now, may sometime be exhausted. It surprises me to find that such an idea has crossed the mind of any one, especially of a highly gifted critic. The very fact that the nineteenth century has not produced many authors whom the world may count among the greatest of all time does not in my opinion justify the remark, "There may come a time when people cease to write."

In the first place, the fountains of literature are fed by two vast worlds, one of action, one of thought, by a succession of creations in the one and of changes in the other. New experiences and events call forth new ideas and stir men to ask questions unthought of before, and seek a definite answer in the depths of human knowledge.

In the second place, if it is true that as many centuries must

pass before the world becomes perfect as passed before it became
what it is to-day, literature will surely be enriched incalculably
by the tremendous changes, acquisitions and improvements that
cannot fail to take place in the distant future. If genius has
been silent for a century it has not been idle. On the contrary,
it has been collecting fresh materials not only from the remote
past, but also from the age of progress and development, and
perhaps in the new century there will be outbursts of splendor
in all the various branches of literature. At present the world
is undergoing a complete revolution, and in the midst of falling
systems and empires, conflicting theories and creeds, discoveries
and inventions, it is a marvel how one can produce any great
literary works at all. This is an age of workers, not of thinkers.
The song to-day is:

> Let the dead past bury its dead,
> Act, act in the living present,
> Heart within and God overhead.

A little later, when the rush and heat of achievement relax, we
can begin to expect the appearance of grand men to celebrate in
glorious poetry and prose the deeds and triumphs of the last few
centuries.

It is very interesting to watch a plant grow, it is like taking
part in creation. When all outside is cold and white, when the
little children of the woodland are gone to their nurseries in the
warm earth, and the empty nests on the bare trees fill with snow,
my window-garden glows and smiles, making summer within
while it is winter without. It is wonderful to see flowers bloom
in the midst of a snow-storm! I have felt a bud "shyly doff her
green hood and blossom with a silken burst of sound," while
the icy fingers of the snow beat against the window-panes. What
secret power, I wonder, caused this blossoming miracle? What
mysterious force guided the seedling from the dark earth up to
the light, through leaf and stem and bud, to glorious fulfilment
in the perfect flower? Who could have dreamed that such beauty
lurked in the dark earth, was latent in the tiny seed we planted?
Beautiful flower, you have taught me to see a little way into the
hidden heart of things. Now I understand that the darkness
everywhere may hold possibilities better even than my
hopes.

A FREE TRANSLATION FROM HORACE

BOOK II—18.

I am not one of those on whom fortune deigns to smile. My house is not resplendent with ivory and gold; nor is it adorned with marble arches, resting on graceful columns brought from the quarries of distant Africa. For me no thrifty spinners weave purple garments. I have not unexpectedly fallen heir to princely estates, titles or power; but I have something more to be desired than all the world's treasures—the love of my friends, and honorable fame, won by my own industry and talents. Despite my poverty, it is my privilege to be the companion of the rich and mighty. I am too grateful for all these blessings to wish for more from princes, or from the gods. My little Sabine farm is dear to me; for here I spend my happiest days, far from the noise and strife of the world.

O, ye who live in the midst of luxury, who seek beautiful marbles for new villas, that shall surpass the old in splendor, you never dream that the shadow of death is hanging over your halls. Forgetful of the tomb, you lay the foundation of your palaces. In your mad pursuit of pleasure you rob the sea of its beach and desecrate hallowed ground. More even than this, in your wickedness you destroy the peaceful homes of your clients! Without a touch of remorse you drive the father from his land, clasping to his bosom his household gods and his half-naked children.

You forget that death comes to the rich and the poor alike, and comes once for all; but remember, Acheron could not be bribed by gold to ferry the crafty Prometheus back to the sunlit world. Tantalus, too, great as he was above all mortals, went down to the kingdom of the dead, never to return. Remember, too, that, although death is inexorable, yet he is just; for he brings retribution to the rich for their wickedness, and gives the poor eternal rest from their toil and sorrow.

Ah, the pranks that the nixies of Dreamland play on us while we sleep! Methinks "they are jesters at the Court of Heaven." They frequently take the shape of daily themes to mock me; they strut about on the stage of Sleep like foolish virgins, only they carry well-trimmed note-books in their hands instead of empty lamps. At other times they examine and cross-examine me in all the studies I have ever had, and invariably ask me questions as easy to answer as this: "What was the name of the first mouse that worried Hippopotamus, satrap of Cambridge under Astyagas, grandfather of Cyrus the Great?" I wake terror-stricken with the words ringing in my ears, "An answer or your life!"

Such are the distorted fancies that flit through the mind of one who is at college and lives as I do in an atmosphere of ideas, conceptions and half-thoughts, half-feelings which tumble and jostle each other until one is almost crazy. I rarely have dreams that are not in keeping with what I really think and feel, but one night my very nature seemed to change, and I stood in the eye of the world a mighty man and a terrible. Naturally I love peace and hate war and all that pertains to war; I see nothing admirable in the ruthless career of Napoleon, save its finish. Nevertheless, in that dream the spirit of that pitiless slayer of men entered me! I shall never forget how the fury of battle throbbed in my veins—it seemed as if the tumultuous beating of my heart would stop my breath. I rode a fiery hunter—I can feel the impatient toss of his head now and the quiver that ran through him at the first roar of the cannon.

From the top of the hill where I stood I saw my army surging over a sunlit plain like angry breakers, and as they moved, I saw the green of fields, like the cool hollows between billows. Trumpet answered trumpet above the steady beat of drums and the rhythm of marching feet. I spurred my panting steed and waving my sword on high and shouting, "I come! Behold me, warriors—Europe!" I plunged into the oncoming billows, as a strong swimmer dives into breakers, and struck, alas, 'tis true, the bedpost!

Now I rarely sleep without dreaming; but before Miss Sullivan came to me, my dreams were few and far between, devoid of thought or coherency, except those of a purely physical nature. In my dreams something was always falling suddenly and heavily, and at times my nurse seemed to punish me for my unkind treatment of her in the daytime and return at an usurer's rate of interest my kickings and pinchings. I would wake with a start or struggle frantically to escape from my tormentor. I was very fond of bananas, and one night I dreamed that I found a long string of them in the dining-room, near the cupboard, all peeled and deliciously ripe, and all I had to do was to stand under the string and eat as long as I could eat.

After Miss Sullivan came to me, the more I learned, the oftener I dreamed; but with the waking of my mind there came many dreary fancies and vague terrors which troubled my sleep for a long time. I dreaded the darkness and loved the woodfire. Its warm touch seemed so like a human caress, I really thought it was a sentient being, capable of loving and protecting me. One cold winter night I was alone in my room. Miss Sullivan had put out the light and gone away, thinking I was sound asleep. Suddenly I felt my bed shake, and a wolf seemed to spring on me and snarl in my face. It was only a dream, but I thought it real, and my heart sank within me. I dared not scream, and I dared not stay in bed. Perhaps this was a confused recollection of the story I had heard not long before about Red Riding Hood. At all events, I slipped down from the bed and nestled close to the fire which had not flickered out. The instant I felt its warmth I was reassured, and I sat a long time watching it climb higher and higher in shining waves. At last sleep surprised me, and when Miss Sullivan returned she found me wrapped in a blanket by the hearth.

Often when I dream, thoughts pass through my mind like cowled shadows, silent and remote, and disappear. Perhaps they are the ghosts of thoughts that once inhabited the mind of an ancestor. At other times the things I have learned and the things I have been taught, drop away, as the lizard sheds its skin, and I see my soul as God sees it. There are also rare and beautiful moments when I see and hear in Dreamland. What if in my waking hours a sound should ring through the silent halls of hearing? What if a ray of light should flash through the darkened chambers of my soul? What would happen, I ask many and many a time. Would the bow-and-string tension of life snap? Would the heart, overweighted with sudden joy, stop beating for very excess of happiness?

INDEX